Studies in German Literature, Linguistics, and Culture

Edited by James Hardin
(South Carolina)

Literature and Film in the Third Reich

Literature and Film in the Third Reich

KARL-HEINZ SCHOEPS

Translated by
Kathleen M. Dell'Orto

First English-language edition,
based on the second German edition
but revised and expanded.

CAMDEN HOUSE

First published 2004
by Camden House

Camden House is an imprint of Boydell & Brewer Inc.
668 Mt. Hope Avenue, Rochester, NY 14620 USA
and of Boydell & Brewer Limited
PO Box 9, Woodbridge, Suffolk IP12 3DF, UK

ISBN: 1–57113–252–X

Library of Congress Cataloging-in-Publication Data

Schoeps, Karl-Heinz, 1935–
 Literature and film in the Third Reich / Karl-Heinz Schoeps; translated by Kathleen M. Dell'Orto. — 1st English-language ed. / rev. and
expanded from the 2nd German ed.
   p. cm. — (Studies in German Literature, Linguistics, and Culture)
Includes bibliographical references and index.
ISBN 1–57113–252–X (alk. paper)
   1. German literature — 20th century — History and criticism. 2. National socialism and literature. 3. National socialism and motion pictures.
4. Motion pictures — Germany — History. I. Title. II. Series: Studies
in German literature, linguistics, and culture (Unnumbered)

PT405.S3495 2003
830.9'358—dc22

2003017324

A catalogue record for this title is available from the British Library.

This publication is printed on acid-free paper.
Printed in the United States of America.

Contents

Illustrations

Introduction

A GERMAN EDITION of this book was first published in 1992 by Peter Lang Publishers in Bern, Switzerland. A second revised and enlarged edition appeared in 2000 by Weidler in Berlin. For the English edition some changes were made in various chapters while the chapter on film and the bibliography were substantially expanded. The present work is the first book in English to provide a comprehensive overview of literature and film within Nazi Germany, ranging from Nazi literature to literature of the Inner Emigration and literature of resistance.

To date there have only been a few attempts at an overview of the literature in the Third Reich, for example, books by Uwe-K. Ketelsen, *Völkischnationale und nationalsozialistische Literatur in Deutschland, 1890–1945* (*Völkisch* National and National Socialist Literature in Germany, 1890–1945 [1976]) and *Literatur und Drittes Reich* (Literature and the Third Reich [1992; second edition, 1994]); Horst Denkler and Karl Prümm, eds., *Die deutsche Literatur im Dritten Reich: Themen — Traditionen — Wirkungen* (Literature in the Third Reich: Themes — Traditions — Effects [1976]); Ernst Loewy, *Literatur unterm Hakenkreuz* (Literature Under the Swastika [1969 and 1987]); and Franz Schonauer *Deutsche Literatur im Dritten Reich* (German Literature in the Third Reich [1961]). Ketelsen's first book is a handbook that appeared in the collection of realia by Metzler Publishers; the individual chapters on various aspects of literature within the Third Reich in his second book have all been published previously in a number of different publications and are not intended as a systematic overview. The Denkler-Prümm book contains twenty-three essays by twenty-three authors on a number of literary topics. Loewy provides excerpts of texts from various literary genres on numerous topics popular with the Nazis, and Schonauer's book, the first attempt at a comprehensive survey, with the intent of being at once polemical and didactic, is somewhat out-of-date today. All of these publications, however, proved very helpful for my study, as were Dietrich Strothmann's and Jan Pieter Barbian's descriptions of cultural policies in the Third Reich and Eric Rentschler's and Linda Schulte-Sasse's books on film in the Third Reich.

The present study is an attempt to start with the knowledge to date and, on the basis of selected and representative examples, to furnish an introduction to the literature within the Third Reich. In the selection of the works, the decisive criteria were themes, the level of familiarity, the prominence of the authors, and the size of the printing runs, although in many cases other works and authors could just as well have been used as examples to illustrate genres, themes, and ideologems. A number of authors and works not considered in the text because of the vast amount of material will at least be mentioned in the biographical and bibliographical index. As the texts themselves are in many cases very hard to locate and, for the most part, unavailable in English translation, they will be the main focus of examination.

In contrast to the works of Ketelsen, Loewy, and Schonauer cited above, not only National Socialist literature but also non-National Socialist literature composed in the Third Reich will be considered. Nazi literature will be discussed by genre so that individual works can, whenever possible, be introduced in their entirety and typical features demonstrated in context on the basis of the individual examples. As Nazi literature does not fall within the political confines of the Third Reich but to a great extent was already extant in 1933, the prehistory of the literature in the Third Reich must also be considered, that is, works of Nazi literature that were composed before 1933. Nazi literature in the broadest sense encompasses all the *völkisch*, nationalistic, conservative works and authors who enjoyed official sponsorship and sizable printings in the Third Reich, even if some of them were critical of official National Socialism, for example, Ernst Jünger. The purpose of this volume is not to develop a theory of National Socialist literature but to offer practical examples in context.[1]

While I have made an attempt to include literature written in camps and ghettos, chapters on theater in the concentration camps and on the activities of the *Jüdischer Kulturbund* (Jewish Cultural Association) must be left for another edition. At this point I can only refer the English-speaking reader to articles by Glen Gadberry ("Nazi Germany's Jewish Theatre," in *Theatre Survey* 21, 1 [May 1980]) and Bruce H. Zortmann ("Theatre in Isolation: The Jüdischer Kulturbund on Nazi Germany," in *Educational Theatre Journal* 24, 2 [1972]), as well as to articles by Rebecca Rovit ("Collaboration or Survival, 1933–1938: Reassessing the Role of the Jüdischer Kulturbund") and Michael Patterson ("The Final Chapter: Theatre in the Concentration Camps of Nazi Germany"), both in Gadberry's book *Theatre in the Third Reich, the Prewar Years: Essays on Theatre in Nazi Germany* (Westport, CT and London: Greenwood Press, 1995). According to Rovit, the most comprehensive history of the *Kulturbund* is still Herbert Freeden's book *Jüdisches Theater in Nazi Deutschland* (Jewish Theater in Nazi Germany) (Tübingen, 1964; Frankfurt am Main, 1985). In particular, Patterson points to the fate of the actor Kurt Gerron, "perhaps the saddest case of a great talent having to compromise with the Nazis" (162). Gerron, whose life and death is well documented in the Jewish Museum in Berlin, had played many roles in films and on the stage. His performances included Tiger Brown in Brecht and Weill's famous *Threepenny Opera* premiere of 1928 in Berlin. He arrived in the concentration camp of Theresienstadt in 1944 and was forced by the SS to stage the review *Karussell* (Carousel) and to direct the Nazi propaganda film on Theresienstadt, *Der Führer schenkt den Juden eine Stadt* (The Führer Gives the Jews a City), before he was gassed in Auschwitz in 1944.[2]

The definition of literature of the Third Reich is controversial, as strictly speaking the literature of the Third Reich did not exist at all, or at least not any more than the drama or the novel of the Third Reich. The difficulty in defining Nazi literature is attributable to the fact that National Socialism never developed a uniform concept of literature and was unable to agree on what constitutes a binding canon of National Socialist Literature. In his essay titled "What is National Socialist Literature?" Ralf Schnell provides the most serviceable definition to date of the literature of the Third Reich from a literary and aesthetic perspective. According to Schnell, this literature contains the following features: a new beginning, dualism (good against evil), returning home, sacredness, literary organization of mass symbols and invisible masses, monumentality and suggestivity, indifference to genre, and imitative and traditionalist features.[3] The difference between *völkisch*, nationalistic literature and National Socialist literature is, in Schnell's view, the "decidedly positive nature of National Socialist literature" compared to the "undirected negativity of *völkisch*, nationalistic literature."[4] In practice, however, not all works that can be classified as literature of the Third Reich exhibit all of these features to the same extent.

Although this volume focuses on the literature within the Third Reich for the period between 1933 and 1945, this period cannot be viewed as a closed era. It is open at both ends: numerous Nazi writers and authors of the Inner Emigration or the Other Germany wrote before 1933 and after 1945; of course, neither group enjoyed much popularity after 1945. On the other hand, the beginning efforts of well-known authors like Günter Eich, Peter Huchel, or Wolfgang Koeppen go back to the period of the Third Reich.[5] Furthermore, the Nazi literature between 1933 and 1945 cannot be viewed as a uniform block despite the Nazis' attempts to force everything into conformity (*Gleichschaltung*). Qualitatively, there were great differences among the Nazi authors; Jünger and Weinheber, for example, are worlds apart from the Nazi propaganda literature of Schumann and Zöberlein. In their writing style most authors returned to traditional forms, but in this regard, there were also exceptions such as Eberhard Wolfgang Möller, who operated with the forms of expressionism and downright Brechtian alienation. The wall separating the authors of National Socialism and those of the Inner Emigration is not as thick as it might seem: both drew on the same traditions and clung to the same forms (for example, the sonnet); ideologically both groups, in many cases, shared an aversion to modernism in any form. According to Ketelsen, the groups that have been so carefully separated in secondary literature, that is, National Socialist literature, the literature of Inner Emigration, and exile literature, actually share a number of common features.[6]

The German writer Ursula Krechel, for example, sensed the "Reich Party Congress style . . . even in texts of writers who had emigrated."[7] Historical novels were not only written by Nazi authors but also by inner and outer emigrants. In a number of cases the same novel was read differently by different groups. The Nazis read Werner Bergengruen's novel *Der Großtyrann und das Gericht* (The Great Tyrant and the Court) as a *Führer* novel, the non-Nazis, as a resistance novel. The inner emigrant Jochen Klepper, whose novel about the Prussian king Friedrich Wilhelm I, *Der Vater* (The Father), was received by the Nazis as glorification of a great leader, was ultimately driven to suicide by the Nazis. Many thought Ernst Jünger's *Auf den Marmorklippen* (On the Marble Cliffs) was a resistance novel, but at the same time, it fit into the fascist aesthetics of violence. Even some works of Ernst Wiechert and Reinhold Schneider were in keeping with a *völkisch*, conservative concept of literature. And Friedrich Reck-Malleczwen, who was murdered by the Nazis in Dachau, was, with his arch-conservative ideology, not far removed from National Socialism.

The terms "Inner Emigration," "National Socialist literature," or "fascist literature" are not free from controversy but in the absence of better terminology, they will be retained here. The present study is divided into chapters mostly according to ideological considerations, although aesthetic aspects are not totally excluded. In order to reach a general and comprehensive verdict on the literature within the Third Reich, more detailed studies of individual works such as that provided by Uwe-K. Ketelsen in his thoughtful analysis of Ernst Jünger's lengthy essay *Der Arbeiter* (The Worker) are necessary. A study of German literature within the Third Reich with chapters organized around aesthetic and literary-historical principles would, I suspect, produce completely different results, breaking down the subcategories of literature of the Third Reich (i.e., Nazi literature), literature of Inner Emigration and resistance, and exile literature and producing different categorizations.

The German version of literary fascism was by no means totally reactionary, but also participated in modernism just as the Italian, French, and American versions with Marinetti and d'Annunzio in Italy, Celine in France, and Pound in the Anglo-American world, although the German version did not attain the same artistic heights. Literary modernism included such ideologically disparate authors as Bertolt Brecht, whom the Nazis drove into exile, and Ernst Jünger, who remained in Germany and was highly esteemed by the Nazis. Brecht's modernist concept of literature in the service of socialism is well enough known, but this is not the case for Jünger's fascist concept of modernism, which Uwe-K. Ketelsen elucidated in his analysis of *Der Arbeiter*. For Ketelsen, the glorification of violence is at the core of fascist aesthetics: "In fascist aesthetics, violence always enters in . . . as part of its structure; violence is a characteristic of fascist aesthetics" (Ketelsen, 263). The fascist aesthetics Ketelsen finds in *Der Arbeiter* is also a constituent element of Jünger's so-called novel of resistance, *Auf den Marmorklippen*. According to Ketelsen, this aesthetization of violence is associated with a distant, amoral (or extra-moral) attitude and a tendency to symmetry, smoothness, and the monumental, which is reminiscent of Albert Speer's monumental architecture (Ketelsen, 264).

Jünger's worker is not the Marxist proletarian but rather the countertype to the bourgeois individual that perished in the firestorms at Langemarck in the First World War (Ketelsen, 270). Jünger's modern and fascist model of society is organized according to military and technological principles; in that society there is no room for the old and outworn concept of the bourgeois individual. Violence and militarization open the way to elementary forces that remain unknown to the bourgeois individual. In contrast to the traditional *völkisch* movement that rejects modernism and takes refuge in the past, Jünger embraces modernism, which he characterizes by breaks and discontinuities. This fragmented reality is mirrored in the structure of Jünger's *Der Arbeiter* and other of his works in which the continuity of presentation is interrupted and replaced by unrelenting clashes of contrasts. In these structural principles, Jünger is not terribly far removed from Bertolt Brecht who, like Jünger, breaks the flow of events into disjointed and contradictory parts. Ketelsen's characterization of Jünger's *Der Arbeiter* could also be applied to Brecht: "Facts and observations are not systematically arranged in his texts; their introduction therefore achieves a certain prominence and comes as a surprise to the reader and causes him to wonder" (Ketelsen, 274). For Brecht, too, the end of the bourgeois individual is near, and Brecht strives to replace him with a new construction (see, for example his play *Mann ist Mann* [Man is a Man]). It comes, therefore, as no surprise that the playwright Heiner Müller, one of the most prominent German postmodernists, traces his roots back to Brecht and Jünger (Ketelsen, 274).

Brecht and Jünger, of course, arrive at diametrically opposed conclusions for the reconstruction of modern society, but they agree in their analysis of modernism, in their call for the replacement of the bourgeois individual with a construction more suitable to technological modernism, and in the fragmented structure of their work. Another German writer, the noted poet Gottfried Benn, essentially a conservative who is not known to have had socialist leanings and who sympathized with the Nazi cause only for a short time, also deserves to be mentioned in this context, as he attempted to incorporate modernism through expressionism into fascist aesthetics (Ketelsen, 335). Even Goebbels, the Nazi minister of propaganda, was at first not averse to the concept of fascist modernism. The concept of modernism that Ketelsen traces in Jünger's *Der Arbeiter* could perhaps also be discovered in other fascist writers such as Eberhard Wolfgang Möller or Hans Rehberg once more detailed studies of their works become available.

Opposite the modernists were the traditionalists who sought to escape from fragmented modernism into the supposedly whole world of the past and classical tradition. They could be found among the *völkisch* nationalists as well as among the inner and outer emigrants and included such diverse authors as Hermann Burte, Hans Friedrich Blunck, Joseph Roth, Ernst Wiechert, Hans Carossa, and Wilhelm Lehmann. This flight from modernism began long before the Third Reich came into existence and did not end with the collapse of the so-called Thousand Year Reich in 1945. As Ketelsen demonstrates, Wilhelm Lehmann's Inner Emigration during the Nazi period, for example, was nothing more than a flight from modernism in general, a modernism he saw embodied in National Socialism. On the other hand, neither the beginning (1933) nor the end (1945) of the Third Reich made a difference in his views.

It is difficult to answer the question of whether works were produced during the Third Reich that can stand the test of time and are still worth reading today. Thomas Mann certainly did not think so when he claimed shortly after the war that all books published in Germany between 1933 and 1945 smell of blood and should be destroyed. This may apply to the propagandistic works by a number of authors, from Anacker to Zöberlein, which today are of historic interest only. Except that initially even Thomas Mann's books were published in Nazi Germany, some dramas by Hans Rehberg, Eberhard Wolfgang Möller, and Erwin Guido Kolbenheyer may have some literary merit, as may some novels by Hans Grimm, Reinhold Schneider, Stefan Andres, and Ernst Jünger, or poetry by Oskar Loerke, Wilhelm Lehmann, or Ernst Jünger's younger brother Georg Friedrich Jünger. Which works of the literature within the Third Reich will remain and deserve to be included in the literary canon? Ketelsen raises the question without, however, providing a satisfactory answer (Ketelsen, 46). To begin with, more detailed studies of authors and works are necessary to give more conclusive proof one way or the other. One thing is clear, however: the literature within Nazi Germany does not adequately reflect the reality of the Third Reich, or in Ketelsen's words, there is "a non-identity between the fictional literary world and historical reality" (Ketelsen, 17). Entire segments of the reality of the Third Reich are blanked out, such as life and death in the concentration camps. Moreover, the poet and author in the Third Reich was supposed to be a leader, a teacher, and a visionary, a *praeceptor Germaniae,* just as he was in bourgeois times (Ketelsen, 18).

In order to show film and literature within the Third Reich in the context of its history as well as its cultural history and ideology, this study includes chapters on the historical and ideological background and the background in terms of cultural policy along with the chapters on literature and film. The deliberations above, however, should be remembered when reading the following pages. Even the chapter on cultural policies should not be taken as a prescription. To be sure, there were a number of cultural bureaucracies, but cultural life in Nazi Germany was not entirely subservient to Nazi propaganda. One need only consider the attention paid to non-National Socialist literature in lending libraries, the timeless pursuit of the classical tradition, and policies concerning film. Ketelsen points out that the Nazis had their greatest successes in the cultural realm (Ketelsen, 56). In general, however, the assertion can also be made that film, literature, and culture in the Third Reich were far from being "the Other," as has been claimed. To the contrary, they were part and parcel of the German cultural tradition. The dates 1933 and 1945, although crucial for the political history of Germany, were far less important for film, literature, and culture.

Notes

[1] For theoretical issues of literary production within the Third Reich, see Uwe-K. Ketelsen, *Literatur und Drittes Reich* (Literature and the Third Reich) (Schernfeld: SH-Verlag, 1992 and 1994). The page citations in the text refer to this study.

[2] See Barbara Felsmann and Karl Prümm, *Kurt Gerron: Gefeiert und gejagt, 1897–1944: Das Schicksal eines deutschen Unterhaltungskünstlers: Berlin, Amsterdam, Theresienstadt, Auschwitz* (Kurt Gerron: Celebrated and Hunted, 1897–1944: The Fate of a German Entertainer: Berlin, Amsterdam, Theresienstadt, Auschwitz) (Berlin: Edition Hentrich, 1992).

[3] Ralf Schnell, "Was ist 'nationalsozialistische Dichtung'?" in *Leid der Worte: Panorama des literarischen Nationalsozialismus* (The Suffering of Words: Panorama of the Literary National Socialism), edited by Jörg Thunecke (Bonn: Bouvier, 1987), 28–45.

[4] Schnell, 40.

[5] Various references are made to these cases of continuity, for example, by Uwe-K. Ketelsen in "Die Literatur des Dritten Reichs als Gegenstand germanistischer Forschung," in *Wege der Literaturwissenschaft* (Paths of Studies in Literature), edited by Jutta Kolkenbrock-Netz, Gerhard Plumpe, and Hans Joachim Schrimpf (Bonn: Bouvier, 1985), 301: "Many influential post-war writers [began] their literary careers in National Socialist Germany . . . and not at all always at the distance insinuated after 1945. After 1945, the texts of Agnes Miegel, Hans Carossa, Josef Weinheber, and Ernst Jünger (if they were considered harmless, and most of them were) still continued for a long time to have the same function in West Germany as the texts of Kolbenheyer, Griese, von Schirach, Agnes Miegel, Hans Carossa, Weinheber, and Jünger had had before 1945." On the reception of National Socialist authors after 1945, see also Hans Sarkowics, "Die literarischen Apologeten des Dritten Reiches. Zur Rezeption der vom Nationalsozialismus geförderten Autoren nach 1945" (The Literary Apologists of the Third Reich. On the Reception After 1945 of the Authors Supported by National Socialism), in *Leid der Worte*, edited by Jörg Thunecke, 435–59. On the beginnings of postwar authors, see Hans Dieter Schäfer, "Die nichtfaschisti-

sche Literatur der 'jungen Generation' im nationalsozialistischen Deutschland" (The Non-Fascist Literature of the 'Young Generation' in National Socialist Germany), in Hans Denkler and Karl Prümm, eds., *Die deutsche Literatur im Dritten Reich: Themen-Traditionen-Wirkungen* (Literature in the Third Reich: Themes-Traditions-Effects) (Stuttgart: Reclam, 1976), 459–503; new version in Hans Dietrich Schäfer, ed., *Das gespaltene Bewußtsein: Deutsche Kultur und Lebenswirklichkeit 1933–1945* (Divided Consciousness: German Culture and the Realities of Life, 1933–1945) (Munich: Hanser, 1981), 7–54. See also Hans Dietrich Schäfer, ed., *Am Rande der Nacht: Moderne Klassik im Dritten Reich* (On the Edge of Night: Modern Classics in the Third Reich) (Frankfurt am Main: Ullstein, 1984).

[6] Uwe-K. Ketelsen, "Die Literatur des Dritten Reichs als Gegenstand germanistischer Forschung," 301. In his article "Probleme einer gegenwärtigen Forschung zur Literatur des Dritten Reichs" (Problems of Current Research on the 'Literature of the Third Reich), Ketelsen even proposes relinquishing the concept of "literature of the Third Reich," at least for the time being, to get away from a schema of delimitation based on polar opposites and in this way to recognize the international context of the era and achieve new research results, see *Deutsche Vierteljahreszeitschrift für Literaturwissenschaft und Geistesgeschichte* (German Quarterly for Literature and Intellectual History), 64 (1990), No. 4, 725. On this subject, see also Rainer Zimmermann, *Das dramatische Bewußtsein: Studien zum bewußtseinsgeschichtlichen Ort der Dreißiger Jahre in Deutschland* (The Dramatic Consciousness: Studies on the Situation in Terms of the History of Consciousness During the Thirties in Germany) (Münster: Aschendorffsche Verlagsbuchhandlung, 1989). Zimmermann views National Socialism as part of an evolving process of experiencing reality dynamically and directly, starting around 1930.

[7] Ursula Krechel in the afterword to Elisabeth Langgässer, *Das unauslöschliche Siegel* (The Indelible Seal) (Darmstadt: Luchterhand, 1979), 230.

1: Historical Overview

AFTER ADOLF HITLER had decided in 1919 to become a politician and began in 1920 to reorganize the German Workers' Party (DAP) into the National Socialist German Workers' Party on the model of a small Austrian right-wing party, it was not at all foreseeable that this party, with him at its head, would seize control of the German Reich a mere thirteen years later, despite Arthur Moeller van den Bruck's conviction that the National Socialist Party, which he had already dreamed of shortly after the turn of the century, would "certainly be part of the German future."[1] The DAP for which Hitler initially acted as the recruiting spokesman and propaganda speaker was in 1919 nothing but an insignificant right-wing party among numerous ideologically similar groups such as the many *bündisch*[2] associations or the *völkisch,* pan-German Thule organization that boasted of Aryan ancestry and operated with runes and swastikas, and whose leader, Rudolf Glauer, called himself Rudolf, Baron of Sebottendorf.[3] This organization also produced later Nazi ideologues like Alfred Rosenberg, Hans Frank, and Hitler's mentor, Dietrich Eckart. The newspaper of the Thule Society, the *Münchener Beobachter* (Munich Observer), was the precursor of the NSDAP newspaper *Völkischer Beobachter* (The Völkisch Observer) as well.[4] Combining nationalism and socialism was a clever propaganda maneuver, and as became evident in time, the combination merged the two essential political currents of the nineteenth and early twentieth centuries into one party, at least in name. The NSDAP attempted to benefit politically from a relationship with these two German movements and to guarantee national continuity to the population, in particular to the great majority of conservative voters. The NSDAP attempted to exploit for its own purposes the uneasiness with capitalistic materialism and bolshevist communism that continued to prevail by ostensibly fusing socialism and German nationalism to form one party. In particular, the NSDAP knew how to turn latent and open anti-Semitism to its political advantage. As the drum beater for this movement, Adolf Hitler had finally found a sphere of activity that suited him.[5]

German nationalism had awakened with the wars of liberation in the early nineteenth century as the German state threw off the Napoleonic yoke. In the course of the restoration after the Congress of Vienna, this nationalism still had a progressive, republican focus. Not until the victory over France and the subsequent establishment of the German Reich by Bismarck in 1871 did nationalism take on a regressive chauvinistic character, and even survived the battles fraught with casualties and the defeat of the First World War. Strength-ened by the terms of the Versailles Treaty of 1919 and by the so-called stab-in-the-back legend, according to which the German army, unconquered in the field, was betrayed by "anarchistic and unpatriotic elements" at home, Hitler continued to thrive in the underground, waiting to surface. Just how thin the Weimar Republic's surface layer of democracy actually was became frighten-ingly clear when it collapsed without word or whimper in 1933. Only after the Second World War had been lost and Germany had been divided did it be-come clear to most Germans where this nationalism had led them.

Almost simultaneously with the reawakening of German feelings of na-tionalism, aspirations for social justice began to stir as industrialization took hold, aspirations that peaked for the first time with Karl Marx's *Communist Manifesto* of 1848. Ferdinand Lassalle's General German Union of Workers of 1836 first gave the socialist movement organizational form; this organiza-tion then merged in 1875 with the Social Democratic Workers' Party founded by Liebknecht and Bebel and, as a result of the Erfurt Program Plan of 1891, gained a platform with Marxism as its foundation and the name Social Demo-cratic Party. After the SPD had been compromised in the First World War by nationalistic overtones and support of the Kaiser's imperialism, the Independ-ent Social Democratic Party was formed, and then subsequent to the Bolshe-vik revolution in Russia, the Spartacus Union; these two organizations combined to form the Communist Party of Germany at the end of 1918.

The struggle between these two political currents, the one left-oriented, bound to Moscow, and associated with the KPD, and other right-oriented, nationalistic, and associated with the NSDAP, particularly dominated the last phase of the Weimar Republic. It ended with a victory for the Nazis on Janu-ary 30, 1933, when Hitler was named Reich Chancellor. Although Hitler and his party attempted to preserve the appearance of legality, this was clearly not the case; the democratic state of laws, to the extent that it existed at all in the twenties, had already been left only a shell by the presidential governments of von Papen and Schleicher. Furthermore, thinking in terms of democracy and a state of laws was not very widespread in this first German republic. In addi-tion, the great majority of the politicians had underestimated Hitler. Even after Hitler's assumption of power and the systematic expansion of that power, most of them were convinced that he would not last long. His book, *Mein Kampf,* if registered at all, was dismissed as the fantastic musings of a political lunatic. The beginning of the German republic, proclaimed on November 9, 1918, by Philipp Scheidemann, the leader of the majority socialists, was al-ready threatened by street fighting between the right and left. In these dis-putes, the SPD, as the majority party that formed the government, had the task of ensuring stability, which it accomplished by deploying the army and the police against the rioters of the right and left. The police and the military came to the aid of various volunteer units that had been formed of soldiers and officers left unemployed after the First World War. They sprang up at any location where there were leftists to fight, in Munich, in Saxony, in the Baltic states, and in the Ruhr region. Among them was also Leo Schlageter who, after his execution by the French in 1923, became one of the most important martyrs of the Nazi movement and was glorified in numerous books. Leftist groups that wanted to transform Germany into a *Räterepublik*[6] after the collapse of the German *Kaiserreich* became the declared enemies of the Weimar Republic because of the brutal treatment meted out to them with the approval of the SPD government. Rightist groups agreed with the measures against the leftists but accused the government of betraying the people of Germany after it had signed the Versailles Peace Treaty.

The victims were primarily leftists and government officials. Rosa Luxemburg, Karl Liebknecht, Kurt Eisner, Walter Rathenau, and Mathias Erzberger were brutally murdered by rightist radicals. Rightist conspirators fared better. After his failed attempt at a revolt against the government in Berlin in March of 1920, Wolfgang Kapp was allowed to leave the country. After his vain putsch in Munich on November 9, 1923, Adolf Hitler received a five-year jail sentence, only eight months of which he had to serve, under quite favorable conditions. In the proceedings against him in February and March of 1924, Hitler succeeded in transforming his position as defendant into the role of a prosecutor of the Weimar regime. The time in jail gave him an opportunity to think about his movement and to write down his thoughts and objectives in *Mein Kampf,* supported by the loyal Rudolf Hess and the *völkisch* oriented Catholic priest Bernhard Stempfle. Hess was later rewarded with the meaningless title "Deputy of the *Führer,*" and Stempfle, with death in the cleansings of 1934, when Hitler eliminated comrades who had gotten in his way. Even before the putsch attempt of 1923, Hitler had either absorbed other national groups or outflanked them with more realistic politics. During his time in jail, the young NSDAP threatened to fall apart. After his release, however, he soon succeeded in restoring the party and having it pledge itself completely to him, and thus consolidating the *Führer* principle on which the Third Reich was fundamentally based.

The currency reform of 1923 and American loans under the Dawes Plan brought about relative stability in the republic, although the very tired phrase "the Golden Twenties" hardly seems appropriate even for this second phase, as the economic problems had by no means been eliminated, and the republican, democratic way of thinking remained restricted to a very small group.[7] The contrast between right and left persisted, even if it no longer captured the headlines. Among the level-headed republicans were politicians such as Stresemann, who served the republic in a variety of roles (usually as Foreign Minister), and the Reich President, Field Marshal von Hindenburg, the conquering hero of Tannenberg, who succeeded the first Reich President, Friedrich Ebert (SPD), in office after the latter's death in February of 1925.

The years of the second phase, from 1923 to 1929, were essentially dominated by governments that stood to the right of the middle. After the American stock market crash in October of 1929, however, it turned out that the relative economic stability was only fragile prosperity based on American capital. Bankruptcies, foreclosures, and unemployment figures shot through the roof, and the *Reichstag* elections of 1930 ended with an enormous gain of votes by the Communists and the National Socialists. The devastating economic situation — in 1932 the unemployment rate reached 44.5 percent — increased membership in both parties. Organized groups of both parties (the SA, SS, Red Front Fighters Union, etc.) staged fierce street battles that finally broke the Weimar Republic. From 1929 to 1933, economic decline dominated the third phase of the republic and increased the antagonism between right and left, as well as emergency measures by the hard-pressed Reich government. Although the first signs of an improvement in the economic situation were already visible at this point, and the NSDAP seemed to have passed its prime, the phase ended with the appointment of Adolf Hitler as Reich Chancellor by the senile Hindenburg on January 30, 1933.

The rightist circles that had hoped to be able to control Hitler by including him in the government, among them primarily Alfred Hugenberg and his German National People's Party, the DNVP, which had entered a coalition with the NSDAP, were soon proven wrong, for Hitler immediately went about solidifying his power with drastic means and abolishing the last remnants of republicanism. All parties were prohibited except for the NSDAP, which was elevated to the official party of the state. With the Enabling Act after the fatal *Reichstag* fire of February 27, 1933, Hitler had unified practically all the power in his own person. Rivals in his own ranks, such as Ernst Röhm or Gregor Strasser, were eliminated as ruthlessly as opposition from other circles. In this, Hitler without a doubt had the support of large parts of the population, which had seen only the decline and erosion of state authority and had only tolerated the republic. Hitler and his party were expected to bring about a rebirth of German greatness and restoration of state authority.

Now it became evident that the socialist aspect of the Hitler movement was only a pretext for taking votes away — successfully — from the social democrats and communists in particular. Otto Strasser, the representative of the social revolutionary wing of the NSDAP, had already been booted out in 1930. Apart from this, Hitler had a very curious notion of socialism: for him it was "something like the national community of people with socially egalitarian tendencies."[8] Aside from a few very general slogans, Hitler's *Mein Kampf,* and the twenty-five points announced by Hitler in February of 1920, the NSDAP had no set platform but instead promised to be everything to everybody. The glue that bound the party together was hatred of Jews and leftists who were made the sole scapegoats for Germany's humiliation and defeat. Likewise, anti-capitalism, just like the initial friendliness towards the church and concern for legality, turned out to be no more than a tactic and a deception to gain votes and time for stabilization.

Gradually Hitler eliminated unemployment primarily by stimulating the armaments industry and the burdens of the Versailles Treaty by, among other things, halting the payment of reparations, occupying the Rhineland without opposition in 1936. In March of 1938 he invaded Austria and incorporated it into the German Reich in violation of international law — without protest from any of the democratic countries (except Mexico) but with the agreement and jubilation of the great majority of the population of both countries. Also, in March of 1939, Hitler dissolved Czechoslovakia without penalty and placed Bohemia and Moravia under German protection. With the march into Poland on September 1, 1939, the disastrous Munich Agreement of September 1938 finally broke down completely; on September 3, 1939, France and Great Britain declared war. Hitler then expanded into the Soviet Union in June of 1941 despite the non-aggression treaty signed in August of 1939. After initial successes and victories, the tide began to turn, particularly after the entry of the United States into the war in December of 1941 and the catastrophic German defeat at Stalingrad in January of 1943. With the landing of the Allies in Normandy in the early morning hours of June 6, 1944, the fate of the Third Reich was sealed. The unconditional surrender took place on May 8, 1945.

The Nazis took violent action against any opposition and all enemies of the Third Reich in internal politics as well. Especially affected were leftists, Jews, confessional Christians of all denominations, and other groups that the Nazis considered inferior. Concentration camps were created for them and in those camps millions of innocent people were murdered up to 1945. Open resistance against the Nazi regime was minimal: the successes of Hitler's internal and external policies as well as the course of the war, which was initially favorable to the Nazis, made it difficult for resistance groups of the right and left to be formed and to gain broad support. Open resistance on a larger scale occurred only in 1944, but after the tragically failed attempt on Hitler's life on July 20, 1944, resistance ended with the total and brutal annihilation of any and all opposition, even if only suspected.

Notes

[1] Joachim C. Fest, *Hitler: Eine Biographie* (Hitler: A Biography) (Frankfurt am Main: Propyläen, 1973), 185.

[2] "*Bündisch*" means belonging to the Youth Movement.

[3] On racially oriented, nationalistic associations, see, for example, George L. Mosse, *The Crisis of German Ideology: Intellectual Origins of the Third Reich* (New York: Grosset and Dunlap, 1964 and 1971), chapters 11 and 12, as well as the caricature

of these movements by Lion Feuchtwanger in "Gespräche mit dem ewigen Juden" ("Conversations with the Eternal Jew"), in his book *Ein Buch nur für meine Freunde* (A Book Only for my Friends) (Frankfurt am Main: Fischer, 1984), 437–459.

[4] On the beginnings of the Nazi movement, see, for example, Karl Dietrich Bracher, *Die deutsche Diktatur: Entstehung, Struktur, Folgen des Nationalsozialismus* (The German Dictatorship: Development, Structure, and Consequences of National Socialism) (Cologne and Berlin: Kiepenheuer & Witsch, 1969), containing numerous additional literature references; or Dietrich Bronder, *Bevor Hitler kam* (Before Hitler Came) (Hanover: Pfeiffer, 1964).

[5] For a detailed and comprehensive description and analysis of Hitler's life and career see Ian Kershaw's extensive and authoritative Hitler biography in two volumes: volume 1: *Hitler 1889–1936. Hubris* (New York and London: Norton, 1998; 1st American edition 1999); volume 2: *Hitler 1936–45. Nemesis* (New York and London: Norton, 2000, 1st American edition 2000).

[6] Soviet-style republics that existed briefly during the revolutionary days in 1919, first in Bremen in February, then in Munich in April under the leadership of the radical left, including the writers Erich Mühsam, Ernst Toller, and Gustav Landauer.

[7] See Jost Hermand and Frank Trommler, eds., *Die Kultur der Weimarer Republik* (The Culture of the Weimar Republic) (Munich: Nymphenburger Verlagshandlung, 1978), 26–27.

[8] Karl Dietrich Erdmann, *Deutschland unter der Herrschaft des Nationalsozialismus* (Germany Under the Rule of National Socialism, 1933–1939) (Munich: dtv, 1980), 25.

2: The Ideological Context

AS TO BE EXPECTED, the literature of the Third Reich reflects its ideology; in contrast to the "manic democratic egalitarianism" of the Weimar Republic, the ideology is founded on *völkisch* national Germanness, hero worship, and the leader principle. However, Klaus Vondung rightly points out that National Socialist literature cannot be defined any more exactly than can National Socialism itself: "National Socialism is not a clearly defined entity."[1] National Socialist literature and National Socialist ideology cannot be cleanly separated from each other because there is a mutual dependence between the two: the literature influences, indeed, forms the ideology, and vice versa. National Socialist literature reflects the lack of consistency of the ideology, for National Socialist ideology is "not a clearly defined system but rather a conglomerate of disparate elements," that is, *völkisch* and anti-Semitic, nationalistic and conservative, social revolutionary, anti-liberal, anti-democratic, and anti-capitalistic elements.[2]

The Nazis often succeeded in exploiting the various movements for their purposes, with open or secret approval, but at times also against the will of individual representatives of these ideologies. One need only remember the conservative resistance to the Nazis and Hitler that reached its culmination in Stauffenberg's assassination attempt on July 20, 1944. Ironically, Stauffenberg had led the torch procession in Hitler's honor in his garrison on January 30, 1933.[3] Ernst Jünger is another example of Nazi exploitation. Although Jünger rejected National Socialism his war journal *In Stahlgewittern* (In Storms of Steel) fit well into Nazi ideology and went through twenty-six printings for a total of 244,000 copies.[4] The experience of Arthur Moeller van den Bruck, the prophet of the Third Reich, was not much different; he refused Hitler's offer of collaboration, but by 1935, 130,000 copies of his main work, *Das Dritte Reich* (The Third Reich), which was first published 1923, had already been printed.[5] Hitler had the Conservative Revolutionary and publicist, Edgar J. Jung, who had propagated numerous Nazi ideas in his main work *Die Herrschaft der Minderwertigen* (The Rule of Inferior Beings, 1927),[6] murdered on June 30, 1934, in the course of the Röhm putsch. Jung was an opponent of Hitler and his comrades, but claims that he and the Conservative Revolution had really made Hitler's assumption of power possible.[7] Jung clearly illustrates that "rejection of Adolf Hitler and his party [. . .]" is "by no means a measure of democratic spirit."[8]

The objective here is not to introduce the various theories on the development of National Socialism,[9] nor to examine in detail the various conservative groups of the Weimar Republic (e.g., German Nationalism, Conservative Revolution, Revolutionary Nationalism, National Bolshevism, German *völkisch* groups, and so on) and their contribution to National Socialism, nor to differentiate the old conservatives from the new conservatives; for that, one can refer to the relevant secondary literature.[10] As Martin Greiffenhagen and others show, the discussion about the role of German conservatism in Hitler's success is continuing. Defenders of the conservatives see themselves as victims; others see the conservatives, regardless of what variety, as the stirrup holders for the Nazis.[11] Be that as it may, it is certain that all anti-democratic groups, not least of all the Conservative Revolution, contributed their part to the rise of the Nazis, which the clever chief ideologues of the Nazis knew how to exploit to establish legitimacy.[12] The Nazis made reference to numerous predecessors from the time of the Kaiser and the Weimar Republic, even to writers and philosophers of the wars of liberation[13] in whose works the Nazis thought they had found material that was useful for their purposes. At the same time, these works often played a decisive role in the ideological development of influential Nazis and numerous National Socialist authors. In these works we find the prefigured ideologems (Vondung) that recur in National Socialist ideology and National Socialist literature.

In a talk given before a group of Old Fighters on February 24, 1938, in the Munich Hofbräuhaus, Adolf Hitler confessed with unusual candor that National Socialist ideology did not really contain anything new. "Much of what was in our platform, or what I proclaimed in this hall on this day eighteen years ago had already been thought up a very long time before that."[14] All of these various elements, however, never coalesced into a unified ideology of National Socialism; they remained "an opportunistic mixture of the most disparate ideological complexes."[15] Many of the ideas propagated in these influential works were applied in reality after the seizure of power, for example, the "destruction of inferior races," the "breeding of an Arian race," and the creation of a *völkisch* racial elite on the model of the German Order.[16] However, "returning to the peasant, Nordic origins of the German people," living without modern technology, and eliminating capitalism were never seriously considered.[17] In the following pages, some of the especially influential works of literary and cultural history with the themes "Reich," "war," and "race" will be briefly presented.

The "old dream of the new Reich" flits through the works of numerous publishers and writers of the twenties and thirties.[18] The most influential of them is undoubtedly *Das Dritte Reich* (The Third Reich) by Arthur Moeller van den Bruck. In the preface to the third edition, which was published six years after Moeller's death, Hans Schwarz attests to the great influence of the main work of this Conservative Revolutionary:

Anyone who follows political journalism in our times will find traces of Moeller's words everywhere, in formulations like "from the strength of living with contradictions," "in turning away from liberalism as the death of nations," "in the nationalization of socialism and the socialization of nationalism," "in revolutionary conservatism," "in the thesis of the rights of young nations."[19]

According to Sontheimer, Moeller's book, first published in 1922, was "practically the bible of young National Socialism."[20] In a time of cultural pessimism after the lost war and Oswald Spengler's famous book *Untergang des Abendlandes* (Decline of the West, 1918), it rekindled the New Conservatives's hopes for the coming of a great age beyond liberalism, Bolshevism, Western democracy, and parliamentary systems. "In place of party guardianship we put the concept of the German Reich. It is an old and great German concept" (IX). As a conservative, Moeller believes "in the power of the leader as an exemplary person" (278). The leader must be decisive to the last in order to identify with the national fate of the people.

> We need leaders who feel that they have become one with the nation, who associate the fate of the nation with their own destiny, . . . and who . . . are determined to shape the future of the nation with their will, with their decisiveness, and with their ambition. (280)

Naturally these leaders will not be elected in a parliamentary, democratic manner; Moeller and the rightists had just experienced such leaders: "the leader concept is not a matter for the ballot but for agreement, which is based on trust" (280). For that purpose new political forms are needed, not the ones introduced in 1918, but instead "forms not from western parliamentary systems, which have as their objective party rule, but the forms of our most German tradition, which is based on leadership" (218).

Of course, just how the choice of a leader will proceed is not stated; the leader simply appears, for leading is in the blood of the conservative person:

> It is rather knowledge of the blood that gives the conservative person the edge: the in-born ability to move in the real world and to assert himself, the in-born overview that derives from the distance separating him from human and state affairs and reserved to him, and the in-born suitability for leadership, which repeatedly is the lot of the conservative person, because it belongs to him. (287)

Moeller called the supporters of the black, red, and gold flag of the Weimar Republic romantics (300), but according to Kaltenbrunner, he was a "late-blooming political romantic," who found himself in "good" European company, like Merezhkovski, Sorel, Marinetti, D. H. Lawrence, or Hamsun.[21] Indeed, it is also no coincidence that Moeller was the editor of the first complete German edition of Dostoyevsky. The Russian poet was "the answer of the anti-liberals and irrationalists on the right to the challenge of Zola, the idol of the left."[22] Russia, Italy, and Germany were for Moeller young countries with a future;[23] it is therefore not surprising that not only Hitler but also Lenin — likewise unsuccessfully — sought Moeller as a collaborator.[24] From here, a trail also leads to the National Bolshevists, but that cannot be pursued further here.[25] However, the trail indicates the diversity of the conservative camp, which did not completely disappear even in the Third Reich, and also the selectivity of the Nazis, for they could not use the entire Moeller, nor the entire Nietzsche nor the entire Jünger.

The broad range of conservatism was a kind of smorgasbord where the Nazis could seek out exactly what they needed — in both literature and politics. In Moeller they found a good deal, but not the teaching about subhumans. They found abundant anti-rationalism and belief in fate, as illustrated in the following passage, which also could come directly from Hitler's *Mein Kampf* (My Struggle): "We humans . . ., whose fate is sealed without our being conscious of it, [are] set to exert our will, depend on our bravery, and listen to the voice of our inspirations. And we speak of foresight because we cannot foresee what is foreseen for us" (31) In Moeller, however, there are also prophetic sentences, such as "the human race is all too inclined to yield to self-deception. The thought of the Third Reich could become the greatest of all self-deceptions" (IX). Neither he nor his numerous readers realized just how right he was. But according to Moeller, if there must be decline and fall, then it should be with great style, and in that point the Nazis were of one mind with him again, especially toward the end of the war: "For all peoples the hour will come when they will die by murder or suicide and no greater end is imaginable for a great people than ruin in a world war which the whole world must wage to conquer a single country" (301). What Moeller meant to apply to the First World War then became, even more than in 1918, the most gruesome of realities in the Second World War, which was instigated by the Nazis.

Such an end requires willingness to sacrifice and courage in the face of death. The heroic glorification of war by Walter Flex, who died in action in 1917 near Oesel Island, came at an opportune time for the Nazis. His war diary *Der Wanderer zwischen beiden Welten* (The Wanderer Between Two Worlds, 1915) became a "national bestseller";[26] by 1942, 912,000 copies had already been published.[27] While Ernst Jünger glorifies in a sober, objective manner the men tempered in the barrages of fire in the First World War, youthful romanticism sets the tone of Flex's book, which is dedicated to his friend, the theology student and war volunteer, Lieutenant Ernst Wurche: "All glory and all salvation in the German future seemed to him [Wurche] to come from the spirit of the *Wandervogel,* and when I [Flex] think of him [Wurche], he who embodies this spirit, pure and bright, I agree with him. . . ."[28] And what constitutes this spirit? "Stay pure and mature" (37). The *Wandervogel*[29] sought edification in untouched nature, and this almost mystical romanticism based on nature also finds its way into the Flex text. In the midst of the events of war at the Russian front in 1915, scenes like the following appear:

> Gunfire rumbles over from afar, but the world of battle from which we were carried away for hours seemed distant and unreal, like a dream. Our guns lay under our dusty clothes in the grass; we were not thinking about them. A sacred sphere embraced the wide, shimmering depths of green pastures and blue waters. (44)

The *Wandervogel,* however, is concerned not only with nature, but also with rejuvenated Germanness and humanity: "The young people of the *Wandervogel* and the Germanness and humanity rejuvenated by their spirit were perhaps closest to his [Wurche's] heart, and around this love circulated the warmest waves of his blood" (37). Wurche, like Flex, is an exemplary and dutiful German officer who does not ask about the background of the war and carries out orders to the point of self-sacrifice, but he also demands absolute obedience. At the same time, he does not demand more of his subordinates than of himself: he lives as an example to his people, and if necessary, he will also die as an example to his people: "Serving as a lieutenant means: living as an example to your people, . . . dying as an example to your people is probably just part of it" (9). Living as an example means being a leader, and the best school for leadership is the trench at the war front: "Living together in the trenches was perhaps the best school, and probably no one will become a real leader who was not already a leader there" (10).

Scattered throughout the text are lyrical passages by Walter Flex, who is called by many the Theodor Körner of the First World War.[30] In Körner's poetry we find not only the wild geese that move northward through the night with shrill cries (Körner lines made famous by a popular song), past the front of fighting men, but also stanzas like the following, which would fit seamlessly into any National Socialist anthology of poetry:

> Brandhelle loht!
> Mord, Haß, und Tod
> Sie recken ob der Erde
> Zu grauser Drohgebärde,
> Daß niemals Friede werde,
> Schwurhände blutigrot.
> Was Frost und Leid!
> Mich brennt ein Eid.
> Der glüht wie Feuersbrände
> Durch Schwert und Herz und Hände.
> Es ende drum, wie's ende —
> Deutschland, ich bin bereit. (89–90)

[Light of fire flares!
Murder, hate, and death,
They spread across the earth
With savage gestures, threatening
That peace will never be,
Hands raised to vow, bloody red.
What frost and pain!
In me sears an oath.
It burns like fire's blaze
Through sword and heart and hands.
End as it will end —
Germany, I am ready.]

His friend falls in action near Calvary, the "city of suffering" (57) — in obvious reference to Christ's sacrificial death. However, his friend stays with him even after death as the "wanderer between two worlds"; the boundary between life and death is lifted: "For great souls, death is the greatest experience" (77). The dead who march together with the living became a characteristic of National Socialist literature and ideology, as in the Horst Wessel song, the official Nazi anthem.

The racial idea that is at the core of National Socialist ideology is found in numerous small and large prophets of a racist ideology. Such prophets were especially popular in periods of crisis, 1873 to 1895, 1919 to 1923, and 1930 to 1933, but the seeds that they sowed only sprouted after Hitler's assumption of power.[31] Even some Jews turned up in the role of wild anti-Semites and provided the Nazis with propaganda material, for example, Otto Weininger with his main work *Geschlecht und Charakter* (*Sex and Character,* 1903), which was, however, censured after the seizure of power, because the author was a Jew.[32] In the multi-ethnic Habsburg state, the *völkisch* racial ideas fell on especially fertile soil, particularly in Vienna, which was the destination of numerous eastern Jews fleeing from pogroms.

Hitler and other National Socialists derived their anti-Semitic ideas about race from the racist Vienna of the period before the First World War, from people like the estate owner Georg Ritter von Schönerer, who demanded special anti-Jewish laws; the Christian socialist Karl Lueger, the Lord Mayor of Vienna from 1897 to 1910; and the runaway Cistercian monk and self-anointed racial apostle Adolf Lanz (1874–1954), who called himself Georg (Jörg) Lanz von Liebenfels and had already raised the swastika flag over his "castle," Werfenstein, in Lower Austria in 1907. Lanz founded a men's order of blond, blue-eyed Aryans and served as the editor of the journal *Ostara,* which Hitler studied avidly during his time in Vienna, although "the whole climate of the Lanz people's 'order,'" as Friedrich Heer explains, did not suit him.[33] In any case, Hitler found in the *Ostara* ideas on racial breeding and sovereign rights of the blond Aryans of noble race designed to protect them from being placed in jeopardy by "racial mixed-breeds" and "sub-humans." Lanz calls them *Äfflinge, Schrättlinge,* and *Tschandalen,* which could be roughly translated as "monkeymen," "satyrs," and "shameful vandals." In his book *Mein Kampf,* Hitler accorded Dr. Lueger the highest praise and acknowledged having laid the foundations of his ideology in his "years of apprenticeship and suffering in Vienna" (1908–1913): "In this period I formed my image of the world and my ideology, which became the granite foundation of my actions at that time. I have had to learn little more than what I created for myself back then and I needed to change nothing."[34] In Vienna, he confessed, his "eyes were opened . . . to two dangers . . . to the existence of the German people . . .: Marxism and Judaism."[35]

Among the prophets of anti-Semitism were Germans like Herman Ahlwardt, Otto Boeckel, who was the first independent anti-Semite in the *Reichstag,*[36] Arthur Dinter, Theodor Fritsch, Julius Langbehn, Wilhelm Marr, the Berlin cathedral and court clergyman Adolf Stöcker, Heinrich von Treitschke, Richard Wagner, and the poet highly respected by Hitler and the Nazis, Johann Dietrich Eckart, who arranged direct start-up assistance for Hitler; he was the only one whom Hitler publicly acknowledged as a mentor. One of the first and the worst was Eugen Dühring, the former rival of Karl Marx: "The Jews are the foulest product of the entire Semitic race, representing a nationality especially dangerous to other peoples."[37] In 1937 Alfred von Terzi wrote in the journal *Hammer,* published by Theodor Fritsch:

> Dühring's achievement in recognizing the Jewish question and in creating a life-affirming socialism tailored to the German [remains] a *great accomplishment that deserves not to be forgotten.* Dühring is the man who was the first German to clearly emphasize, on the basis of his idea of personality, the *notion of the leader.* He is likewise in accord with Adolf Hitler in very many other ways.[38]

In Dühring's blind hatred of Jews, with "'eradication' and 'blood-radical' as his favorite words," he went so far as to proclaim "genocide to be a 'higher law of history'" and to elevate "the Jewish question to an 'existential question.'"[39]

Dinter's anti-Semitic "historical novel" *Die Sünde wider das Blut* (The Sin Against Blood, 1917), one of the most radical and most influential works,[40] is dedicated to "the German Houston Stewart Chamberlain," who had opened Dinter's eyes to the "race question," as he confesses in the epilogue. The anti-Semitism of this book is not even exceeded by that of Zöberlein's novel *Der Befehl des Gewissens* (The Command of Conscience), discussed further in the chapter on novels. The main character of this novel, Hermann Kämpfer, is "systematically destroyed by Jews."[41] His father loses his property as the result of land speculation by the Jewish broker Levisohn, and Hermann's marriage to the blond Elisabeth is ruined by the crime of having Jewish blood. Hermann dedicates himself completely to the battle against the "poisonous and destructive influence which the Jews exert directly and indirectly by the power of their money, through the press, writing, and theater, through the offices of judges and teachers on German feelings and thought, on German customs and views, and on German trade and traffic" (275). In anticipation of the National Socialist Aryan paragraphs, he demands legal exclusion of the Jews from public life: "The Jews are foreign to us in blood and spirit and must be viewed as foreigners and be treated as foreigners under special laws, if we are not to perish because of them" (276). In order to lend authenticity and emphasis to his tirades, which are thinly disguised as a novel, he adds notes and further literature citations on the question of race to the book.[42]

In 1890 an anonymous work appeared that was written "by a German" and according to Ketelsen "exerted considerable influence on the formation of petty-bourgeois ideology in the Wilhelminian era": Julius Langbehn's *Rembrandt als Erzieher* (Rembrandt as Educator).[43] "Of all the essayists on ideology, J. Langbehn is most interesting for the question of literary history."[44] In the preface to the 1943 edition of the work, the title of which is derived from Nietzsche's title *Schopenhauer as Educator,* the book is praised as "his greatest legacy to the German people," for

> the foundation for the Rembrandt German is his Germanness, the close tie to his native soil, which is expressed in his fondness for the peasantry and his aversion to all elements of foreign origin (Jewry). His great mentor here was Paul de Lagarde, whom he passionately revered; building on the latter's works, he has come close to grasping the racial ideas of today.[45]

As did Gottfried Benn later, Langbehn is also seeking a way out of a world that has been fragmented by modern natural science: "One thirsts for synthesis" (2). For him the road to salvation is through art and artists. The "heroes of the mind, ancestors of the people, representatives of those of its qualities of character which are destined at present and in the period just ahead to come to the surface of history . . . they are the *educators* of their people" (7). Langbehn sees all these qualities embodied in Rembrandt; for Langbehn, the Dutch painter is "the most German of all painters and even the most German of all German artists" (10). He is "the prototype of the German artist; thus, he and only he, as the perfect model, satisfies the wishes and needs vaguely perceived by the German people of today in the spiritual realm — even if it is to some extent unconsciously" (10). The great thing about Rembrandt is his lack of any plan: "That is essentially the only true artistic plan" (11). Langbehn considers this lack of any plan to be a good political plan as well, "and perhaps the only good political plan . . . a German plan in the true sense of the word" (11), since it leaves free play to the intuition of the genius. It would appear that the "artist" Adolf Hitler made

Langbehn's plan his own, for despite his twenty-five points and *Mein Kampf,* the Nazi Party had no clearly defined party platform.

For Langbehn, that which is genuine German slumbers in the Low German soul; the refinement and renewal of the German people are to emerge thence, for even in the Prussian sphere foreign racial elements are still mixed in (120). In the Low German sphere, the qualities of peasant, artist, and king are combined: "In the peasant the earthly comes together with the heavenly, the outer with the inner life of the human being, the king, with the artist" (119). He finds all these qualities embodied in Rembrandt, his colors, "black and white, light and dark, are elegant, cool, decisive, and above all Low German colors" (240) In the colors black and white, the Prussian national colors, the Low German lands show, according to Langbehn, that they are the "political as well as the spiritual link between Prussia and Germany" (240). Langbehn, too, longs for a leader, a "secret *Kaiser*":

> Time needs an extraordinary mover and shaker who can set the dead masses in motion; to him is due rule over all. Of course not in the manner of a tyrant, but like Bismarck ruled Germany: by putting into effect the feelings, wishes, and orders of his people, at times even to all appearances against its will. (235–36)

The leader must be an artist and have the creative abilities: "If such a 'secret *Kaiser*' comes, he will have to have the gift for leading and forming. In this way he will present a decided contrast to the present paper age" (237).

The way to the rebirth of Germany — Langbehn strictly rejects the un-German term "renaissance" in the course of demanding purification of the German language — is, however, blocked by the Jews; his book ends with wild tirades of hatred against this "putrefaction" on the German body: "The political health must have a showdown with the political putrefaction" (275). The "destructive Jewish spirit" has, according to Langbehn, wormed its way in everywhere, even in art: "And as in politics, likewise in art. The Jewish character, which so likes to sympathize with Zola, runs, like the latter, completely counter to the purely German essence of a Walter von der Vogelweide, Dürer, or Mozart" (275). He rants like Hitler that not only the press but also the theater is "jewified": "The German theater itself, which is now predominantly in the hands of the Jews, has as a result become unproductive, trivial, and in part unseemly . . . Extreme measures are necessary here!" (277). His proposal: following the example of the Jesuits, the German officer corps, and the fraternities, remove the Jews from government service and other important positions, and a "proof of Aryanism": "The proof in question would be supplied by the particular applicant's swearing an oath. The present stage of German development is approaching such a solution to the problem" (278). In this context, Rembrandt, too, becomes a racial model: "Rembrandt is a real Aryan (280), as he comes from the "cradle of Aryanism," the "entire Germanic northwest, that is, the Low German lands" (280). From here, according to Langbehn, who was born in Schleswig, the rebirth of the German people is to begin: "Starting from where a people was born, there it will be reborn," through "the Aryan blood, . . . which has the most moral 'gold' in it" (280). The myth of the leader, of blood and soil that blossomed in the Third Reich, is already clearly evident in Langbehn's book, although many of its significant representatives were neither from the Low German lands nor did they fit the Aryan ideal of "racial purity."[46]

This unusual book by an unusual person struck a nerve at the time and articulated the widespread discomfort with Wilhelminian society: "Unsystematic, erratic, eclectic, but with great gestures showing insight into world history and extensive education, the author formulates and summarizes what was discussed within the petty-bourgeois and educated middle class of the time, vaguely and laden with emotion, but discussed all the same."[47] The connection to National Socialism came about because this movement also considered itself a reaction to the general uncertainty that set in with the social changes at the end of the nineteenth century. However, Ketelsen warns justifiably of "declaring Langbehn the 'intellectual forerunner' of the National Socialism," as the Nazis developed "a thoroughly ruptured relationship with Langbehn and his book."[48]

However, even non-German anti-Semitic works and authors attracted considerable attention in German-speaking areas, including the *Protokolle der Weisen von Zion* (Protocols of the Wise Men from Zion), a fake document from Eastern Europe that first appeared in Russian newspapers in 1903 as a "document," and above all, *Die Ungleichheit der Menschenrassen* (The Inequality of the Human Races; in French, "Essay sur l'inégalité des races humaines," 1853) of the French Baron Joseph Arthur Gobineau (1816–1882) This work was translated into German in 1901 by the race researcher Ludwig Schemann on the advice of Richard Wagner,[49] and the *Die Grundlagen des Neunzehnten Jahrhunderts* (Foundations of the Nineteenth Century, 1899) by the Englishman Houston Stewart Chamberlain. The work of the Englishman and later son-in-law of Richard Wagner enjoyed considerable popularity and had large printings until 1945; the twenty-eighth printing, for example, appeared in 1942. With the noticeable exception of the years between 1922 and 1932, coincidentally the most stable period of the Weimar Republic), the book, which was highly praised by Hitler, Rosenberg, and other Nazi greats, was reprinted almost every year. For all of that, the book by the cultivated Englishman, who had lived in Germany and Austria since 1870 and was on friendly terms with numerous persons in high positions, is far removed from the primitive racial hatred of Langbehn, Dühring, Streicher, editor of the National Socialist newspaper *Der Stürmer*, or Zöberlin, discussed further in the chapter on the novel. While Chamberlain was writing his main work — other works of his treat Kant, Goethe, and botany — the influences from Vienna and Wagner were the greatest.

In an ambitious study, Chamberlain attempts to follow the various cultural currents from the beginning of our calendar to the nineteenth century, to bring into focus the main features of the century that in his opinion are characteristic. In that undertaking, Germans and Jews play a decisive role, the Germans as creators "of our entire civilization and culture of today"[50] and the Jews as the threat to them. His attitude towards Jews, however, is entirely ambivalent; he admires the "racial purity" that they have been able to maintain over centuries, particularly the Sephardic Jews,[51] but he considers them, "like the Emperor Tiberius or Friedrich II von Hohenstaufen," a "*national* danger" (397). In particular, after emancipation, "the Jew rushed in, stormed all position and planted . . . the flag of his eternally foreign being on the breach of our real unique character" (382). He does not, however, seek to blame the Jews: "Should we revile the Jews for that? That would be just as ignoble, unworthy, and unreasonable. The Jews deserve admiration, for they have acted in keeping with the logic and truth of their individual character" (382). He attempts to prove on the basis of history that the "great and destructive influence of the Jews . . . until deep into the nineteenth century" was made possible by the complicity of numerous non-Jews: "kings and princes who needed money, down to the Metternichs and Hardenbergs" (401–2). The Jews provide Chamberlain with "a truly admirable example of loyalty against themselves, against their own nation, and against the belief of their fathers" (402). He lays the blame on himself and his own kind: "We ourselves were the criminal helpers of the Jews; that was the case and still is the case today; and we ourselves betrayed that which the most pitiful residents of the ghetto held sacred, the purity of inherited blood" (402). A primitive anti-Semitism that makes "the Jews the common scapegoat for all the evils of our times" is of no help (19). The "Jewish danger" emanates from the Germanic peoples, and only they can do something to stop it: "We produced it ourselves and must overcome it ourselves" (19). The means to do that is a new religion, for "our entire Germanic culture is growing ill from lack of a true religion" (19).

The uneasiness with modern civilization and the complaint about the fragmentation and democratization of a society without myths are shared by Alfred Rosenberg, the chief ideologue of the Third Reich, who in his main work *Der Mythus des 20. Jahrhunderts* (The Myth of the Twentieth Century, 1930) calls for a rebirth of Nordic, *völkisch* myth.[52] If that does not happen, in his view, the occident will inevitably sink into racial chaos:

> Either we will rise up through revitalization and up-breeding of the ancient blood, combined with an increased will to fight, to a purifying proficiency, or the last Germanic occidental values of civilization and

statecraft will sink into the dirty human flood of the international cities, grow crippled on the burning, sterile asphalt of brutalized inhumanity, or seep away to South America, China, the Dutch Indies, and Africa as an infectious germ in the form of emigrants, bastardizing themselves.[53]

However, he sees a sign of hope: "The blood which died starts to revive. In its mystical sign, a new cell structure of the German people's soul unfolds" (1). Opposite systems of rational and intellectual analysis, the entire bloodless intellectual trash heap of purely schematic systems, Rosenberg places the organic and timeless unity of the *völkisch* soul of the people:

> We posit the following organization according to the laws of life: 1. racial soul, 2. *Volkstum*, 3. personality, 4. cultural group, whereby we are not thinking of a progression from top to bottom but rather circulation pulsing through. The racial soul cannot be grasped with the hands and yet is represented in the community of the people bound by blood, is crowned by and symbolically concentrated in the great personalities, who through creative activities produce a cultural group, which in turn is borne by the race and the racial soul. . . . With this insight, the organic philosophy of our times escapes from the tyranny of rational schemata. (697)

Rosenberg's book traces in a completely unsystematic manner the origins of the Nordic soul of the race in its various forms, from the "legendary Atlantis," from "North Atlantic traces in Egypt," from "Nordic Helas," to the Germanic people, the mystic Meister Eckhart, Richard Wagner, and Adolf Hitler. History is combed for Nordic blond types; even Jesus is Aryanized and freed of "Jewish slag." With just such intensity Rosenberg traces through history all elements "foreign to the species," such as Pauline Christianity and the Old Testament, Catholicism, Marxian Socialism, Capitalism, Feminism, and all other "-isms" — except for National Socialism.

His sharpest attacks are directed at "Jewish parasitism . . . from Joseph in Egypt to Rothschild and Rathenau, from Philo through David ben Selomo to Heine" (463). For him the "subhuman state of Jews" is also displayed in the area of art: "Jewish art is 'nigger' art in every respect . . . imitation, technique, pretense, effect, quantity, virtuosity, everything that is desired, just no genius, no creative power" (365). In contrast, true art, in Rosenberg's view, rises from the mythical depths of the *völkisch* racial soul, which does not lose itself in individual psychology but instead willfully experiences the cosmic laws of the soul and forms them spiritually and architectonically, as "revealed in Richard Wagner" (433). Wagnerian art is, however, only one expression of the "racial soul of the people," which is eternally at work and which permeates every creation that is "true to its nature":

A Nordic heroic legend, a Prussian march, a composition of Bach, a sermon of Eckhart, a Faust monologue, [these are] only different expressions of one and the same soul, creations of the same will . . ., eternal forces which first joined together under the name of Odin, and in modern times were embodied in Friedrich[54] and Bismarck. And for as long as that is so, and only for that long, will Nordic blood act together with the Nordic soul in mystical union, as the precondition for any creation true to its nature. (680)

The swastika is the symbol of the "old-new myth" (689). Rosenberg's book, which was already "essentially complete" in 1925 and whose beginnings extend back to 1917, had already reached a printing total of 553,000 copies by 1937. It is dedicated "to the memory of two million German heroes, . . . who were killed in the First World War for a German life and a German Reich of honor and freedom" and whose memory the Nazis considered dishonored and sullied by the "Jewish democratic shopkeeper souls."

The ancestral gallery of National Socialism can be expanded as desired, but the objective here was only to provide a brief look at the complex problem.[55] Not only the literature but also the ideology of National Socialism, to the extent that it can be called that at all, was almost completely ready at the time of the seizure of power in 1933. Anti-Semitism, right-wing radicalism, and fascism were by no means limited to Germany,[56] but as the result of certain political, historical, and social conditions they took on their worst forms in that country. Even after 1945, these tendencies did not disappear completely from the screen, neither in Germany nor in other countries; Brecht's epilogue to his work *Der aufhaltsame Aufstieg des Arturo Ui* (The Resistible Rise of Arturo Ui, 1941) formulates: "The womb out of which that crept is fertile still!"[57]

Notes

[1] Klaus Vondung, "Der literarische Nationalismus. Ideologische, politische und sozialhistorische Wirkungszusammenhänge" (Literary National Socialism. Ideological, Political, and Social-Historical Interconnections), in *Die deutsche Literatur im Dritten Reich* (German Literature in the Third Reich), edited by Horst Denkler and Karl Prümm (Stuttgart: Reclam, 1976), 44. See also Kurt Sontheimer in his standard work, *Antidemokratisches Denken in der Weimarer Republik* (Anti-Democratic Thinking in the Weimar Republic), 2nd edition (Munich: Nymphenburger Verlagshandlung, 1962, 1968), 134. "National Socialist ideology was never a uniform doctrine that could even vaguely be compared with the closed system of Marxist ideology."

[2] Klaus Vondung, 46.

[3] See Arnim Mohler, quoted in Martin Greiffenhagen, *Das Dilemma des Konservatismus in Deutschland* (The Dilemma of Conservatism in Germany) (Munich: Piper, 1977), 294.

[4] Karl Prümm, *Die Literatur des Soldatischen Nationalismus der 20er Jahre (1918–1933)* (The Literature of Soldierly Nationalism in the Twenties [1918–1933]), 2 volumes (Kronberg im Taunus: Scriptor, 1974), 101.

[5] See Gerd Klaus Kaltenbrunner, "Vom 'Preußischen Stil' zum 'Dritten Reich': Arthur Moeller van den Bruck" (From "Prussian Style" to the "Third Reich": Arthur Moeller van den Bruck), in *Propheten des Nationalsozialismus* (Prophets of National Socialism), edited by Karl Schwedhelm (Munich: List, 1969), 153 and 157.

[6] His "Richtlinien zur inneren und äußeren Erneuerung deutschen Volkes und deutschen Staates" (Guidelines for Inner and Outer Renewal of the German People and the German State) is based on *völkisch* racial ideas, leadership of an elite, and the imperialistic drive to the east; see Edgar J. Jung, *Die Herrschaft der Minderwertigen: Ihr Zerfall und ihre Ablösung* (The Rule of Inferior Beings: Its Decline and Its Dissolution) (Berlin: Deutsche Rundschau, 1927), especially 333–341.

[7] See Kurt Sontheimer, 283.

[8] Kurt Sontheimer, 283.

[9] A good introductory overview on that subject is provided by Wolfgang Wippermann, ed., in his book *Kontroversen um Hitler* (Controversies about Hitler) (Frankfurt: Suhrkamp, 1986).

[10] Especially Kurt Sontheimer, *Antidemokratisches Denken in der Weimarer Republik*, or Karl Prümm, *Die Literatur des Soldatischen Nationalismus der 20er Jahre (1918–1933)*, especially 1–81.

[11] See Martin Greiffenhagen, *Das Dilemma des Konservatismus in Deutschland*; Ernst Nolte, ed., *Theorien über den Faschismus* (Theories on Fascism) (Cologne and Berlin: Kiepenheuer & Witsch, 1967); or Richard Saage, *Faschismustheorien* (Fascism Theories) (Munich: Beck, 1976). For Armin Mohler, "the relationship of the 'Conservative Revolution' to political events after 1933" remains unexplored, see Armin Mohler, *Die konservative Revolution in Deutschland 1918–1932. Ein Handbuch* (The Conservative Revolution in Germany, 1918–1932. A Handbook), 2nd completely revised and expanded edition (Darmstadt: Wissenschaftliche Buchgesellschaft 1972; 1st edition, 1950), 3. The difference between theories of totalitarianism and theories of fascism cannot be treated here; for that subject, see for example Reinhard Kühnl, *Deutschland zwischen Demokratie und Faschismus* (Germany between Democracy and Fascism) (Munich: Hanser, 1969), especially 143–163 ("Faschismus — Versuch einer Begriffsbestimmung" (Fascism — Attempt at a Definition of the Concept). Grossly failing to recognize political realities, Conservative Revolutionaries like Edgar Jung even hoped to exploit the Nazis for their own anti-democratic ends; see Sontheimer, 287.

[12] Keith Bullivant, "Aufbruch der Nation: Zur 'Konservativen Revolution'" (Emergence of the Nation. On the "Conservative Revolution"), in *Das literarische Leben in der Weimarer Republik* (The Literary Life in the Weimar Republic), edited by Keith Bullivant (Königstein im Taunus: Scriptor, 1978), 44.

[13] In contrast to the period after 1900, however, the *völkisch* had become "inexorably bound to the democratic" in the wars of liberation from 1813 to 1815, in the words of Jost Hermand in "Ultima Thule," in Jost Hermand, *Orte. Irgendwo. Formen utopischen Denkens* (Places. Somewhere. Forms of Utopian Thinking) (Königstein im Taunus: Athenäum, 1981), 61.

[14] Quoted in Joachim Petzold, "Die Entstehung der Naziideologie" (The Development of Nazi Ideology), in *Kontroversen um Hitler*," edited by Wolfgang Wippermann (Frankfurt am Main: Suhrkamp, 1986), 169.

[15] Jost Hermand, "Ultima Thule," 70.

[16] On this subject, see Alfred Rosenberg, "Der deutsche Ordensstaat" (The State of the German Order), in Alfred Rosenberg, *Gestaltung der Idee, Blut und Ehre, II. Band: Reden und Aufsätze von 1933–1935* (Giving Form to the Idea: Blood and Honor, volume II: Speeches and Essays from 1933–1935), edited by Thilo von Trotha, 8th edition (Munich: Zentralverlag der NSDAP, Successors of Franz Eher, 1938), 70–89, and Jost Hermand, "Ultima Thule," 81–82.

[17] See Jost Hermand, "Ultima Thule," 71.

[18] On that subject, see Jost Hermand's book *Der alte Traum vom neuen Reich: Völkische Utopien und Nationalsozialismus* (The Old Dream of the New Reich: Racial Utopias and National Socialism) (Frankfurt am Main: Athenäum, 1988), English translation by Paul Levesque and Stefan Soldovieri as *Old Dreams of a New Reich: Volkish Utopias and National Socialism* (Bloomington, Indianapolis: Indiana UP, 1992), in which the author traces Reich utopias in numerous German nationalistic novels of the future. According to Hermand, "in the fifty years between 1895 and 1945, the period when this transformation of older German nationalist ideas into more chauvinistic and imperialist concepts reached its high point, approximately two or three hundred of these novels appeared with some of them running through many editions and being read by hundreds of thousands if not by millions" (xv in the English edition).

[19] Arthur Moeller van den Bruck, *Das Dritte Reich* (The Third Reich), 3rd edition (Hamburg: Hanseatische Verlagsanstalt, 1931), XVI. The page references in the text refer to this edition.

[20] Kurt Sontheimer, 241. A further effective, if abstruse, book was Friedrich Hielscher's *Das Reich* (The Reich) (1931); for that book see Kurt Sontheimer, 230.

[21] See Gerd Klaus Kaltenbrunner, 140–141.

[22] See Gerd Klaus Kaltenbrunner, 145.

[23] On that subject, see Moeller's book *Das Recht der jungen Völker* (The Rights of Young Nations) (Munich: 1919)

[24] See Gerd Klaus Kaltenbrunner, 157.

[25] On that subject, see Arthur Mohler, *Die konservative Revolution in Deutschland 1918–1932. Ein Handbuch*, 47–53. Karl Radeck, a member of the Communist Party of the Soviet Union and the Germany expert of the Communist International gave a speech in 1923 on "Schlageter, the wanderer to nowhere," to which Moeller replied. One of the most important representatives of the national Bolshevist wing of the NSDAP was Gregor Strasser, who was murdered in 1934 by Hitler.

[26] Alfred Prugel, "Ein Wanderer ins Nichts: Walter Flex" (A Wanderer to Nowhere: Walter Flex), in *Propheten des Nationalsozialismus,* edited by Karl Schwedhelm, 138.

[27] Walter Flex, *Der Wanderer zwischen beiden Welten* (The Wanderer Between Two Worlds), 869,000th to 912,000th copies printed (Munich: Beck, 1942).

[28] Walter Flex, 12. The page citations in the text refer to this edition.

[29] The *Wandervogel* movement, which was part of the German Youth Movement from around 1900, developed its own lifestyle independent of adults, with trips, folk music, folk dancing, and camps. The movement, which was similar to today's scouting organizations, subscribed to the leadership principle and at first included boys only, but later also girls.

[30] Karl Theodor Körner (1791–1813, killed in battle) was the author of patriotic poetry during the wars of liberation against Napoleon.

[31] On that subject, see Karl Dietrich Bracher, *Die deutsche Diktatur* (The German Dictatorship) (Cologne and Berlin: Kiepenheuer & Witsch, 1969), 47–48.

[32] After long years of obscurity, "Otto Weininger is the subject . . . of new interest" in Italy, France, and in the Federal Republic, according to Joachim Riedl in *Die Zeit* (The Times), 50 (December 13, 1985). On this subject, also see the play *Weiningers Nacht* (Weininger's Night), written by the Israeli playwright Joshua Sobol in 1982, and first performed in Düsseldorf in 1985. Paulus Manker edited the Vienna version with essays and text in 1988.

[33] See Friedrich Heer, *Der Glaube des Adolf Hitler: Anatomie einer politischen Religiosität* (The Belief of Adolf Hitler: Anatomy of a Political Religiosity) (Munich and Eßlingen: Bechtle, 1968), 709. On Lanz-Liebenfels, see also Wilfried Daim, *Der Mann, der Hitler die Ideen gab: Von den religiösen Verirrungen eines Sektierers zum Rassenwahn des Dikators* (The Man Who Gave Hitler the Ideas: From the Religious Confusion of a Sectarian to the Racial Madness of a Dictator) (Munich: Isar Verlag, 1958). Hitler himself never mentioned Lanz by name; he even issued an order in 1938 prohibiting him from writing. Liebenfels died in 1954.

[34] Adolf Hitler, *Mein Kampf* (My Struggle) (Munich: Eher Successors, 1933, XVII edition of the popular edition), 21.

[35] Adolf Hitler, 20.

[36] On that subject, see Karl Dietrich Bracher, 35–42.

[37] Quoted in Günther Hartung, "Völkische Ideologie" (Völkisch Ideology), in *Weimarer Beiträge* (Weimar Essays), 33, 7 (1987), 1181. As is well known, Friedrich Engels put a clear end to this rivalry in 1878 with his anti-Dühring book about Mr. Eugen Dühring's fundamental change of science.

[38] Quoted in Gerd Klaus Kaltenbrunner, "Vom Konkurrenten des Karl Marx zum Vorläufer Hitlers: Eugen Dühring" (From Rival of Karl Marx to Predecessor of Hitler: Eugen Dühring), in *Propheten des Nationalsozialismus,* edited by Karl Schwedhelm, 38.

[39] Gerd Klaus Kaltenbrunner, 52.

[40] The size of the printing in 1934 was 260,000 copies; see Donald Ray Richards, *The German Bestseller in the 20th Century: A Complete Bibliography and Analysis 1915–1940* (Bern: Lang, 1968), 58.

[41] Artur Dinter, *Die Sünde wider das Blut* (The Sin Against Blood), 15th edition (Leipzig: Matthes und Thost, 1921), 272. The page citations in the text follow this edition.

[42] These include Houston Stewart Chamberlain (*Die Grundlagen des neunzehnten Jahrhunderts* [The Foundations of the Nineteenth Century], 1899), Arthur Gobineau

(*Versuch über die Ungleichheit der Menschenrassen* [Attempt on the Inequality of the Human Races], 1853), Otto Weininger (*Geschlecht und Charakter* [Sex and Character], 1910), Adolf Bartels (*Die deutsche Dichtung der Gegenwart* [German Literature of the Present], and Theodor Fritsch (*Handbuch der Rassenfrage* [Handbook of the Race Question], 1887). Under the pseudonym "Artur Sünder" (Sinner), the satirist Hans Reimann published in 1921 a parody of Dinter's novel with the title *Die Dinte wider das Blut* (Ink Against Blood) (Leipzig: Steegmann, "39th wildly messed up edition"). In the preface to his book, which is dedicated to the *"German* Moriz Abraham Gardinenbetrug,"* Reimann gives the assurance that "the author of the parody and its publisher" are "verifiably blond, blue-eyed, and uncircumcised, and in every respect the opposite of Jews." In the parody, the university lecturer and chemist, Dr. Hermann Stänker, tries, among other things, to destroy Semitococci with Teuton blood.

[43] Uwe-K. Ketelsen, *Völkisch-nationale und nationalsozialistische Literatur in Deutschland 1890–1945* (Völkisch National and National Socialist Literature in Germany, 1890–1945) (Stuttgart: Metzler, 1976), 34.

[44] Uwe-K. Ketelsen, 33.

[45] Julius Langbehn, *Rembrandt als Erzieher* (Rembrandt as an Educator), 24,000th to 34,000th copies printed (Weimar: Duncker, 1943), VI–VII. The page citations in the text refer to this edition.

[46] On that subject, see Dietrich Bracher, *Die deutsche Diktatur,* 60; "Neither Hitler himself nor his closest associates, such as his chief ideologue Alfred Rosenberg or the top man in annihilation of Jew, Reinhard Heydrich, satisfied the postulate for National Socialist command in its most important requisites: race, cult and ancestry."

[47] Uwe-K. Ketelsen, *Literatur und Drittes Reich* (Literature and the Third Reich) (Schernfeld: SH-Verlag, 1992), 135.

[48] Ketelsen, 45.

[49] See Dietrich Bronder, *Bevor Hitler kam* (Before Hitler Came) (Hanover: Pfeiffer, 1964), 288.

[50] Houston Stewart Chamberlain, *Die Grundlagen des neunzehnten Jahrhunderts* (Munich: Bruckmann, 29th edition, 1942), 8. The page citations in the text refer to this edition.

[51] "Whoever wants to learn with his own eyes what a noble race is and what is not should have the poorest of the Sephardim brought to him from Salonika or Sarajevo . . . and should place him next to any Baron Rothschild or Hirsch: then he will be aware of the difference between nobility lent by race and that granted by a monarch" (325–326). At the same time, Chamberlain also considers "certain limited mixtures of blood" necessary "for the refinement of a race" (334).

[52] On the myth concept, see Theodore Ziolkowski, "Der Hunger nach dem Mythos. Zur seelischen Gastronomie der Deutschen in den Zwanziger Jahren" (Hunger for Mythos. On the Spiritual Gastronomy of the Germans in the Twenties), in *Die sogenannten zwanziger Jahre* (The So-Called Twenties), edited by Reinhold Grimm and Jost Hermand (Bad Homburg vor der Höhe: Gehlen, 1970), 169–201, and Hans Schumacher, "Mythisierende Tendenzen in der Literatur 1918–1933" (Mythicizing Tendencies in Literature from 1819–1933), in *Die deutsche Literatur in der Weimarer Republik* (German Literature in the Weimar Republic), edited by Wolf-

gang Rothe (Stuttgart: Reclam, 1974), 281–303. For the term "*völkisch*," see Günther Hartung, "Racial Ideology," 1174–1185, and George L. Mosse, *The Crisis of German Ideology* (New York: Grosset & Dunlap, 1964, 1971), 4.

[53] Alfred Rosenberg, *Der Mythus des 20. Jahrhunderts* (The Myth of the Twentieth Century), 107,000th to 110,000th copies printed (Munich: Hoheneichen-Verlag, 1937), 82. The page citations in the text refer to this edition.

[54] Frederick II of Prussia is meant here, or Frederick the Great, also called "Frederick the Only" by Rosenberg.

[55] For further literature on that subject, see Karl Schwedhelm, ed., *Propheten des Nationalsozialismus;* Dietrich Bronder, *Bevor Hitler kam;* and Karl Dietrich Bracher, *Die deutsche Diktatur.*

[56] On that subject, see especially Wolfgang Wippermann, *Europäischer Faschismus im Vergleich 1922–1982* (European Fascism Compared, 1922–1982) (Frankfurt am Main: Suhrkamp, 1983), or Ernst Nolte, ed., *Theorien über Faschismus* (Theories on Fascism) (Cologne and Berlin: Kiepenheuer & Witsch, 1967).

[57] On that subject, see Heinz Brüdigam, *Der Schoß ist fruchtbar noch . . . Neonazistische, militaristische, nationalistische Literatur und Publizistik in der Bundesrepublik* (The Womb is Still Fertile . . . Neonazi, militaristic, nationalistic Literature and Journalism in the Federal Republic) (Frankfurt am Main: Röderberg, 1964).

The presidents of the Reichsschrifttumskammer:
Hans Friedrich Blunck (1933–35), above; Hanns Johst
(1935–45), below. Courtesy of Bundesarchiv, Koblenz.

3: Literature and Cultural Policies in the Third Reich

Control Agencies and Control Mechanisms

THE NATIONAL SOCIALIST culture policies centered around Adolf Hitler's remarks on cultural policies in his governmental declaration of March 23, 1933. In that declaration, he demanded the "elimination of the destructive heritage of cultural decline" and the "preparation of the soil and clearing of the path for creative cultural development in the future."[1] From these statements emerged the two main functions of National Socialist culture policies: cleansing and support; *culture* policies became culture *policies* (Strothmann, 258). The Nazis attempted to justify their cleansings with the assertion that the Jews in the Weimar Republic dominated in all areas of culture. As Strothmann shows, this assertion in no way corresponds to the facts, for in the area of literature alone *völkisch* books were already among the most frequently purchased books in the period from 1918 to 1933. In the top spots in 1932 were not, for example, Franz Werfel or Alfred Döblin but Werner Beumelburg, Edwin Erich Dwinger, and Hans Grimm (Strothmann, 92). Likewise, in the publishing business, Jews owned by no means all the publishing houses. Known publishing houses like Westermann, Insel, List, Diederichs, and others did not have any difficulty producing and selling *völkisch* national literature (Strothmann, 93). "The thesis of Jewish and at the same time 'red dominance' of the German literature operation was pure invention to provide a rationale for the control power as an obligation of the state and party and to justify that power to the public" (Strothmann, 94). The following chapter presents some of the control agencies and control mechanisms of the state and party that served these purposes and often had overlapping functions. Likewise, the effects of the intervention of these agencies on the literature of the past and the present are illuminated briefly. A look at representative literary histories and the state of German studies in the Third Reich also illustrates those effects.

As Jan Pieter Barbian establishes in detail in his pioneering work *Literaturpolitik im "Dritten Reich": Institutionen, Kompetenzen, Betätigungsfelder* (Literary Policies in the "Third Reich": Institutions, Competencies, Fields of Activity), the National Socialist influence on cultural policies began a year before the official seizure of power in January of 1933 with organizations like Alfred Rosenberg's *Kampfbund für deutsche Kultur* (Fighting League for German Culture), founded at the beginning of 1928; the *Abteilung für Rasse und Kultur* (Department for Race and Culture); the *Volksbildung* (People's Education) department; and the *Propagandaleitung* (Propaganda Management) within the Reich leadership of the NSDAP, as well as Wilhelm Frick's Interior and People's Education ministry in Thuringia. With his decree "Against the Negro Culture for the German *Volkstum*," Frick, later the Minister of the Interior, voiced his objection to the "contamination by the non-cultures of foreign races." By using the power of state to implement his racist culture policies, he created a model that could be transferred after 1933 to the entire Reich. His Culture Commissar, Dr. Hans Severus Ziegler, defined "culture" as the "incarnation of all racially conditioned intellectual, spiritual, and ethical values of a people and furthermore of all the works created from those values, works that are presented as gifts to a people by its creative personalities" (quoted in Barbian, 68). Poetry, literature, and all of the other arts are to serve as a tool of the state in educating the people on "race and *Volkstum*" (Barbian, 68).[2]

The enormous exertion of influence by the National Socialists on cultural policies began immediately after the seizure of power. One of the first casualties was the Literature Section of the Prussian Academy that had been established in March of 1926 by a decree of the Prussian Culture Minister Carl-Heinrich Becker. After the Jewish members had been thrown out in May of 1933, a number of *völkisch* national writers like Werner Beumelburg, Hans Friedrich Blunck, Hans Grimm, Hanns Johst, and Erwin Guido Kolbenheyer took their places. Several non-Jewish authors who did not want to sign the declaration of loyalty initiated by Gottfried Benn left, including Thomas Mann and Ricarda Huch; the president, Heinrich Mann, had already been driven from the Academy on February 15. In the following years, the Literature Section became the football in the game of power politics and lost all meaning. The German section of the international PEN Club met a similar fate; it was disbanded in November of 1933. The *Schutzverband deutscher Schriftsteller* (Protective Association of German Writers) (SDS), which was founded in 1909 and was the most important special interest association of German writers in the Weimar Republic was changed in June of 1936 into the *Reichsverband deutscher Schriftsteller e.V.* (Reich Association of German Writers, Registered Association) (RDS), which later became the *Reichsschrifttumskammer* (Reich Chamber of Literature) (RSK). The public book burning on May 10, 1933, was not, as often claimed, planned by either the state or the party; the "operation against the un-German spirit" was planned and carried out by the student association and with active participation of some university teachers. Goebbels did give a fire speech at the opera ball in Berlin to mark the occasion, but the uncontrolled operation did not entirely fit into his scheme of things; in the first years of National

Socialist power, attention was still paid to some extent to internal order and benevolent recognition abroad.[3]

The most influential cultural authority in the Third Reich first saw light in April of 1933 with the foundation of the Reich Ministry for Public Enlightenment and Propaganda under Joseph Goebbels. Reich Minister Goebbels also assumed leadership of the *Reichskulturkammer* (Reich Chamber of Culture) (RKK), which had been ceremoniously launched on November 15, 1933, and which consisted of seven subdivisions each directed by a president: A *Reichsschrifttumskammer* (Reich Chamber of Literature) (RSK), a *Reichspressekammer* (Reich Chamber of the Press), a *Reichsrundfunkkammer* (Reich Chamber of Radio), a *Reichstheaterkammer* (Reich Chamber of Theater), a *Reichsmusikkammer* (Reich Chamber of Music), a *Reichskammer für bildende Künste* (Reich Chamber of Visual Arts), and a *Reichsfilmkammer* (Reich Chamber of Film). The highest-ranking committee of the RKK, the Reich Culture Senate, which included the presidents of the individual chambers, several publishers, and authors like Heinrich Anacker, Edwin Erich Dwinger, Richard Euringer, Hanns Johst, Eberhard Wolfgang Möller, and Gerhard Schumann, was subordinate to the president, Goebbels.

In guiding literature, the RSK worked closely with the Literature Department of the Propaganda ministry, which as Department III was able over the years to gain control of the important tasks of the Reich relating to culture *policy,* but not without disputes with Philipp Bouhler's *Parteiamtlicher Prüfungskommission zum Schutze des nationalsozialistischen Schrifttums* (Official Party Review Commission for the Protection of National Socialist Literature) (PPK), which was founded in April of 1934. Thus Wilhelm Haegert, the last head of the department, succeeded in centralizing all book censorship in his office. The main function of the department was to oversee all aspects of all German-language literature inside the country and abroad. As this department had complete censorship authority, including paper allocation after initiation of the war economy in 1939, it became the highest control jurisdiction for literature in the Third Reich, with sole responsibility for prohibiting books; however, it shared other monitoring tasks with other authorities. The PPK had lists of prohibited books drawn up, sent writers on lecture tours, held the Weimar poets' meeting, and attempted to breathe life into a "European Writers' Association," in 1941, which nevertheless seemed more like a stillbirth, especially as Hans Carossa, who was named president against his will, exhibited neither desire nor initiative.[4]

The presidents of the RSK were the writers Hans Friedrich Blunck (until 1935) and Hanns Johst (until 1945). The task of the RSK was, in addition to representation of writers as a professional group, supervision of all phases of book production and book distribution from author to publishers and then to bookstores and libraries, even to book reviews. Everyone involved in this process had to be a member of the RSK or he/she would be prohibited from practicing his/her profession. According to Paragraph 4 of the First Regulation for Implementation of the RKK Law of November 1, 1933, the same rule applied to all of the other chambers: "Anyone who is involved in the creation, the reproduction, the intellectual or technical processing, the distribution, the preservation, the sale, or the mediation of the sale of cultural objects must be a member of the individual chamber which has the responsibility for his activity" (Strothmann, 28). The RSK and the other chambers had their monitors and spies in every Reich district. According to Strothmann, the RSK had around 35,000 members in 1941, of them 5,000 writers, 5,000 publishers, 7,000 book dealers, 10,300 employees in publishing houses and bookstores, 2,500 in lending libraries, 3,200 book sales agents, 1,500 in people's libraries, and 400 lecturers (Strothmann, 29). In the RSK there were at first no Arian paragraphs; in 1934, 428 "non-Aryans" were still admitted. By the end of 1935, however, the number of "non-Aryans" had already been reduced to all of five (Barbian, 370–71).

The "gentle wave" pursued for tactical reasons ended in 1935 as the chamber presidents without Party affiliation like Blunck, who did not join the Party until 1937 and Richard Strauss, president of the Reich Chamber of Music, had to resign. Hanns Johst, who maintained close relations with Himmler, became president of the RSK, and with him initiated a stricter manner of dealing with "non-Arian" and "ideologically unreliable" members of the RSK; members in those categories were automatically excluded and hindered from practicing their professions. According to the guidelines that Hans Hinkel, the Special Commissioner of the Propaganda ministry for the "dejewification" of German cultural life, issued in 1936, "all full Jews, three-quarters Jews, half Jews, one-quarter Jews, persons married to full or three-quarters Jews, and persons married to half Jews or one-quarter Jews" were to be excluded from the individual chambers of the RKK by May 15, 1936.

In practice, these guidelines were actually softened by Goebbels. The Nuremburg Laws hit "full Jews" with full force, but in the case of half Jews and persons married to full Jews the president of the RKK (that is, Goebbels) could grant special dispensations. "'One-quarter Jews' and person married to 'half Jews' only had to be excluded if they had trespassed 'against the state or against National Socialism or otherwise [!] shown that they are favorably inclined to Jewry'" (Barbian, 372). In this manner, Stefan Andres, who was married to a "half-Jewish woman," managed to get a special dispensation in 1937 without any problems, likewise Werner Bergengruen, who was married to a "three-quarters Jewish woman." Even Jochen Klepper, who was married to a "full-Jewish woman," received, on the basis of his successful novel *Der Vater* (*The Father*), a special dispensation, which he had won on appeal. Nevertheless, he committed suicide with his family on December 10, 1942, because he could no longer bear the pressure. The commentary of the RSK: "Cancel the special dispensation," "Taken care of" (Barbian, 374). In the case of other authors the prohibition to practice their professions was also handled unevenly. Thus, Alfred Andersch, who as a youthful functionary of the German Communist Party was imprisoned in Dachau Concentration Camp, received a "release certificate" from the RSK in February of 1943 for his first literary works. The expressionist author Kasimir Edschmid was also able to hold his head above water until the end of the Third Reich with nonpolitical travel books (Barbian, 379). Somewhat more complicated was the case of Arnolt Bronnen, the friend at one time of Bertolt Brecht, who at the beginning of the thirties changed political sides and actively supported National Socialism. His new comrades nevertheless made his life difficult. He was classified as a "half Jew" and excluded from the RSK in 1939. He did succeed in proving his Aryan ancestry and, after a legal battle, in having his exclusion from the Chamber repealed in 1941, but on a direct order from Hitler he was prohibited from any further literary activity (Barbian, 384–85).

Overall, the picture of admissions of Aryan writers who encountered difficulties for political or aesthetic reasons is "diffuse" (Barbian, 385). In assessing the political reliability of the writers, the RSK consulted the Gestapo, the Security Service (SD), and the SS, as well as the Party offices, which as a result gained influence on culture policies. In controlling writers, the authorities did not shrink from threats to use force, for example, against Ernst Wiechert and even against Hans Grimm, who called himself a "National Socialist outside the Party" (Barbian, 408). Wiechert had openly opposed the Party and Grimm did not shy away from criticizing defects in the culture bureaucracy.[5] The RSK published a series of journals, including *Der deutsche Schriftsteller* (The German Writer), *Das Börsenblatt für den deutschen Buchhandel* (The German Book Trade Gazette), and *Die Bücherei* (The Library), as well as numerous lists of prohibited and undesirable literature that constantly had to be updated to the current status. The "List 1 of detrimental and undesirable literature" was prepared starting in 1938 by specialists in the bibliographical department of the German Library in Leipzig on behalf of the literature office of the Propaganda ministry (Barbian, 527). Being placed on the index, however, did not automatically spell the end professionally for the authors in question, for example, Edschmidt, Lampe, Lernet-Holenia, or Thiess. At the same time, numerous careers were terminated by it, for instance, those of Irmgard Keun, Joachim Maaß, and even Hanns Heinz Ewers, the author of the *Horst Wessel* book, whose publications prior to 1933 were prohibited (Barbian, 412–16).

A third oversight authority in addition to the RSK and the Literature Office of the Propaganda ministry was the *Reichsministerium für Wissenschaft, Erziehung und Volksbildung* (Reich Ministry for Science, Pedagogy, and Public Education) under the direction of Bernard Rust. The task of this ministry was to take over supervision of the entire school system and responsibility for teacher and school libraries, and to develop suitable materials for school instruction. Over Goebbel's protests, Rust also assumed control of the *Reichs-stelle für volkstümliches Büchereiwesen* (Reich Office for the Popular Library System). Such control ensured "that all of the libraries" operated "in the spirit of the National Socialist state" (Strothmann, 33). Here it must be taken into consideration that the situation looked quite different in practice. The popular libraries were by no means libraries for the National Socialist struggle; pronounced National Socialist literature took up a relatively small space (around 16 percent) compared to the classics and light fiction, which made up the greater part of the holdings (19.5 percent and 52.5 percent).[6]

The most important control and oversight agency on the part of the Party was the *Reichsstelle zur Förderung des deutschen Schrifttums* (Reich Office for Promotion of German Literature) under the leadership of Alfred Rosenberg, the chief ideologue of the party and *Beauftragter des Führers für die Überwachung der gesamten geistigen und weltanschaulichen Schulung und Erziehung der NSDAP* (Official Representative of the Führer for the Oversight over All Intellectual and Ideological Training and Education of the NSDAP). The *Reichsstelle Rosenberg* (Rosenberg Reich Office), later renamed the *Amt Schrifttumspflege* (Office for the Cultivation of Literature) and the *Hauptamt Schrifttum* (Main Literature Office), did not have the power to prohibit but still represented the most extensive control authority, which with its numerous subsections monitored the entire cultural sphere. It arose from the *Kampfbund für deutsche Kultur,* which Rosenberg had already founded in 1929, before Hitler's seizure of power (Strothmann, 38). The founding members included Alfred Bäumler, Hanns Johst, Hellmuth Langenbucher, and Rainer Schlösser (Strothmann, 39).

With his Reich office, Rosenberg sought a position of power similar to the one that his rival Goebbels had in the state, but he did not achieve success. The Rosenberg Reich Office derived its mission from the effort to thwart criticism of National Socialism hidden in literature and to keep Nazi doctrine pure. From 1940 on, Rosenberg's official title was accordingly *Der Beauftragte des Führers zur Sicherung der nationalsozialistischen Weltanschauung* (The Official Representative of the Führer for Protection of National Socialist Ideology) (Strothmann, 37). The mission of the Rosenberg Office, however, extended far beyond official party literature; it included "the systematic appraisal of more recent German literature from the standpoint of policy and ideology, artistry, and popular education as well as the support of deserving works" (Strothmann, 38). The central readers' department, the largest section of the Reich Office, monitored belletristic literature; the first head of the readers' department was Hellmuth Langenbucher, who was "a kind of literature Pope" in the Third Reich (Barbian, 272). At the beginning of the war, this readers' department encompassed fifty main readers and a lecturer staff of over 1,400 readers distributed over the entire Reich (Strothmann, 40). In the journals published by the Rosenberg Office, *Bücherkunde*

(Book Lore) and the annual gazettes with the opinions of the experts, the literature screened was divided into "deserving support" and "undesirable"; the latter lists sometimes provided Department VIII in Goebbel's ministry with the basis for prohibition. The last great operation of the Rosenberg Office was its raid of "ownerless" Jewish private libraries whose holdings were used to piece together the library of the *Institut zur Erforschung der Juden-frage* (Institute for Research on the Jewish Question), which was founded in 1939 in Frankfurt am Main (Strothmann, 42).

The Rosenberg Office collaborated with numerous other offices, but mostly with the PPK under the chairmanship of the *Reichsleiter* Philipp Bouhler. With a smaller staff but with censorship authority (like the Literature Department in Goebbel's ministry, but unlike the Rosenberg Office), the PPK was to "keep the foundations of a political community healthy, strong, and capable of development." Its area of responsibility comprised, besides party literature, also "scientific and lexical publications, school books, calendars, and belletristic works, in particular novels about the Nazi period of struggle and celebratory poetry" (Strothmann, 43). In the *Nationalsozialistische Bibliogra-phie* (National Socialist Bibliography) published by the PPK, not only party literature but also "belletristic literature" was considered (Barbian, 314).

To the control offices mentioned were added countless review offices in the various party organizations; however, their authority was considerably more limited (see Strothmann, 47–48). Thus, the *Deutsche Arbeitsfront* (German Labor Front) (DAF) under Robert Ley set up its own literature department and took over several publishers, such as the Hanseatic Publish-ing Company, Langen-Müller Publishers, Book and Theater Publishers, Avenarius Publishers of Leipzig, and made millions with travel and adven-ture books as well as technical literature. In 1942, the DAF owned twenty publishers, seven printers, two book clubs, and a paper factory (Barbian, 340). Max Amman, president of the Reich Press Chamber, *Reichsleiter* for the Press of the NSDAP, and master of a "gigantic publishing empire" (Barbian 342), exerted great influence on culture policy with his Franz Eher Central Publishers. In the area of literature for young people, the Reich Youth Leader Baldur von Schirach also won his say (Barbian, 358).

Even Heinrich Himmler, the leader of the SS, had ambitions to meddle in the cultural field with his research and teaching program called *Ahnenerbe* (Ancestral Heritage), which initially intended to restore the cultural heritage of the Germanic past and make it relevant in the present. The program began in 1935 with the study of early German culture and history, but it soon extended its tentacles into a variety of fields ranging from runic in-scriptions and racial "science" to rocket science and biological experimenta-tion on concentration camp inmates, that is, from serious scholarship to criminal activities. The program involved numerous renowned scholars and scientists and included such illustrious names as Wernher von Braun and

Hans Schneider, who became a respected Germanist after 1945 under his new name Hans Schwerte.[7]

As in the socialist camp, a kind of debate about expressionism also arose at the beginning of the Nazi regime in the dispute between Goebbels and Rosenberg about *Gleichschaltung* of cultural policies, when the fronts had not yet completely hardened. In the course of this debate, primarily young National Socialist artists within the *Nationalsozialistischer deutscher Studentenbund* (National Socialist German Student Association) (NDS) attempted against Rosenberg's instructions to save German expressionism in painting (Marc, Nolde, Pechstein, Pankok, Schmitt-Rottluff) for the culture policy of the Third Reich, with the silent support of Goebbels.[8] As Klaus Vondung explains, this debate did also have effects on literature, particularly through Gottfried Benn's "Speech on Marinetti" and his "Confession of Loyalty to Expressionism."[9] Hitler ended the battle in a highly personal manner with a speech at the Reich Party Congress in September of 1934 in Nuremberg. In this speech, Hitler objected to the "corrupters of art" "who oppose tradition," "the cubists, futurists, dadaists, etc.," but also to the "backward-lookers" and romantic, Germanic, *völkisch* scatterbrains like Fidus, Fahrenkrog, and Lanzinger.[10]

Officially, there was no censorship in the Third Reich, as various Nazi greats emphasized repeatedly, for example, Karl-Heinz Hederich, at one time director of the PKK and Department VIII, "Literature," in Goebbels's Reich Ministry for Public Enlightenment and Propaganda: "We do not want censorship and therefore no dependent publishers who do not know what they are supposed to do and always just squint at the letter of the law; instead, we want publishers who are our loyal helpers in common task" (Strothmann, 118). Philipp Bouhler only wanted to stand "at the side" of the publishers, "advising and helping," as he explained in an address to the fourth Annual Book Week (Strothmann, 118). He only wanted "to resort to the most extreme means in situations where there is bad will or incompetence" (Strothmann, 118). Denunciations were relied upon, as was the certainty that writers would develop the right awareness of what could be published in the Reich and what not. Even as late as 1934, Goebbels announced that art is free, of course within the framework of national laws of life.[11] The publishers were not nationalized in the Third Reich as in Bolshevism, which was demonized by the Nazis to maintain the fiction of a publishing industry independent of the state. After the book burning in May of 1933, the expulsion of Jewish citizens from German culture and the German state, and the establishment of a wide variety of control agencies by the state and the Party, such independence was out of the question from the very beginning of the Nazi regime. The controls applied not only to the publishing industry but also to all areas of culture and literature. In the field of literature, the attempt was made to control not only book production but also book distribution, authors, and readers. In this process, the current cultural material was screened critically, and the past was "cleansed" of "undesirable elements." Central to control of literature were the various means of support for literature. The lists of prohibited works were not published but only sent to trusted parties, as the appearance of being a nation of culture was to be preserved. Besides, censorship that did not operate openly resulted in constant uncertainty and thus promotion of self-censorship.

The criteria for the division of literature into authors "deserving support," "undesirable" authors, and "prohibited" authors were determined on the basis of their ideology and the race to which they belonged, as well as of themes and suitability of their books to be weapons in the propaganda battle of National Socialism. Aside from several ideological catchwords such as *Volk* (nation), *Blut* (blood), *Rasse* (race), and *Heroismus* (heroism), National Socialism did not develop any normative aesthetics that everyone would have to follow, compared to socialist realism (Strothmann, 82). The evaluation criteria for literature resulted, as Karl-Heinz Hederich formulated, "only from what is necessary . . . for the National Socialist movement in its struggle for Germany" (Strothmann, 305). The book was no longer considered a linguistic work of art, but a political training tool in the service of National Socialist ideology. Support went to works that represented such themes as "battle," "allegiance," and "sacrifice," as well as "the myth of soil," "leaders," "blood," and "race." At the same time the theme scale varied according to political necessity, for example, annexation and *Volkstum* in 1938, suppression of anti-Bolshevik themes after the Stalin-Hitler Pact of 1939, and war literature and the literature of perseverance after 1939. Weak or sickly heroes, experiments in the aesthetics of form, and psychological and anti-war portrayals were shunned. The central evaluation categories in art, "race," and "heroism" were put forward by Hitler in his cultural program of March 23, 1933: "1. Heroism rises up passionately as the future shaper and leader of political fates. It is the mission of art to be the expression of this determining spirit of the times. 2. Blood and race are again the source of artistic intuition" (Strothmann, 324). The healthy is to celebrate new triumphs, as Hanns Johst pronounced at a "Demonstration for German Literature" on the occasion of the 1936 Olympics: "Healthy is the heroic order!" (Strothmann, 324).[12] After the seizure of power, Jewish and leftist authors were labeled and condemned as "parasites on the people" and "corrupters of the German soul" (Strothmann, 309); the "eternally middle class and humane individuals," who were guided by aesthetic and cosmopolitan considerations of mind were defamed and declared undesirable authors. The literary historian Adolf Bartels provides a formulaic summary of the criteria of National Socialist literature: "All literature should be national; if it is not, it is good for nothing" (Strothmann, 332). Books like *Der Befehl des Gewissens* (The Command of Conscience) by Hans Zöberlein, discussed in the chapter on the National Socialist novel, was singled out by the *Völkischer*

Beobachter (*Völkisch* Observer) as an exemplary work of National Socialist literature: "It is the work of an old soldier and National Socialist fighter, outstanding as well in its unassuming and simple language. A work that can be said to be among the best books on the postwar period that was written in the National Socialist spirit" (Strothmann, 328).

According to today's evaluation criteria, Zöberlein's book is one of the nastiest pieces of botched work in National Socialist literature. However, such critical criteria were not valid between 1933 and 1945. So that no critical comments could turn up in book reviews, Goebbels prohibited art criticism in 1936 and replaced it with an "art report" that was to presume "respect for artistic work and creative accomplishment" (Strothmann, 276). Not critical understanding, which was according to Johst only an expression of "superficial persuasion and Jewish equivocation," was decisive, but rather "instinct" (Strothmann, 264). Criticism was considered "un-German" (Strothmann, 285). Only those "observers of art" who were regarded to be firmly seated in the saddle ideologically were admitted. In this way, "a number of pockets of resistance" were cleared out and a "concealed opposition was driven" out of them, as Hellmuth Langenbucher noted (Strothmann, 284); up to this point, the middle-class press had sometimes succeeded in directing hidden criticism by means of book reviews at *volkhafte Literatur*, at literature "focusing on the people" (Strothmann, 300–301).

Observing art rather than criticizing it, *Kunstbetrachtung*, became a further means of control for National Socialist culture policies. Other forms of influence included "mandatory membership in the RSK, prohibitions on writing, advance censorship of certain book types and in the case of authors with dispensations, scrutiny of almost the entire year's production, paper approval, regulations on trade, closings and mergers of companies, prohibition and recommendation lists, book propaganda campaigns ('poet action,' book exhibits)" (Strothmann, 81). Added to these were literature prizes,[13] conferences for poets like the Weimar Poets' Days (1938–1942), outfitting and supervision of public libraries of all kinds (with attempts at influencing even private household libraries), Days of the Book, journals like Rosenberg's bibliography, etc. Poets were to become "soldierly education officials" whose mission according to Hanns Johst was "to shape Germans, to make Germans irresistible" (Strothmann, 88). Writers who did not prove ready for or capable of the task in the eyes of the Nazis were in the Nazis' view Jews and "privileged non-Aryans," part of the Jewish "clan," "Jew comrades," or "spiritual Jews," including the "salon Bolsheviks," as well as the "individuals of eternal yesterdays" among the religious writers and "citizens of the world" (Strothmann, 90). They were excluded from the RSK and their names appeared on lists of prohibited or undesirable books.

After book burnings, emigration of countless authors (Strothmann mentions 250), and various cleansing operations, the book market in 1938 was practically "cleansed" and *gleichgeschaltet*. After this time only a few titles appeared on the prohibited indexes, even though some publishers continued to publish "undesirable" books (Strothmann, 94). All authors, publishers, book dealers, and library directors were monitored via their mandatory membership in the RSK and could at any time be prohibited from practicing their professions. These measures affected numerous authors who had remained in the Reich, such as Gottfried Benn (prohibition on writing in 1936), Werner Bergengruen (excluded from the Chamber in 1937), Kasimir Edschmid (prohibition on lectures in 1933 and denial of paper in 1940), Bernt von Heiseler (denial of paper in 1942), Ricarda Huch (indicted in 1937 because of her support of Käthe Kollwitz), Hermann Kasack (prohibition on lectures), Erich Kästner (admission rejected in 1939), Jochen Klepper (excluded from the Chamber in 1937), Elisabeth Langgässer (prohibition on writing in 1939; as a "half-Jewish woman" she had to perform several years of forced labor), Reinhold Schneider (prohibition on printing in 1941; starting in 1943 under indictment by the *Reichssicherheitshauptamt* [Reich Security Main Office, the central office of the SS]), Rudolf Alexander Schröder (prohibition on lectures in 1941), Ehm Welk (concentration camp detention, prohibition on writing until 1937), and Ernst Wiechert (concentration camp detention) (Strothmann, 95). However, as mentioned above, there were a number of special dispensations.

Of the many recommendation and prohibition lists, the ones published by Department VIII of the Propaganda ministry as well as by the Rosenberg Reich Office and the PKK stand out. Department VIII, or rather the RSK subordinate to it, published three lists: 1. list of damaging and undesirable literature (from 1935 to 1941, from 1939 on as the "annual list"; from 1942 on, book dealers and large and small libraries received instructions directly from the Gestapo); 2. list of publications unsuitable for juveniles and libraries; 3. catalogue of English and North American books (Strothmann, 218). The Rosenberg Reich Office and the PKK periodically published the annual gazette with the opinions of the experts in which literature was evaluated according to ideological criteria and was given rankings such as "positive," "conditionally positive," conditionally negative," "negative," "trivial," or "outdated." All of the lists agree in their rejection of authors who are Christian, emphasized artistic form, or otherwise not *völkisch*. In addition to these black lists, there were also special white lists, especially the National Socialist bibliographies published by the PKK, which were primarily intended to promote literature focusing on the people and authors of war, homeland, and historical novels by authors such as Anacker, Beumelburg, Blunck, Carossa, Dwinger, Griese, Grimm, Kolbenheyer, Lersch, Möller, Schumacher, Stehr, Steguweit, and Zöberlein.

Among all these National Socialist agencies for control and oversight there were from the outset overlaps and conflicts of competence, and it borders on the miraculous that the culture policies of the Third Reich functioned at all. The various offices agreed with each other only that Jews and political opponents of National Socialism had to disappear. These conflicts occasionally allowed clever publishers to evade censorship, but on the other hand also allowed Hans Friedrich Blunck to use the excuse after 1945 that he had been an anti-Nazi seated on the chair of the RSK.[14] Uwe-K. Ketelsen warns rightly in describing National Socialist culture policy with a strictly instrumentalist focus, as doing so could give the (false) impression that the entire culture policy of the Third Reich was tightly organized and aligned. That was by no means the case, and between claim and reality yawned a wide gap.[15] "The grim struggle in the area of culture policy among Rosenberg, Goebbels, and other top functionaries of the NSDAP (. . .) determined decisively the character" of that policy, so that even Adolf Hitler felt compelled to observe at the culture conference at the Reich Party Congress of the NSDAP in 1938 that the cultural accomplishments in the Third Reich limped along far behind those in the political, social, and economic areas.[16]

National Socialist Histories of Literature

Literary history was also combed for ideological angles and when necessary bent into shape according to the instructions of the culture authorities; histories of literature also became a control means for literature policy. It is therefore not surprising that between 1930 and 1945 "fifty histories of literature of in part considerable size" appeared, "some in several editions"; the histories "sought to connect immediate contemporary literature to tradition."[17] Added to that was a series of influential histories of literature that had appeared before 1930, such as those of Adolf Bartels and Josef Nadler. The wave of histories of literature crested in 1941 with the publication of the five-volume monumental work *Von deutscher Art in Sprache und Dichtung* (On the German Manner in Language and Literature) edited by Gerhard Fricke, Franz Koch, and Klemens Lugowski. Collaborating on this work were a number of well-known German scholars who had remained in the Reich, such as Paul Böckmann, Heinz Otto Burger, Herbert Cysarz, Paul Kluckhohn, Fritz Martini, Julius Petersen, Robert Petsch, Benno von Wiese, and others.

Among the abundance of histories of literature, the following are especially worth noting, as they were produced by authors who were prominent at the time and were usually published in several editions: Adolf Bartels, *Geschichte der deutschen Literatur* (History of German Literature, 1900, 19th edition 1943)); Hans Naumann, *Die deutsche Dichtung der Gegenwart* (German Literature of the Present, 5th edition 1931); Hellmuth Langenbucher, *Volkhafte Dichtung der Zeit* (People's Literature of the Time, 6th edition, 1941); Franz Koch, *Geschichte der deutschen Dichtung* (History of

German Literature, 4th edition, 1941); Walther Linden, *Geschichte der deutschen Literatur von den Anfängen bis zur Gegenwart* (History of German Literature from the Beginnings to the Present, 1937); Paul Fechter, *Geschichte der deutschen Literatur von den Anfängen bis zur Gegenwart* (History of German Literature from the Beginning to the Present, 1941); Norbert Langer, *Die deutsche Dichtung seit dem Weltkrieg: Von Paul Ernst bis Hans Baumann* (German Literature Since the World War: From Paul Ernst to Hans Baumann, 2nd edition, 1941), and Arno Mulot, *Die Deutsche Dichtung unserer Zeit* (German Literature of Our Time, 2nd edition, 1944). Shortly before the collapse, Mulot still wanted to lend support to "the enormous struggle over the fate of our people" with his work and "to contribute to the self-contemplation that strengthens and tempers, and thus to the unconditional will to fight and prevail."[18]

In the fourth edition of the fourth volume of his monumental *Literaturgeschichte des deutschen Volkes: Dichtung und Schrifttum der deutschen Stämme und Landschaften* (Literary History of the German People: Poetry and Literature of the German Tribes and Landscapes, 1st edition between 1912 and 1928), which was published in 1941, Josef Nadler had finally moved from tribe to race. In his basic concept for the work, he supports the race and annihilation policy of the National Socialists with blunt sentences such as the following: "All of the West European people's states of the Middle Ages that are striving youthfully upwards have torn out the Jews among them by their roots. [. . .] The belief, will, and order of the National Socialist work are directed at pushing all of the living cells from foreign races out of the body of the people and restoring the dominant position to the original, tribal Germanic, racial Nordic internal core."[19] Another history of literature written completely in the spirit of National Socialism, *Die deutsche Gegenwartsdichtung im Aufbau der Nation* (German Contemporary Literature in the Building of the Nation, 1935) flowed from the pen of the active German scholar and Party comrade Heinz Kindermann. According to Jens Malte Fischer, Kindermann was "one of the most ambitious Nazi scholars of *Germanistik*" and "a Germanistic desk murderer who beat the drum for the regime until the bitter end."[20]

The histories of literature in the thirties and forties were in agreement on the eradication of Jewish, communist, and other outlawed authors. On the other hand, there was no agreement on what actually constituted a National Socialist literature canon and how the "National Socialist" writers were to be evaluated. Thus, Uwe-K. Ketelsen examined a series of literary histories and determined that "among the approximately 2,000 names listed in the expressly cited ten histories of literature [. . .]" there are "only a scant 25 which all ten [. . .] consider worth mentioning," including authors like Bartels, Billinger, Binding, Blunck, Bröger, Carossa, Ernst, Frenssen, George, H. Grimm, Johst, E. Jünger, Kneip, Kolbenheyer, Lersch, Löns,

Miegel, Ponten, von Scholz, I. Seidel, Stehr, E. Strauss, von Strauss and Torney, Vogt-Diederichs, and J. Winckler. Nine of these histories of literature share another twenty-one authors, for example, Beumelburg, Burte, Dwinger, Griese, Schauwecker, and others, including Huch and Rilke. Pure propaganda writers are missing, as are many *völkisch* writers, who might be expected in such a canon after the seizure of power. All of those named have in common that they are poets, and in Fechter's formulation "write from the totality for the totality."[21] From this uncertainty about who belongs in a history of literature in National Socialism, it is evident that not even National Socialists knew what National Socialist literature actually was.[22] Predominant were the epigones of middle-class realism and not the authors of the Conservative Revolution. That did not change when a modernization of the canon was undertaken in 1940; the histories of literature were only expanded to include a few new authors like Möller and Schumann. Even then, there were still no fixed criteria for a literature of the Third Reich. "Outlining a separate, genuine previous history of the literature of the Third Reich" met with just as little success.[23] Instead, the middle-class literature tradition, including Schiller, Hölderlin, Kleist, and Grabbe, was relied upon. In the following pages, two representative histories of literature, Helmuth Langenbucher's *Volkhafte Dichtung der Zeit* (People's Literature of the Time) and Adolf Bartel's *Geschichte der deutschen Literatur* (History of German Literature), are to be presented in more detail.

Hellmuth Langenbucher held important positions in the Rosenberg Reich Office as the director of the *Gesamtlektorat,* the main reading department and main reader of the main reading department for belletristic literature. Among other things, he was also the chief editor of the *Das Börsenblatt für den deutschen Buchhandel* (The German Book Trade Gazette) and *Weltliteratur* (World Literature), as well as editor of *Die Welt des Buches: Eine Kunde vom Buch.* (The World of the Book: A Guide to the Book). In addition to the history of literature mentioned, he was the author of other histories of literature, such as *Nationalsozialistische Dichtung* (National Socialist Literature), *Deutsche Dichtung in Vergangenheit und Gegenwart* (German Literature in the Past and Present), and *Dichtung der jungen Mannschaft* (Literature of the Young Team). The first edition of his *Volkhafte Dichtung der Zeit* (People's Literature of the Time) appeared in 1933 and was conceived of after the seizure of power as a polemical fighting document against the decadent literati of the "system period" as the Nazis called the Weimar Republic, and the "false alignmenteers" (79) whom he contrasted to the real German poets who in his opinion were suppressed in the "system period." As for those who feared that there would be a spiritual void after the countless "racially alien" authors had been driven from the German temple of the Muses, he wanted to "open their eyes to the actual presence of such a wealth of German literature" (1st edition, 9). In the appendix of his thin volume is a short overview of the development of the "German Academy of Litera-ture" and a book list of "Literature of the Time," published by the Rosen-berg Reich Office. Langenbucher derogatorily describes the entire group of writers expelled in 1933 as literati who in his view bear the principal guilt "for our people's collapsing from within and going astray"; our people "had almost fallen victim" to those tendencies (1st edition, 68).

German literature, which bloomed in "seclusion" in the "system pe-riod," can — according to Langenbucher — develop freely and unhindered after 1933 and count on the protection and support of the new Germany. For Langenbucher, the words of the poet that the "literati" had debased count again after the seizure of power: "The goal is . . . to again elevate the words of the poet out of the profane everyday world to the prophetic, to make the poet unconditionally dedicated to his people and to the mission with which his people is willing to entrust him, and to make the people unconditionally dedicated to its poet and to the elevating and purifying forces that flow out of the words of the poet and into the life of the people" (1st edition, 15). The change in direction, to Langenbucher, means libera-tion from the "slick dissection of the soul according to Freud, the vain self-admiration, and the overeagerly excusatory understanding of all human perversities" in the literature that has predominated up to now and return "to the literature that was from time immemorial subject to the harsh laws of a manly conduct in life and sustained by a true sense of fate" (1st edition, 90). Langenbucher considers himself safe "from the worst," "namely from the can-do-it-all conformity of the now forgotten individuals who left Ger-many" (1st edition, 91). However, according to Langenbucher, a new danger threatens in the form of a flood of pseudo-national publications that are "patriotic trash" by false prophets, changelings, and brown opportunists who are now attempting in their works to create the illusion of the true *Volkstum* by introducing as many swastikas, brown shirts, *Führer,* national sayings, compound words with the prefix "*ur-*" (original), and the "smells of earth" as possible into their books (1st edition, 91).[24] Among the authors who are now free to proceed, Langenbucher included Rudolf G. Binding, Emil Strauß, Paul Ernst, Hermann Stehr, Wilhelm Schäfer, Hermann Burte ("one of the few poets of the present who has recognized the meaning of race for the life of the people" — 1st edition, 45), Hans Friedrich Blunck, Erwin Guido Kolbenheyer, and Will Vesper.

The consolidation of National Socialism and its culture policy is re-flected in the further editions of Langenbucher's history of literature in which polemics noticeably recede and the description of "literature focusing on the people" takes up an ever greater amount of space. In the third edition of 1937 as well as in the 5th edition of 1941, both "written for the layman" (22), the traditional division into genres is thrown overboard: "No particular explanation is necessary for why a division by genres (poetry, drama, novel) is today no longer justified" (12). The same applies for the epochal concepts used up to now, and for the classification by "isms": "I was also able to omit the use of the traditional designations in histories of literature for concepts, epochs, and schools. There is not a single one of those confusing "isms" that today, in the cultural life of the new Germany, would have any justification for its existence" (12–13).

In contrast, Langenbucher's history of literature is subdivided by themes, such as "Volk und Dichter" (The People and Poets); "Der Kampf um Gesetz und Würde der Dichtkunst" (The Struggle for the Laws and Dignity of Literature) (including Paul Ernst and Wilhelm von Scholz); "Der deutsche Mensch" (The German Being) (including Wilhelm Guido Kolbenheyer, Emil Strauss, Hermann Stehr, Ina Seidel, Rudolf G. Binding, Gustav Frenssen, and Josefa Berens-Totenohl); "Volk an der Arbeit I: Deutsches Bauertum" (The People at Work I: The German Peasantry) (including Friedrich Griese, Richard Billinger, Karl Heinrich Waggerl, Ludwig Thoma, and Lulu von Strauß und Torney); "Volk an der Arbeit II: Deutsches Arbeitertum der Faust und der Stirn" (The People at Work II: German Workers of the Fist and the Mind) (including Heinrich Lersch, Hermann Claudius, Hans Carossa, and Josef Weinheber); "Landschaft und Stammestum als völkischer Lebensgrund" (Landscape and Tribalism as the *völkisch* Reason for Living) (including Agnes Miegel and Ernst Wiechert [who of course failed to realize the hopes placed in him, 309], Georg Britting, Josef Friedrich Perkonig, Max Mell, Kuni Tremel-Eggert, Jakob Schaffner, Hermann Eris Busse, Heinz Steguweit, Heinrich Zerkaulen, Hermann Löns, and Helene Voigt-Diederichs); "Der geschichtliche Werdegang des deutschen Volkes" (The Historical Development of the German People) (including Hans Friedrich Blunck, Börries von Münchhausen, Wilhelm Schäfer, Will Vesper, Otto Gmelin, Bruno Brehm, Curt Langenbeck, and Hans Rehberg); "Der Selbstbehauptungskampf des deutschen Volkes" (The Struggle for Self-Affirmation of the German People) (including Hans Grimm, Josef Ponten, Adolf Meschendörfer, Heinrich Zillig, and Gustav Leutelt); "Schicksalswende" (Change in Fate) (including Isolde Kurz, Rudolf Huch, Karl Bröger, Franz Schauwecker, Ernst Jünger, Edwin Erich Dwinger, Walter Flex, and Hans Zöberlein); and "Die neue Lebensordnung des deutschen Volkes" (The New Order of Life of the German People) (including Stefan George, Dietrich Eckart, Georg Stammler, Hanns Johst, Richard Euringer, Heinrich Anacker, Ludwig Friedrich Bartels, Eberhard Wolfgang Möller, Gerhard Schumann, and Werner Beumelburg).

In the first chapter, Langenbucher attempts to define the concept *Volk* (People) in light of German history. In doing so, he makes Görres, Arndt, Fichte, and Jahn the ancestors of the concept of *Volk* as used in National Socialism (26–27). All of the definitions of *Volk* can, according to Langenbucher, be reduced to a basic formula: *Volk* means "what is common to all people of German blood" (29).[25] Langenbucher sees as the mission of the poet his submission to the concept of the people, from which all his creativity derives and to which all his creativity returns. But what is meant by *Volk* remains vague and nebulous despite all attempts at definition. According to Kolbenheyer, the key concept of National Socialism, *Volk*, defies definition.[26] In the definition of Paul Ernst, *Volk* completely becomes myth. A people is for him not the "sum of the individuals," but has its own personality, which can be clearly delineated, with its own unique character and fate, which must accomplish specific tasks known only to God in the big human world. . . . The accomplishment [of these tasks] through mysterious movements within that people, movements which need not be clear even to it and the causes of which it does not have to know."[27] A similarly mystical role is assigned to the poet, who is chosen by Ernst to be a prophet and leader: "This life of the people is directed by the leaders, who have a higher level of awareness than the whole. . . . The poets are among the most important leaders; . . . the will of the people, which is dull and unknown, becomes clarity and awareness in them."[28]

Adolf Bartels's *Geschichte der Literatur* (History of Literature) paved the way for a history of literature according to National Socialism. It was first published by Westermann in Braunschweig in 1900 and then appeared in a number of editions up to 1945; the nineteenth edition, for example, came onto the market in 1943. The work illustrates in an exemplary manner how the history of literature was viewed, and was supposed to be viewed, from a National Socialist perspective. Adolf Bartels has earned the dubious honor of having studied literature using a racial approach. In the preface to the edition of 1919, Bartels expresses the hope that his work "can become a book for the education of the nation that clearly shows the *völkisch* wherefrom and where-to and helps slowly guide the necessary German renewal upwards" (VI). In the preface of 1937, Bartels quotes the honors he received for his "part in the building and rebirth of the people" for which Hitler awarded him the Eagle's Shield of the German Reich (IX).

While Langenbucher restricts himself only to the new *völkisch* literature, Bartels begins with the origins of the "Aryan race." The material is spread over ten books and is divided according to traditional categories, but with strong ideological and anti-Semitic coloration. Thus, "Young Germany" is dismissed as "an essentially Berlin Jewish product" from the salon of Rahel Levin, whose married name was Varnhagen (325). The Jewish influence on German literature, according to Bartels, began in the "Age of Romanticism" "as the Schlegels made themselves at home in the Berlin Jewish salons" (325), and from that point on "until our time its hold has never again been fully broken" (325). For Bartels, literature is "the revelation of a nation's own essence" (325), which will be destroyed by the Jews "from the inside out, parasitically residing in the body of the nation" (326). He concedes some degree of superficial virtuosity to Heine and Börne, for a Jew who happens to get "German upbringing . . . can in some circumstances become somewhat capable" (327). Nevertheless, Bartels considers in particular their "un-German feuilletons" a curse for German literature. Both "have adopted German culture, to the extent possible for them, but in spirit they have remained real Jews" (326). Bartels grants Heine world renown, but he is of course not "a German poet but a Jewish poet who makes use of the German language" (330). Heine is regarded by Bartels as the father of the "decadence of the nineteenth century . . . and Young Germany, the so-called school, was decadence" (327). Bartels views himself as completely in agreement with Wolfgang Menzel and the latter's anti-Semitic invectives, which Menzel directed against Heine and Börne in his "Literary Magazine" and which essentially contributed to the prohibition of the Young Germans in 1835: "Menzel was completely right when he raised his voice against them" (327).[29] Menzel then has Bartel's sympathy, for the former, as the "enemy of French liberalism and of Jewry . . ., was one of the first to discover the meaning of race for the development of humanity" (338).[30]

The opposite of the supposed decadence of the Young Germans is for Bartels German Romanticism and the patriotic pathos of the literature from the wars of liberation. For Bartels "romantic" and "German" are identical: "Romanticism is the German Renaissance," which still in his time is not complete (226). According to Bartels, Romanticism in turn builds on the Storm and Stress movement, which had already overcome the French influence and "had taken possession of the concept of literature of the people and nature as opposed to the literature of art and culture, creating a new German literature that was no longer reflection but sensuousness, passion, nature, and at its core national, German, Germanic" — even though Storm and Stress still lacked "a complete understanding of the special unique character of the people and the forces contained in it" (226). The literature of the wars of liberation has for Bartels a function similar to that of the national literature after 1933, when in the view of the National Socialists the aestheticism and cosmopolitanism of the Weimar Republic were defeated and the German people were reborn. In the view of Bartels, with the wars of liberation "the national rebirth was . . . accomplished, cosmopolitanism and aesthetic culture were defeated . . . the German people found themselves again; the time of German disgrace was over" (262–63).

After the descent of the Young Germans into decadence, as mentioned, Bartels sees a new upswing in German literature with the "great realists" in the first half of the nineteenth century, including Willibald Alexis, Charles Sealsfield, Jeremias Gotthelf, Adalbert Stifter, Friedrich Hebbel ("the most significant literary phenomenon to appear in Germany since Goethe's death, and one of the greatest German personalities ever," 391), and Otto Ludwig.

Not even Bartels can dispute the talent of Bertold Auerbach, the creator of the village tale, but he shows his irritation with the "humanity Jew" (385).

As Bartels complains, however, a national literature by no means went hand in hand with the founding of the German Reich and national unification. On the contrary, increasing "industrialism" resulted not only in "social distress and deterioration of the race but also something almost like an interruption of culture, as industrialism destroyed the old German humanistic, individualistic culture, without, however, being able to put something of equal value, indeed, anything at all new and stable, in its place" (457).

With capitalism, "corrupting Jewry" came to the fore; "the desolate founders' era" (*Gründerzeit*) took form, "which together with the economy based on profiteering and corruption afforded pretty much the most disgusting spectacle in all of German history" (459). Instead of "earnest German feeling and genuine national pride," Bartels finds only hollow patriotic phrases (459) or "incendiary social democracy," which, in Bartel's eyes, believed that it had a lease on the social question. Connecting nationalism and socialism to defend against Jewry was attempted by few, among them the court chaplain Stöcker, or in the beginning, Friedrich Naumann (544). However, "a national movement that knew what race is" gradually took form. In could not prevent the collapse of 1918, but then became dominant under National Socialism (460).

The "leading lights" in the Bismarck Reich, according to Bartels, were "again not poets . . . as in the period of Young Germany"; they included Arthur Schopenhauer, Richard Wagner, Otto von Bismarck, Helmuth von Moltke, and Ernst Haeckel. Otherwise he sees in the last third of the nineteenth century mostly decline, as "the 'nature' within the *Volkstum* was no longer able (perhaps because of worsening of the race) to repel or expel the putrescent material, and that was the case in the late sixties when liberalism, with its industrial, scientific, democratic, radical tendencies . . ., only had a flattening and destructive effect" (482). In the mid-eighties, Bartels does see signs of "recovery" resulting from "improvement of the race" and "strengthening of the national organs," but they did not persist (482–83): "Complete recovery after the illness has . . . by no means been achieved again, even now, despite the initial upswing in the World War and the penetration of National Socialism since 1919. But Hitler will help us through it" (483). In the literature of decline Bartels includes authors like Spielhagen, Karl Emil Franzos, and Heinrich Leuthold. The first counteractions to decadence, industrialization, and capitalism, which "are really of benefit to us" (506), originated with Wilhelm Heinrich Riehl (506). They came likewise from Konrad Ferdinand Meyer, one "of the few greats of the entire period," who proved as few had "that the natural Germanic spirit can also achieve the most pronounced effects of a literature of culture in the grandest style" (508, 510). Bartels views Ernst Adolf von Wildenbruch, the author of numerous dramas based on German prehistory, as another national champion: "Wildenbruch's rise can safely be characterized as a victory of the national and poetic spirit over the French Jewish spirit of feuilletonism" (522). For Bartels, Wildenbruch's achievement is to be found in his having contrasted an aristocratic ideal to the democratic "laissez faire" spirit. Nietzsche is too academic and European for Bartels, but as an idea his master morality is "certainly extraordinarily fruitful, all the more so as it ties in effortlessly the race theory for which a scientific foundation is to be laid" (546).

German naturalism is not flatly condemned but instead is carefully removed from the "superficial reporter-style naturalism" of Zola (570). Gerhart Hauptmann, the "greatest poet of German naturalism" is cautiously praised, as he created "genuine, touching images based on his precise knowledge of the people of the lower classes in his homeland," especially in his drama *Die Weber* (The Weavers). In Bartels eyes, however, "he was also a one-sided pessimist and at the same time labored mistakenly under confused ideas about humanity, he had no belief in the indestructible power of the German people, and he allowed himself, as a spirit with little independence, to be deceived by international, democratic phrases" (573). Naturally Bartels disapproves of the poets of the "fin de siècle," especially the Viennese Jew, Arthur Schnitzler. Schnitzler is in Bartel's view "representative of the fine Jewish decadence that often occurred in Viennese society in particular and under certain circumstances could be appealing" (579), "but we Germans still cannot take it completely seriously" (580). For Bartels, the "high point of German decadence" is reached with Wedekind's dramas *Frühlings Erwachen* (Spring's Awakening) and *Erdgeist* (The Earth Spirit) (586); they represent "a kind of stylized cynicism." *Frühlings Erwachen* "is reminiscent of Lenz's *Hofmeister* (The Tutor), but is even less suitable for the theater, if that is possible, than that work and also already shows the effects of all the evil spirits which then reduce Wedekind's works . . . to bacchanalia of insolence" (586). According to Bartels, Rilke, too, despite great lyrical artistry, inclines too decidedly to decadence and aestheticism; in Rilke's novel, *Die Aufzeichnungen des Malte Laurids Brigge* (The Notebooks of Malte Laurids Brigge), Bartels sees only the "history of the illness of an idiotic aristocrat" (590). Nevertheless, even Bartels cannot get around conceding to naturalism and symbolism overall that they are "literarily extremely interesting and as a transition period are undoubtedly also historically significant, . . ." although they have of course given "the German people little (of lasting value)" (604).

In his determined hunt for Jews in German literature, Bartels does not even spare Thomas and Heinrich Mann: "The brothers Heinrich and Thomas Mann from Lübeck led . . . up to Jewry — their father was an important merchant and senator, but their mother was Portuguese, thus possibly not without Jewish and Negro blood, and both married Jewish women" (667). In Heinrich Mann's novel *Der Untertan* (Patrioteer) Bartels sees "nothing more than an impudent caricature of German life," which "aroused his rage"; Heinrich Mann is "obviously . . . on the black list today" (668). In the case of Thomas Mann, Bartels has somewhat more difficulty. Thomas Mann is for him "undoubtedly something more than just a person of masterly talent," but has "basically nothing to offer, at least . . . nothing for our development" (668). Bartels especially has it in for "Jewish Expressionism" and its "Jewish publishers" Kurt Wolff and Samuel Fischer:

> And coming now to the literature of these "latest poets" themselves — Pinthus published the symphony of the latest literature "Menschheitsdämmerung [The Twilight of Humanity]" in 1920 with Ernst Rowohlt, Berlin — here the suspicion intrudes, as in the case of the modern directions in painting, futurism, and cubism, that perhaps only inability, I would almost like to say Jewish inability, created the new style, and that furthermore the international or "cosmic" tendency, the complete disregard for the *Volkstum* is a Jewish contribution accompanying the new art.

Of Franz Werfel Bartels says disparagingly: "The Jew Franz Werfel was made out to be the great light of the entire movement, perhaps indeed the greatest of today's poets, of course, only by Jews and comrades of Jews" (703). In the case of Reinhard Goering, Bartels is not certain whether he is a Jew; Bartels's "proof" shows once more with what "scholarly" methods he approaches his material: "He, too, seems to me to have Jewish blood, as in the 'Seeschlacht (The Sea Battle)' he had one sailor addressed as 'You, Jew' reply 'You, Christian.' The cadences of his language also appear to me to be Jewish" (710). In any case, Bartels regrets that the piece was not prohibited during the War, for "it was preparation, perhaps conscious preparation, for the revolution which then first broke out among the sailors" (711). Bartels objected even more explicitly to the Jewish writer Friedrich Wolf: "I considered him very dangerous" (712).

Other important writers of the time are touched upon only briefly and without commentary, for example, Georg Kaiser, Carl Einstein, Gottfried Benn, and Bertolt Brecht. It appears that Bartels' anti-Semitic polemics intensify the further his interpretation gets into modern times. Tucholsky is dismissed as a "genuine Jewish wise guy" and Ernst Toller as "a Jewish ne'er-do-well" (741). Bartels considers the comedy *Der fröhliche Weinberg* (The Merry Vineyard) by the "half Jew" Carl Zuckmayer to be "morally questionable and also politically tendentious," as it attempts to poke fun at the *völkisch* movement with the figure of the assessor Knuzius, "who lies drunk on a manure heap for an entire act" (742). Erich Kästner is suspicious, as his irony reminds Bartels of Heine and points to his "Jewish origins" (742). At the pinnacle of new German literature are, according to Bartels, the war books. However, Remarque's anti-war book *Im Westen Nichts Neues* (All Quiet on the Western Front) slipped in among the proud phalanx of works by Ernst Jünger, Werner Beumelburg, and Edwin Erich Dwinger, "a rather nasty representation of the soldier's life" from the "Jewish publisher Ullstein" (744). In his hunt for Jews, Bartels at times overshot his target by so far that he was forced to take back some of his unproven statements.[31]

Bartels contrasts the "decadent" and "jewified literati" to the literature of the German *Volkstum* that gained the upper hand after 1933. In doing so, he adds his own works, such as *Die Ditmarscher* (The People from Ditmarsch), to the works of Burte, Blunck, Beumelburg, Dwinger, Schumann, and others. However, for Bartels the millennium of national literature has not arrived yet. For that reason, he closes the nineteenth edition of his history of German literature (1943) with the hope for a time "in which political and literary, poetic greatness come together in our land — something which has not happened here since the days of the Hohenstaufen" (791) — and with a sermon directed at the German people: "No, you German people, don't let yourselves be confused by the high-sounding words of the 'moderns,' stay true to your German *Volkstum,* purify it, deepen it, keep it sacred!" (792). In an examination of "Jewish and *völkisch* Literature Studies" in 1936, one of the new generation of poets, Gerhard Schumann praises Adolf Bartels for having already recognized National Socialism in 1923 as the rescuer of Germany.[32]

Germanistik (German Language and Literature) in the Third Reich

Today it is hard to imagine that Bartels was ever taken seriously, but the large size of the printings proves it. His example, by no means an exception in the literature studies of the time, illustrates perhaps most blatantly how the field of *Germanistik* in the Third Reich had prostituted itself and had been in the service of literary control. Thus, Beate Pinkerneil points out that August Sauer and his student Josef Nadler had already publicized a connection between nationalism and racism three decades before the seizure of power of the National Socialists.[33] The nationalization of *Germanistik* that set in at the end of the nineteenth century leads into the "claim to unlimited authority of the Germanic-German master ideology" (Pinkerneil, 92). *Germanistik* in the Third Reich operated according to Pinkerneil "in a closed system of irrationalism, the individual categories of which claim to have the force of legal norms. The racial-biological community of the people, as the only, inescapable destiny forms its center" (Pinkerneil, 91). Klaus Vondung in *Völkisch-nationale und nationalsozialistische Literaturtheorie* (*Völkisch* National and National Socialist Literary Theory) and Eberhard Lämmert et al. in *Germanistik — eine deutsche Wissenschaft* (*Germanistik* — a German Scholarly Pursuit) bear witness to that. According to Klaus Vondung, "*Germanistik* in Germany dedicated itself to National Socialism in 1933 with greater zeal than all the other university disciplines" (105). Accordingly, we read the following in 1933 in the *Zeit-schrift für deutsche Dichtung* (Journal for German Literature), published by the Association of Germanists that was founded in 1912 and was renamed the "Society for German Education" after 1933: "We have been the pioneers for the new, which was promised back then and now has been realized."[34] The "movement for instruction in German civilization" (*Deutschkundebewegung*), which had its roots in German Romanticism, had become the leading field at German universities, after their numbers were cleansed of "undesirable elements almost without protest."

For the majority, however, Thomas Mann's reproach in his farewell letter to his friend of many years, Ernst Bertram, applied even before 1933: "The last thing that you can be accused of is that you went in the direction that the wind blew. Your direction was always 'right.'"[35] Ernst Bertram is just one of many illustrious names of scholars from the 1920s, including Karl Vietor, Herbert Cysarz, and Josef Nadler, who at least for a time served as intellectual stooges to the Nazis, as Lämmert recognized with embarrassment (Lämmert, 20–21). Ernst Bertram did not behave any differently from most of his colleagues in German studies — perhaps even better, for he was never a member of the Party, realized his error, and withdrew to his poet's existence much like Benn.[36] Indeed, *Germanistik* was apparently especially susceptible to National Socialism, for "in contrast to the professors of other disciplines, almost none of the scholars in German had to resign their positions. In this field, there were hardly any so-called members of foreign races, to say nothing of pronounced leftists."[37]

Germanistik, or *Deutschwissenschaft* (the scholarly study of German), in the Third Reich[38] thought of itself as "a scholarly pursuit of the *völkisch* essence and the protector of the intellectual and cultural core of the nation" (Vondung, 106). Thus in Karl Vietor's view in 1933, the time had come in which "scholars of *Germanistik*" "finally were in a position to make of their scholarly endeavors in research and teaching what they should be according to their purest destiny and their noble origins in the 'German movement': the scholarly study of the German people for the German people."[39] The renowned literary scholar Heinz Kindermann, who taught in Königsberg, Münster, and Vienna, agreed: "The new awareness of worth and system of order has obviously also changed our perception of the meaning of German literature. Race and *Volkstum*, these values for the growth of mankind, are now also decisive for the meaning of poetry, for the meaning of any literature."[40] Art is linked to biology: "The birth of literature from the people is thus a fact of artistic biology of which we are again aware — after going astray on a wide variety of tracks."[41] According to Kindermann and many others, the poet stands next to the leader; his creativity flows "out of the hereditary traits of his race, his people"; he expresses "what the others only sense intuitively." Therefore, he is subject "to the same responsibility as the statesman, as the leader of the people" (Kindermann, 18). Literature of the people — according to Kindermann — arises from the people, courses through the genius of the forming artist, and returns again to the people: "Circulation of blood and the soul occurs in this process" (Kindermann, 18).[42]

In his article *"Die Auswechslung der Literatur"* (The Renewal of Literature) in 1935, Paul Fechter supports the efforts to "root out the official literature of the middle-class left that was prevalent up to 1933," to help the literature, which was in his opinion "oppressed" in those days, make a breakthrough; the literature that was once so victorious is to be rooted out, disappear, and surrender the field to the German literature that was suppressed and passed over before now.[43] Therefore, it comes as no surprise that even well-known Germanists supported the campaign staged by the "German Student Association," "against the un-German spirit," which culminated in the book burning of May 1933.[44] Thus, Ernst Bertram composed a poem for this event that includes the line: "Into the flames with that which threatens you!"[45] In Bonn, Walter Schlevogt, the leader of the student association, demanded the "rooting out of all un-German intellectual products" with strong support from Hans Naumann, a professor for German and Nordic languages, who thanked the student association in a speech in the Bonn market square for acting so decisively.[46] In his speech, he declared, among other things: "When man is faced with an emergency and there is danger ahead, action must be taken without all too much hesitation. If one book too many flies into the fire to-night, that does not hurt as much as one too few flying into the fire would. What is healthy will rise up again of its own accord."[47] According to Naumann, Germany had become ill with rationalism; therefore he called for return to the original depths of irrationalism: "It was precisely the cleverly contrived art of the civilization literati who are alien to our kind. German art comes out of irrational depths. It comes out of the depths of *Parzival* and *Faust*. And it is the access to these depths that the gates are to be opened once again."[48] He ended his speech with a call for *völkisch* deeds and a hail to the *Führer* and Germany: "We appeal to the artistic spirit of *völkisch* activity. Hail then to new German literature! Hail to the highest leader! Hail, Germany!"[49] In Göttingen, the Germanist Gerhard Fricke sounded off similarly in his inflammatory speech. He saw in Hitler's seizure of power a "Copernican change" and greeted the new Germany full of anticipation: "We are waiting for the new and we believe in the future. Adolf Hitler has shown a world which has fallen prey to materialism that today the idea and the burning will are stronger than any other forces on earth."[50]

The renewal announced by Fechter is evident from the name change. *Germanistik* became *Deutschwissenschaft*, the study of German; the internationally recognized journal *Euphorion* was Germanized to *Dichtung und Volkstum* (Literature and *Volkstum*). The new editors, Julius Petersen and Hermann Pongs, made the following comment on that change: "The new name . . . intends to express that even the scholarly study of literature shall always keep the essence of the *Volkstum* before its eyes as the fundamental value that bears and nourishes all the values of aesthetics, literary history, and intellectual history."[51] To bolster the concept of the *"Volkstum"* literary scholars referred to Herder and the Grimm brothers, among others. The First World War, with its "storms of steel" that helped weld together a new community of the people, was added to that: "In the volleys of the World War the German *Volksgemeinschaft* was founded spiritually."[52] As Vondung proves, Germanists did not even shy away from supporting pan-German plans for expansion (125). With the outbreak of the Second World War, "the mobilization of the German humanities" was proclaimed, and as the leading scholarly field, *Deutschwissenschaft* was intimately involved. The objective, in the formulation of Franz Koch in the foreword of *Von deutscher Art und Dichtung* (Of German Heritage and Literature), was "to permeate intellectually what the sword had conquered."[53]

As Norbert Hopster has demonstrated, even the German teachers in the schools became instruments of political control.[54] According to Walther Linden, the new educator is "to be a recruiter and drum beater for the great community goals, a 'propaganda minister' on a small scale."[55] The "inclination to 'conservative' literature 'focusing on the people'" and the "vehement criticism of 'international,' 'corrupting' literature" that the Cologne German studies scholar Karl Otto Conrady establishes in an "un-ceremonial remembrance" on the occasion of the 600th Anniversary of the University of Cologne for Ernst Bertram and Friedrich von der Leyen, his predecessors, also apply to other renowned Germanists in the Third Reich. At the same time, it should not be overlooked how difficult the situation was for many of them, for example, for von der Leyen, who in 1936 was forced out of his position by the Nazis.[56]

Classicism and Romanticism in the Third Reich

After the seizure of power, *Wilhelm Tell* was performed as the national liberation and *Führer* drama, as it "embodied the longing for a strong and free German people"; until 1941, it was among the most performed Schiller dramas (414). The quotes on the thousand-year ownership of property, the dear fatherland, and the Rütli oath were especially popular, for they anticipated most decidedly what the National Socialists now seemed about to accomplish. For example, the *Völkischer Beobachter* reports in extensive detail about the Rütli scene on the occasion of the *Tell* performance in Dresden on June 2, 1934: "The most decisive scene of Schiller's *Tell* for the theater of today is the Rütli scene. Here a national cult act was most visibly brought to the German stage at an early point . . . Friedrich Schiller, the writer of the Classicism period, stepped among us as the *völkisch* poet of the present"

(416). On April 20, 1938, *Wilhelm Tell* was produced at Vienna's Burgtheater in honor of the German-Austrian, Adolf Hitler, on the occasion of his first birthday after the *Anschluß*, the annexation of Austria in March of 1938, as the pan-German *Führer*. The *Neue Wiener Tageblatt* (New Vienna Daily Gazette) regarded this performance as thanks "from the depths of our hearts to our *Führer*, Adolf Hitler. *Sieg Heil!*" (418). *Wilhelm Tell* was not only considered a drama celebrating a leader, but also a drama of *völkisch* family policy and an educational drama of a "healthy *Volkstum*" (418). A *Tell* performance in Eger in Czechoslovakia, then the "Sudetenland," turned into a demonstration of German national ambitions (419, 421).

After 1941, however, *Tell* was no longer performed on the express wish of Hitler; the murder of a tyrant and the celebration of separatism in *Tell* "made Schiller over night into the 'state enemy' of National Socialism" (422). As Ernst Osterkamp demonstrated in his article "Klassik-Konzepte: Kontinuität und Diskontinuität bei Walter Rehm und Hans Pyritz" (Concepts of Classicism: Continuity and Discontinuity in Walter Rehm and Hans Pyritz),[57] Goethe and Classicism were by no means uncontested among the German studies scholars in the Third Reich. While the Freiburg Germanist Walter Rehm sought to preserve the classic ideal of education and humanity, especially in his book *Griechentum und Goethezeit* (Hellenism and the Period of Goethe) of 1936, his Berlin colleague Hans Pyritz judged "Classicism to be an alienation of the German from himself, as a loss of identity of the German to humanitarian ethics."[58] Walter Rehm still saw in Classicism "self-discovery of the German in the spirit of German humanity" (161). In contrast, Pyritz was of the opinion "that the German would first discover himself at the point when he turned away from the spirit of Classicism."[59]

Bartels, who once again is quoted as illustrative for many others, equates German Romanticism with Germanness: "What is it then, the Romantic spirit? I believe that it can simply be called the Germanic spirit, despite its being reminiscent of Romanesque; Romanticism is the German Renaissance" (226). The Romantics have located the essence of the German *Volkstum* deep within the German soul: the Romantics penetrated deep into the region of the subconscious "and discovered in the individual himself the other ego, the unconscious, in which the heritage of the *Volkstum* is primarily found" (227). For Bartels a "decidedly national literature . . . in the Germanic spirit" begins with Romanticism (227). Bartels considers Heinrich von Kleist one of the most outstanding representatives of Romanticism; "as a genius by nature, he stands head and shoulders above the Romantic haze and becomes an 'eternal' poet and therefore also a modern one" (247–48). For Bartels's student, and the Reich Dramatic Advisor (*Reichsdramaturg*) Rainer Schlösser, the very name Kleist sounds like a concentration of enormous elementary force in one syllable, it is dynamite and the destructive force of steel casing all in one!"[60] Above all in Eichendorff's folk songs

Schlösser sees "specific and healthy Romanticism," in contract to the "hypo-critical society" of the salon. Schlösser finds in Eichendorff "a piece of vir-ginal, untouched, original homeland, pervaded by the breath of Nordic natural bliss, blessed by the touch of the great unknown God" (145). Eichendorff avoided, according to Schlösser, the "ordinary winding spool of Liberalism" and is even named a Party comrade by him: "He was really accorded confirmation for the first time by us National Socialists" (146).

Hölderlin, too, is misrepresented one-sidedly as a promulgator of patriotic willingness to sacrifice. For Franz Koch, "in Hölderlin the still slumbering German *Volkheit* (folkdom) had opened its eyes and recognized the Greek person as the living dream of its own blood."[61] In Hölderlin, Koch sees the "heroic poet who wants 'what unifies' and the prophet and seer of future unification of his Germans . . . sinking into the night of madness," whose laments about the Germans spring "from burning love for the people" (162–63). Even for less radical Germanists such as Heinz Otto Burger, Hölderlin's work reaches its peak "in the proclamation of the coming day of the Ger-mans."[62] The *Nationalsozialistische Monatshefte* (National Socialist Monthly Magazine), the "central political and cultural magazine of the NSDAP," edited by Alfred Rosenberg, skillfully plundered Hölderlin, to "improve the ideological brew and make it mostly more palatable to the educated middle class" (Cl. Vol. 1, 341). For Matthes Ziegler, in the volume dedicated to "Zarathustra, Meister Eckhart, Hölderlin, Kierkegaard" (Vol. 5, Number 47, 1934), Hölderlin was "an inspired artist of Nordic heroic belief in God" (Cl. Vol. 1, 341). In 1943, as the war casualties became greater and the end loomed, Hölderlin was invoked by Franz Koch as the one who died as a model for a misled youth: "For in the memory of Germany he lives, rediscov-ered and awakened to new life by that youth, which shed its blood at Lange-marck and Verdun, as the archetype of him who had to die young because the gods loved him" (Cl. Vol. 1, 342). Heinz Kindermann joined in, calling for determination to stay the course in "the fateful Hölderlin commemorative year," 1943: "Around us roars chaos, a new order of values must be battled for bitterly against the forces of extinction. The one stands by us in this strug-gle for life or death . . . in a time when everyone must give his all to save what is most precious, that is Hölderlin" (Cl. Vol. 1, 344).

Notes

[1] Quoted in Dietrich Strothmann, *Nationalsozialistische Literaturpolitik* (National Socialist Literature Policies), 4th edition (Bonn: Bouvier, 1985; 1st edition, 1960), 62 (cited in the text as Strothmann and the page number). For the following re-marks, Strothmann's work was a valuable aid for me, as was the study of Jan Pieter Barbian *Literaturpolitik im "Dritten Reich": Institutionen, Kompetenzen, Betäti-gungsfelder* (Literary Policies in the "Third Reich": Institutions, Competencies,

Fields of Activity) (Frankfurt am Main: Buchhändler-Vereinigung GmbH, 1993; revised and updated edition, Munich: dtv, 1995), cited in the text as Barbian and the page number. Barbian's comprehensive work (916 pages) goes considerably beyond Strothmann's valuable study, as it is based on the latest findings and insights into archival materials not yet available to Strothmann. Klaus Vondung's judgment on Strothmann (Klaus Vondung, *Völkisch-nationale und nationalsozialistische Literaturtheorie* (Völkisch National and National Socialist Literature Theory) (Munich: List, 1973), 152: "His thorough examination remains of basic importance for this subject") therefore still only applies with limitations, for Barbian is able to show several serious errors in Strothmann (Barbian, 26–27). For the special situation regarding cultural policies in Austria before the annexation, which cannot be considered here, see Klaus Aman, *Der Anschluß österreichischer Schriftsteller and das Dritte Reich: Institutionelle und bewußtseinsgeschichtliche Aspekte* (The Annexation of Austrian Writers to the Third Reich: Institutional Aspects and Aspects relating to the History of Awareness) (Frankfurt am Main: Athenäum, 1988).

[2] On that subject also see Uwe-K. Ketelsen, *Literatur und Drittes Reich* (Literature and the Third Reich) (Vierow near Greifswald: SH Verlag, 1992 and 1994), 289, and Georg Bollenbeck, "Das Ende des Bildungsbürgers" (The End of the Educated Citizen), in *Die Zeit* (The Times), 3 (January 14, 1999), 29–30.

[3] On the book burning, see Barbian, 128–141.

[4] On that subject, see Barbian, 442–445, and Hans Carossa, *Ungleiche Welten* (Unequal Worlds) (Frankfurt am Main: Suhrkamp, 1978; first edition with Insel, 1951), 105–9.

[5] See Barbian, 398–409.

[6] According to Volker Dahm of the Munich Institute for Contemporary History at a symposium on the Inner Emigration, Hofstra University, US, 16 October 1999.

[7] For more details on *Ahnenerbe,* see Michael H. Kater, *Das 'Ahnenerbe' der SS 1935–1945. Ein Beitrag zur Kulturpolitik des Dritten Reiches* (Cultural Heritage Program of the SS, 1935–1945. A Contribution to the Cultural Policies of the Third Reich) (Stuttgart: Deutsche Verlags-Anstalt, 1974).

[8] On that subject, see Hildegard Brenner, *Die Kunstpolitik des Nationalsozialismus* (The Art Policy of National Socialism) (Reinbeck: Rowohlt, 1963), 63–86. For the Expressionism battle in the socialist camp, see, for example, Hans Jürgen Schmitt. *Die Expressionismusdebatte* (The Expressionism Debate) (Frankfurt am Main: Suhrkamp, 1973).

[9] See Klaus Vondung, 155.

[10] See Brenner, 82–83.

[11] This is very reminiscent of the East German leader Erich Honecker's well-known statement in 1971 that there are no taboos in the literary sphere if the fixed positions of socialism are the starting point.

[12] This quotation also shows what an important political value the Olympics were in Nazi ideology.

[13] For example, the "National Prize for Art and Science" established by Hitler was considered a replacement for the Nobel prize, which German citizens were no longer allowed

to accept after the writer Carl von Ossietzky, who was taken away to a concentration camp, infected with tuberculosis there, and died of it in 1938, was honored with one.

[14] See Ernst Loewy, *Literatur unterm Hakenkreuz* (Literature under the Swastika) (Frankfurt am Main: Fischer, 1985 and 1987; 1st edition, 1966), 307. As Glenn R. Cuomo explains, Blunck was more moderate in the exercise of his office than his successor, the SS *Oberführer* (later *Gruppenführer*) Hanns Johst, who was close to the *Reichsführer* of the SS, Heinrich Himmler. Among other things, Blunck attempted to prevent the Aryan Paragraph and to obtain a kind of "national park for writers"; see Glenn R. Cuomo, "Hanns Johst und die Reichsschrifttumskammer, ihr Einfluß auf die Situation des Schriftstellers im Dritten Reich" (Hanns Johst and the Reich Literature Chamber. Its Influence on the Situation of the Writer in the Third Reich) in *Leid der Worte: Panorama des literarischen Nationalsozialismus* (Suffering of Words: Panorama of Literary National Socialism), edited by Jörg Thunecke (Bonn: Bouvier, 1987), especially 109–113.

[15] Ketelsen, *Literatur und Drittes Reich*, Chapter 11, 286–304.

[16] Ketelsen, *Literatur und Drittes Reich*, 296.

[17] Ketelsen, *Literatur und Drittes Reich*, 76.

[18] Quoted in Wilfried Barner, "Literaturgeschichtsschreibung vor und nach 1945, alt, neu, alt/neu" (The Writing of Literary History Before and After 1945, Old, New, Old-New), in *Zeitenwechsel: Germanistische Literaturwissenschaft vor und nach 1945* (Changing Times: The Study of German Literature before and after 1945), edited by Wilfried Barner and Christoph König (Frankfurt am Main: Fischer, 1996), 122.

[19] Quoted in Wilhelm Voßkamp, "Kontinuität und Diskontinuität. Zur deutschen Literaturwissenschaft im Dritten Reich" (Continuity and Discontinuity. On the Study of German Literature in the Third Reich), in *Wissenschaft im Dritten Reich* (Scholarship in the Third Reich), edited by Peter Lundgren (Frankfurt am Main: Suhrkamp, 1985), 151.

[20] Jens Malte Fischer, "'Zwischen uns und Weimar liegt Buchenwald.' Germanisten im Dritten Reich" ("Between Weimar and Us Lies Buchenwald." Germanists in the Third Reich), in *Merkur* 41, 1 (January 1987), 20–21. The quotation in the title comes from Richard Alewyn's preface to his Goethe lecture, which he held in 1949 at the University of Cologne after his return from exile. Kindermann's Jewish teacher Max Hermann died in 1942 in Theresienstadt Concentration Camp. In 1954 Kindermann was reinstated in his position at the University of Vienna.

[21] Ketelsen, *Literatur und Drittes Reich*, 86–87.

[22] On the theme of histories of literature in the Third Reich, see Barner, 119–149.

[23] Ketelsen, *Literatur und Drittes Reich*, 93.

[24] Langenbucher is referring here directly to Hitler's speech at the Culture Conference of the Reich Party Congress of the NSDAP in 1933 in Nuremberg in which the *Führer* energetically expressed his opposition to such people: "The National Socialist movement and state leadership must not tolerate in the cultural area, either, that ne'er-do-wells and charlatans change their flags and then, as if nothing had happened, move into the new state in order to once again make grand speeches there in the area of art and culture policy. . . . But we know one thing, that the representatives of the ruin that lies behind us may under no circumstances suddenly become the

standard bearers of the future. Either the monstrosities that they produced back then were really an inner experience, in which case they belong in medical safekeeping as a danger to the mental health of our people, or it was only speculation, in which case they belong in the appropriate institution for fraud." Quoted in Vondung, 86.

[25] In Jacob Grimm, to whom Langenbucher refers several times, *Volk* still means "the embodiment of people who speak the same language." Quoted in Eberhard Lämmert, et al, *Germanistik — eine deutsche Wissenschaft* (*Germanistik* — A German Scholarly Pursuit), 2nd edition (Frankfurt am Main: Suhrkamp, 1967), 22.

[26] See Langenbucher, 1st edition, 19.

[27] Paul Ernst, "Das deutsche Volk und der Dichter von heute" (The German People and the Poet of Today), in *Des deutschen Dichters Sendung in der Gegenwart* (*The Mission of the German Poet in the Present*), edited by Heinz Kindermann (Leipzig: Reclam, 1933), 19.

[28] Paul Ernst, 19–20.

[29] On that subject, see Jost Hermand, "Das junge Deutschland" (Young Germany), in *Von Mainz nach Weimar 1793–1919* (From Mainz to Weimar, 1793–1919), edited by Jost Hermand (Stuttgart: Metzler, 1969).

[30] Paul Fechter in his *Geschichte der deutschen Literatur: Von den Anfängen bis zur Gegenwart* (The History of German Literature: From the Beginnings to the Present) (Berlin: Knaur Nachfolger Verlag, 1941) made statements about Heine similar to those of Bartels, just not in as obvious a way as Bartels: "A very clever Jewish word talent without inhibitions seizes the formulas of authenticity, and uses them, but cannot create new ones on his own" (510). For Franz Koch, too, the penetration of the "civilization literati into German literature, and thus its demise begins with the mostly Jewish Young Germans"; see Franz Koch, *Geschichte deutscher Dichtung* (The History of German Literature), 5th edition (Hamburg: Hanseatische Verlagsanstalt, 1942), 198.

[31] On that subject, see Strothmann, 330–31.

[32] See Voßkamp, 152.

[33] Beate Pinkerneil, "Vom kulturellen Nationalismus zur nationalen Germanistik" (From Cultural Nationalism to National German Studies), in *Am Beispiel "Wilhelm Meister": Einführung in die Wissenschaftsgeschichte der Germanistik* (Using the Example of "Wilhelm Meister." Introduction to the History of the Field of German Studies), Vol. 1, *Darstellung* (Description), edited by Klaus L. Berghahn and Beate Pinkerneil (Königstein im Taunus: Athenäum, 1980), 75–97. (Vol. 2, *Dokumente* [Documents]).

[34] Quoted in Karl Otto Conrady, "Deutsche Literaturwissenschaft und Drittes Reich" (German Literature Studies and the Third Reich), in *Germanistik — eine deutsche Wissenschaft*, edited by Eberhard Lämmert (Frankfurt am Main: Suhrkamp, 1967), 73.

[35] Quoted in Klaus Vondung, *Völkisch-nationale und nationalsozialistische Literaturtheorie* (*Völkisch National and National Socialist Literature Theory*), 105. On the continuity of German studies before and after 1933, see Wilhelm Voßkamp, 140–62. Voßkamp says in summary: "The discontinuity in political development in 1933 does not correspond to one in the history of scholarship; continuity in the development of German studies at German universities has prevailed since the first decades of the twentieth century" (152).

[36] See Jens Malte Fischer, 24.

[37] Jost Hermand, *Geschichte der Germanistik* (History of German Studies) (Reinbek near Hamburg: Rowohlt, 1994), 99.

[38] According to Lämmert, the term "Deutschwissenschaft" (the scholarly study of German) came into use between 1910 and 1920; see Lämmert, 9.

[39] Quoted in Conrady, 75. Despite all criticism, Conrady rightly points out the accomplishments of this generation of German scholars, which are evident, for example, in Paul Kluckhohn's research report "Deutsche Literaturwissenschaft 1933–1940" (German Literature Studies, 1933–1940) from 1941. Kluckhohn's text is reprinted in *NS-Literaturtheorie: Eine Dokumentation* (National Socialist Literature Theory: Documentation), edited by Sander L. Gilman (Frankfurt am Main: Athenäum, 1971), 244–264. Vietor had already left Germany in 1935, deceived and disappointed by the Third Reich.

[40] See Heinz Kindermann, "Das Schrifttum als Ausdruck des Volkstums" (Literature as the Expression of *Volkstum*), in *Kampf um die deutsche Lebensform* (Struggle for the German Way of Life), edited by Heinz Kindermann (Vienna: Wiener Verlag, 1941, 1944), 12.

[41] Kindermann, 14.

[42] For Heinz Kindermann, see also Mechthild Kirsch, "Heinz Kindermann — ein Wiener Germanist und Theaterwissenschaftler (Heinz Kindermann — a Viennese scholar of German Studies and Theater," in *Zeitenwechsel*, 47–59.

[43] Paul Fechter, "Die Auswechslung der Literatur" (The Renewal of Literature), in Sander Gilmann, 240.

[44] On the leading role of the students on the book burning, see among others Joseph Wulf, *Literatur und Dichtung im Dritten Reich: Eine Dokumentation* (Literature and Poetry in the Third Reich: Documentation) (Frankfurt am Main: Ullstein, 1983), 44–63.

[45] In Ernst Loewy, 18.

[46] See Joseph Wulf, *Literatur und Dichtung im Dritten Reich: Eine Dokumentation*, 52. Further details regarding Naumann and other German studies scholars can be found in Norbert Oellers, "Literatur und Volkstum. Der Fall der Literaturwissenschaft" (Literature and *Volkstum*. The Fall of Literary Scholarship), in *Literatur und Germanistik nach der Machtübernahme* (Literature and German Studies after the Seizure of Power), edited by Beda Allemann (Bonn: Bouvier, 1983), 232–54.

[47] Quoted in Voßkamp, 140–141.

[48] Quoted in Voßkamp, 141.

[49] Quoted in Voßkamp, 141.

[50] Quoted in Voßkamp, 143.

[51] Quoted in Voßkamp, 114.

[52] According to Walther Linden, quoted in Vondung, 124.

[53] Quoted in Werner Herden, "Zwischen 'Gleichschaltung' und Kriegseinsatz. Positionen der Germanistik in der Zeit des Faschismus" (Between "Alignment" and Use in War: Positions of German Studies in the Time of Fascism), in *Weimarer Beiträge* 33, 11 (1987), 1878. In addition, Herden concerns himself with three other

prominent scholars of German studies and their views on the Third Reich: Franz Hübner and Julius Petersen, who despite their sympathy for the new Reich still wanted to ensure a free space for scholarship, and Franz Koch, a rabid Nazi, who was embroiled in controversy with his colleague Petersen and even accused him of intellectually sabotaging the Third Reich — see Herden, 1876–77.

[54] Norbert Hopster, "Ausbildung und politische Funktion der Deutschlehrer im National-sozialismus" (The Training and Political Function of German Teachers in National Socialism), in *Wissenschaft im Dritten Reich*, edited by Peter Lundgren, 113–139.

[55] Quoted in Hopster, 123.

[56] See Karl Otto Conrady, *Völkisch-nationale Germanistik in Köln: Eine unfestliche Erinnerung* (*Völkisch* National German Studies in Cologne: An Un-Ceremonial Remembrance) (Schernfeld: SH Verlag, 1990), 72. Just how great the influence of von der Leyen was anyway becomes clear from the outrage with which Ernst Alfred Philippson, one of von der Leyen's students and a professor at the University of Illinois, reviewed Conrady's book in the U.S., where Phillipson had emigrated before the Nazis (source: personal conversation).

[57] Ernst Osterkamp, "Klassik-Konzepte: Kontinuität und Diskontinuität bei Walter Rehm und Hans Pyritz" (Classicism Conceptions: Continuity and Discontinuity in Walter Rehm and Hans Pyritz), in *Zeitenwechsel*, 150–170.

[58] Osterkamp, 161.

[59] Osterkamp, 161.

[60] Rainer Schlösser, "Das einfaltige Herz: Eichendorff als Geschichtsschreiber unseres Innern" (The Simple Heart: Eichendorff as the Historian of Our Interior Being), in *NS-Literaturtheorie*, edited by Sander Gilman, 142. The page citations in the text refer to this edition.

[61] Franz Koch, *Geschichte der deutschen Dichtung*, 179. The page citations in the text refer to this edition.

[62] Quoted in *Klassiker in finsteren Zeiten*, volume 1, 332. Quoted in the text as "Cl. Vol. 1" and page citation.

Hans Grimm, author of the novel *Volk ohne Raum* (A People Without Space), from which the Nazis took the catch phrase. Courtesy Bundesarchiv, Koblenz.

4: The National Socialist Novel

THE NOVEL IN particular made possible the detailed representation of the ideology of National Socialism. As bestseller lists from the twenties and thirties show, the novel surpassed all other genres.[1] This chapter will show, on the basis of several selected novels, what subjects were dealt with in the novels that were welcome to the Nazis for ideological reasons. It makes no difference that some of the novels were already written before Hitler's official seizure of power in 1933. Decisive is only the ideology expressed in the novels and the fact that several editions and many thousands of copies of the novels were distributed in the period from 1933 to 1945 and reached a large segment of the reading public. Karl Prümm provides several examples of this: "In 1936, 500,000 copies of Edwin Erich Dwinger's novels were printed. Through the distribution mechanisms of the Party, the total number of copies of Zöberlein's works printed had reached 800,000 by 1940, while Beumelburg had already exceeded the million mark in 1939."[2] The National Socialist novel concerns itself with themes similar to those of the National Socialist drama: the community-building experiences of war and battle ("Steel Romanticism") from the First World War or from the period of struggle of National Socialism before the seizure of power, the peasantry of German blood and soil, Aryan people of the north and Jews, historical champions of the Reich idea, important leaders and founders of the Reich from German history, and martyrs of the Reich. Several examples of these theme groups will be represented in the following pages.

War and Battle

Among the most popular themes was the experience of the front and the camaraderie that had been established in the First World War, and its decline in a mollycoddled Weimar Republic. As Karl Prümm shows, "war themes" ranked "quantitatively even before such accustomed subjects as 'blood and soil,' 'homeland and people.'"[3] The anti-democratic front-line collective with its authoritarian structures of leader and followers was the prototype in the Third Reich for a National Socialist community of the people. Thus, the literature scholar Hermann Pongs sees an "underground connection" between the "elemental matter of war, which is reclaimed as the destiny of the people, and . . . the great people's movement that leads to a new Germany of the people."[4] The novels that illuminate the front-line spirit of the First

World War in more detail, such as *Die Gruppe Bosemüller* (The Bosemüller Group, 1930) by Werner Beumelburg, *Die Armee hinter Stacheldraht: Das sibirische Tagebuch* (The Army behind Barbed Wire: The Siberian Diaries, 1929) by Edwin Erich Dwinger, *Aufbruch der Nation* (Rise of the Nation, 1929) by Franz Schauwecker, *Sieben vor Verdun* (Seven before Verdun, 1930) by Josef Magnus Wehner, and *Der Glaube an Deutschland: Ein Kriegserleben von Verdun bis zum Umsturz* (Belief in Germany: Experiencing the War from Verdun to the Overthrow, 1931) by Franz Zöberlein have already been treated extensively by Karl Prümm[5] and need not be considered here. Of this group of "novels of the front-line spirit," the novel *In Stahlgewittern* (In Storms of Steel) by Ernst Jünger that was so popular and successful under the Nazis, as well as the following novels from the "period of struggle," will be discussed: *Die letzten Reiter* (The Last Cavalrymen) by Edwin Erich Dwinger, *Der Befehl des Gewissens* (The Command of Conscience) by Hans Zöberlein, *Der Hitlerjunge Quex* (Hitler Youth Quex) by Karl Aloys Schenzinger, and *Horst Wessel* by Hanns Heinz Ewers.

A literarily quite ambitious war book that highlights the spirit of camaraderie at the front and the soldierly heroism of the First World War is Ernst Jünger's war diary *In Stahlgewittern* (1920), which was printed numerous times up to 1945 (the twenty-fourth edition in 1942). For Karl Prümm, this book is a prime example of "soldierly nationalism" in the Weimar Republic.[6] Ernst Jünger himself, who participated as an officer in both world wars, was far too much of an aesthetic aristocrat to become an enthusiastic follower of the Nazis; in 1944 he was even released from the army as "unfit for service," as he was close to the resistance group around General von Stülpnagel.[7] However, as Uwe-K. Ketelsen correctly remarks, "intellectual Fascism/National Socialism" was "not necessarily identical to political Fascism/National Socialism; in fact, the former could even be at odds with the latter."[8] "Heroic Realism" and what Loewy called "Steel Romanticism" made *In Stahlgewittern* very popular reading in the Third Reich as well. For Russell A. Berman, this book in particular exhibits the special characteristics of fascist literature in which the middle-class, liberal individual is replaced by the soldierly, national collective.[9]

The question of origin, meaning, and objective of the war plays no role in the context of Jünger's aesthetics, as they transcend any rationally progressive thinking and move into mystical realms. Battle scenes are stripped of their individual content and transposed into the contemplative aesthetics of statics and repetition.[10] The detailed description of mangled bodied only has an aesthetic function on a superficial level. Drawn by a "sweetish smell," Lieutenant Jünger examines a "bundle hanging in the barbed wire." He finds a half-decayed French soldier: "Fish-like decayed flesh glistens greenish-white out of the tattered uniform."[11] These and other grisly images are by no means intended to convert the reader to pacifism. Jünger describes everything only with a cool distance, just as if walking on a meadow path in the Champagne, except that he is now in the trenches: "I strolled . . . along the devastated trench" (23). There is no question of an emotional reaction. Feelings play almost no role in this book, at most in a very distant manner. An English mine has, for example, "an unpleasant effect on the nerves" (34). After a gas attack, the first-person narrator Jünger has "the icy feeling that the conversation was no longer with human beings but with demons. One roams around as if in a gigantic dumping ground on the other side of the borders of the known world" (120). The horrors and death that the author witnesses in the war do not give rise to indescribable terror in him. On the contrary, the sweet smell of corpses, mixed with the acrid haze of explosives, produce in him "an almost clairvoyant excitement" (96). When in the field hospital a comrade in the next bed dies, he is not at all sad: "I felt here for the first time that death is a big thing" (122). A heavy barrage gives him "the feeling of the inevitable and of absolute necessity as if facing an eruption of the elements" (99). Jünger does not mention a word about the fact that wars are instigated by people, about how they develop, or about who profits from them. Terrible battle scenes are described in detail, but the suffering of the victims does not interest him:

> In such moments the human spirit triumphs over the most violent manifestations of matter, the frail body, steeled by the will, stands up to the most terrible storm. (104)

As is well known, Adolf Hitler also wished his German youths to be "hard as Krupp steel." War cannot be conducted with soldiers who have feelings. As the model for conduct, a steel-helmeted messenger is presented who reports in a monotone voice from the front. In his voice is nothing "but great, manly indifference. With such men it is possible to fight" (95). The finality of death is neutralized by his being drawn into the fateful, elementary circle of life to which war also belongs: "Somehow even the very simple soul sensed that his life is being directed into eternal circulation [and] is a meaningful event" (151). War does not produce unspeakable sorrow for Jünger, but an aristocratic and manly elite, as he acknowledges after the battle at the officers' table:

> Here, where the intellectual supporters and champions of the front came together, the will to victory became concentrated and took form in the features of weather-hardened faces. An element was alive here that underlined the desolation of war yet spiritualized the objective pleasure in danger, the chivalrous urge to do battle. In the course of four years, the fire smelted out an increasingly pure and increasingly bold warrior force. (148)

War ennobles; the front-line soldiers became "princes of the trenches with hard, determined faces, jumping back and forth, recklessly, so sinewy and lithe, with sharp, blood-thirsty eyes." Even with all the otherwise pre-dominant objectivity, this front spirit is elevated, even as the all-creator, into the mystical, religious realm: "The brassy spirit of attack, the spirit of the Prussian infantry, hovered over the masses" (237). A defender "who puts his bullets through the body of the attacker at five steps away . . . is under the influence of powerful primal drives" (256). The often cited spirit of camara-derie is by no means the equivalent of rankless egalitarianism. For Jünger the difference between the leaders and the led is also fundamental. Colonel von Oppen, for example, is a born leader: "Colonel von Oppen was a living example of the fact that there are people who are born to give orders. He was a representative of the leading race" (236).

The aristocratic, soldierly chivalry at work throughout the diary also extends to the English opponents. At the sight of an English sergeant stoically smoking his pipe, both of whose "legs were almost torn off by the fragments of a hand grenade," Jünger writes, "Here, too, as wherever we encountered the English, we had the pleasant impression of brave manliness" (132). In the preface to the English translation of his book (the fifth edition of which already appeared in 1929), Jünger made his admiration of the English clear: "Of all the troops who were opposed to the Germans on the great battlefields, the English were not only the most formidable but the most manly and the most chivalrous."[12] The French, on the other hand, are not "opponents" for Jünger, but the "enemy"; their trenches were "shrouded with an ancient enmity" (204).

Towards the end of the war, Jünger noted a "crumbling of war disci-pline"; even a "Prussian dressing down" no longer intimidated the inner "moral swine." Jünger sensed that the meaning of the war had changed. What that meaning was, however, was never said; it remained a riddle: "The war presented new riddles. It was a strange time" (278). The bitter end loomed: "With every attack, the enemy presented more powerful arma-ments; its strikes came faster and heavier. Everyone knew that we could no longer win" (296). Only the inventors of the stab-in-the-back legend appar-ently did not know, or consciously kept the legend alive — such as the Nazis, to capitalize on it politically.

What the National Socialists took from the book for their purposes was the praise of war as the creator of soldierly, heroic warriors. In the introduc-tion to the English translation, R. H. Mottram recommends that the book be read as the historical document of a German front-line officer, with his limited perspective, and as an anti-war book.

Edwin Erich Dwinger's novel *Die letzten Reiter* (The Last Cavalrymen), published in 1935 by Eugen Diedrichs, is dedicated to "General Field Mar-shall von Mackensen, the last cavalry general of the Great War." The book shows how the spirit of camaraderie and of the front live on after the war in the so-called *Freikorps* (volunteer corps), which had made it their mission to destroy Bolshevism inside and outside the German Reich. The volunteer corps consisted mostly of former front-line soldiers who were not able to make the transition from an authoritarian to a democratic form of government and from military existence to civilian life in the Weimar Republic, although the new state was not at all as oriented to the liberal left, as many of the unemployed officers of the former imperial army believed.[13]

Adolf Hitler wrote the following about the role of the volunteer corps in the Weimar Republic:

> As the matadors of the revolution in the days of December, January, and February of 1918–1919 felt the ground shake under their feet, they looked around for people who were prepared to strengthen by force of arms the weak position that the love of their people offered them. The "antimilitary" republic needed soldiers.[14]

As their own supporters consisted only of "thieves, shirkers, and deserters" — according to Hitler — they called, in their need, the much disparaged front-line soldiers who then voluntarily once again put on their soldier's uniforms, "in the service of 'public peace and order,' as they thought," "in order to offer resistance, with their helmets pulled on, to the destroyers of the homeland."[15] It is well known that the voluntary corps, and the government that had called them, were severely criticized by the left. Although Hitler thoroughly praised the idealism and the good faith of the men of the voluntary corps, he also criticized the voluntary corps, as he was aware of the ironic contradiction that here men who "fiercely hated the revolution" began "to protect, and thus to practically fortify, that same revolution." Of course that could only happen because those people failed to see what Hitler had known all along: "The real organizer of the revolution and the person who actually pulled the strings" was "the international Jew."[16]

Dwinger's novel *Die letzten Reiter* was one of his most successful works; 230,000 copies had been printed by 1940.[17] It portrays the fate of the voluntary corps that fought Bolshevism in the Baltic states and felt "betrayed" by the Entente and the Weimar Republic. At the center of the story are the men of the "Mansfeld Mounted Volunteer Corps," which with sacrifice and great effort advanced as far as Riga, and then markedly decimated and beaten, again reached the German border, where they were treated like pariahs. The volunteer corps comprised "former African colonists," students, farmers, and "mercenaries by blood" who wanted to save "the Occident from being overrun by Bolsheviks."[18] Here in the Kurland, a fertile province in former East Prussia, they want "to dig a well from which the true German springs forth" (46) and to produce a generation that rolls up Weimar Germany and once again erects Potsdam Germany. This "noble" task appeals to them more than becoming "traveling wine salesmen . . . in this proletarian republic" (15).

The veneration for the rural landed aristocracy that runs through the entire novel intensifies to an apotheosis when Dwinger compares the suffering

column of captured nobles on the way to Riga to Christ's journey to Golgo-
tha. The Prussian nobility's lifestyle and way of thinking are to be exemplary
for a new Germany, for here the natural relationship between leader and
followers is still evident to Dwinger, not the egalitarian, treasonous, narrow-
minded spirit of the Weimar Republic, embodied above all in Erzberger, who
ostensibly sold out Germany in Versailles.[19] Germany must arise once again
with its old greatness; that is only possible by a revolution from the right in the
old front-line spirit, a revolution that pits the so-called classless society of the
Marxists against a "natural" order of leaders and followers, infused with a spirit
of camaraderie that stands ready to sacrifice. However, "with collars and ties
there is no camaraderie" (319). That requires a uniform: "The uniform is
being in step, the uniform is community, the uniform is leadership" (320).
The separate individual must be extinguished; his independent will must be
broken, even if he perishes in the process:

> To achieve this state, in which he has neither wife nor children, in
> which he forgets life with all its enticements, one method had proven
> indispensable, which is called, in a word, "Breaking!" It is the same
> method . . . that is used for young horses. Every so often one doesn't
> make it, but for us it is not the "I" that counts but the "we!" (152)

To the leaders belong followers who are idealistic, trusting, strong, and
prepared to sacrifice. The shining examples are the men who died in action
in the First World War, especially the young volunteers who marched singing to their deaths before Langemarck in Flanders.[20] For them death was
fulfillment, "for us, the survivors, promise! . . . Oh, if it would really grow,
this legacy of Langemarck, then it would also finally succeed, for there is no
stronger force" (114–15).

As does Jünger, Dwinger views war not as something terrible, but as
fulfillment and a process of purification, as a catharsis; Langemarck and war
as the preliminary step to greatness can no longer be grasped rationally. Of
course, Dwinger is not trying to appeal to reason. To the contrary, he consciously rejects "bloodless reality" and reason. The problem as Dwinger sees
it is in fact precisely that at the time of the Weimar Republic in Germany
cool reason prevailed. And reason means technology, civilization, and destruction of the soul of the people. That is precisely what the volunteer
corpsman Reimers wants to escape, first in the youth movement around
1900, as a *Wandervogel,* and now in the volunteer corps. Here in the open
landscape of the Kurland, he believes that he has found what he was seeking,
"fruitful space for the soul" (173). And here he also sees the deeper meaning
of the youth movement:

For the first time it [the Youth Movement] allowed instinct to break free and into the totality of life, for the first time it decided to move beyond reason. It no longer made knowledge its guidepost, but rather the rising up of its youthful feelings! It washed away all the experiences passed on by fathers; it laughed at all the safeguards against the demonic nature of the unconscious! (173–74)

The German state must be reformed by a "revolution from irrational forces . . . not from reason, but from the soul" (174–75). Only Germany is acquainted with such a rejuvenation process instigated by the revolt of youth: "That above all is Germany's most distinctive characteristic." The slag that is civilization is to be thrown away by such a revolution, for "civilization means old" (175). In the process, the end justifies the means, even brutal force:

Thus, let's rejuvenate ourselves — if there is no other way — with a dash of barbarism! And even if some things go down the drain, civilization can always be rebuilt, but crushed youth is forever lost! (175)

Of course all of that is not to happen for the sake of financial dividends, as is the case for other peoples, but for a higher purpose:

Only for us Germans that is different; only we alone want it [power] to make the world better . . . every German feels that with his entire soul; for every German that is the final destination. (417)

The volunteer corps in the Baltic states, which see themselves as the last outposts of the true Germany, are going under, despite such "wild daredevils" as Lieutenant Schlageter, and with them, a world and an ideology. Technology, materialism, and Bolshevism are advancing. However, the book does not end with that, but rather with the admonition to take up the battle against chaos in order to save Germany. Dwinger wants to solve the problem of the masses that will very necessarily follow from "the incorrectly understood over-acceleration of our technology" and "with the approaching end of high capitalism" (430). Russia is seeking to address the problem "in its way"; "we must attempt to do so in ours" (430). In Russia the solution is called Bolshevism; Germany needs another "which we can call German without shame: people, state, work — that must be the religion of our times" (431). The "religion of being a people" stands in contrast to "dehumanization by technical civilization." The volunteer corps see themselves as champions of the former and as the last bastion of the Occident against Bolshevism.

The reprinting of the novel in 1953 at the high point of the Cold War is attributable to the anti-Bolshevik, not anti-Russian, tendencies of the novel. In contrast to the Prussian and the Baltic nobility, the Reds are portrayed as absolute barbarians. They have no culture, they do not know how to conduct themselves, they live like animals in palaces, they amuse themselves with "gun wenches" in nobility's beds, and they torture their prisoners horribly to death. They cannot even fight properly. If the volunteer corps encounter vigorous resistance by the Reds, then they are German worker battalions or German communist sailors. In the Great War even wounded Russian troops were different: they prepared themselves quietly for the hereafter. Now they scream and curse "inhumanly." "For the first time Reimers realized, shuddering deep inside, just what Bolshevism had taken from these simple human beings" (83). The White Russian officer Platoff, who was fighting in the German volunteer corps, sees in Bolshevism "a tremendous eruption of primitive bestiality, which is continually fueled by uncontrolled demagogy!" (177). As a system, Bolshevism is the absolute opposite of the irrational, intuitive elemental force of the people that is touted as the last resort of Germany; Bolshevism is a "system of the ultimate rationality, . . . a force of such rational will to destruction . . ., that it could only be overcome with the dedication of crusaders" (178).

From the perspective of literary aesthetics, the novel hardly rises above the level of ordinary pulp fiction. The figures remain stereotypes, often characterized only by a particular way of speaking, such as Truchs or the cavalryman Christian, who always pronounces the letter "(German) I" as "ü" (Sücher lübt er sü [Sicher liebt er sie — of course he loves her]," 310). Cavalryman Feinhals has a "tuberous potato head"; Walter is a "bourgeois Philistine" and is deprecated with the following description: "His near-sighted eyes blinked behind a pince-nez; a Vandyke decorated his chin, the typical sign of a functionary" (355). The language, too, remains stereotypical: officers have knife-sharp voices, and cannon mouths gape thirstily (315). "Pensive," "delicate," and "dreamy" are the preferred adjectives for pseudo-Romantic passages. The circular structure of the novel underlines the progress-averse ideology of the novel: the story begins at the old positions of the German army of 1917 and returns to them at the end.

In its demand for restoration of the people from the spirit of camaraderie of the front-line soldier's experience and restoration of the natural order for leader and followers, the novel reflects significant characteristics of National Socialism. One of its most terrible aspects, however, has no place in Dwinger's novel: anti-Semitism. Instead, Dwinger's entire hatred is directed as the "sub-humans" of the "Asiatic hordes" of Bolshevism.

Hans Zöberlein's novel *Der Befehl des Gewissens* (1936) also deals with battle. However, it is no longer concerned with the First World War, but with the struggle against the "Red Soviet Republic" in Munich and the struggles from the early phases of Hitler's Party, as the subtitle already indicates: *A Novel about the Turmoil of the Post-War Period and the First Uprising*. According to Günther Hartung, the novel is "one of those novels of development that embody the National Socialist ideology most completely, and of those, it is the one with the most consistency."[21] For Ernst Loewy,

Zöberlein's books are "among the most shameless works of Nazi literature."[22] Especially the all-pervasive anti-Semitism makes reading the approximately one thousand pages an almost unbearable effort. During the Nazi period, however, Zöberlein was a highly praised author whose works were printed and distributed in large numbers. *Der Befehl des Gewissens,* for example, was in its thirteenth printing in 1941, encompassing the 261,000th to 280,000th copies.

The novel *Der Befehl des Gewissens* has markedly autobiographical features; it depicts the path of the shoemaker's son and front-line soldier with the pregnantly symbolic name Hans Krafft to passionate National Socialism in the critical years from 1919 to 1923. The story of the novel is told quickly. Hans Krafft returns from the front, joins a volunteer corps, and fights against the Red Soviet Republic in Munich. After first attending a school for architecture, he becomes an associate in an architectural office, and then an independent architect. After a long search, he believes that he has found the answer for himself and Germany in Hitler's National Socialism. As a result of his declaration of loyalty to the swastika, however, he has professional difficulties to the point where he must give up his position and work as a simple bricklayer. To blame for his misfortune, and that of Germany, are of course in his eyes the Jews. He lives with his wife Berta, nee Schön, and her child in a workers' sector of Munich that he intends to take away from the Reds with his SA comrades in bitter street fights and win over for Hitler. After many setbacks and difficulties, the movement grows, until the fateful Hitler putsch in Munich in November of 1923, at which point the book ends. SA and NSDAP have sixteen dead to mourn and are outlawed. The promise of the dead, however, must be fulfilled, as the motto of the book declares: "The struggle for Germany goes on." The rest of the voluminous book consists of a description of battle scenes and street battles against the Reds, sentimental home and love scenes, Party meetings, and agitation against Jews, Freemasons, and the Weimar Republic.

At home, Hans meets only swindlers, Reds, Jews, Freemasons, moral corruption, drug use, and decadence. The camaraderie of the front among those hardened in barrages of fire is gone; front-line soldiers are ridiculed and discriminated against: no one understands them. Only Hans Krafft sees through everything, for his eyes have a "baffling way of looking at and seeing through all things."[23] He runs around restlessly, waiting for "some miracle, an uprising, a rebellion" (44). In his searching and doubting, Hans Krafft feels related to Faust (252), and he finds his Gretchen in the "noble spirit" Berta Schön. Friedel from Hessen, who is affable and thoroughly honest, and who chatters on in dialect, asks Hans to go with him to the Baltic states in the volunteer corps in order to fight against the Bolsheviks, for against them "only one thing works, the most brutal raw force, because they are devils, worse than devils" (47). Hans, however, wants to finish his architectural studies first. In Munich he sees with disgust the affected behavior of the Reds because of the "so-called political murder of the Jew Eisner" (68). Now, "as one of the vilest of Jews, who had betrayed his people and country, was carried to his grave" (69–70), more people are crying than at the Crucifixion of Christ. The book often deteriorates, as here, into primitive tirades of hatred; Zöberlein usually does not even take the trouble to have such uncontrolled outbreaks issue from the mouth of one of his characters and thus be integrated into the structure of the book.

In his representation of the Reds, too, Zöberlein works with the tawdriest of clichés. The Red Commissars stand for placing the hard-working and the lazy, honest people and cheats, the smart and the stupid all on equal footing; they plunder, murder, violate, and practice free love, which gives them venereal diseases (116). At the same time, they are cowardly and decadent, and lurk around in swindler hangouts with women of dubious character. Their leaders are of course Jews who betray their colleagues whenever it is to their own advantage. They pretend to everyone, however, that they are acting in the interest of the people; some loyal, trusting front-line soldiers even join them — such as Krafft's comrades Max and Fritz. The voice of the people, however, demands the iron fist to put an end to the "Soviet pig pen." That is then taken care of by the volunteer corps, in which "true democracy" prevails. Old ranks and branches of service no longer apply within the corps; there is only "the most tremendous democracy, which here has taken on a warlike aspect" (140). The farmers who fight on the side of the volunteer corps are "clear, open, and upright" and not "shady, untruthful, and sullen" like the Reds (214). The "Red rabble" must be "destroyed like plague rats — even if my own brother were among them!" (185). The volunteer corps were fighting not for the "political cabbage heads" of the Weimar Republic, but for "a very — very grand and lofty goal! Germany in honor and freedom!" (186). The goal of the Reds, on the other hand, is "the destruction of everything that is beautiful, good, and noble" (220). Today the German people are divided into employers and employees, according to Zöberlein. The spirit of camaraderie must overcome this split. However, the way of achieving that will not be easy: The best did not return from the war and "much, much blood must still flow before these separate people have become one again" (229). The situation is serious but not hopeless. The "good healthy blood" is still circulating in the old war comrades, who with their wives can produce the new German: "A new German could, through us soldiers, grow out of our wives. In one generation the German people could become more beautiful, bigger, and more magnificent than before" (247). The new time that Zöberlein sees is not based on reason but grows out of the irrational, "out of the depths of souls," out of the blood: "Not what is in the brain, but what is at work in the blood is the building material for a new era" (263). But according to Zöberlein, this "building material" is threatened by the Jews. With the Jewish question, the core of the novel, and its absolute low point is reached. Worse anti-Semitism cannot be imagined. It runs through the entire book, but is concentrated especially in the chapters "The Jewish Question" and "Mirjam."

In the chapter "The Jewish Question," Berta is looked at lustfully by "dirty Jews." Full of loathing, she turns to Hans: "These Jewish swine will be the death of us; they are mucking up our blood completely" (298). Hans replies: "And blood is the best and only thing we still have" (298). Then Berta asks the crucial question of National Socialism: "Hans, what do you think about the Jewish question?" (298). Berta is convinced "that this is the most burning question for us. The touchstone on which everything genuine and not genuine in the German must be separated" (298). Berta waits intently for Hans's answer, "as if she expects from him a decision about life and death" (298). However, she had nothing to fear; her Hans is of the same mind. He has never liked Jews: "That is in our blood. The Jews are, for our way of feeling, dirty, obscene, and dishonorable — in short, the exact opposite of us" (299). With "us," Hans means all true Germans, not only Berta and himself. For Berta, Hans, and Zöberlein, the Jews are "vermin," which can only thrive on the manure of the Weimar Republic (299). After this experience in the swimming pool, the two row out into the lake in order to throw themselves naked into the water in view of their beautiful homeland and to wash off the "Jewish filth" (300).

In the chapter "Mirjam," which is almost at the midpoint of the novel, Zöberlein succeeds in intensifying his racial hatred to the mythical.[24] At a party, Hans meets the beautiful daughter, Mirjam, of the General Director Kupfer, a Jew; she immediately attempts to ensnare him. However, an apothecary friend warns Hans of this "gliding cat," for she is infected with the "Jewish pestilence, . . . syphilis" (495). In his subsequent conversation with the unfortunate Mirjam, "an icy whiff of decay" wafts to Krafft, "as from a deep, ancient dungeon under the earth" (509). "Shuddering," Hans recognizes therein "the curse of eternity" that weighs on the Jews — according to Zöberlein. After Hans has escaped from the claws of Mirjam, with great effort and with trust in his German Berta, the apothecary explains to him why Mirjam, as a Jewess, had to act that way: for her race to survive, Jews need fresh blood to regenerate their sick blood. Otherwise the Jews would die of their inbreeding. "A new branch is quickly grafted on from other blood, and the thing proliferates further. . . . The Jews no longer live only from our work but from our blood as well. That is the principle behind their immortality up to now; with that principle, they deceive nature. They call it breeding, but it is fornication, for is not a process of refinement but rather a process of degeneration" (512). Zöberlein offers a solution for this problem: "The tree that bears poisonous fruit must be chopped down and thrown into the fire. Here there must be no mercy. Mercy is a weakness here" (515). Zöberlein compares the healthy German blood to the "parasitic" and "degenerate" blood: "Our gods look different. The earth trembles when they set foot on it once again" (515). *One* source for the views of the apothecary is his reading of Paracelsus. Another is Adolf Hitler; in Hitler, he sees the doctor for the sick body of the people. Hitler has, in his opinion, the ability to divine the fateful, prefigured laws of nature that lend him invincible powers (517). Inspired by Hitler, Berta also writes to Hans from Munich. "This Hitler is the prototype of the upright German. This man is the spokesman and the accuser in the name of all good front-line soldiers" (441). She even compares him to Luther:

> His plan . . ., [and] the guidelines of the National Socialist German Workers Party, are as tremendous . . . as the nailing up of Luther's theses on the church in Wittenberg must have been back then, even greater, farther seeing, more tremendous. . . . (448)

When Hans then hears Hitler, the latter affects him like a divine force of nature:

> He is like light, air, and dew that awakens in us amazement at the new budding and blossoming which we cannot do alone, any more than a seed could do it alone on its own without soil, sun, and rain. He is more than a speaker; he is a person who radiates power and awakens life, a creative spirit. (545–46)

Hitler will clear out the "messy heap of parties" and the Republic. The parties and the government are, according to Zöberlein, only auxiliary troops of the French; instead of acting, they only wave the "black, red, and mustard flag" (572) as he derisively calls the Republican colors black, red, and gold. The crucial scoundrels are again the Jews, above all Rathenau — who was then, logically, murdered by right-wing terrorists. Hans Krafft found what he was searching for in Hitler's National Socialists, for they wanted "men, not a mob of voters" (660). The solution for Germany's problem according to Zöberlein lies not in democracy but in dictatorship: "The shortest way goes through dictatorship of a strong man" (660). Hans Krafft joins the Hitler Party. He talks and suffers for his leader until Hitler's putsch in November of 1923 puts a temporary end to his activity. Yet the dream of the Reich remains: "Adolf Hitler will lead you there" (990). The book ends with this vision; it is the vision of the "poet" Dietrich Eckart, who died because of "so much betrayal": "A passionate German heart is broken" (989). Dietrich Eckart was greatly admired by Zöberlein as "a powerful master poet in the new spirit of the times" (783) who wrote the "splendid" new storm song of the SA:

> Sturm! Sturm! Sturm!
> Läutet die Glocken von Turm zu Turm! (784)

[Storm! Storm! Storm!
The bells ring from tower to tower!]

How different this "noble poetry" is from the "Jewish asphalt literature that corrupts the morals" (633). Zöberlein's book illustrates vividly what the nature of the new spirit is and what literary accomplishment it brings forth. The new spirit, however, is not so new; Zöberlein does not in any point go beyond Artur Dinter's "novel" *Die Sünde wider das Blut* (The Sin against Blood) from the year 1917, which already attempted to portray "the defilement of German Aryan blood" by "Jewish blood" in a thinly veiled plot about the sufferings of the German *völkisch* hero Hermann Kämpfer. This is expanded on further in chapter 2, The Ideological Context.

More than 244,000 copies of Karl Aloys Schenzinger's novel *Hitlerjunge Quex* (Hitler Youth Quex), published in 1932, had already been distributed by 1940, serving as the basis for one of the most popular films of the National Socialist era. This topic is also discussed in the chapter on film. *Hitlerjunge Quex,* written "from May to September of 1932" is a martyr novel from the "time of the struggle" shortly before the seizure of power by the Nazis. It is directed primarily at young readers for whom the history and development of the fifteen-year-old main character Heini Völker are intended to serve as a model for imitation.

Heini Völker lives with his caring mother and his unemployed father in the Berlin worker's sector of Moabit, which is controlled by communist organizations to which Heini and his father also belong. However, Heini is only reluctantly involved; the disorderliness, lack of discipline, and crudeness of his comrades disturb him. He longs for order and discipline, as he sees demonstrated by the policeman on the corner or the Reich army: "He liked the municipal police. They looked so orderly, clean, and austere; the leather things shone. They brought to mind order, breeding, and discipline, as could still be read about in old stories. He liked the Reich army even better, when the guard changed or presented the honor company at the *Reichstag*."[25] Brightly polished policemen reminded Heini of a group of youths who had recently passed by him, spic-and-span, lively and fresh, a flag at their front (8). As Heini becomes disgusted with the wild antics of his communist youth group, he sneaks away and meets a group of young people who are very different:

> Directly in front of him, ordered in rows, stood young men like him. Every one of them held next to him a pennant on a long pole, vertical toward heaven, black pennants and bright red ones with zigzag symbols on the ground of the cloth. Each one looked like the other, short pants, bare knees, a brown shirt, a bandana wrapped around each neck.

He heard words like "movement" and "leader," and the German anthem ("Deutschland, Deutschland über alles") ran "like a hot wave over him" (44).

Now, for the first time, he becomes aware of his Germanness, here in the middle of the German forest: "This was German soil, German forest, these were German youths, and he saw that he stood to the side, alone, without help, not knowing what to do with these sudden intense feelings" (44–45). He would like to belong to these youths, and he cannot get the word "order" out of his head (45). He succeeds in making contact with the Hitler youths. In the process, he learns that they do not want a society with classes either, but instead, in contrast to communist internationalism of all the proletariat united in the class struggle against exploiters, they seek a natural and national community of all German people that is based on racial purity, discipline, and order. One of the of the Hitler youths explains to him:

> I want to train myself, outside and inside, so that the courage within is matter-of-fact. I want to feel my blood and that of the others who have the same as I do. We must become a natural community again. We only have bastards left. The word "people" has become laughable. (60)

However, there are difficulties and dangers. Heini learns about the fate of the Hitler youth Norkus who was beaten to death by communists while distributing flyers and thus became the heroic shining example of the movement. Heini's father is a communist and naturally does not want to see his son in a brown shirt. The communist leader Stoppel does everything possible to prevent Heini from changing over. But it is already too late; Heini has reached his decision. The final break with his old comrades comes when he betrays the planned attack on his new brown friends to those friends. Heini's mother can no longer stand the strain; she turns on the gas valve and commits suicide. Heini only narrowly escapes death by gas and lives after that under the protection of his brown comrades, whose uniform he wears with pride. The community of Hitler Youth becomes a replacement for his family.[26] The unit leader makes clear to him what the uniform means: "It is the clothing of the community, the idea, the integration. . . . It makes everyone equal; it gives everyone the same thing and expects the same thing of everyone. Anyone who wears such a uniform has to give up his own will; he has to obey" (164). Heini, however, is ready: "He wanted orders, he wanted to obey" (176); for he believes now in the people and the leader. He carries out all orders of the central office conscientiously and quickly, which earns him the name "Quicksilver" or "Quex."

His former Red mentor tries once again to get Heini back, but in vain: Heini believes in the leader and the flag. In retrospect, the mentor's answer to that is the only one possible: "You're crazy! Completely" (199). Heini stays with the swastika flag and even rises to leader of his group of comrades. However, his former colleagues have not forgotten his betrayal: after a flyer operation he is killed on the dark way home and becomes a martyr of the movement.

The background of this novel is the street battles between the communists and the Nazis in the final stage of the Weimar Republic and the violent acts on both sides. Heini's development and decision in favor of the Nazis, the supposed bringers of salvation and order, are intended primarily to inspire worker youth to follow the same path — and many of them did. Certainly the film and the book of Hitler Youth Quex had a part in that development. The book does not have any literary value, but as an exciting propaganda work it did not miss its mark.

Schenzinger's book on Hitler Youth Quex is illustrative of an entire series of works in which a hero ends tragically in battle for the good cause. As in these works the basic schema of the war novel is transferred to the area of internal politics. Ketelsen also speaks of "civil war novels."[27]

Hanns Heinz Ewers's *Horst Wessel: Ein deutsches Schicksal* (Horst Wessel: A German Fate, 1933) also takes place toward the end of the twenties, during the period of struggle between the Nazis and the Communists for dominance in Berlin. Ewers concentrates on the last two years in the life of the SA man Hans Wessel, honored by the Nazis as a martyr and author of the Nazi hymn *Die Fahne hoch* (Raise the Flag). As Ewers intimates in the epilogue, the inspiration for this novel came from the *Führer* himself: "It was he, who a year ago in the Brown House gave me the inspiration, who designated me to portray the 'battle for the streets.'"[28] Although Ewers, according to his own statement, relies on diaries, letters, archival documents, and personal interviews, his book is a pure propaganda work and not a historical novel. The author indulges in subjectively painting things black or white: The SA men are uniformly represented as regular German guys and the Reds either as Germans who have gone astray or as swindlers, Jews, and pimps. In 1934, over 200,000 copies of the book had been printed.[29] Ewers's *Horst Wessel* served as the basis for a film and a radio play, both in 1933.

The novel begins in October of 1928. Horst Wessel — "his face was tanned, the sharply bent nose was noble. His forehead was high; his eyes shone brightly" (11) — has given up his fraternity Normannia and his law studies in order to dedicate himself completely to the National Socialist struggle for Germany. His motto is the line of the National Socialist bard Dietrich Eckart: "Germany awake!" (10–11). He is determined to stand at the side of Goebbels in his battle as the leader of the Fifth Storm Trooper (SA) Unit and to take control of Berlin away from the Reds. His missionary zeal comes from his father, the Lutheran minister Dr. Ludwig Wessel, from whose sermons he has drawn many a consoling word when his brown frenzy to convert threatens to flag. For him there was never any doubt about what side he was on in the battle for a new Germany:

> He came to the Nazis in complete awareness; it was entirely clear to him that the future belonged only to them or to the communists. The

two had in common their revolutionary and unbourgeois character, and the courage to fight for a great idea: in the one case for world dominance of the one proletarian class; [and] in the other for a free Germany to include all classes and professions. (33)

Wessel thoroughly agrees with some of the socialist goals of Marxism: secure work, high wages, short working hours, games, sports, and pleasure in leisure time. However, all of that remains one-sided, bloodless, and cerebral in the case of the Reds; it does not depend on a mysterious, mystical, ultimate cause in heart and soul (39).

A shining example to all of the SA-men in Berlin is the Rhinelander Dr. Joseph Goebbels whom Hitler personally sent to Berlin:

> They loved *their doctor,* Joseph Goebbels; felt one with him and part of him. And Goebbels, he was the stand-in for the *Führer,* was part of Hitler. Such was the belief of this youth: Germany, the true, the genuine Germany, the Germany with the splendid past and, despite all disgrace, with a great future — that was called Adolf Hitler and Goebbels and all the others around him — and the SA as well! They were one, one body and one spirit, one hope and one dream, solidly forged and not to be rent. (38)

Horst Wessel, the writer of the texts of numerous Nazi songs, feels a particular affinity to Hitler and Goebbels in the "artistic realm," as one of his SA comrades puts it:

> It is actually remarkable, . . . that all of our leaders have something to do with art. I don't understand much about it, but I do feel it. Hitler is certainly an artist; otherwise he never could have thought up the flag and never could have put the SA on its feet. Our doctor — he likes nothing better than when he does not need to give speeches in the small SA group but instead recites some kind of poetry to us instead. And you, Horst, the devil take it, it's the same with you. (40)

Art here takes on the functions of mystification and clairvoyance that lend the Nazi leaders greater insight than the simple SA man. For long stretches, Ewers's book provides heroic descriptions of SA marches through the streets of Berlin and street battles against communists and the police, which are not worth relating in any detail. Horst Wessel intermittently seeks power and strength from his understanding mother, to whom he feels especially close, or from his Erna, one of the prostitutes rescued by him from the morass, with whom he lives and who spies on the Reds for him. This act of saving a good girl from the underworld controlled by Red pimps exemplifies the salvation of the German people by the SA, the initials of which could also mean "Salvation Army" (97). For his "noble" deed, the Reds denounce Horst Wessel, and even his own SA people keep their distance from Erna.

Horst Wessel, however, remains true to her. Ewers tries to make clear repeatedly that the Reds are not to be believed. According to him, their reports of Nazi misdeeds and Jewish pogroms that appear in the Communist paper *"Rote Fahne"* (Red Flag) are entirely invented — to provide evidence to that effect, Ewers has a socialist eyewitness take the stage.

In order to get to know the proletarian milieu better, the minister's son Horst Wessel takes jobs as a taxi driver and as a shoveler. With real calluses on his hands he hopes to have greater appeal to workers — with some success; according to Ewers, the battle of the Reds becomes noticeably focused on Horst Wessel, who is recruiting more and more people from them. The death of his brother Werner, who wanted to save a comrade during a snow storm in the Riesengebirge, a mountainous region between Germany and Czechoslovakia, foreshadows Horst Wessel's own end and gives Ewers the opportunity to conjure up the mysticism of a National Socialist death. Goebbels and the SA leader speak at the grave:

> "You understood that the German student must stand next to the German worker, when the battle is about freedom and an honorable and true socialism." And the drums, the drums roll dully. Glowing red, the torches light up the graveyard. (196)

Betrayed, Horst Wessel is finally brought down by the Reds: "The string-pullers in the Karl Liebknecht House played their little game and played it well" (227). Else Cohn, "an anti-fascist girl, a small, ugly person" (214), insists on directly carrying out the order of Kronstein, the leader of the Reds in Warsaw, that Horst Wessel be eliminated immediately. Without Ewers needing to say so expressly, it should be clear to the reader that the Nazi hero fell victim to a Jewish, international, Marxist conspiracy. The executioners were Red pimps and criminals who murdered Wessel from behind in his room. The Red press then spread the rumor, according to Ewers, that the pimp Wessel died in a fight with a colleague.

In the hospital Wessel struggles with death for several weeks more, has the Kaiser's son Prince August Wilhelm taken into the SA, and dies in the arms of his mother. Countless teeth-gnashing SA men with "grim" faces take leave of Horst Wessel, who is laid out in a brown room, encircled by candles, Nazi banners, and fraternity flags. At the grave, Hermann Göring and Joseph Goebbels, among others, speak: "And when the SA stands assembled at the great roll call, when the name of every individual is called, the leader will then call your name, Horst Wessel! And everyone, all the SA men will answer, as in one voice: 'Here!' — For the SA — it is Horst Wessel." The novel does not close there, however, but with an apotheosis-like transfiguration of the hero that stands alone in its trashy sentimentality:

The mother dreamed again. Erected high above, a giant cross, on the cross beam, entwined with a swastika. Horst stood below in his brown storm trooper uniform; he held his cap in both hands, and looked up earnestly. And she knew: when the misery of the people demands a sacrifice — it is always the bravest, it is always the noblest and the best who are chosen. And always, always, this is the end: *down below, before the cross, stands a mother.* (288–89)

In the epilogue, Ewers draws a parallel to the national freedom fighter of the wars against Napoleon, Theodor Körner, seeking in this manner to give historical dignity and legitimacy to his Horst Wessel.

Despite the theme, the large number of orders, and the large printings, Ewers's book was not very popular with the Nazis; in the end it was even banned and Ewers was dismissed as an "opportunistic belletrist."[30] This was not because of the bad style of the novel, but because of the disreputable professional past of the author. To the "clean" Nazis, a writer of dubious repute such as Ewers really did appear unsuitable to be the biographer of their national hero. In a review of the book that appeared in 1933 in *Die neue Literatur* (*The New Literature*), Ewers's writer colleague, the Nazi poet Will Vesper, wrote, among other things:

> On the basis of information from the family of Horst Wessel, Hanns Heinz Ewers made a novel in the form of newspaper accounts on the life of the youthful martyr, the Theodor Körner of the National Socialist movement; and he made it skillfully, to the extent that the powers of the clever writer of light fiction allow. The fact that Hanns Heinz Ewers, of all people, could write such a novel cannot be considered without painful feelings.

Vesper accuses Ewers of only having acknowledged his Germanness a short time before and then having trumpeted it publicly in order to make good business deals. Vesper continues:

> Indeed, we would have wished for the passionate fighter Horst Wessel, who courageously sacrificed his life for all of Germany, that he had been spared being grasped by fingers that still all to clearly smelled of "morphine," "mandrake," "vampires," "dead eyes," and similar things.[31]

As to be expected, criticism also came from the left. No less a figure than Bertolt Brecht wrote an extensive description of Ewers's novel in 1935 titled "Die Horst-Wessel-Legende" (The Horst Wessel Legend). In his essay, Brecht takes up the pimp theme, illuminates it from the economic perspective, and views the pimp and exploiter milieu as symptomatic for the entire Nazi movement, which is fittingly illustrated by Horst Wessel and the appropriate author:

To produce a final description of the life of the young hero, Joseph Goebbels sought an expert and turned to a successful pornographer. This expert, a man by the name of Hans Heinz Ewers, had among other things written a book in which a corpse is dug up and raped. He seemed extraordinarily qualified to write the history of the dead Wessel's life. There were not two people with so much imagination in Germany.[32]

With biting mockery, Brecht ponders the proletarian twists of the pimp Wessel living in the workers' sector; he wanted to pull the people and the prostitute Erna up to his level. However, Wessel is in Brecht's eyes not just an ordinary pimp but also a political one and therefore is typical for the entire Nazi movement.

Just as the ordinary pimp inserts himself between the working prostitutes and their renters, supervises the business deal, and brings order to the business, so, too, does the political pimp insert himself between the workers and their buyers, supervise the act of selling the ware, an employee, and bring order to the business. Indeed, there is scarcely any better school for National Socialism than pandering. National Socialism is political pandering.[33]

With Horst Wessel, the National Socialists thus erected a monument to themselves, of course, but not at all in the way they imagined:

The National Socialists have really gotten hold of something with Horst Wessel. In him the ruling triumvirate, consisting of a lackadaisical student, a discharged officer, and a Reich army informant, has found the symbol of their movement, the young hero of whom it can be said: thinking of him, one immediately thinks of the movement, and thinking of the movement, one immediately thinks of him.[34]

The Historical Novel

Historical novels played an important role in the Third Reich because they provided the regime with some sense of legitimacy on the basis of examples from history. At the same time, no serious consideration was given to history as the Other; history is only viewed as the history of salvation as it relates to the present.[35] To this class belong novels like *König Geiserich* (King Geiserich, 1936) by Hans Friedrich Blunck, the *Paracelsus-Trilogie* (Paracelsus Trilogy, 1917–1925) by Erwin Guido Kolbenheyer, *Tristan und Isolde* (Tristan and Isolda, 1911), and *Parzival* (Percival, 1911) by Will Vesper, *Bismarck gründet das Reich* (Bismarck Founds the Reich, 1932), *Mont Royal: Ein Buch vom himmlischen und vom irdischen Reich* (Mount Royal: A Book of the Heavenly Kingdom and Earthly Empire, 1936), *Kaiser und Herzog: Kampf zweier Geschlechter um Deutschland* (Emperor and Duke: The Battle of Two Families for Germany, 1936), *Reich und Rom: Aus dem Zeitalter der Reformation* (Reich and Rome. From the Age of the Reformation, 1937), and *Der König und die Kaiserin: Friedrich der Große und Maria Theresia* (The King and the Empress: Frederick the Great and Maria Theresa, 1937) by Werner Beumelburg. There were also historical biographical novels about great leader figures such as Caesar, Cromwell, Hannibal, Henry the Lion, Franz von Sickingen, Scharnhorst, and Prince Eugene by the Austrian bestseller author Mirko Jelusich (1886–1969), the "'house and court poet' of the Austrian NSDAP."[36] In the following pages the two novels *Mont Royal* and *Reich und Rom* by Beumelburg are treated in some detail.

Werner Beumelburg was among the most popular authors of the Third Reich. In 1939 his books had already gone beyond the million mark;[37] 328,000 copies of his novel *Sperrfeuer um Rom* (Barrages Around Rome, 1929) alone had already been printed by 1940.[38] With his historical novels, Beumelburg wanted "to awaken . . . consciousness of the meaning of German destiny and to lead . . . the people to the sources of its historical origins," a mission that he had also set for himself as editor of the *Schriften an die Nation* (Writings to the Nation).[39]

In *Mont Royal,* Beumelburg takes the reader back to "the time of the greatest humiliation" (6). The novel takes place in the years between 1680 and 1700, as great disunity prevailed in the Empire, the German Emperor turned back the Turks before Vienna, and "his Most Christian Majesty" Louis XIV cleverly used the unrest to tear off large parts of the Empire. To consolidate French power, the architect Vauban built a mighty fortress at Trarbach on the Mosel River: Mount Royal. From here, the French controlled and suppressed — according to Beumelburg — the German population and attempted to expand France to the Rhine and beyond; even Brandenburg, which was on the rise under the Great Electors and Frederick III, could do little in opposition. The story of Jörg and his brother Martin from Trarbach on the Mosel River is placed in this historical framework. At the beginning of the novel, Jörg joins the Dutch troops under the Huguenot Messr. de Sierge at Boppard on the Rhine to advance with them against the Turks before Vienna. Jörg distinguishes himself in battle against the Turks and receives an ivory neck chain from the dying de Sierge to remember him by; later he passes the neck chain on to Gaston de Sierge, the son of the honored leader. Gaston is a French officer and later becomes Jörg's most dangerous and bravest opponent. After his return from Vienna, Jörg himself becomes a French soldier for a short time, but deserts to the Brandenburgs whom he hopes will liberate his country. When that does not happen, he returns unnoticed to his home on the Mosel to fight as a saboteur, guerilla, and partisan against the French and for a German Reich, not least of all against his brother Martin, who as a Benedictine monk is only interested in a heavenly kingdom. Jörg is seized by the French and tortured, but escapes and dies as a visionary and champion of the German Reich in the vicinity of Boppard, from where he started. In a time of conflicting interests, Jörg wants to stir up longing for the eternal and united German Reich:

> People must be made ready to strive for the eternal rather than for the present. A call must be made to them; someone must come who leads them and opens their eyes . . .; they should learn that there is an earthly empire in which they must prove themselves before the heavenly kingdom is opened to them. But he who pursues the heavenly over the earthly is a traitor to them. . . . Every individual has longing within him, and all these longings must be brought together to form a great will, and it may be that in the process much cruelty and blood will come over the world, but the end will be the great justice that it is about. . . . Every person should love his destiny more than himself and should obey the principle that drives him. . . . But the justice that we seek is the Reich. Let our Reich come, yes, let it come! (72–73)

On a moonlit night in his dreams, Jörg sees the transformation of the fortress Mount Royal into a mythical picture of nature: "The mountain had fallen silent again and had returned home to its thousand-year rest, and on its top stood the dark fir trees like a lake of unfathomable depth" (178). To create the Reich, faith is necessary above all else: "One must die for the Reich and for belief in the Reich. But this belief must be so strong that it cannot be shaken by anything, for the Reich can only grow out of such belief" (104). The idea of the Reich of eternal Germany will become the new religion. Other Nazi authors make that clear already in the titles of their works, such as Zöberlein in his novel *Der Glaube an Deutschland* (Belief in Germany, 1931). All confessions of faith can be reduced to the common denominator Adolf Hitler, who already in 1923 in *Mein Kampf* (My Struggle) wrote of the necessity of belief as "the vast majority consists neither of philosophers nor of saints."[40] Of course, Hitler demands that this belief must be fixed to a particular political program: "A political program must be formed from general ideas, and a particular political belief from a general ideology."[41]

As university professor Dr. Karl Plenzat announces to his readers in his introduction to Beumelburg's *Geschichten vom Reich* (Stories from the Reich), Jörg's longing for the Reich was fulfilled under Hitler: "This Reich, which has finally come into being today, which is still struggling and yet at the same time already taking form, is the Reich that has lived in the longing of men aware of their Germanness in all times." According to Plenzat, it "grew out of the struggle against the universalist Reich idea that was turned in another direction by the power of foreign races . . ., and determined by Roman ecclesiasticism or Jewish capitalism, proceeded from the Roman Empire and not from the world of the people, with its own characteristic nature."[42] The anti-Roman tendency and the *völkisch* idea as embodied in the healthy German peasant lad Jörg are clearly evident in Beumelburg's novel, which is, however, free of any anti-Semitic polemics. Beumelburg's novel *Mont Royal* was apparently quite popular; it was even published especially for the army by the high command of the army. Excerpts from the novel appeared separately, for example, as the story "Unser Reich komme" (Let Our Reich Come) in Beumelburg's *Geschichten vom Reich* and as a specially printed story with the title *Jörg*.[43] In his introduction Kurt Kölsch even stylizes Jörg upwards to one "of the few unforgettable figures of literature, such as Grimmelshausen's Simplizissimus or Charles de Coster's Til Ulenspiegel."[44]

Beumelburg's novel *Mont Royal* contains clear allusions to the reformer Martin Luther, whom the Elector Frederick the Wise had brought as Squire Jörg to the Wartburg to protect him from his enemies. The fraternal feud between Jörg and Martin mirrors the struggle between an earthly empire and a heavenly kingdom. The parallels between Luther and Brother Martin become very clear at the point in the novel at which Beumelburg has Brother Martin struggle in his monk's cell with his God: "He struck and tortured himself in his cell, such that his moans could be heard in the middle of the night. He struggled with God that He might grant him the grace of conviction and knowledge so that he would raise the cross again and drive Satan back into his caves" (215). It is therefore not surprising that Beumelburg wrote a Luther novel with the title *Reich und Rom* (1937) of which 35,000 copies had been printed by 1940.[45]

The novel begins with the German *Reichstag* in Lindau in 1496 and ends with the *Reichstag* in Speyer in 1526. Those were the years of unrest and change that, set in motion primarily by Luther's sermons and writings, held great possibilities for the German Reich, possibilities that were squandered by the Luther's vacillating position, the capitalistic machinations of the Fuggers, the Papists, the intrigues of the French King Francis I and the disunity of the princes, the fragmentation of the peasantry, and the weakness of the Empire — at least as Beumelburg sees it.

In the conflict among the selfish interests of the various parties as well as in the opposition between the earthly empire and the heavenly kingdom, the longing for a German Reich of one's own and a German church of one's own lost out. Missing above all was an extraordinary leader who would have been in a position to cut the Gordian knot of selfish interests:

> Throwing the torch of a heretical religion into this fermenting mass, into this vat, filled to the top with incendiary ideas, with dissatisfaction, and with the demand for independent power of its own meant starting a revolution which would end in chaos unless there were men, or one man, who could take control of it and force it into some form.[46]

Kaiser Maximilian was too old to recognize that he could have used Luther's "Heresy" against the Pope to strengthen the Empire. In not understanding that, he missed "the great and irretrievable hour in which a distinctly German empire and German faith could have been born" (90). After Maximilian's death in 1519, the Germans transferred their hopes and longings for a German empire to Emperor Charles V, Maximilian's successor. However,

> he did not know a great deal about Germany . . . (156). No one had ever told this young man a word about the fact that the Germans expected him to be their savior, their liberator. . . . Not a single word had gotten to him about the great longing, that is to say, passion, with which the Germans in their need clung to him, of whom it was said that he came with the irrepressible will to place the German Empire at the top of the Occident and to free it from the claws of his enemies internally and externally. Not a line ever got to him from the hundred documents and drafts about how to reform this Empire from top to bottom, [or] that the power of the devil had to be broken, the selfishness of the princes, the greed of the banks, the corvée debts of the Church, and the miserable disintegration a thousand times over in all areas. (158)

Martin Luther was not the man, either, who could, with a strong hand, help the idea of the Empire break through in these chaotic times. This "inconspicuous little Monk from Wittenberg," to whom the people, in its "craving for truth," ran in droves, "was slender, pale, unsettled, and unsure of himself" and had "certainly never thought a great deal" about the meaning of his heresy (96). He was in conflict with himself and did not think of himself being called to be the champion of a secular empire: "How, he thought, should the pure word and the true doctrine be mixed with worldly things?" (104). The Empire echoed with the cry: "Down with Rome! The Empire to the Germans! A German Emperor! A German church! Freedom of conscience and freedom in faith!" (140). But as Beumelburg had Luther's adversary Eck recognize, Luther was not the man "who posed great danger" (139–40). And yet Luther was finally forced to enter the conflict between "reformation and revolution, a secular empire and an ecclesiastical empire, and to demand secular reforms in addition to ecclesiastical reforms, as in particular in his pamphlet 'To the Christian Nobility of the German Nation.'" For Beumelburg, this pamphlet represents "a tremendous reform program for internal recreation of the Empire,"

> for the renewal of morals, [for] the limitation of property ownership, for the destruction of the rule of capital, for a return to the simple and *volkstümlich*, for the revitalization of national feeling and the ruthless destruction of any foreign rule in the areas of religion and finance. (167)

The same Luther, however, the author of the revolutionary pamphlet and staunch opponent of the powerful Emperor Charles V in Worms (for whom "those Germans" were "so inscrutable, so dangerous, so uncomfortable," 242), is again plagued by doubts when he sees how the new faith is becoming a "game ball for political forces" (354). He calls in beseeching words for balance: "It was a justification for his own benefit" (356). The development of his reformation, which he did not foresee and did not want, slipped from his hands. In his rage he finally let himself be carried away and wrote the dubious manifesto "Against the Murderous and Thieving Hordes of Peasants," which later left his conscience no more rest, and which caused irreparable damage to his work (393). For Beumelburg, the vacillating Luther was also not the man who could gain control "over all of the forces struggling with one another" and help the idea of the Empire to victory — despite his contributions. He provided great impetus and was a pioneer, but he failed.

One of those who took up Luther's cry and despite many weaknesses became a fiery champion of the secular Empire was, in Beumelburg's view, Ulrich von Hutten. This von Hutten, "a representative of the young Germany," regretted that German youth, which hungered for great deeds, fell without leaders into listlessness (107). He called the capitalist Fuggers the "courtesans of the princes" and the cardinals "idlers clothed in purple" (150). "He understood something about the people and its sentiments, . . . screamed for arms for this Empire" and for "intellectual renewal . . ., if the fatherland was to be saved" (153). He feared that Luther's reformation and thus the hope for a new Germany would come to nothing and therefore planned to bring Luther, with the help of Franz von Sickingen, to his fortress, the Ebernburg. Allied with Luther, he hoped to call "the German nation to arms" against the "rabble" of princes, clerics, and Romans. In a vision, a national, anti-capitalistic, new German Empire appeared before him, "heralding Church reform in the same breath with reform of the Empire, elimination of monopolies, freeing of the peasants, introduction of duties, uniform coinage, removal of all non-Germans from German offices, and seizure of Church properties" (224). However, Hutten's plans for a German national state and a German national church also failed because of the selfishness of the German princes, not least of all that of his former friend Franz von Sickingen. "In Sickingen's hands, a German revolution became an armed uprising of a disowned knightage against princely territorial power" (285). However, not all hope for a German national revolution had been buried yet:

> The common man now seemed to succeed in what Sickingen did not like and what the people from Wittenberg fearfully avoided. The German revolution against the Church, the rule of princes, the limits of the estates, [and] capitalism, and against Roman law and for a German Empire had arrived, and it appeared that it would be a victorious breakthrough. (372)

That is how Beumelburg sees the Peasants Wars. Their leaders, such as Thomas Münzer, Wendelin Hippler, and George Meltzer are, as men of the people, genuine champions of the idea of the Reich. According to Beumelburg, Thomas Münzer was "the first who preached about the Holy Gospel and the Thousand-Year Reich which is now beginning, and that they all must be brothers and free from tyrants" (331). Beumelburg singles out the fourteen articles of the peasant leaders Wendelin Hippel and Friedrich Weigand from the year 1525 as particularly significant and deals with them extensively:

> At the beginning and the end of their reform they placed the German nation and the German Empire under a German Emperor. They created a plan that we today can only read and be deeply moved, when we think what happened afterward in reality, for centuries long. (326)

However, the peasants also lacked a leader that stood above the others; betrayal and a lack of strict leadership was their undoing. The idea of the nation remained underground for centuries. Everyone — the Emperor, the imperial regiment, Hutten, Sickingen, the estates, the princes, the Wittenberg reformers, and the peasants — had missed their chance: "Each one individually missed his hour, and all together squandered the one great, decisive, irretrievable hour of the German nation" (384). At the *Reichstag* in Speyer in 1526, talk was only of matters relating to faith, no longer of the Empire, and no longer of reforms: "The individuals calling for the Empire all lay in their graves" (435). Instead of appealing for German unity, they decided that "everyone . . . [could] do or not do what he wanted. In complete awareness, they condemned the Empire of the Germans to terrible suffering throughout the centuries, because they did not believe in the Empire" (436). Beumelburg ends his book on that note, implying of course that with the Nazi Reich the end to the suffering and the hour of fulfillment had come, provided that belief in the Reich is firm.

Beumelburg's novel is a mixture of history, fiction, and propaganda in which the individual parts are not always joined seamlessly to each other; that is particularly the case for the quotations inserted from historical documents. Among the strongest parts of the book are the sections on the peasant uprisings in Southern Germany. Here Beumelburg can represent in epic breadth the uprising of the concentrated and uncontrolled force of the people that was sacred to National Socialism — at least in their literature. From this point, a line can be drawn without difficulty to another important genre of the novel that was particularly popular in the Nazi period: the homeland and peasant novel. In the twenties and thirties, the peasant novel became "the most read genre overall."[47] The absolute peak in the production of the peasant novel was reached in the years 1934 to 1938.[48]

The Peasant Novel

The development of the peasant novel from the early nineteenth century to the Third Reich is varied and cannot be described with a single comprehensive label, as Gerhard Schweizer and Peter Zimmermann show. The Nazis also had difficulty aligning the individual works ideologically.[49] One and the same work was often subject to opposite interpretations. Thus, both Adolf Hitler and Lenin considered the novel *Der Büttnerbauer* (The Cooper Peasant, 1895) by Wilhelm von Polenz as one of their favorite books.[50] What the Nazis liked about the peasant novels was the close bonds to the people, the blood and soil themes, flight from the problems of industrial society, and longing for the simple life. According to Alfred Rosenberg, "the idea of a people's honor, which cannot be grasped with the hands," is rooted "in the soil of a nation," "that is, in its living space."[51] His mentor, Adolf Hitler, also viewed the peasant class as the "foundation of the entire nation" and the best "protection against all social ills."[52] As Zimmermann demonstrates, the Nazis needed such works to cover up the contradictions between plan and practice; for, as is well known, the Nazis advocated thoroughly bourgeois, capitalist production methods and industrialization.[53]

From the wealth of materials, the novel *Der Femhof* (The Fehme Farm, 1934)[54] by Josepha Berens-Totenohl will be discussed in more detail in the following pages. By 1940, 160,000 copies of the novel had been printed[55] and it was among the most widely distributed novels in the Third Reich, together with the peasant novels *Der Wehrwolf* (The Werewolf, 1910) by Hermann Löns (over 565,000 copies printed by 1939), *Vom Hofe, welcher unterging* (The Farm that Went Under, 1912) by Hermann Burte (over 140,000 copies printed by 1939), and *Bauernstolz* (Peasant Pride, 1901) by Lulu von Strauss und Torney (over 100,000 copies printed by 1938). Schonauer reports that "a total of almost a half million copies of *Der Femhof* and the novel *Frau Magdalene* (Mrs. Magdalene) by Berens-Totenohl had been printed and sold" by 1942.[56] Both novels were still being republished in 1957 under the title *Die Leute vom Femhof* (The People of the Fehme Farm).[57]

The novel *Der Femhof* is set in the upper Lenne Valley of the Sauerland, a hilly region in the western part of Germany, around the middle of the fourteenth century. The times are full of unrest: the Duke of Mark and Arnsberg and the Archbishop of Cologne are feuding with each other; the roads have been made unsafe by roaming highwaymen and gypsies. "In the high mountains and narrow gorges" of the Sauerland, rumors are circulating about the secret runes and birds. Before this backdrop, the action centers primarily around the free Wulf farm on the Lenne River: "Here resided the clan of the Wulfs, arrogant, free, and self-contained."[58] In their veins roared "strong, bold, wild blood" (14). The Wulfs had increased their numbers, defied all dangers, and kept the farm free. However, the strong clan of the

Wulfs is coming to an end; the Wulf peasant has only one daughter, Magdalene: "But now the strong oak is for the first time not putting out any tips of its own" (18). The question of succession is now becoming of burning importance. The Wulf peasant decides that Magdalene will marry Erik of the Stadeler farm. Magdalene, however, is made of the genuine wood of the Wulf family tree. She resists her father's will and intends to marry Ulrich, who had saved her on a stormy night from the floodwaters of the Lenne and has lived since then on the Wulf farm. Ulrich had owned a farm in Westphalia, but lost it after he killed the impertinent local noble Bruno in self-defense in Brakelerholz on the Weser River. Now the daughter stands up to her father; will is pitted against will. Ulrich is also boiling over; he can no longer stand to be closed up inside the house: "He had to go out into the open; he had to be able to let the fire burning up his life blaze under the heavens!" (135). In the clear starlit night he climbs up through the forest to Owl Rock. There he meets the Wulf peasant, who attacks Ulrich with a dagger, but is defeated. Ulrich leaves the farm, wanders about lost, applies to be a mercenary for the Duke of the Mark, Adolf, deserts into the mountains as he is pursued, and is finally surrendered in absentia to the Fehme under pressure by the Wulf peasant at the Fehmic Court, which meets in the open under a large linden tree and is presided over by Duke Gottfried von Arnsberg. The Wulf peasant tracks Ulrich down in the mountains, kills him in a mad rage, but then succumbs himself in the process. The farm, now called the "Fehme Farm," blossoms under the son of Ulrich and Magdalene.

The person actually pulling the strings is the fat shady trader Tobias, called Robbe. Robbe is not from the region; he has a southern way about him, a tooth gap in a grinning mouth and a narrow, lurking gaze. This shifty groveler ("*robben*" means "creep, grovel") extorts the Wulf peasant at will, as he knows about a youthful transgression of the peasant. The young Wulf had once, for one "white-hot" fall, forgotten his blond, rich, but quiet peasant bride Margarete over a "wild raven-haired gypsy witch" (40). After he had gotten her with child and his lust was satisfied, he came to his senses, left her, and was overcome with "righteous hatred" for her, the fiery-eyed seductress of a free peasant: "The righteous instinct of his peasant's blood raised this terrible sword to avenge the sin against his being" (41). In any case, Berens-Totenohl sees it that way: Not the peasant is guilty but the gypsy woman who dared to contaminate a free German peasant's blood. Now the Wulf peasant pays money for silence through the intermediary Robbe. It never becomes clear whether Robbe is a Jew or a gypsy; the word "Jew" is never mentioned in the novel — in contrast to the unbearable Jew-baiting in Zöberlein's novel that was discussed earlier. The defiant, free, powerful peasants firmly rooted in the soil of the homeland whom Berens-Totenohl praises fit the Nazi ideology; she confronts them with the shifty, groveling, unreliable, roving foreign elements in the figures of the exploitative traders and gypsies: "The peasants of the mountains shake from the raging of the weather, but they only fall if the roots are disintegrating, if there is no more gripping of the soil and there is no more strength for defiance" (43).

The novel takes place for the most part on a rather trivial level, as Schonauer correctly writes: "The peasant myth, the example of Berens-Totenohl shows it clearly, is nothing more than the projection of tawdry and sentimental petit bourgeois notions and wish dreams."[59]

Berens-Totenohl's novel *Der Femhof* is connected primarily by the name of the central figure, Wulf, to Herman Löns's most popular and also considerably better peasant novel *Der Wehrwolf,* which centers around the peasant Harm Wulf. The wolf angel, a rune with a shape similar to a swastika, which serves as the protective house sign of Löns's Wulf peasants, also decorates the Fehme Farm of Berens-Totenohl. Löns also takes the story of his novel from the German past. His werewolves are heath peasants from Ödringen who band together in a protective society against the marauding soldiers of the Thirty Years War (1618–1648): "And now we want to become brothers in need and death, life and property, so that all are for one, and one for all, but all of us [are] for everything that lives around and in the quarry and is of our kind."[60] Their chief is Harm Wolf; their sign is the wolf angel. After they had lost their belongings, property, and families, they saw no other way than to answer force with force. Löns makes clear in his peasant chronicle that they long for peace, that they are tired of killing and do it only in self-defense. Löns's novel takes place in a violent time; the representation of brutality and force, which borders almost on glorification, fits well into views of the ideologues of Social Darwinism when they insist on the law of the fittest — as the Nazis did.[61] It was therefore not difficult for the latter to force Löns's *Wehrwolf* into the ideological straitjacket and to hitch the writer and war volunteer who died in action on September 26, 1914, near Reims before their wagon. Thus, Alfred Rosenberg places the *Wehrwolf* next to Goethe's *Faust:* The "werewolves" act, as Faust does, "according to their innermost emotional and racial will to freedom."[62] As Günter Hartung explains, the *Wehrwolf,* "which Walter Linden rightly called a '*völkisch* basic book,' . . . gave the volunteer corps and Fehme associations models of behavior; the youth movement, a sign (the 'wolf angel'); and finally, the last attempt at resistance to the Allies in 1945 by the Hitler Youth, a name and symbol. The breadth of its effects can scarcely be overestimated."[63] The number of copies of the novel printed had reached more than 565,000 in 1939.[64]

It would be misleading to designate the novel *Volk ohne Raum* (A People Without Space) by Hans Grimm as a purely Nazi novel and to place it next to Zöberlein's shoddy works. And yet it belongs in this chapter, as it fit exactly into Nazi ideology, with its demand for living space for the German people. And after its appearance in 1926, it became one of the most influential books of the Nazi period: by 1942 the total number of copies printed had reached 540,000. In 1956 it was reprinted.[65]

The novel tells the story of the peasants' son Cornelius Friebott, called Nelius, from Jürgenshagen, a village on the Weser, who must emigrate to South Africa because of a shortage of land; he attains respectability and prosperity there, but after the defeat of the First World War returns to a broken Germany and is killed in the middle of his speech about the need for German colonies shortly before November 9, 1923, the day of the Hitler putsch in Munich, by a socialist stone-thrower.[66]

Uwe-K. Ketelsen calls the work, with some justification, a "colonial homeland novel."[67] The novel can also be read as a *völkisch* novel of development and education in which not the individual education of the main character Cornelius Friebott is the central focus, but his education for the *völkisch* collective.[68] Actually the novel crosses over all the individual categories, as it treats most of the themes that were of importance to the Nazi state. As the central theme of the novel relates to blood, soil, and the peasantry, it belongs most prominently in the chapter on the peasant novel, unless it is to be placed in a special category of colonial literature, as Peter Zimmermann does.[69]

Hans Grimm spent five years as a business apprentice in Port Elizabeth, South Africa, and another eight years — until 1910 — as an independent businessman in East London in Cape Land. During this time he collected the experiences necessary for his main work, or as Langenbucher put it in 1937, "the experiences and impressions which were the determining factors for his future poetic task," and which allowed "him to see earlier and clearer than many others the difficulty of the German destiny in the world."[70] "People without space" became one of the best-known slogans of the Third Reich, and Hans Grimm, although he was not a member of the NSDAP, became a kind of "classic national author."[71] Hans Grimm did have his differences with Goebbels, but his ideas were very close to National Socialism. For example, he declared in 1932: "I see in National Socialism, with a few others, the *first,* and until now *the only genuine* democratic movement of the German people."[72] Edgar Kirsch adds in his dissertation *Hans Grimm als Wegbereiter nordischer Gedankenschau* (Hans Grimm as a Champion of the Nordic View of Ideas) from 1937: "In these three basic questions, race, Jewry, and Aryan (Northman), Grimm agrees with the principles of the *Führer* not only in the results, but also in the considerations which must lead to those results."[73]

The question regarding the necessary "living space" for the German people was one of the most significant problems that the Third Reich intended to resolve by availing itself of all means. On that subject we read in Grimm's main work: "The entire German country is small and already overcrowded with shoving people, and bread must be taken where it can be found."[74] Without living space, the German people will become alienated from their own nature as a result of the dependent work for wages and "never again be able to be masters of the fate of their own land and barons of their arms" (19). For Grimm, the answer lay in the re-acquisition of colonies: "Indeed, if only these grandchildren of peasants were British and knew that the broad expanses of Canada, and Australia and New Zealand and South Africa were behind them and [that they] thus had some other choice beside the walk to the factory and the big city!" (19). Without living space, the human being suffers damage to body and soul: "In the crowded and cramped conditions, each creation and each body and each soul becomes ill" (309). Nelius, too, is forced to work for wages. He goes to Bochum in the Ruhr region and becomes a miner. After a mine accident, he accuses the mine management of inhuman behavior because of greed for profits; he is fired, arrested, and thrown in prison.

However, neither the path out of proletarian confinement through class struggle and socialism, as suggested by the socialist Martin Wessel, or the pietism recommended by his master in Bochum are options for Nelius and Grimm. As the homeland no longer has any space to offer him, Nelius immigrates to South Africa. When he gets to South Africa, however, he finds two different societies there, too: the world of the native peasantry, that is, the Boers and the world of the profit-hungry English merchants:

> A widely dispersed bunch of tough, much deceived and therefore distrustful, self-reliant peasants who had become one with their new land in sun and need, and packs of mobile middlemen supported by the foreigners; in opposition to each other are: two languages, two fatherlands, two economic views, even two beliefs in being chosen by God. (189)

According to Grimm, these two empires are destined to collide. Cornelius Friebott fights in the "Boer War" on the side of the Boers, is captured by the English, and loses his wife and child in English "concentration camps." According to Grimm, this war is about the power of the "money bags" who want to shamelessly exploit the mineral resources of the Boer lands. Behind these efforts are "of course" the English and the Jews: "The game was instigated by the English and the Jewish money people" (439). The question is whether the "love of the soil" or the "love of money bags and trade" will become the "fate of the homeland" (440). In the opinion of the "money bags," according to Grimm, the German influence in the Boer lands is becoming too great and must be pushed back (439).

The captured Boers, among them Cornelius Friebott, are taken to the island St. Helena. There they are subtly sounded out by German and Polish Jews who are being used as spies, Jews "who left the Boer republics so that they would not have to perform military service" (501). In the prisoner-of-war camp, Nelius thinks about Germany's fate: "The nobility, local nobility, and army have not grasped the intellectual obligation in this country, . . . what is to become of us without German intellectual leadership? — Isn't it true that German culture can now only be found in newspapers and books?" (508). After his release from prison, Friebott meets an English worker named Kennedy in Johannesburg who wants to see him, and all Germans, removed from the British colonies and advises:

> Are you Germans such weaklings that you have to ride on foreign backs? Your state should get for you what it needs for you; that is my opinion. Were our colonies brought to us or given to us as gifts? But old England was up early and dared and paid with blood, and it was not bothered by scolding. (573–74)

The speech of the Englishman is Grimm's call for the German people to do the same as the English, to use the law of the fittest to gain "living space" and not to care about the opinion of foreign countries. As Friebott makes clear to his earlier friend, the socialist Martin Wessel, who followed him to South Africa, the great flaw in socialism is that the point of departure is class, not the people: "Socialism started with classes rather than with peoples. International social democracy had too little regard for peoples, perhaps because its founder was a Jew" (575). International socialism based on class struggle is thus to be replaced by National Socialism on a *völkisch* basis. If Germans are not to be cheated out of their German nature, Friebott realizes in the course of his national education, they must renew themselves of their own accord: "Kennedy is right, we must stop running to others, we must go to ourselves, we must, we must, we must. Otherwise the renewal energy will be diverted from Germany and sucked off!" (594–95). Still worse, without a renewed Germany — according to Grimm — there is no hope for the world that — also in the view of the National Socialists — is to recover through German nature: "And otherwise, if we stop completely, there will certainly never be any help for the world!" (595).

Friebott decides to leave Cape Land, which is controlled by the English and Jewish "money bags," for German Southeast Africa — today's Namibia. Before his departure, he visits the German merchant Hans Grimm, who hopes to find "a little food for his soul" on his farm near East London, far outside city life and English customs foreign to his nature (632). In a final discussion with Grimm, Friebott summarizes, as follows, the results up to now of his search for a path to his own identity, as well as to national identity: "But as I now weigh everything and repeatedly attempt to understand, there is something that Germany cannot get around: Germany must win over its masses, and that means that Germany must win over its little people" (658). But he also knows that a new leader is necessary for that:

> Ah, if I only knew the way myself: I only know that the German destiny
> is still completely unfinished and young, and that our old leadership
> class forgot the foremost position and the very great majesty of the
> community of the people, because of all the service to the princes, and
> looking up, and hoping for honors. And I know that the people them-
> selves are confused. I am to that point. It is important that we go on
> and find a way. (659)

This, then, is the stage of development Friebott has reached at the end
of the first part, "Heimat und Enge" (Homeland and Close Confinement).

The second part, "Deutscher Raum" (German Space), begins with a
reminiscence of the narrator Grimm, giving the author's perspective on the
beauties of the German colony Southwest Africa: "I see red, yellow, and
green colors under blue heavens: the red of the deep sand and the yellow of
high, hard grass and the green of the various thorny trees" (663). In nostal-
gic retrospect from the last stage of Weimar Germany to imperial Germany,
he complains that the heroic deeds of the officers of the German Empire
such as Friedrich von Erckert and his people struggling for living space in
German Southwest Africa against rebellious Hottentots in 1907 and 1908
have been completely forgotten. Cornelius Friebott had participated in these
battles, and through him Grimm takes the reader back to that time. Naturally it does not occur to Grimm that "the Hottentot" was perhaps only
defending his country against foreign invaders, "because as a human being
he is of less worth than we are" (707). Of course, not only the German
colonists thought that way, but in the context of racist Nazi propaganda,
such statements are of special import, as is Grimm's warning about miscege-
nation. His solution for South Africa is apartheid:

> Anyone who has lived for many years in South Africa in more devel-
> oped circumstances not only knows, but also comes to believe strongly,
> that the whites and the coloreds should not mix if the white race is to
> last in intellectual dominance, with its small but irreplaceable human
> qualities of cheerfulness, objectivity, and mysticism. (714–15)

In German Southwest Africa, Friebott also finds what he missed at
home: a genuine community of the people:

> And here there is only the black, white, and red flag; and here there are
> no parties; . . . and here we are allowed to start again where our old
> German forefathers left off, in the wide-open spaces, and yet to remain
> people of the present. (809)

After years of work in Lüderitzbucht, Friebott has finally saved the
money for his own farm, which he takes over in 1911, at the age of 36. In
his free time he occupies himself with books such a *Die Buddenbrooks* by
Thomas Mann and *Die Erschütterung der Industrieherrschaft und des Indu-*

striesozialismus (The Breakdown of Industrial Dominance and of Industrial Socialism) by Gerhard Hildebrand, books that contribute to his further education. In Hildebrand he sees the affirmation of his theory that industrial work is alienating and only peasant work is liberating (922–23).

In the third part of the novel, "Volk ohne Raum," Friebott visits his old homeland again for the first time in sixteen years. When visiting the Social Democratic Party congress in Chemnitz, he encounters Hildebrand, who at that very moment is standing before the party court because of his favorable attitude toward colonies. Friebott senses "a strange connection" to the man who places living space and the peasantry above class differences and who is excluded from the party for that reason (954).

Despite all the politicking, however, room still remains for romanticism, German romanticism. In Reinhardswald near Kassel, Friebott meets the chaste Melsene while taking a walk; he forms a sentimental attachment to her under the well-meaning eyes of her mother. However, after a wistful leave-taking from Melsene, Friebott comes across his old socialist friend Martin Wessel, who had in the meantime been deported from South Africa to Germany after a strike; according to Friebott, he has learned nothing more, not noticing how other peoples only pursue their own national interests under the banner of internationalism: "But that we should be such jackasses as to repeatedly hitch ourselves to foreign wagons for the sake of internationalism, that is what I am resisting" (1002). Disappointed by Germany, Friebott returns to German South West Africa. He is there at the outbreak of the First World War, which he welcomes because it will create space for the German people:

> Cornelius Friebott thought: The space that the German people lack will be gained through this terrible war. This war is nothing more than a war about space. And it is almost laughable that the Germans do not seem to know what they lack and what the issue is. (1073)

However, after ten months of heroic resistance, the German colony, "disgracefully" left in the lurch by the fatherland, succumbs to the superior force of the enemy, the Boers and the English. Friebott, who had killed a Bushman robber in self-defense, was sentenced by an English court, first to death and then to ten years in the penitentiary; he is taken to prison in Windhuk. The Germans present at sentencing shake their heads and ask themselves: "How is that possible? — How could it have come to this? How can the purest and most honorable and most capable and most diligent people on earth receive such entirely base treatment?" (1110). Friebott, however, lives with the conviction that "when Germany is far enough along, then all the torment in the world will stop. . . . Germany will undo the wrong when its day comes" (1113 and 1116–17).

Friebott finally succeeds in staging a fantastic escape from prison and Africa to Germany. At home, however, he is faced with the disgrace of the lost war and all of its negative consequences: "This is now the year in which the peace treaty began to take effect, with the surrender of the old German territories, with the profound disgrace, with the extradition list" (1150). To blame for the misfortune is above all international Marxism:

> This is now the year in which the seeds of Marxist doctrine and of being led around by the nose intellectually by foreigners sprouted, both factors having hindered a real freedom movement in the German Empire for a generation, and began to wreak terrible havoc on German labor and on the German people. (1150)

Prisoners of war, colonists, and merchants return "to the over-crowded, diminished, aimless homeland," "so that the quarreling of too many, the need, and the cramped conditions there become hopelessly entangled" (1150–51). Blatherers, bureaucrats, and partisan disputes dominate the scene; the old Germany, the Emperor, "and everything that was once proud" are now disparaged and ridiculed (1185). Among those returning is the merchant Hans Grimm, who now begins to write about his African experiences. He, too, is irritated by the homeland (1232) where now only "swindlers, good-for-nothings, and traitors" are at work (1244), the same ones who in 1918 stabbed the men at the front in the back. It becomes increasingly clear to Hans Grimm and to his novel character Hans Grimm "that henceforth numbers and the ability to perform, and not heritage, bestow rights in the distribution of the earth among the peoples" (1243–43). In Germany, Friebott and Grimm meet once again; both hold the same view about space and the people. Friebott travels through German lands with his message about the need for German living space, while Grimm begins in December of 1920 with his novel *Volk ohne Raum* — it is for him a "calling" (1285). Melsene, too, whom Friebott has found once again and married, has become "a believer," as she tells Grimm in a letter: "I believe that the entire German people will understand one day and will demand its rights and take them by force from the rest of the world" (1288–89). The novel ends in 1923 with the death of Friebott and Melsene's appeal and legacy to the reader not to forget the sacrificial death of Friebott and of the two million killed in action in the First World War, for all of them died "for the same thing" — living space (1297).

Despite the many printings and the obvious parallels to National Socialist ideology, Grimm's novel *Volk ohne Raum* — as well as other colonial literature — was not received by the official Nazi authorities with unqualified joy. The *Richtlinien für Kolonialwerbung* (Guidelines for Promotion of Colonies) issued by Goebbels at the end of 1933 say, among other things:

Future colonial possessions overseas are to serve for the acquisition of raw materials and colonial products for the German economy and not as settlement territories for German farmers. Promotion of any other kind is to be prevented under any circumstances. Furthermore, it should be noted that colonial propaganda is not today an urgent life-or-death issue of our people.[75]

Living space for the German people was to be found in the east, not in overseas territories:

Thus we National Socialists are consciously breaking with the foreign policy direction of the pre-war years. We are taking up where it was left off six hundred years ago. We are stopping the eternal movement of the Germans to the south and west of Europe and are directing our gaze to the land in the east. We are finally bringing to an end the colonial and trade policies of the pre-war period and are moving on to the territorial policies of the future. However, when we speak today of new land and territory in Europe, we can only be thinking primarily of Russia and the states around its perimeters that are subject to it.[76]

Hitler, the National Socialists, and Hans Grimm agreed that a healthy farmer class, as the foundation for the entire nation, requires living space to develop, and that Germany, which had become too cramped, has the natural right of the stronger to assert these claims:

The position must be taken, coolly and soberly, that Heaven cannot have intended to give one people fifty times as much land and territory on this earth as the others. In this case, political borders must not stand in the way of the borders of eternal law.[77]

However, while Grimm sees this living space in colonies, the National Socialists want to acquire it in Eastern Europe. Despite these differences, the Nazis could appreciate Grimm's work:

Hans Grimm's *Volk ohne Raum* is one of the works in our literature which will last through the ages and in which future generations will learn about the nature of our people, the eternal force of its being and the voice of its blood, and thrill at the weight and greatness of its fate.[78]

The Northern Renaissance

The National Socialists hoped for regeneration of the German people by harking back to its northern origins: "Today the same racial soul that once lived in Zarathustra is re-awakening with mythical force in the heart and in the north of Europe. The northern way of thinking and northern racial breeding are today, too, the answer to the Syrian Occident."[79] A prominent representative of the so-called "Northern Renaissance" in literature was the

Northern German Hans Friedrich Blunck, who in his trilogy *Die Urvätersaga* (The Saga of the Forefathers, 1926–1928) traces the mythological origins of the Northmen.

In the first book of *Die Urvätersaga,* "Gewalt über das Feuer" (Control over Fire), Blunck goes back to the mythical period of human prehistory. It is the

> saga of man who was called out of the depths by God. It extends back further than our remembering words and begins at a time when man had just tamed fire, when he threw himself in hordes on the black, steer-like lion and struggled with it on its cliff edges, [and] when, waiting confused and impassive for daylight, [he] for the first time opened his mouth to sing.[80]

The focus of the story from those dark times is on the hunter Börr, born of the mother Mo. Börr lives in caves, tames fire, fights with other hordes, builds a kind of house, suffers during enormous natural catastrophes, marries Arra, and with her has the son Mann. Man still understands the language of nature, although the first signs of a split between man and nature are beginning to become evident. However, he lives like nature, subject to the same law, according to which only the fittest survive. Life means struggle, struggle with nature, struggle with other human hordes, and above all struggle against the lion, the ruler of the earth. Börr, the courageous hero, blessed by the "Great Man-Wanderer," succeeds in conquering the lion in a bloody battle and making man the ruler of the earth. Here is a typical battle description in which the human horde throws itself in an atavistic frenzy on the king of the cave:

> And they threw themselves, howling with fear and rage, on it, and as the hunter Börr and the boys fell down before the terrible claws and teeth of the cat that seemed destined to win; they clung in a black mass over the lord of the cave, clawed and bit a firm hold where they could get to his hide, and [they] turned and twisted, a tangle of bleeding, twitching bodies, around the king of the earth. (78)

Finally, man won but the battle continues; instead of the lions, man now becomes the worst enemy of man (86). Nor do women stand back in this; roaming hordes of women are often more bloodthirsty and crueler than the "man, who establishes a new order after the wild deed" (86). There is also conflict between the forces of darkness and light. According to Blunck, however, the gods sent the mediator between the gods and the earthlings, the loyal messenger and warner Eckart, to aid man (111). The mystery of the flame, this "flaming beard, flickering eye," which had its origins in the "Great Hunter," permeates man, "it burns in his blood" (21), and binds him to eternal forces: "Rebelliously man felt the call of an event waiting beneath the flame (25). . . . Flames create righteousness behind the eyelids and flicker in blood and brain — the flames, or he who threw them at the feet of men" (30). Just how well this and other passages of the novel fit into the flame cult of the Nazis is clearly evident — only consider the popular campfires, solstice fires, torch-lit processions, etc.

In Blunck's book, language also comes from mystical-mythological primal depths. An unknown Foreigner (= God = the Great Man-Wanderer = Fast Runner = Great Hunter = Word Giver) makes the earth a drum so that "the sound echos back powerfully from the depths of the earth." Börr senses the nearness of the Foreigner like rapture: "He did not want to stop tasting this deep, roaring dance of the trilling spear and of his blood" (40). And the God touched the lips of man, which now connected the sounds to shape language instead of continuing to babble. With the help of the gods, men developed art, in the form of cave drawings, and music. At the end, the "Great Wanderer" finally brings Börr to him on the other side of the rainbow (118).

In the second book, "Kampf der Gestirne (Battle of the Stars) that takes place once again in the distant past, the battle is expanded into the cosmos as the battle of light against dark: "Gods and giants battle each other in the blue distance. The bright lights of day and of night seemed to be the highest beings open to the senses of men" (150). Battle and the law of the fittest also controlled the life of men. The stronger enemy Lärmer kills the light worshiper and hunter Elk at night. But Elk's son Ull kills Lärmer in a wild battle. The giant Ull now becomes the dominant figure of the book; he "wants to make sure that there are offspring sacrificing from his blood everywhere." In his excessive pride he even attempts to capture the sun. Ull and his men live as farmers, fishermen, and hunters in pile dwellings and go out to abduct women and on extended pillaging expeditions; in their world, the weak and cowardly are killed. King Ull's appearance alone teaches people fear: "His linen shirt open at the neck, the otter skin thrown back over his shoulders, a massive stone weapon in his amber-bedecked belt" (173). However, after the dawn has revealed itself to him and has brought Solmund to him, he calls himself Diuvis, "that is, he who is called by eternal Heaven" (178), and he founds an empire of the sun, in which he, with Solmund, "will bring man good fortune according to the dreams that he had" (178). After the wild journeys of his life, he feels the urge "to spread his joy to many, to be a friend of heaven, and for his Queen, to be lord of all peoples" (179). Everything in him fevers for the sun; sunrise becomes a consecration:

> While Ull still feels the consecration of the earth, the gates to the heights open; with brownish glow the twilight arches over the dark forests of the earth. And as he bows down humbly before the morning, he sees the world's burning light in person, opening its lid and looking out, flaming, over the treetops in the distance. (174)

With this bombast, Blunck simply wants to say that the sun is coming up. Of course, for him, dawn is the hour "when creation becomes perceptible and real" (194). After a short time, Solmund bore her giant a daughter, Osatara, "who at birth already had long light hair" (181). Her blond hair seems to Diuvis to be the earthly reflection of the divine that would be passed on from generation to generation (181). Diuvis seems to be at the peak of his power. "Wild was the belief of Diuvis and full of fervor for the mighty day star [e.g., the sun]" (182) that rules over everything and is honored at the solstice ceremonies: "But over everything rose, according to the ancient mysteries, Diu, the radiant heaven, and his daughter whose wheel, hammered out of yellow stone, was carried into the land on a high wagon in spring in the days of change" (198–99). However, evil is not banished; the unstable Goll grows to be a serious enemy to Diuvis and is a worshiper of the night and the moon. A battle arises between Ull/Diuvis and Goll, a battle between the elements of light and dark:

> Night and day, earth and longing — terrible in their power, raging in their anger, and blind in their hatred for each other. . . . It was as if two earths struggled primordially with each other, so terrible was the dull sound of the falling bodies, stamping feet, and moaning chests. (204)

Ull wins because his belief is stronger, not because he is the more powerful: "Only Ull's belief was greater" (204). Belief in what, Blunck does not reveal. However, the book cannot be grasped with rational explanations anyway. Osatara grows up to be the Nordic person of light, daughter of the sun, with blue eyes and blond hair (208–9). Her father Ull swears to her that he intends to "completely destroy" the unstable gods of the night. He does not even stop at his own wife Solmund: he kills her, when he finds traces of the night in her.

Diuvis wants to know from the warner and magician Bra why he is not yet lord of the world. Bra answers him that a long road must still be traveled: "Much life arose in the depths, and much that is light and much that is evil will still cross the path of men, Diuvis!" (231–32). Bra gives him to understand that many heroes must still be sacrificed before the savior finally comes: "Many heroes will stand up and bleed to death, until the last takes you home" (232). Diuvis does not attain the goal either; his daughter Osatara loves Imber, "who prays to the night" and who drives out Diuvis with his superior power. Imber rules with Osatara, becomes a mighty king, and reconciles day and night. However, after him his empire also collapses because man was too fickle and had no firm beliefs; for as the prophet Bra assured King Diuvis, only an unshakable belief in fate helps: "Only one thing protects the peoples: the power to believe in the good stars and in the eternal father who lives behind them" (231). From here, a direct line leads to other Nazi confessions of faith, such as Hanns Johst's "Ich glaube" (I believe), or that of Adolf Hitler, who wrote of belief in *Mein Kampf:* "Because belief helps elevate man above the level of an animal existence, it does in truth contribute to stabilizing and securing his existence."[81]

The fate of the giant and smith of the gods, Weland, Dunnar's son, who was cast out by the gods, is the subject of the third book, "Streit mit den Göttern" (Fight with the Gods). The time is undefined, but the events unfold in the Nordic region of the Frisians, the Saxons, the Goths, and other tribes. But as in the previous books, the life of men consists of battle and cruelty. Thus, King Niod, "next to the gods the most powerful prince among the twelve tribes of the North" (259), has Weland's tendons pierced because the latter surprised Niod's daughter Baduhild at the holy stone (262), and orders that Weland work for him as a smith and carve rune stones. Weland, however, plots revenge and murders Niod's young sons (271). Weland flees from Niod and Wodan's anger to the crag Rauchzahn off Helgoland, crafts bird wings, and is plagued by evil trolls, monsters of the deep and of darkness. Weland attempts to escape from Wodan's curse, but he must fulfill his destiny (286), bring misfortune, and withstand many battles before, in very great distress, he flees from the island of Rauchzahn with the help of his wings. Now he roams restlessly over the plains and through the Weser Mountains, and bringing pain, he kills King Niod and longs for wings to carry him up to the sun. For a time he finds peace as an agricultural laborer in the blood and soil of peasant work: "How good the work felt, how the forces of earth rose in him!" (331). But the spell of the gods drove him on: "Who can do anything about fate?" (342). Finally, the gods have mercy. Wodan, the father of the gods, wishes to release Weland from the curse, if he flies over the gods (361). Thereupon Weland begins to craft wings as he did back then at Rauchzahn. On a stormy morning, he rises into the air with his beloved, Sintgund, "like a great wonder, into the clouds with rushing wing strokes" (363) and up over the gods, thus reconciling them.

Although Hans Blunck, the first head of the Reich Chamber of Literature (1933–1935) does not directly support the National Socialists in this book, the novel *Die Urvätersaga,* with its flame and light-dark symbolism, its fate theme, the glorification of battle, the strength of Nordic men and gods, and the cult of sun, earth, and blood fits right into National Socialist ideology. As Langenbucher puts it in 1941, Blunck's works, "thanks to the unwavering connection of the author to the forces of the people," are "also interpretations of the life of the people as a community and as testimony to the obvious rootedness of the author in the essential heritage of his people."[82] An uninformed reader of today without any knowledge of history might want to read the novel differently, perhaps like a Tolkien novel, but not a reader who is somewhat familiar with the language and ideology of the Nazi period. Sentences such as, "up above in the clouds strides a great white plowman and throws the giant clods apart," as an image for wind and clouds are too tell-tale and too closely associated with Nazi vocabulary to be read any differently.

Notes

[1] See Donald Ray Richards, *The German Bestseller in the 20th Century: A Complete Bibliography and Analysis 1915–1940* (Bern: Lang, 1968).

[2] Karl Prümm, "Das Erbe der Front. Der antidemokratische Kriegsroman der Weimarer Republik und seine nationalsozialistische Fortsetzung" (The Legacy of the Front. The Antidemocratic War Novel and Its Continuation Under the National Socialists), in *Die deutsche Literatur im Dritten Reich* (German Literature in the Third Reich), edited by Horst Denkler and Karl Prümm (Stuttgart: Reclam, 1976), 157.

[3] Karl Prümm, "Das Erbe der Front," 139. For the theme of war and literature, see Wolfgang C. Natter, *Literature at War, 1914–1940. Representing the "Times of Greatness" in Germany* (New Haven and London: Yale UP, 1999).

[4] Quoted in Karl Prümm, "Das Erbe der Front" (Legacy of the Front), 157.

[5] See Karl Prümm, "Das Erbe der Front."

[6] Karl Prümm, *Die Literatur des Soldatischen Nationalismus der 20er Jahre (1918–1933)* (The Literature of Soldierly Nationalism in the Twenties [1918–1933]), 2 volumes (Kronberg im Taunus: Scriptor, 1974). For the interpretation of *In Stahlgewittern* (In Storms of Steel), see 92–129.

[7] As Karl O. Paetel reports, Jünger did refuse "to take part in the preparations for the putsch." Quoted in Wolfgang Kaempfer, *Ernst Jünger* (Stuttgart: Metzler, 1981), 34. The reasons for his refusal to join the poet's academy after 1933 were more personal than political; with his ideas, "he remains connected to the regime on a 'higher' level," as Kaempfer says, 34. For further information and literature, see Kaempfer's book on Ernst Jünger. See also Günter Hartung, *Literatur und Ästhetik des deutschen Faschismus* (Literatur and Aesthetics in German Fascism) (Berlin: Akademie Verlag, 1983), 69–77.

[8] Uwe-K. Ketelsen, "Die Literatur des 3. Reichs als Gegenstand germanistischer Forschung" (The Literature of the Third Reich as the Subject of Research in German Literature), in *Wege der Literaturwissenschaft* (Directions of Literary Scholarship), edited by Jutta Kolkenbrock-Netz, et al. (Bonn: Bouvier, 1985), 299. Ketelsen's remark here is meant for Benn but also fits Jünger.

[9] See Russel A. Berman, *The Rise of the Modern German Novel* (Cambridge, MA and London: Harvard UP, 1986), 216; "Jünger's version of fascist modernism is purest in his pre-1930 writings, such as the war memoirs *In Stahlgewittern* . . . which represents the ideal type of a fascist epic, the substitute for the novel of bourgeois subjectivity in a postsubjective cultural context."

[10] On that subject, see Russell A. Berman, 225.

[11] Ernst Jünger, *In Stahlgewittern*, 24th edition (Berlin: Verlag von E. S. Mittler & Sohn, 1942), 22. The page citations in the text refer to this edition. For Karl-Heinz Bohrer, this and similar scenes in the novel are part of Jünger's "aesthetics of horror," see Karl-Heinz Bohrer, *Die Ästhetik des Schreckens* (Aesthetics of Horror)

(Munich: Hanser, 1978), and also on that subject, Kaempfer's criticism of Bohrer in *Ernst Jünger*, 164–68. Aestheticizing war and horror, as Jünger does here, was quite widespread, and not only in Germany. Think only of the images of decay in the poems of the early Benn. Even in early 1942, André Gide wrote of Jünger's war diary: "Ernst Jünger's book on the war of 1914, In Stahlgewittern, is incontestably the most beautiful war book that I have read, having complete candor, honesty, and nobility," quoted in Karl-Heinz Bohrer, 520. In reading it should be noted that Ernst Jünger reworked the book several times; of the five versions, "the final version has essentially nothing more in common with the first edition," according to Karl Prümm in *Die Literatur des Soldatischen Nationalismus im 20er Jahre (1918–1933)*, 90–91. The first edition was more military memoir literature with names, ranks, reflections on strategy and tactics with criticism of the leadership, etc. The literary shaping only came in later editions, see Karl Prümm, 102–103.

[12] Ernst Jünger, *The Storm of Steel: From the Diary of a German Storm-Troop Officer on the Western Front*, translated by Basil Creighton (London: Chatto & Windus, 1929), xii–xiii.

[13] On that subject, see Jost Hermand and Frank Trommler, *Die Kultur der Weimarer Republik* (The Culture of the Weimar Republic) (Munich: Nymphenburger Verlagshandlung, 1978), 14–34.

[14] Adolf Hitler, *Mein Kampf* (My Struggle), 17th printing of the popular edition (Munich: Franz Eher Nachfolger, 1933), 584.

[15] See Adolf Hitler, 585.

[16] See Adolf Hitler, 585.

[17] See Donald Ray Richards, 54.

[18] Edwin Eugen Dwinger, *Die letzten Reiter* (The Last Cavalrymen) (Jena: Diedrichs, 1935), 14. The page citations in the text refer to this edition.

[19] Matthias Erzberger, born in 1875, was to the right the most hated man: as the originator of the peace resolution, as the visible embodiment of the Weimar coalition, as the indictor of the German leadership in the World War, against which he gave an important speech in July of 1919 in the National Assembly, see Karl Dietrich Erdmann, *Die Weimarer Republik* (The Weimar Republic), 7th edition (Munich: dtv, 1980, 1987), 135. The representative of the center and Reich minister was murdered by fanatical nationalists on August 26, 1921; "the assassins, members of the Consul Organization, a secret society that succeeded the disbanded Ehrhardt Brigade (which had occupied the government sector of Berlin in March of 1920 in the course of the failed Kapp putsch), escaped to overseas" (Erdmann, 161).

[20] On that subject, see Günther Rühle's commentary on Heinrich Zerkaulen's work *Jugend vor Langemarck* (Youth Before Langemarck), in *Zeit und Theater* (Time and Theater), volume 3, *Diktatur und Exil* (Dictatorship and Exile) (Berlin: Propyläen, 1974), 742–754.

[21] Günter Hartung, *Literatur und Ästhetik des deutschen Faschismus*, 115.

[22] Ernst Loewy, *Literatur unterm Hakenkreuz* (Literature Under the Swastika), 7,000th to 8,000th copies printed (Frankfurt am Main: Fischer, 1987), 329.

[23] Hans Zöberlein, *Der Befehl des Gewissens* (The Command of Conscience), 38th edition (Munich: Zentralverlag der NSDAP, Franz Eher Nachfolger, 1942), 43. The page citations in the text refer to this edition.

[24] In the second volume of his socio-psychological analysis of Fascism, *Männerphantasien* (Men's Fantasies) (Frankfurt am Main: Verlag Roter Stern, 1978), Klaus Theweleit quotes extensively from this chapter; 20–22 and 487–92.

[25] Karl Aloys Schenzinger, *Hitlerjunge Quex* (Hitler Youth Quex) (Berlin: Zeitgeschichte Verlag Wilhelm Andermann, 1932), 7. The page citations in the text refer to this edition.

[26] On that subject, see Renate Jaroslawski and Rüdiger Steinlein, "Die 'politische Jugendschrift.' Zur Theorie und Praxis faschistischer deutscher Jugendliteratur" (The "Political Book for Young People." On the Theory and Practice of Fascist German Juvenile Literature), in *Die deutsche Literatur im Dritten Reich,* edited by Denkler and Prümm, 314.

[27] Uwe-K. Ketelsen, *Völkisch-nationale und nationalsozialistische Literatur in Deutschland 1890–1945* (Völkisch National and National Socialist Literature in Germany, 1890–1945) (Stuttgart: Metzler, 1976), 70.

[28] Hanns Heinz Ewers, *Horst Wessel: Ein deutsches Schicksal* (Horst Wessel: A German Fate) (Stuttgart and Berlin: J. G. Cotta'sche Buchhandlung Nachfolger, 1933), 290. The page citations in the text refer to this edition.

[29] See Donald Ray Richards, 20.

[30] See Klaus Vondung, "Der literarische Nationalismus. Ideologische, politische und sozial-historische Wirkungszusammenhänge" (Literary National Socialism. Ideological, Political, and Social-Historical Interconnections), in *Die deutsche Literatur im Dritten Reich,* edited by Horst Denkler and Karl Prümm, 45.

[31] Quoted in Joseph Wulf, *Literatur und Dichtung im Dritten Reich: Eine Dokumentation* (Literature and Poetry in the Third Reich: Documentation) (Frankfurt am Main: Ullstein, 1983), 162.

[32] Bertolt Brecht, "Die Horst-Wessel-Legende" (The Horst Wessel Legend), in Brecht, *Werke: Große Kommentierte Berliner und Frankfurter Ausgabe* (Works: Large, Commented Berlin and Frankfurt Edition), edited by Werner Hecht et al., volume 19 (Berlin and Weimar: Aufbau, 1997 and Frankfurt am Main: Suhrkamp, 1997), 382.

[33] Bertolt Brecht, 386.

[34] Bertolt Brecht, 389. For more details see Karl-Heinz Schoeps, "Die Horst-Wessel-Legende," in *Brecht-Handbuch,* volume 3, *Prosa, Filme, Drehbücher,* edited by Jan Knopf (Stuttgart: Metzler, 2002), 276–282.

[35] On that subject, see Helmut Vallery, "Enteroisierte Geschichte. Der nationalsozialistische historische Roman" (History Without Heroes. The National Socialist Historical Novel), in *Leid der Worte: Panorama des literarischen Nationalsozialismus* (Suffering of Words: Panorama of Literary National Socialism), edited by Jörg Thunecke (Bonn: Bouvier, 1987), 90–107. Vallery shows in addition how the political development of the Third Reich is reflected in the themes of historical novels. According to Vallery, however, historical subjects were by no means the exclusive

domain of the National Socialists; from the middle of the twenties to the forties, all the political camps from the Inner Emigration to exile had them in common.

[36] Johannes Sachslehner, *Führerwort und Führerblick: Mirko Jelusich: Zur Strategie eines Bestsellerautors in den Dreißiger Jahren* (Leader Words and Leader Looks: On the Strategy of a Bestseller Author in the Thirties) (Königsstein im Taunus: Hain, 1985), 40. On that subject, see the review by Klaus Zeyringer, in *Monatshefte* 79, 4 (1985), 523–24.

[37] See Karl Prümm, "Das Erbe der Front," 157.

[38] See Donald Ray Richards, 57 and 104.

[39] See Werner Beumelburg, *Mont Royal* (Mount Royal) (Published by the High Command of the Army, Internal Affairs Section, no date), 6. The page citations in the text refer to this edition.

[40] See Adolf Hitler, 416.

[41] See Adolf Hitler, 418.

[42] Werner Beumelberg, *Geschichten vom Reich* (Stories of the Reich), edited by Karl Plenzat (Leipzig: Hermann Eichblatt Verlag, 1941), 3.

[43] Kurt Kölsch, *Jörg,* Published by the National Labor Front, National Socialist Association Kraft durch Freude (Strength Through Joy) (Stuttgart: Verlag Deutsche Volksbücher GmbH, 1943).

[44] See Kölsch, 12.

[45] See Donald Ray Richards, 105.

[46] Werner Beumelburg, *Reich and Rom* (Reich and Rome), 16,000th to 30,000th copies printed (Oldenburg in East Frisia and Berlin: Stalling, 1937), 95. The page citations in the text refer to this edition.

[47] Gerhard Schweizer, *Bauernroman und Faschismus* (The Peasant Novel and Fascism) (Tübingen: Vereinigung für Volkskunde E. V. Schloss, 1976), volume 42, 7.

[48] See Peter Zimmermann, *Der Bauernroman: Antifeudalismus-Konservatismus-Faschismus* (The Peasant Novel: Anti-Feudalism-Conservatism-Fascism) (Stuttgart: Metzler, 1975), 159. Here Zimmermann describes the distribution of the 614 peasant novels in the period from 1830 to 1970 that he examines.

[49] See Gerhard Schweizer, 21.

[50] See Gerhard Schweizer, 20, and George L. Mosse, *The Crisis of German Ideology* (New York: Grosset & Dunlap, 1964), 27.

[51] Alfred Rosenberg, *Der Mythus des 20. Jahrhundert* (The Mythos of the Twentieth Century), 107,000th to 110,000th copies printed (Munich: Hoheneichen Verlag), 1937), 531.

[52] See Adolf Hitler, 151.

[53] See Peter Zimmermann, *Der Bauernroman,* 3.

[54] The Fehme was a secret court in medieval times.

[55] See Donald Ray Richards, 62.

[56] Franz Schonauer, *Deutsche Literatur im Dritten Reich* (German Literature in the Third Reich) (Olten and Freiburg: Walter-Verlag, 1961), 89.

[57] See Ernst Loewy, 288.

[58] Josefa Berens-Totenohl, *Der Femhof* (The Fehme Farm), 161,000th to 285,000th copies printed (Jena: Diederichs, 1941), 41. The page citations in the text refer to this edition.

[59] See Franz Schonauer, 90.

[60] Hermann Löns, *Der Wehrwolf* (The Werewolf) (Jena: Eugen Diederichs, 1926), 95.

[61] On that subject, see Klaus Eberhardt, *Literatur-Sozialcharakter-Gesellschaft: Untersuchungen von präfaschistischen Erzählwelten zu Beginn des 20. Jahrhunderts* (Literature-Social Character-Society: Studies on the Prefascist Story Worlds at the Beginning of the Twentieth Century) (Frankfurt am Main, Bern, and New York: Lang, 1986), 70–85, and George L. Mosse, 25–26.

[62] See Alfred Rosenberg, 436.

[63] See Günter Hartung, 47–48.

[64] See Donald Ray Richards, 178. In 1976, the *Wehrwolf* was republished in Munich in the "Heyne Nostalgia Library."

[65] See Ernst Loewy, 299.

[66] On the history of German colonies, see Horst Gründer, *Geschichte der deutschen Kolonien* (History of the German Colonies) (Paderborn: Schöningh Verlag, 1985), UNI Pocketbook 1332 of the Tübingen University Library Work Group for Scholarship.

[67] Uwe-K. Ketelsen, *Völkisch-nationale und nationalsozialistische Literatur in Deutschland 1890–1945*, 73.

[68] On that subject, see Russell Bermann, 210. For Bermann, Grimm's novel, together with Gustav Frenssen's *Jörn Uhl*, Ernst Jünger's early work, and Artur Dinter's *Die Sünde wider das Blut* (The Sin Against Blood), are examples for "fascist modernism," which provides stability to the uprooted individual in a regressive ideology of the *völkisch* national collective: "Bourgeois subjectivity and its cultural modes are outflanked by a literary strategy that invokes the regressive temptations of a pre-individuated state in the service of post-individual domination" (231).

[69] See Peter Zimmermann, "Kampf um den Lebensraum. Ein Mythos der Kolonial- und der Blut-und-Boden-Literatur" (The Struggle for Living Space. A Myth of Colonial Literature and Blood-and-Soil Literature), in *Die deutsche Literatur im Dritten Reich,* edited by Denkler and Prümm, 165–82.

[70] Hellmuth Langenbucher, *Volkhafte Dichtung der Zeit* (People's Literature of the Time), 6th edition (Berlin: Junker and Dünnhaupt, 1941), 613.

[71] See Ernst Loewy, 299.

[72] Quoted in Joseph Wulf, *Literatur und Dichtung im Dritten Reich,* 337.

[73] Quoted in Joseph Wulf, 338.

[74] Hans Grimm, *Volk ohne Raum* (People Without Space) (Munich: Albert Langen and Georg Müller, 1926), 19. The page citations in the text refer to this edition.

[75] Quoted in Peter Zimmermann, "Kampf um den Lebensraum. Ein Mythos der Kolonial- und der Blut-und-Boden-Literatur," in Denkler and Prümm, *Die deutsche Literatur im Dritten Reich,* 170.

[76] Adolf Hitler in *Mein Kampf,* quoted in Peter Zimmermann, 170.

[77] See *Mein Kampf,* 152.

[78] See Langenbucher, 463.

[79] See Alfred Rosenberg, 33. In his book, Rosenberg uses "Syrian" and "Jewish" as synonyms.

[80] Hans Friedrich Blunck, *Die Urvätersaga* (The Saga of the Forefathers) (Jena: Eugen Diederichs, 1934), 3. The page citations in the text refer to this edition.

[81] See *Mein Kampf,* 216.

[82] See Langenbucher, 415.

Eberhard Wolfgang Möller before a bas-relief of his grandfather.
Möller was author of the play *Rothschild siegt bei Waterloo*
(Rothschild Wins at Waterloo), and of the *Frankenburger Würfelspiel*
(Frankenburger Dice Game), one of the most successful *Thingspiele*.
Courtesy Bundesarchiv, Koblenz.

5: The National Socialist Drama

IN *MEIN KAMPF*, Hitler complains, among other things, about the demise of culture and the "intellectual degeneration" of art. The "bolshevism of art" is for Hitler the herald of "political collapse" in Germany. In his opinion, it is the duty of the state to prevent "the people from being driven into the arms of intellectual insanity."[1] According to Hitler, this disease has also affected the theater in general:

> The theater sank visibly deeper and would probably have already disappeared as a cultural factor back then, if the court theaters, at least, had not opposed the prostitution of art. Aside from them, and several other praiseworthy exceptions, the stage productions were such that it would be more expedient for the nation to avoid attending them at all. (284)

Hitler likewise complains about the decline of the classical writers in his time:

> But of course, what are Schiller, Goethe, or Shakespeare compared to the heroes of contemporary German literature! Old, worn-out, and outmoded, no, outdated phenomena. For that was the characteristic feature of this time: not only did they only produce more filth themselves, but they also sullied everything really great from the past besides. (285)

Hitler believes that this "filth" is to be found not only in the theater, but in all areas. He therefore made it his own responsibility to lead Germany out of this "filth." Literature, and not least of all, theater, had to contribute to that effort. For it was the theater in particular that Hitler saw as an instructional institution that had to "be there primarily for the education of the youth" (284). By harking back to the past, Hitler promised Germany a glorious future.

The direction was also set for literature. Accordingly, the critics with a National Socialist bent saw only decline and decay in the theater of the Weimar Republic. Helmut Wanderscheck's comments are quoted here as a paradigm for many others: "The drama was degraded to a play for a political purpose."[2] Any and all connections to eternal laws of drama and eternally human values were set aside; "the people were intellectually and spiritually sick. . . . The drama became a plaything in the hands of rootless international literati" (3). "Epic theater" in particular came under attack:

> Driven by party politics, epic drama in its basic structure and its nature, led to the complete destruction of the drama as an art form. . . . It did not grow out of life or experience, not out of the depths of the people's soul or out of the desire of militant youth. (3–4)

With the seizure of power by the National Socialists, a new day was also supposed to dawn in theater: "A change in the world is at the same time always a change in art! With the victory of National Socialism, the transformation of German theater also took place to an extent not even imagined up to that point. A realm of non-art, un-art, and art replacement was extinguished" (7). Theater should once again be rooted in the immortal soul of the German people; staging plays will again become a "magical process" (10). Drama becomes myth: "The political morality of National Socialism becomes the basis for *völkisch* myth in drama" (13). Fate again enters into the dramatic arts: "The connection of the dramatist to the fate of his people returns him to drama dominated by fate" (15). Also important in this process is the return to poetic language in drama, after language was "profaned and debased to the level of the ordinary newspaper editorial" by naturalism, expressionism, and dramas with a political agenda. (16) The purpose of theater is no longer instruction but "edification and redemption" (18). That is accomplished most perfectly in tragedy; as the Reich drama advisor (*Reichsdramaturg*) Schlösser declares, "The stage is a site of tragic ideas, [and] as the most exalted idea of which the human spirit can conceive, [the site of] the idea of tragedy, which, by touching profoundly, achieves the greatest edification."[3]

These remarks suggest the development of a uniform National Socialist drama theory. But as Ketelsen shows correctly, there actually never was "*the* drama of the Third Reich."[4] The briefness of the period from 1933 to 1945 (and of that, around five of the years were war years) and the confusion about jurisdiction within the official offices prevented development of a uniform concept. Furthermore, for the drama as for the novel, 1933 was not the beginning of a new era. Numerous dramas written before 1933 fit seamlessly into the total fabric of National Socialist goals. The difference in the period before 1933 was only that these dramas were now given special preferential treatment and works running counter to National Socialist ideology were banned. But even the theater promoted by the National Socialists was not uniform. The multitude of opposing directions within the national, conservative, *völkisch,* National Socialist drama resulted not only from the rivalry among the official authorities responsible for theater — the diverging views of Rosenberg and Goebbels are well known[5] — but also from the different models followed by the authors:

> People used the Greek classic writer for orientation and interpreted them in the "spirit of the times," swore by Shakespeare as the absolute Nordic-Germanic poet, developed a decided preference for Nordic tragedy, . . . [and] enthusiastically embraced the writers of German classicism, or damned them.[6]

Authors drew on Wagner, the German Youth Movement, Paul Ernst, even expressionism — of which Hitler so thoroughly disapproved — and Bertolt

Brecht (see Eberhard Wolfgang Möller). That led variously to frictions, complications, and bans on performance, which after 1945 provided many authors with an alibi. The only common ground of all these different trends was the ideology of the Third Reich. It cannot be emphasized enough that many authors did not have to be aligned after 1933: they already had been a long time ago and of their own volition. In 1933, their hour had come; they did not feel that they were being patronized from above, but rather that they were collaborating in constructing the building of state, totally unlike those authors who traditionally viewed themselves as a counterweight to the power of state, or simply did not bother about it. However, there is no question that the National Socialists attached extraordinary importance to the theater:

> At no time did the state do more to promote theater than between 1933 and 1945. In 1936, 331 theaters were operating in Germany. Some of them (theaters of the people) were newly built or renovated. Special subsidies of the Reich (12 million marks in 1936) improved their equipment. Large-scale theater advertisement began. Reich theater festival weeks took place from 1934 on, alternating among Berlin, Hamburg, Munich, Bochum, and Essen, and in 1938, Vienna.[7]

At the 1937 Reich Theater Festival Week in Düsseldorf, Goebbels declared very proudly: "Germany is the leading theater country in the world."[8]

Theater did not stay limited to buildings specially constructed for that purpose; the entire country was overrun with theater. In a broad sense, and with a double meaning, the entire National Socialist movement can be seen as theater. Marches, various kinds of uniforms and decorations, flags, banners, drums, flag dedications, torch-lit processions, playing taps, Reich Party congresses, and Hitler speeches were nothing more than "grand theater." That is the view expressed by Joachim Fest in his Hitler biography about Hitler's "circensian need for flourishes, fanfare, and grand entrances" and his inclination "to see his life as a series of grandiose stage appearances where, before the audience, which is holding its breath, he extends his arm in the glow of the stage lights and once again declaims the role of the great hero anew."[9] Of course, this was only for the purpose of covering up reality — as most of the Nazi dramas did. That is the explanation for the National Socialists' rejection of the dramas since naturalism that exposed reality.

Hitler's gestures and voice, even his fits of anger, were also theatrical devices consciously employed to achieve certain effects. Court theater, and even the theater director Max Reinhardt, who was driven out of Germany for racial reasons, left their marks on Hitler's theatrical mission, which was masterfully caricatured by Bertolt Brecht in his play *Der aufhaltsame Aufstieg des Arturo Ui* (The Resistible Rise of Arturo Ui) and by Charlie Chaplin in his film *Der große Diktator* (The Great Dictator). Hanns Johst, head of the

Reich Chamber of Literature from 1935 to 1945 and one of the prominent Nazi authors and important culture functionaries recognized this tradition in no uncertain terms. The Nazi marches with flags, fanfares, and Hitler's beseeching rhetoric made the matter all too clear to him: "That was Max Reinhardt."[10] According to Joachim Fest, Hitler was "basically a theater person." He became intoxicated especially with catastrophes and worldwide conflagrations as he knew them from Wagner's *Götterdämmerung* (Twilight of the Gods), which were then later transformed into grim reality. Nazism, Hitler, and Theater are thus intimately connected to each other. Likewise, National Socialist theater does not appeal to reason, but to feelings: *religio* replaces *ratio,* as Hanns Johst declared in the essay "Vom neuen Drama" (On the New Drama) in 1928:

> I demand that the last act of the future dramas not proceed realistically, not materially, and not dogmatically to the very end, but instead I see a drama that has within it the power, the intellectual and spiritual power, to overwhelm all participants to such a degree that at the end the members of the audience do not finish the evening by storming the coat check, but that this drama instead begins to dissolve in them like an elixir. That they feel their experiences overshadowed by the encounter with something metaphysical. . . . Only belief makes the world as a whole bearable; all other methods of understanding can only shatter. . . . The future theater will have to become a cult, or the theater will have come to the end of its mission, its living content of ideas and will only be carried along as a kind of petrified fossil in the cultural shuffling. The future drama will live! The distress, the despair, [and] the misery of our people require help. And help does not come in the end effect or in the most profound sense from begging for banknotes of high denominations, but help comes instead from the rebirth of a community of belief.[11]

Johst's own drama *Schlageter* is the most vivid example of his theory, as we will see. But the theory also applies to the majority of the other National Socialist dramas.

In the following chapter, a few important examples are selected from the wealth of authors and directions, are assigned to particular thematic groups, and are analyzed in some detail. Ideology as well as the prominence of the author and the theme and form of the play were all important for selection. To avoid long ideological definitions, all such works of *völkisch,* conservative, national authors who were widely read and received official support are subsumed under National Socialist drama. The dramas to be presented are arranged in particular thematic groups.

Battle and Proof of Worth

The Schlageter material was an extremely clever choice by Johst. He struck a nerve in many Germans, not only the National Socialists, who looked back with bitterness on the period of disgrace and suffering immediately following the First World War. The historical Schlageter, a front-line officer who became unemployed in 1918, the hero of volunteer corps's (*Freikorps*) operations in the Baltic States and in the Ruhr Region, was executed by a French firing squad on May 26, 1923, in the Golzheim Heath near Düsseldorf for sabotage against the French occupation troops in the Rhineland. The sentence gave rise to outrage and protests. The Reich government in Berlin contested its legality. The International Red Cross, the Pope, the Queen of Sweden, and the Archbishop of Cologne intervened in vain. Johst fashioned this Schlageter into a champion and martyr for the Third Reich, to the "first soldier of the Third Reich,"[12] who joyfully went to his death for Germany and his convictions. The play is personally dedicated to the *Führer* upon his expressed wish "in loving admiration and unchanging loyalty." Of course, Johst interpreted the facts liberally. The real Schlageter was by no means as patriotic and heroic as Johst portrayed him. Schlageter did organize national secret societies in Danzig, but at the same time served as an informant for the Polish intelligence services. Finally, his behavior before the war court was hardly heroic and exemplary: to save his own head, he betrayed the men fighting with him.[13]

Johst presents on the stage in four acts the transformation of Schlageter from a student in political economy to a national fighter. Actually, it is more a rediscovery of the old spirit of the front, for Schlageter's former comrade in arms and present fellow student Friedrich Thiemann knows that under the academic facade beats the heart of his old comrade, which he need only coax out with earthy sayings. Thiemann storms against ink-spattering academics and capitalists who, instead of machines guns and grenades, operate with fountain pens and stock market quotes: "Pencil and fountain pen, those are the weapons to advance one's career! . . . (83) The stock market as a battlefield, the dollar as battle cry! How noble by comparison is a machine gun!" (89). For him the year 1918 was not a devastating defeat, but instead an extended "home leave" (84). The efforts for democratization of the Weimar Republic are for Thiemann only a dumb confidence game and weakening of the battle spirit:

> I know that stuff from 18 . . . [1848] fraternity, equality, . . . freedom . . . beauty and dignity! You catch mice with cheese. Suddenly, in the middle of parleying: Hands up! You are disarmed . . . You are a republican voter herd! — No, get ten feet away from me with the whole ideology mess . . . Here we shoot with live ammunition! When I hear culture . . . I take off the safety on my Browning! (87)

When the weak, groveling German Socialist Party politicians of the Republic, who only think of their own careers, can only pull themselves together enough to declare passive resistance as the French march into the Rhineland, Schlageter gives in to the pressure by Thiemann and joins the active resistance of former comrades, as his heart orders him: "The good conscience of the Reich . . . today is only found in revolutionaries!" (108). The tender bonds of love for Alexandra Thiemann do not hold him any longer, either; his love for Germany is stronger. He blows things up for Germany and hopes that as a result the German people will awaken and seize power (106). Alexandra, who is German to the core, fully understands. The politicians eager to live up to the Versailles treaty, however, set the police on Schlageter and his party comrades: "Germans turn Schlageter over to the knife . . . Germans catch his comrades like stray dogs!" (137) and hand them over to the French, who drag him before a French court-martial. After this last disgrace, Professor Thiemann bursts out: "I promised German boys that it would be Germany, Germany, above everything!! And now this Germany is lower than any dog!" (131). Even His Excellency General K., always making a loyal effort to serve the Republic, even against his better judgment, now hears the new columns, "March steps . . . Beginning . . . Germany, awaken!!" (138).

Johst does not show the actual sabotage acts, or the proceedings against Schlageter, either, but he does show his execution in a highly emotional, apotheosizing final scene that is extremely effective dramatically. With his back to the audience, Schlageter stands "tall, his hands tied behind his back with a rope, the end of which drags on the ground, as if he were holding up the whole earth" (138) in the "place of skulls [Calvary]" (138). The salvo of the French firing squad passes through Schlageter into the audience. He dies with the word "Germany" on his lips:

> A last word! A wish! Order!
> Germany!!!
> Awaken! Catch fire!!
> Blaze up! Burn enormously!

The premiere of the play on April 20, 1933, for Hitler's first birthday as Reich Chancellor, almost ten years after the execution of the historical Schlageter, became a performance for the inauguration of National Socialism. Instead of applauding, the members of the audience rose from their seats and, together with the actors, sang the Germany song ("Deutschland, Deutschland über alles") and the Horst Wessel song ("Die Fahne hoch" — Up With the Flag). Besides Hitler, the elite of the Nazi state and numerous literary luminaries of that state, such as Blunck, Kolbenheyer, and Schäfer, were in the audience. On the stage stood the celebrities of the Berlin State Theater under the direction of Franz Ulbricht: Lothar Müthel (Schlageter), Emmy Sonnemann (Alexandra Thiemann), Albert Bassermann (General), and Veit Harlan (Thiemann). Alfred Kreienberg, the theater critic for the Berlin *"Tägliche Rundschau"* (Daily Review), wrote the following about this performance on April 22, 1933:

> Carefully weighed literary criticism has no place here. This play and its performance are like a rousing speech, being slapped on the shoulder, being pulled down, being pulled up. Comrade, your hand! This Schlageter stands at the beginning a new art that will be of the people or will not be at all. This Schlageter has some of the fire that can ignite German consciences. The Kleistian fire. The nation's purgatory. Schlageter is the new man, the young German man. His death is resurrection; his possessions are comradeship, loyalty, and fraternity.[14]

What extraordinary significance Schlageter and Johst's Schlageter drama had for National Socialism is evident from a speech by Alfred Rosenberg at the Reich congress of the National Socialist cultural community on June 7, 1935. In this speech, Schlageter became a symbol of the awakening Germany.

> Johst, . . . the poet of "Schlageter," who glorified the man whom we, too, will remember at this Reich congress, in his complete, unconditional self-renunciation and willingness to fight for the German people, has become the symbol of the awakening young Germany. In his drama, Hanns Johst has created a moving memorial to the martyrdom of National Socialist Germany.[15]

Schlageter was the last play of the former expressionist Johst, who after 1933 dedicated himself primarily to tasks relating to party policy, especially as director of the Reich Chamber of Literature from 1935 to 1945. Even if today the ideas and ideology of the play no longer have any meaning, Hanns Johst must still be credited with the skill of an artisan in the composition of his *Schlageter*.

Heinrich Zerkaulen's play *Jugend von Langemarck* also deals with selfless willingness to sacrifice. Here, too, the basis is a historical event: in an attack that was completely senseless from a military standpoint, regiments of young volunteers, singing and with a great number of casualties, stormed the enemy outpost locations near Langemarck in Flanders on November 9, 1914, without, however, being able to break through the enemy front. Hitler erected a monument to these young volunteers in *Mein Kampf*. When he was a young soldier at the Flanders front, he writes, he was himself inspired to attack by the sound of the Germany song being sung by the regiments of young volunteers:

> Out of the distance the sounds of a song reached our ears and came closer and closer, leapt across from company to company, and just at the point when death was very actively gripping our ranks, the song reached us, and we continued to pass it on: Germany, Germany, above all else,

above all else in the world! Two weeks later we returned. Even our way of walking was now different. Seventeen-year-old boys now looked like men. The volunteers of the List Regiment had perhaps not learned to fight correctly, but they did know how to die like old soldiers.[16]

Langemarck, Leo Schlageter, and Horst Wessel became slogans and cue words to invoke the spirit of the front, camaraderie, and the willingness to make sacrifices in the National Socialist Reich. For that reason it is not surprising that the Langemarck story was dramatized a number of times, for example, by Edgar Kahn in *Langemarck* (1933), by Max Geißler-Monato in *Flandern 1914* (Flanders 1914, 1933), and by Paul Alverdes in *Die Freiwilligen: Ein Stück für Langemarck Feiern* (The Volunteers: A Play for Langemarck Celebrations, 1934). References to the spirit of Langemarck are also found in numerous other works of National Socialist literature, for example, in Dwinger's novel *Die letzten Reiter* (The Last Cavalrymen). The Langemarck theme is, at the same time, only one particularly striking example of the literature of the First World War from the *völkisch*, conservative, national perspective. Towards the end of the Weimar Republic, as Erwin Breßlein shows, "a simply enormous number of war plays . . . flooded"

> the book market and theaters, with the ideological intention of contrasting the liberal democratic state and social system to a military, revolutionary conservative system and of placing in the latter an almost messianic expectation of salvation for Germany's internal and external restoration.[17]

As part of the intensified revival of memories of the First World War, which began toward the end of the twenties, a virtual Langemarck cult also developed. Starting in 1927, right-wing university circles had already celebrated "the Day of Langemarck." In the Third Reich, Langemarck became "the symbol of the German love of fatherland and willingness to serve to the death. Cultivating these idols is the purpose of the Langemarck celebrations."[18]

Heinrich Zerkaulen, born in Bonn in 1892 to a father who was a shoemaker, went to the eastern front himself as a war volunteer. He was inspired in 1933 to write his Langemarck drama by a speech Franz von Papen gave to the Berlin student body on the occasion of Langemarck Day and which Zerkaulen heard on the radio:

> To me it was as if a curtain had been torn open that had hidden an experience from view for nineteen years. Almost physically, I felt a fist reaching for my heart. In that hour I knew that I would write the play of consecration for Langemarck . . . My "Youth of Langemarck" was born of the experience and of the storm surrounding the emergence of a new Germany in 1933.[19]

The action of Zerkaulen's *Jugend von Langemarck* is divided into three acts and an epilogue. The first act is set on August 7, 1914, in the house of the widowed factory owner Luise Gärtner. An atmosphere of awakening and enthusiasm for the war prevails; no one wants to hold back at this point, when "all of Germany is marching." In this time of national exaltation, however, Franz Gärtner is, according to the will and testament of his deceased father, supposed to take over the fabric factory and switch over to production of fabric for uniforms. The dramatic conflict of the play is thus defined. Enthusiastic about the war, Franz of course wants to join his friends as a volunteer for the war but is supposed to stay home and run the business, which is critical to the war effort. Conflict also arises on a private level: Franz's enthusiasm for the war also mars his relationship to his mother and his love for the chaste Christa. Franz's mother appeals to his sense of responsibility and family honor to keep him at the factory, as his father had ordered. Franz, however, is overwhelmed by an entire people's sense of awakening. He feels the war "roar . . . in blood and brain . . . so that you would like to tear open your chest in order to hold out your heart."[20] War creates a community of the people without class differences, "so that a student can be familiar with a worker simply because they are marching together, finally together again in the same experience, so that social standing and titles mean nothing; the soldier is everything" (156). Over all of them, however, flies the mystical symbol of the flag: "So that the flag means more to the individual than life" (156).

After a cool good-bye to his mother and a "very tender, and emotionally charged discussion" with Christa, Franz rushes to the front in Flanders where the next two acts take place. The troops consist mostly of young fraternity students, but among them is also the worker Karl Stanz with whom Franz becomes friends. The slightly older, experienced soldiers of the squad and the non-commissioned officer Lehmbruck view the youths in their enthusiasm with sympathy but also with a certain skepticism. Lehmbruck does not understand what is going on in these young war volunteers:

> If Lehmbruck only knew what the intoxication is like . . . Yes, brother, we are intoxicated. You and I . . . all of us, all. The blood of our fathers from centuries before intoxicates us. All those who gave their lives for their home soil, those at Fehrbellin, those at Roßbach, those at Leuthen, Jena, those at Sedan, they are with us — in us! Their legacy, the secret of their blood, that is in us like an anchor; we just did not know it. But now, when a wrong is being done to our soil, when our flags wave in the wind, when the drums go at our borders — then it suddenly tugs, that anchor. The blood of our fathers, their will, their dying for the honor and the freedom of Germany — all that intoxicates us.

What drives Franz and his war comrades are the mystical voices of the forefathers, of the blood, and of the soil. Before this mystical, primal source, all the class barriers naturally break down: workers and students "*join their hands together. . . . Their hands remain firmly holding each other:* nothing but comrades!" (164). The national community of the people defeats the Marxist class society. Franz is torn from this front experience by the order to return home and to take over his father's business, which is critical to the war effort. For Zerkaulen and like-minded persons, that is of course a tragedy, intensifying their inner conflicts. The young soldiers "tear open their service coats, all of them having underneath their fraternity ribbons," and protest against this order: "We are German students! With God as our witness and on our colors, Captain" (171). The captain remains unimpressed: orders are orders.

In the third and final act, Zerkaulen takes us to the position of the English. The stage directions tell us that "the entire third act" is "to be played at a hectic, tense pace" (172). Nevertheless, time remains for a sentimental anecdote, which an English observer tells in a hail of shells. In Bixschoote, he witnessed the German soldiers reaping the grain between the fronts, not in order to see, shoot, and attack better, but for love of the seed and the soil: "When the German smells grain, he smells his soil, even in the middle of enemy territory. He cannot stand to see fruit spoil; he has to harvest it. The German does not do anything without having a deeper reason" (173). At the same time, Zerkaulen makes it clear between the lines just how inwardly poor and sober the English are. He does grant them, however, that they are chivalrous, unlike the French. When the English capture Karl Stanz while he is with a German patrol, he is not afraid: "The Englishman is a decent soldier" (181). The English feel safe, probably rightly so, as an English second lieutenant indicates: "Be careful of the courage of the Germans — but courage can also be madness. To want to attack us here would be madness. We would have a field of bodies before us in short order —" (184). But the Germans actually do attack, and while singing to boot. The third act is highly dramatic as, despite British fire, the first German soldiers appear in the English trenches and are joyfully greeted by Karl Stanz: "Comrades! Victory!" (185). With the two last lines of the Germany song on their lips ("Germany, Germany, above all else, above all else in the world"), which "is transformed into roaring, elemental song," the young war volunteers overrun the English positions, now with the fraternity ribbons over their uniforms" (185). Zerkaulen has the war action of his play end with the false impression of total German victory. In reality, however, the German attack bogged down under the fire of the English, with unspeakable casualties — it was, as the English second lieutenant quoted by Zerkaulen correctly indicated, "madness."

The epilogue returns to the beginning of the play. We find ourselves again in the living room of the Gärtner house. Christa and Luise Gärtner are in black; Franz was killed in action at Langemarck — although Zerkaulen never explains how he got around the order to go home. His mother has reconciled herself: "His death taught me that no one can go against his own inner order. And no one can give more for others than his life. He gave his life for the most sacred thing that he possessed. For his Fatherland" (186). Having returned from the field, Karl Stanz, who like Franz in act I, enters the stage living room in battle dress, takes over the factory; the circle is closed. Stanz hesitates, but Mrs. Gärtner makes it his sacred duty: "Above victory and defeat, above pain and joy, duty is always there. Duty, which sees the goal behind the goal. The essential thing, and that into eternity, is that he be humble in his own feelings in order to be able to do his own duty fully" (192). Thus, according to Zerkaulen and the Nazi ideology, duty stands even above feelings. Karl, however, also obligates his feelings to the national task: he feels that he is a link in a long chain of men who died in action, of all the men who died in action in the four years of the war. With some effort, Zerkaulen builds a bridge over the supposed low spots of the Weimar Republic, to the present, 1933, and to the memory of the dead at Langemarck:

> And then times come again, times of break-down and misfortune in which our people are only held together by their history. Then they will wake up — the dead, the mighty army of the dead. Then they will march to the great roll call of their people. Then their names will be called, individuals, man by man, the ones who were unknown until now, the nameless ones . . . Then their old flags will wave, ghostlike; then a song will be heard, an old song, the legacy of Langemarck. Then they will take the lead as holy leaders, showing their people the way — the way across the abyss. (193)

With the "outer and inner order" Karl Stanz "awakens, . . . passionate and very clear-headed," to do his duty — and with him, Zerkaulen hopes — , the audience in the theater and the entire German people. Of course few realized at the time that this legacy led not over the abyss, but into it.

On November 9, 1933, the day commemorating Langemarck and the Hitler putsch in Munich, the piece was performed for the first time on a number of stages simultaneously in Dresden, Bremen, Kassel, Darmstadt, Halle, Lübeck, Hagen, Greifswald, Beuthen, and Bonn. At many locations, the premiere, just as that of the *Schlageter* drama, was associated with a celebration of national remembrance that began by honoring the dead of Langemarck; student fraternities in full regalia often participated.[21] The dramatic weaknesses that this play contains to a much greater extent than *Schlageter* were overlooked by many critics in favor of the heroic national content, on account of which the play took its place next to Johst's *Schlageter* or Bethge's *Marsch der Veteranen* (March of the Veterans).

Not only the fate of the dead, but also that of the living front-line fighters were dramatized by *völkisch*, national, conservative authors. In contrast to the left-wing liberal critics of how veterans were treated in the Weimar Republic, such as Georg Grosz or Ernst Toller, who view veterans as the victims of capitalist intrigues, right-wing authors accuse the Weimar Republic of a lack of *völkisch* convictions favorable to the fatherland because it ignores the former front-line soldiers. One of these national authors is Friedrich Bethge, himself a veteran of the war, who treats his own experiences in his play *Marsch der Veteranen* (original title: *Hungermarsch der Veteranen* (Hunger March of the Veterans) in order to once again gain attention and respect for the spirit of the front. As Bethge reports in the preface to the play, a newspaper report of April of 1932 from the United States and Gogol's novel *Dead Souls* served as the source material for his play.[22] In April of 1932, American war veterans went to the White House in Washington to demonstrate in a peaceful manner for the improvement of their situation. They were driven away with tanks and tear gas, but found respite on the estate of a patroness in Maryland. "For the National Socialist and front-line soldier, this had to be the perfect material for drama," Bethge explains (196). As the result of "coincidentally reading Gogol at the very moment when planning the drama, Bethge decided, because of the similarity of the material, to move his drama to the time of Napoleonic Russia, "in order to gain temporal and artistic distance" (197). To portray Petersburg society, Bethge borrowed from Tolstoy's *War and Peace;* the Prussian Governor General is modeled on the American Chief of the General Staff, Douglas MacArthur. Schiller's *Räuber* (Robbers) and Hauptmann's *Weber* (Weavers) were also literary godparents. Despite all the historicizing, it always remains clear that Bethge means the front-line soldiers during the Weimar Republic and wants to illuminate their fate from a national perspective.

The play is divided into three acts. Former front-line soldiers of the czar, among them some with limbs shot to bits, ask the minister in the czarist capital Petersburg for money so that they can live. For those in power, however, everything else is more important. When the veterans are repeatedly put off until a later time, they take their fate into their own hands. Acting as "noble robbers" under the leadership of the cadet sergeant Ottoff, they ambush a czarist money transport to recover their "outstanding pay." Taken to task by the leader of the escort, his former captain Kopejkin, Ottoff replies to the question of what kind of men the "robbers" are: "Soldiers — shot until unfit — starving — coarsened — down at the heels — yet soldiers! But they are not to blame — only the luminaries in Petersburg [are]! — A curse on those who allow soldiers to go hungry!" (219). Ottoff proposes a provocative solution to the veteran problem: "*Shoot all the soldiers when the war is over — and the citizen will have peace!!*" (219). In the melee, one of the robbers by the name of Georgieff is killed; now all the veterans — both the robbers and the escort — kneel down by the dead man. Next to the body of their dead comrade, they all praise "obedience, honor, loyalty to the death" (220). Captain Kopejkin becomes the leader of their common cause: "I will not yield from the common cause, nor yield from honor; [I will] not keep company with the luminaries of the Empire, who are responsible this death, for the misery, so help me God!" (220). Ottoff, however, goes a separate way from him: "The ways part but not the goal" (220). Ottoff wants immediate action; Kopejkin wants to wait until the movement is stronger. The dramatic conflict is thus defined. Some veterans secretly decide in favor of Ottoff, but most stand by Kopejkin: "We will follow you — to the death" (221). With the body of the dead soldier Georgieff, the band goes to the capital to execute the last will of the dead soldier Georgieff, who accompanies them as a martyr: "He lives! — He is in our midst!" (221).

The second act is set in the palace of the Minister Smerkoff. His daughter Lisaweta sings a "simple and touching" folksong. The governor, a former Prussian officer, is moved: "A folksong like that goes to the heart — even of the soldier! But not the music of the salon, where people insanely outdo themselves lying" (223). Outside below the windows the marching song of the veterans becomes audible — "blind men, one-armed men, men with one leg on crutches":

> In steinernen Palästen
> Ihr Mächtigen, merkt auf!
> Halt' ein in euern Festen,
> Hier nimmt es seinen Lauf.
> Feld, Äcker, euch zu Frone,
> Sie tranken unsern Tod;
> Jetzt fordern wir zu Lohne:
> Gebt uns der Felder Brot! (224)

> [In stone palaces,
> You, the mighty, pay attention!
> Stop your festivities,
> Here it takes its course.
> Fields, farmland, in your service
> They drank our death;
> Now we are asking in return:
> Give us, of the fields, bread!]

In the palace unrest spreads; the estate owner, Baron Plassinoff, who recently had "a thousand hectares of wheat and corn burned," "to prevent a fall in prices" (224) wants to have the veterans riddled with bullets. The minister tries to divide the veterans and play them off against each other: Ottoff against Kopejkin. If Ottoff's group can be successfully provoked to use force, then the minister has cause to intervene. Kopejkin is for peaceful negotiation. The only one on the side of the government who seriously attempts to solve the problem of the veterans is the governor — but then he was a Prussian officer before he became a Russian general.

The third and final act takes place in the tent camp of the veterans in front of the palace of the minister. While Kopejkin negotiates inside the palace, Ottoff, to whom Kopejkin, conciliatory and trusting, had turned over the command, kills Plassinoff, who has been insulting the veterans. Only the refusal of the line troops to shoot disabled veterans can prevent a blood bath. When Kopejkin has Ottoff arrested, Ottoff shoots him as a traitor. Kopejkin dies, a "blood witness" for the demands of the veterans. The veterans move to Lisaweta's estate, and to add emphasis to their demands, threaten to "always come back."

Like Johst's *Schlageter* and Zerkaulen's *Langemarck,* Bethge invokes the comradely spirit of the front in the hope that it will form a community of the people that overcomes all divisions. In each of the three plays, dead comrades, fashioned into martyrs, are supposed to arouse the emotions of the audience and to have the effect of providing examples. Unlike Johst and Zerkaulen, Bethge does not start with concrete events that still remain in the memories of contemporaries. Nevertheless, *Marsch der Veteranen* became Bethge's most successful play. The premiere, with a newly revised script, took place in 1935 in Augsburg (January 30) and Frankfurt am Main (February 2). Despite initially reserved reviews, the play was staged in over sixty theaters. After it was performed during the Munich Theater Weeks in 1936, it became one of the "main dramas of the new movement."[23] In awarding the National Book Prize to Bethge, Goebbels, the Minister for Enlightenment and Propaganda, stated on May 1, 1937: "The *Marsch der Veteranen* is a song of praise for Prussian breeding and soldierly obedience . . . *Marsch der Veteranen* can be considered a first fortunate realization of the stage writing sought by National Socialist culture policies."[24] Viewed from the standpoint of literature and drama, Johst's *Schlageter* is undoubtedly the most successful of the three works discussed, even if Johst was not the "great German poet" whom he thought himself to be.[25]

The ideological goal of these plays was the formation of a national community of the people, with the leaders and the led, from the comradely spirit of the front to which all class thinking was subordinated, so that the legacy of the dead and the veterans of the First World War could take effect — in conscious opposition to the middle-class, democratic Weimar Republic. The spirit of the front was, as Bethge put it in 1937, the "basic experience of the dramatist," especially in the first phase of National Socialist theater.[26] The dramas presented here are only a small selection from a wealth of plays with the spirit-of-the-front theme, such as Eberhard Wolfgang Möller's *Douaumont oder die Heimkehr des Soldaten Odysseus* (Douaumont or the Return Home of the Soldier Odysseus, 1929), Richard Euringer's *Deutsche Passion* (German Passion, 1932), Hans Rehberg's *Preußische Komödie* (Prussian Comedy, 1932), Paul Joseph Cremer's *Die Marneschlacht* (The Battle on the Marne, 1933), Sigmund Graff's and Carl Ernst Hintze's

Die endlose Straße (The Endless Street, 1928), Edwin Erich Dwinger's *Wo ist Deutschland* (Where is Germany, 1934; based on his 1932 novel *Wir rufen Deutschland* [We Call to Germany]), and Kurt Kluge's *Ewiges Volk* (Eternal People, 1933). The same themes that Zöberlein or Jünger treated in novels appear here under the stage lights. The spirit of the front is, after all, the leitmotif underlying Hitler's *Mein Kampf*. It is apparent that the legacy of the dead comrades is at the same time being used as preparation for a new war, for example, when in the plays the joyful death of a martyr for the community of the people replaces the natural fear of death. The army of the men killed in action marches with the living; the partition separating life and death is to be torn down: "Thus, death passes over into life."[27] The paradox from Zerkaulen's *Langemarck*, "We die in order to live," is transformed into a national, mystical, military ancestor cult, a *völkisch* religion replacing "soft" Christianity, whose vocabulary is nevertheless used frequently, for example in *Schlageter*, where the hero is taken to the "place of skulls [Calvary]." However, the longed-for community of the people remained an idle wish-dream, or was consciously used as a means of misleading gullible people. In reality, the capitalist economic system with its division into classes continued to exist even under the Nazis. Bethge pilloried the rapacious capitalist Baron Plassinoff and gave him his just desserts, but even Zerkaulen's *Langemarck* play, certainly unintentionally on the part of the author, bears witness in the example of the Gärtner family's factory, to the power and significance of capitalist businesses.

National Socialist Dramas in Historical Garb

The virtues that were associated with the spirit of the front and were highly praised by the National Socialists, that is, the readiness to die, the willingness to sacrifice oneself, courage, loyalty, faith, and heroism, believed lost in the Weimar Republic, were sought and found not only in the First World War and the following period of struggle, but especially in the early epochs of German history. The period of a new beginning and re-orientation in the "political theater of the seizure of power" was followed in 1935–1936 by a marked shift toward historical material or "historically draped contemporary plays."[28] In going back to historical material, with a preference for great personalities that supposedly possess special characteristics, the drama was intended to lend the Third Reich historical legitimacy. It was by no means a flight from history. In *Weg zum Reich* (The Way to the Reich, 1940), published by the *Reichsführer* of the SS, the following was written:

> And the new Reich, the beginning of which we are witnessing, is, after decades of decline and degeneration, erecting the new building of the nation on the foundation of its life and its mission. We now understand

why the leading men of the new state repeatedly refer to the prehistory and early history of our people as the foundation of the new building.[29]

For the National Socialist scholar of literature, Hermann Wanderscheck, the historical drama starts with Hegel, for whom "the historical location for the political drama" is "at the great historical turning points, where the individual human being either performs the tasks of world history or is the tool of forces working counter to them."[30] Accordingly, Wanderscheck requires the following:

> Therefore, for the national theater only those political and historical dramas are foreordained and meaningful that represent the great personality who shapes fate or suffers its blows, who shapes the conception of the world or destroys it, as a phenomenon that comes about at a time of transformation in politics and intellectual history.[31]

The National Socialist historical drama returns to the roots of the "German racial soul" and follows its struggle against disintegration and alienation by forces "foreign to its nature" such as Christianity (especially in its Papal-Catholic version), capitalism, democracy, and Judaism. As Breßlein shows, the National Socialist historical dramas are concentrated at certain historical junctures:

> A guided tour through the drama landscape could begin with Widukind, encounter Walter von der Vogelweide and Henry the Lion, has to stop at Henry IV and his disputes with Pope Gregory VII, must consider Henry VI on his field campaigns in Sicily, comes to Luther and the Peasant Wars, [and] with early Prussian figures enters a new phase that reaches its high point with Frederick II and its low point with Jena and the conditions in 1806–1807, the low point at the same time providing a new sign of hope in the rise of the Baron von Stein and other Prussian reforms; the tour must consider General von Yorck and Heinrich von Kleist, and it ends first with the efforts to resolve Germany's national question using authoritarian Prussian means counter to the bourgeois, democratic tradition, that supposedly was the ambition of all true Germans in the nineteenth century.[32]

Consequently, Martin Luther,[33] Ulrich von Hutten,[34] Thomas Münzer,[35] the Prussian General York[36] from the Napoleonic wars of liberation, Heinrich von Kleist,[37] Emperor Henry IV,[38] and particularly the Prussian rulers,[39] were especially popular. Added to that were several deserving Germans abroad, such as Jakob Leisler,[40] as well as the "honorary German" leaders and founders of empires Oliver Cromwell[41] and Thomas Paine.[42]

Emperor Henry IV proved to be shaping fate and suffering its blows at the same time in his journey of sacrifice in 1077 to Pope Gregory VII in Canossa. As indicated, this story was dramatized several times, most forcefully by Erwin Guido Kolbenheyer in his play *Gregor und Heinrich* (Gregory and Henry), which he dedicated to the "German spirit in the process of being resurrected." It was written in the years 1933–1934 and was performed simultaneously in Dresden, Mannheim, Hanover, Erfurt, Königberg, and Karlsruhe on October 18, 1934.

In *Gregor und Heinrich,* Kolbenheyer represents the struggle for the Empire, a theme that was particularly topical after 1933, as carried on by the young Henry IV against Rome. In contrast to the traditional interpretation, Kolbenheyer transforms Henry's pilgrimage to Canossa, around which the drama centers, from a defeat into a victory for Henry and the Empire. National Socialist historiography then also took over this interpretation. The story, written by Kolbenheyer in the language of that early time, is divided into five acts, each of which is divided in turn into several scenes.

The monk Hildebrand, who has just become Pope Gregory, intends to consolidate the power of Rome over the Empire before Henry IV becomes too strong. At issue is power over the world; the decision is between "the Apostolic See or the throne of the barbarians on the other side of the mountains."[43] Gregory, too, seeks to gain the favor of the people: "Only from the fervor of the people can the Church be elevated . . . In the breath of their voices, in the flash of their eyes, [and] in the pulsing of their blood lies the salvation of the Church" (256). If Henry succeeds in bringing the princes and the people over to his side, "the work of elevating the Holy Church is lost, and it will remain the maidservant of the world, the Church, which is destined to be the sole ruler" (272).

After his victory over the Saxons, Henry appears to be at the peak of his power. He wants to use the opportunity to overcome the obstinacy of the princes and together with them build the German Empire: "My lords, we have a victory, and out of this victory shall arise the Holy Empire of the German Nation" (284). Henry invokes the providential dispensation of the hour: "God has placed us in this hour, which our destiny shall take by force, through us!" (284). He sees the Empire threatened by the Pope in Rome, who is reaching out for it: "That will never happen; that someone outside the Empire is reaching out his hand and touching the Empire in the every man's breast and is placing his hand on the Crown with foreign power, intending to use force" (284). Most of the princes, however, are thinking of their own advantage. Henry nevertheless takes up the fight with Rome and in a brilliant scene has Pope Gregory cursed out in Rome through an envoy. In response, Gregory hurls the ban of the Church against Henry. Thereupon the princes refuse to serve him and convince him to undertake the pilgrimage to the Pope. As the proud Henry considers going to Rome with military might and the support of his Lombard vassals, Bishop Benno von Osnabrück warns him: "Lord Henry, the Empire will not be won with foreign weapons. And even if he were master of all the world, the German king will not win his Empire; it must be won with German arms in the German way" (313). Instead of force of arms, he recommends penitential clothing, for by humbling himself he will be raised. The Pope must grant a penitent expiation; otherwise he is denying his Christianity. Henry is supposed to overcome his opponent Gregory with this strategy. Henry follows this advice, divests himself of all splendor, and goes in a snowstorm over the pass of Mount Cenis to Italy, as all other roads are blocked. In great misery and humiliation, Heinrich's consort Berta realizes that the Empire will only be formed from inside and with difficulty by chosen individuals: "It is God who does not intend for a person to have an empire unless he has it within himself . . . The night of this road is imposed upon us so that the Empire might grow from you in the light of day, [the Empire] which you unbeknownst have born within your breast" (318). In a similar fashion, Hitler felt that he was chosen and capable, with the idea of the Reich in his heart, of passing through the darkness of the Weimar Republic, the "transition empire" (according to Wanderscheck) toward the bright light that breaks with his seizure of power on January 30, 1933; small wonder that *per aspera ad astra* (through difficulties, to the stars) became a popular saying in the Third Reich.

In the fifth and final act the play reaches its climax in the encounter of Henry and Gregory and their struggle for the German Empire; everything else is secondary to that. For Gregory, the struggle with Henry is of absolutely critical importance for his rule and for the supremacy of the Roman Church; for "on the other side of the northern mountains is the foundation to which the ship of the Church is anchored. Rome is the building, but the foundation, . . . the foundation is Germania. Thence, from the spring of barbarian youth, flows the new humanity" (325). It is Gregory's intention to force Henry to his knees and to defeat him at an imperial diet in Augsburg. But that does not happen; in Canossa, the proud Henry subdues himself and in a three-day pilgrimage, barefoot and in penitent's clothing his adversary as well. Yet Gregory has recognized — according to Kolbenheyer — that Henry is not really coming to him as a penitent sinner: "You do not seek the peace of your soul! You want the Empire!" (327). Driven into a corner by the apparently penitent Henry, Gregory cannot deny him forgiveness and thus the Empire. Henry leaves feeling certain of the results:

> The *Empire* has become powerful in me and strong . . . Let me go in peace, Bishop of Rome, to found *my* Empire on this man Henry . . . The Kingdom of Christ has a body and soul, be the master and refuge of the soul, Bishop of Rome, and leave to the King what is the King's. (334)

Although Kolbenheyer's reinterpretation of history cannot be sustained — Canossa *was* a defeat for the Emperor — the effectiveness of the play on a dramatic, theatrical level cannot be denied. The material contains dramatic conflict, and Kolbenheyer represents Gregory as an equal to Henry, without lapsing into a trite representation strictly in terms of black and white. In this drama, Kolbenheyer is concerned with far more than simply establishing Henry's diplomatic victory; he is concerned with the overall fate of Nordic-Germanic existence. For him, Canossa is "one of the heroic events of history," for

> what is dramatic about the extraordinary event is that, in an overwhelming historical act, the core essence of the middle countries for the first time in a scope that can be called European went up against our race's Nordic-Germanic essence in an intellectual decision; at stake here was subordination of the north, which probably would have led to a completely different development of the Empire and the people. The decision, however, went in favor of the German core essence ("Wesen").[44]

Of course the Nazis also saw the German essence, which was to bring about the world's recovery, threatened by the Romanic French, and naturally, the Jews and the Slavs.

The Nazis interpreted Kolbenheyer's play as an "illustrative allegory" for the fateful battle of the German people in which they were now engaged. Contemporary critics certified "that the poet who wrote this drama of the soul . . . that this German creator had penetrated deep into the essence of our German *völkisch* nature"[45] — deeper yet than Paul Ernst, who was highly respected by the Nazis, had done in his Canossa play.[46] For Wanderscheck, Kolbenheyer's *Gregor und Heinrich* is "the most essential, and for the drama of the present, the most significant play. . . . As a political drama, Kolbenheyer's forceful dramatic chess game belongs in the very first rank of responsible historical drama of the present."[47]

An astonishing number of Nazi dramas are set in America or go back to American material — for example, Bethge's *Marsch der Veteranen,* Hanns Johst's *Thomas Paine* (according to Wanderscheck, "the first political drama of the new Germany"[48]), Eberhard Wolfgang Möller's *Kalifornische Tragödie* (California Tragedy), about Jakob Suter, whose farm is trampled by greedy gold seekers, and Curt Langenbeck's *Der Hochverräter* (The Man Who Committed High Treason), a play about the German American Jakob Leisler, whose fate is also portrayed by Hans Friedrich Blunck in his drama *Kampf um New York* (Battle for New York, 1938) and his novel by the same name in 1951.

With Jakob Leisler, Langenbeck was taking up a subject from the prehistory and early history of New York. Jakob Leisler, the son of a minister of the Frankfurt-Bockenheim reformed congregation, came to New Amsterdam in 1660 as a soldier in the service of the Dutch West Indies Company. As a merchant, he gained respect and wealth in the city, which would be captured a few years later by the English and renamed "New York." After William of Orange, a Protestant, ended the rule of Jacob II of the House of Stewart, a strict Catholic, in the Glorious Revolution of 1688, there was also unrest in the colonies. The English General Governor in Boston was sent back to England, his deputy in New York, Nicholson, was arrested, and Leisler, as the leader of the Protestants, was selected to be governor and was to lead the government until the new

English governor arrived. Nicholson carried on intrigues in London against Leisler and with the help of the Loyalists arranged to have him murdered. The plot was unsuccessful, and the leaders of the uprising, Bayard and Nicholls, were sentenced to death for their participation, but were pardoned by Leisler. When the new English governor Henry Sloughter finally arrived in New York, he had Leisler arrested for high treason and had him executed in 1691. In 1695, Leisler was completely rehabilitated by an English commission of inquiry and was buried with all honors in the Dutch cemetery in 1698. As the 300th anniversary of German immigration was celebrated in 1983, one of his descendents, Walter Leisler Kiep, a West German politician belonging to the Christian Democratic Union, laid a wreath on his grave. With the "awakening of the German people's soul" after 1933, when interest in the German abroad was heightened, the Leisler story once again became topical and was taken up by two prominent National Socialist writers: Hans Friedrich Blunck in his drama *Kampf um New York* (Battle for New York, 1938) and Curt Langenbeck in *Der Hochverräter* (The Man Who Committed High Treason, 1938).

In his "tragic play," Langenbeck follows the external course of events rather closely, pouring the story into a strictly traditional mold, mostly iambic hexameter following the Greek drama, and dividing it into seventeen scenes, which according to his directions were to be played through without an intermission in about two and one-half hours. The classic unities of place — the docks in New York, time — a few days in 1691, and action are maintained. The tightness of the action is also underlined by the stage sets: "The architecture is to be in broad outlines and severe."[49] In spite of the historical material, clear connection to the present is demanded: "Historical accuracy (in costumes as well) is not desirable" (381).

At the beginning of the play, Jakob Leisler is waiting restlessly, but with complete trust in the English king, for the arrival of the new governor. Leisler is no rebel, but a true servant of his master: "Meine Pflicht ist, das Errungene / Dem König zu verteidigen [My duty is to defend for the king / what has been won]" (384). Leisler has enemies, especially his antagonist Cornelius Nicholls, whom Leisler has put in chains because Nicholls was involved in the murder attempt against him. Leisler's daughter Meisje, once Nicholls's beloved, tries in vain to mediate. As three English frigates are sighted, Leisler has the actions taken against Nicholls, which are meant to promote order, confirmed by the city elders: "Immer bedarf ein Führer der Gnade / Mehr als die andern, die ihn nur tun sehn, / Und sein Gebet verteidigt dem *Helden* / Sieg und Schuld [A leader always needs mercy / More than the others, who only see him act, / And his prayer defends the *hero's* / Victory and blame]" (387). Leisler wants Nicholls to withdraw his letter to the king, as it represents an insult to the king. But Nicholls refuses, as Leisler was not appointed by the king. Leisler accuses Nicholls of failing to cooperate and of inciting the people. Nicholls and Leisler embody the dramatic conflict between business and morals:

Nicholls is the deal-making intriguer without conscience; Leisler, on the other hand, is the honest moralist acting in good faith. To Nicholls, only success counts, particularly in business. Leisler detests that attitude; to him, it cannot serve as the basis for a new world:

> Das seh ich, seh's mit Abscheu! Aber Nicholls, *nicht*
> In diesem Zeichen soll die neue Welt erwachsen,
> Im Zeichen dieses hündischen Erfolges nicht!
> Denn sie soll gut sein. Von Europas Laster frei. (390)

> [I see that, see it with disgust! But Nicholls, *not*
> Under this sign should the new world grow,
> Under the sign of this abject success!
> For it should be good. Free of Europe's encumbrance.]

Nicholls has only disdain for Leisler's belief in the good in man; he is a cynical egoist: "Man is bad!/ Miserably bad is his world" (390).

The three frigates, however, do not bring the governor, as hoped, but only an advance party under Major Ingoldsby, who scornfully refuses to see Leisler's messenger Sergeant Joost Stoll. Portentous clouds gather, but Leisler considers everything a misunderstanding; he wants to personally pass command of the fort and the city to the governor. Asked by Meisje for advice and assistance, the elders of the city answer in the manner of the chorus in a Greek tragedy, interpreting the course of events:

> Keinem ehrlichen Mann ist gegönnt,
> Großen Gewinn zu haben auf Erden und
> Herrschendes Dasein, wenn nicht die Fackel ihm
> Des Leidens vor der Seele glüht. (400)

> [No honorable man is granted
> To have great gain on earth and
> A life of rule, if not the torch of suffering
> Does blaze before his soul.]

In the style of a Greek oracle, the first elder predicts a gloomy future:

> Wehe sage ich voraus und blutige Torheit,
> Denn feigwütender Frevel liegt eingezeugt
> Uraltersher, und wer noch das Rechte will,
> Lebt dem Verhängnis am nächsten. (400)

> [Woe I prophecy and bloody folly,
> For cowardly raging wickedness is there, bred in
> From ancient times, and whoever wants right,
> Lives closest to calamity.]

In this way Leisler's role is, after the model of the ancient tragedy, elevated to the extreme heights of the fated hero — as Langenbeck already suggests in the motto of the play, which is borrowed from Aeschylus: "Who would be without suffering."

Ingolsby also meets Leisler only with arrogance and disdain. All of Leisler's conciliation attempts fail; they collide, as both sides consider themselves the rightful representative of the Crown. Again the elders of the city, functioning as a chorus, accompany the action in order to elevate it to the level of fate and timelessness. In the instant in which Leisler knocks Ingolsby to the ground, the rightful governor, Sir Henry Sloughter, arrives, has Leisler arrested, and executed, together with Stoll, who had stabbed the mocking Ingolsby to death. Even Meisje's pleas no longer help; the tragedy moves relentlessly towards the conclusion. Mcisjc swcars to now devote her life to honoring the memory of her executed father:

> So will ich leben . . .
> Nicht Blüte mehr noch Frucht; nur Leiden und Gehorsam;
> Ihm, der durch Schuld geheiligt steht, die Ehre pflegen
> Und Balsam aus so bittrem Tod, der mich zerreißt,
> Herniederbringen in die Qual der armen Menschen.
> Vernichtet, wie ich bin, kann ich doch *sein* und dienen. (436)

> [I want to live thus . . .
> No longer blossom nor fruit; only suffering and obedience;
> Tend to the honor of him who is sainted by blame,
> And balsam from so bitter a death, which rends me asunder,
> Bring down to the misery of the poor human beings.
> Destroyed as I am, yet can I *be* and serve.]

Leisler accepts his sentence as the punishment for his lack of humility, but not for his deeds. He dies knowing that he has been chosen by fate to be a martyr for loyalty and performance of duty, and that his sacrifice will ignite a sacred fire in the people for centuries to come:

> Gott steht gewaltig hier in unsrer Mitte glühend,
> Und recht ist, was durch ihn mit uns geschieht für alle,
> In denen Edelmut und tapfre Würde nicht
> Verschüttet wurde von dem Grimm der bösen Zeiten!
> Es gibt noch Wunder, künd ich euch, ihr
> Menschenskinder! Und nichts ist euch verloren noch geraubt, solang
> Mein Schicksal wie ein Opferfeuer brennt und Herzen
> Versammelt, die es hegen wollen für ihr Volk. (437)

[Mighty God stands in our midst, glowing,
And right is what happens to us through him for all
In whom nobility and brave dignity were not
Buried by the fury of evil times!
There are still miracles, I tell you, you
Children of man! And naught is lost or stolen from you, as long as
My fate burns like a sacrificial flame and collects
Hearts that want to tend it for their people!]

Like Schlageter, he dies from the bullets of the firing squad, but instead of "Germany awake," his last words are "Hail, New York!" The play closes with the commentary of the elders, who again broaden what has happened to the heroic, timeless, and universal:

> Hart büßen die Guten,
> Weil sie nicht besser waren.
> Grausam zu sterben,
> Werden sie gerufen
> Und zahlen mit Leiden
> Für die andern mit.
> Schmachvoll aber ist,
> Nicht gerufen werden.
> Seinen Helden
> Hat der Herr
> Mit heiligem Lächeln
> Ewig Gedächtnis
> Schützend gestiftet. (437–38)

> [The good pay the penalty,
> Because they were not better.
> They are called
> To die cruelly
> And to pay with suffering
> For the others as well.
> But it is dishonor
> Not to be called.
> To his heroes
> The Lord has,
> With a holy smile,
> Protectively granted
> Eternal remembrance.]

The present version of the drama is the third, as the author states in the *Frankfurter Braune Blätter* (Frankfurt Brown Pages) of 1938–1939. From version to version, he reduced the number of characters, shortened the period of time that the play covers, and tightened the artistic form.[50] After 1945, Langenbeck published his play *Der Hochverräter* as resistance literature, with the rationale that he had portrayed the character of Ingoldsby as a Party boss.[51] In returning to the strict form of the Greek tragedy, he had attempted to revive contemporary drama. In his work about drama theory, *Wiedergeburt des Dramas aus dem Geist der Zeit* (Rebirth of the Drama from the Spirit of the Times, 1940), he wrote, among other things, about the meaning of tragedy: "That is the meaning of tragedy: to show the human being how he is most lost; how he can be pitched into misfortune, *not although*, but *because* he has every intention of doing right." Left to his own devices, "he must accomplish everything that he believes to have been instructed [to do] by himself, with his willingness to sacrifice, with his reliability and strength and humility."[52] After years of decline, Langenbeck saw himself at a historical turning point at which the people were prepared "to get back to their origins again, and sensitive and obedient enough for a new *völkisch* religion."[53] The historical turning point is of course 1933, and the bringer of the doctrine of salvation is Adolf Hitler, who illustrated to the Germans their fate. The premiere of the play took place simultaneously in Düsseldorf and Erfurt on March 15, 1938.

The germ cell of the Third Reich was, in the view of the National Socialists, the Prussian state. It is therefore not surprising that numerous authors attempted to dramatize Prussian material. Among them, Hans Rehberg, with his Prussian cycle, is the most prominent figure. Together with Möller and Langenbeck, Rehberg is recognized as a "politically and historically indispensable dramatist in the new mold" who "is fighting for the renewal of theater."[54] In contrast to Langenbeck, who follows the traditions of antiquity, Rehberg takes Shakespeare as his model: "Rehberg, however, declared himself in favor of a modern Shakespeare theater with extreme demonic intensity."[55] Rehberg was a nationalist and had been a member of the NSDAP since 1930; however, his Prussian dramas did not completely fit the heroic image of the Prussian ruler promoted by the National Socialists. He was a quite willful dramatist and therefore highly controversial. On April 6, 1938, the *Berliner Börsen-Zeitung* (Berlin Financial Newspaper) wrote: "There is probably no other German dramatist of the present about whom such a battle of opinions has raged as about Hans Rehberg and the works in his Hohenzollern series.[56] It even reached the point where Alfred Rosenberg declared: "Rehberg is without doubt a gifted dramatist, but he does not want to bend, even though we have often warned him. It is time; he must be throttled."[57] However, Hanns Johst, Josef Goebbels, and especially the actor/director Gustav Gründgens held their protective hands over him.

For propagandists of the Third Reich, Frederick the Great, besides Bismarck, was an immediate predecessor of Hitler; they all founded a German empire under one leader. How pale in contrast seemed the Weimar Republic under Ebert, as Hitler remarked in *Mein Kampf:* "As long as the historical memory of Frederick II as an example has not died out, Friedrich Ebert will only be able to stimulate very limited attention. The hero of Sanssouci is to the former Bremen pub owner as the sun is to the moon; only when the rays of the sun are extinguished is the moon able to shine."[58] Alfred Rosenberg expressed similar views in his main work, *Der Mythus des 20. Jahrhunderts* (The Myth of the Twentieth Century, 1930): "It is no coincidence when today in particular, in the midst of a new, terrible plunge into the abyss, the figure of Frederick the Great appears to shine with a radiant luster."[59] For Rosenberg, it is precisely this Prussian ruler who embodies all of the virtues of genuine Germanness and of the German "racial soul":

> Personal bravery, inexorable resolution, a sense of responsibility, penetrating intelligence, and a sense of honor, as was never before with such mythical greatness chosen to be the guiding star of an entire life . . . The face of Pericles and the head of Frederick the Great are two symbols for the range of a racial soul and of an ideal of beauty that originated from the same racial equivalent.[60]

It is therefore quite obvious that Frederick the Great would be praised to German youth as a leading figure. Even in defeat, Frederick was invoked, especially his most difficult hour after the defeat of Kunersdorf in 1759. When Roosevelt died on April 12, 1945, some Nazis believed this was a turning point similar to that after the death of the Czarina in the Seven Years War.

Rehberg's Prussian dramas are to be seen, and judged, against this background, including the last play of the cycle, *Der siebenjährige Krieg* (The Seven Years' War), written in 1936–1937. In it, Frederick the Great by no means appears as the superhuman hero figure who spouts pithy national maxims. To the contrary, at a masked ball in the Breslau palace, he appears in a Don Quixote costume wearing a coat with windmill blades (II, 2). On the other hand, it should be considered that the historical course of the Seven Years War was not exactly suited to emphasize Friedrich's heroic greatness with a radiant victor's pose. Even Frederick's entire skill as a field commander would not have protected Prussia from defeat, if several strokes of luck had not come to his aid, especially the death of Czarina Elisabeth. After the defeat at Kunersdorf, for example, Rehberg's Frederick thought seriously about suicide. And yet in his drama Rehberg lets Frederick's greatness shine through; pulling entire peoples with him, he is great in his downfall — like Phaeton from Greek mythology, to whom reference is made several times in the play. Furthermore, Frederick, who suffers with his people, proves to possess exemplary human greatness. That is also how the prologue is to be understood, which states in part:

Anders der Genius!
Ihn zwingen die Flügel!
Aber gewaltiger noch
Zwingt er sie wieder.
Ihm leuchtet die Sonne!
Aber gewaltiger noch
Stürmt er ins Dunkel.[61]

[Different, the Genius!
Wings compel him!
But more forcefully still
He compels them back.
The sun lights his way!
But more forcefully still
He storms into darkness.]

Rehberg assumes thorough knowledge of the historical events so that his play can focus more on the internal action and commentary to the action, which causes Wanderscheck to remark critically: "A 'Seven Years War' calls for an outstanding director concerned with stage position, such as Gustav Gründgens, who creates action, whereas Rehberg only provides commentary to the action."[62] It is precisely the commentaries and allusions, as well as the frequent change of scene from the Prussian camp to the Austrian and Russian camps that make the play difficult to access.

The play begins with Frederick's darkest hour, the loss of the Battle of Kunersdorf in 1759. In an impressive beginning scene, the events of the war are recounted from the point of view of the body-strippers who are robbing the corpses in the darkness after the battle and in the process encounter the victor, the Austrian General Laudon. He laments the dead and his failure to achieve total victory because the Russians did not place at his disposal the soldiers necessary to pursue the beaten Prussian king. He did not succeed, as Baron Starhemberg comments in the second scene, "in catching the sun" (447). Laudon hates Frederick, who once rejected him, and wants to destroy him, the king and the person. For that reason he had the Phaeton letter, which was captured on the battlefield, sent to Frederick; in it, Henry, the king's brother, expresses his despair: "Phaeton has fallen," a sentence that the beaten Frederick cannot forget. His officer, Ewald von Kleist, attempts to console him in the pain of defeat:

His fate, Your Majesty, nevertheless changed a world. Peoples were destroyed, became ashes; mountains burned. But the impertinent doubters of his time had to admit: He is the son of the god Helios! Unlucky, yes, but proving his descent from the gods to all the world, Phaeton was a god. And when on a headstone, Your Majesty, the words "Not completely victorious, he died of the great effort" are written, future

generations will know that one of Phaeton's linage lies here, and he
changed a world. And no one who reveres human greatness in his heart
will continue on his way without respect. (452)

Kleist assures his king that the army now as ever believes in the genius of the
king. The Jews will supply the necessary money through their international
connections, as the "one-eyed Jew Ephraim" assures, if only the profit is
right. These words give Frederick new courage; he assembles his generals to
hear from them whether they have the strength to conquer Silesia, especially
in battle against Russia, "for Russia under the Czarina Elisabeth, General, is
a nightmare, death, if she does not die soon. The others are only enemies;
she is fate" (456). His brother Henry advises peace; Frederick becomes
indignant: "Anyone who feels in his heart that life could be lived without
victory, I will not keep. I have enough means to take my friends along in my
misfortune" (457). However, Frederick displays human greatness; he for-
gives his brother for the Phaeton letter: "My respect for your military genius
allows me to forget Phaeton" (458). His soul wants to mourn, also because
he once had to take the command away from his brother August William
because of his incompetence. But now he must remain hard: "Fall later, soul,
control your mourning, put on your laurels which I hung on your walls"
(459). Frederick's human greatness also becomes evident when he wants to
reconcile the young Austrian officer Count Starhemberg with his General
Laudon, Frederick's worst enemy. Rehberg places this human victory above
victory in battle, for which many Nazis could not forgive him:

> O, if this century curses you, Frederick, and does not grasp your dig-
> nity, if this century can only view your wild deeds through the cloudy
> glass of the suffering that you imposed on it, Germans will one day
> proclaim your humanity to all the world. And over and over, eternally,
> until the day when trumpets are put to lips to announce the departure
> of the last of this godly lineage and of the German people. Victory!
> What is victory in battle?! Prescient General Laudon! You must reach
> still higher and knock the stars together. (462)

How deplorable, in contrast, seems the atmosphere at the corrupt and
dissipated court of the czar. The Czarina Elisabeth drinks, whores, and loves
other women. Czarina Catherine II, who took over the government after the
short rule of her husband Peter III, does not prove to be much better. The
death of Elisabeth brings new hope, especially when Peter III, who is
friendly towards Germany, assumes the throne. Even after Peter's murder,
the Russian General Tschernitscheff promises the Prussian king to keep his
troops out of the battle. Austria, just as exhausted as Prussia, offers peace
and the surrender of Silesia, whereupon Frederick immediately thinks about
aid for the devastated Silesian regions. At the end of the play, Frederick gives
his enemy Laudon his hand in reconciliation.

The last two acts, summarized here very briefly, also contain a number of theatrically effective scenes, such as the boyar dance before Czarina Elisabeth, with Prussian sounds mixed in and at which a dancer in the mask of Frederick shows up and Elisabeth has him shot to death on the spot, or the masked party in the Breslau palace, with a commentary by two harlequins.

Worthy of note and significant in the framework of National Socialist ideology is the second encounter between Frederick and his brother Henry in the third scene of the second act. The English ambassador Mitchell has just given Frederick notice of the cancellation of financial support because England has achieved its war goals in the New World and has beaten France, no longer needing Prussia's assistance. Frederick replies to Mitchell sarcastically: "I'm happy to have been England's friend in times of need and to have helped her conquer half the world" (476). As a result Frederick's situation worsens visibly. Again Henry pushes for conclusion of a peace treaty and for surrender of Silesia, so as not to run the risk of losing everything. But Frederick appeals to Henry's military honor and has him swear eternal loyalty and obedience to the Prussian flag, to extend beyond his understanding and his death; even if everything falls to pieces, "the earth" will, according to Frederick, "belong to us, [and] if not to us, [to what comes] after us" (478). However, the play does not end with this heroic pose, but with the words of Frederick to Laudon: "We have gotten so old, General" (500). What a contrast compared to the end of Johst's *Schlageter*, Zerkaulen's *Jugend von Langemarck*, or Langenbeck's *Der Hochverräter*.

The premiere took place on April 7, 1938, with a brilliant cast under the direction of Gustav Gründgens, who himself played the role of Frederick, in the State Playhouse in Berlin. Paul Fechter wrote about the play in the *Berliner Tageblatt* (Berlin Daily Journal): "He did not present the old Fritz as the Fridericus films portrayed him but showed a man given to the ecstasy of feeling, a man who in war feels the rest of his youth floating away and holds himself and his work together with a firm hand."[63]

Capitalism and Judaism

The Jew, only appearing peripherally in Rehberg, becomes the main character in Eberhard Wolfgang Möller's play *Rothschild siegt bei Waterloo* (Rothschild Wins at Waterloo, 1934). It makes no difference that Möller considered his drama to be primarily an attack on capitalism and did not stoop to hateful anti-Semitic tirades as did, for example, Zöberlein in his novel *Der Befehl des Gewissens* (The Command of Conscience), 1937, discussed in the chapter on novels. In the environment of anti-Semitic propaganda, however, Möller's piece must also be considered as such. Möller had already attacked capitalism in plays such as *Kalifornische Tragödie* (Californian Tragedy, 1930) and *Panamaskandal* (Panama Scandal, 1930). In *Kalifornische Tragödie*,

Möller shows how the hard-won property of the German-Swiss immigrant Johann Jakob Suter (actually Johann August Suter) was destroyed by greedy elements in the California gold rush around the middle of the nineteenth century: "The later politically oriented debate about gold, which is only the symbol for capitalism as a vital function, is already unmistakably evident in *Kalifornische Tragödie*."[64] In the play *Panamaskandal,* Möller shows how unscrupulous speculators and politicians exploit the idealism of the builder Lesseps. This play was understood to be a "challenge to soulless, irresponsible capitalism to unscrupulous speculation, [and] to political intrigues and disintegrating parliamentarianism"; in the Weimar Republic, when "the National Socialist movement" was still struggling "hard for Germany and for political power," the play "took on groundbreaking dramatic significance," or at least that is how Wanderscheck saw it.[65]

Eberhard Wolfgang Möller, who was born in 1906 in Berlin, the son of the sculptor Hermann Möller, was among the leading (and most talented) dramatists of the Third Reich, who have today been completely forgotten. Despite his important position and high-level connections, he was not spared from criticism. His play, *Der Untergang Karthagos* (The Decline of Carthage, 1938), in which he describes the end of Hasdrubal, who is fighting against a capitalist, middle-class regime, was seen by many as a warning and had to be withdrawn. After sharp attacks on Möller in the SS-oriented journal *Weltliteratur* (World Literature) in which he was labeled a cultural Bolshevist because of his poem "Der Tote" (The Dead Man), he was sent to the front to prove himself as a war correspondent for the Waffen SS. The young Möller modeled himself on dramatists such as Hauptmann, Büchner, Strindberg, Wedekind, Kaiser, Johst, and even Brecht and Bakunin. But the main influence was Paul Ernst, whom he had met personally at his parents' house and whose renaissance he propagated in the thirties. In the war, he struggled through to the realization that "tragedy is the most worthy symbol of a life whose meaning is battle."[66]

As Möller explains in the preface, his play *Rothschild siegt bei Waterloo* is based on the anecdote according to which the Jewish banker Rothschild exploited the Battle of Waterloo for bank speculation and thus was the actual victor. On the battlefield Wellington and Blücher did win out over Napoleon, but in reality, all three were losers. The victor was

> a sinister third power that made numbers out of human beings, stock exchange items out of men, profit out of life, [and] capital out of blood . . . It is the anecdote of an entire century in which all the concepts are turned around, numbers are made into gods, material possessions become the ideal, service becomes gain, and risk takes the place of danger, bluff takes the place of engagement, and trickery takes the place of strength.[67]

In six scenes, the play shows Rothschild with his timid bookkeeper O'Pinnel on the battlefield of the war in Belgium, Rothschild during the stormy crossing to England, and Rothschild on the battlefield of the stock exchange in London, where he cheaply buys up the stocks that have fallen through the floor because of the clever false report of Wellington's defeat and resells them again at high prices at the news of the actual truth, Wellington's victory. For his deeds, Rothschild is to be honored by the misled English finance commissioner Herries: "You rushed over here, putting your own life at stake, to warn the English economic establishment of a catastrophe, and to protect it" (123). At that moment, O'Pinnel, who was believed lost and was made a laughing stock by Rothschild until then ("O'Pinnelchen [Little O'Pinnel]"), appears and becomes the moral victor of the play over Rothschild, who at the end stands there, alone and abandoned. Before the assembled honorable guests, O'Pinnel confronts the great financier and hurls his own and Möller's opinion at Rothschild's face: "You are a scoundrel . . . The dead did not fall so that you could make your money off them. And in such a shabby manner . . . You stole . . . an honorable burial . . . from the dead" (125–29). Rothschild, who intends to casually dismiss O'Pinnel as an insane complainer, becomes ever more nervous and screams at him, "You villain, you dishonorable villain!" O'Pinnel responds to that coolly: "Sir, honor is something that does not have anything to do with business deals. As I have slowly come to understand, you unfortunately got that confused at Waterloo" (130). O'Pinnel has the last word: "Anyone who does not have [millions] gets out of the way of such a man" (133). The laughter of the audience, which had previously laughed at O'Pinnel together with Rothschild — the play is often characterized as a comedy — gets caught in their throats and is transformed into contempt for Rothschild, although the transformation comes all too suddenly, for a certain greatness in the person of Rothschild cannot be denied even in Möller's play. In those times and in the environment of Nazi propaganda, however, the play was understood with the intended meaning, and the real connection to the Weimar Republic from the Nazi perspective was clearly evident: "This Jewish Rothschild from Waterloo is the same demon who goes about his shady business in the shadows of a thousand other battles, stirs up and seduces the peoples, [and] profits a million times over in dividend coupons from the terrible exploitation of soldiers' blood."[68] The Reich drama advisor Schlösser agrees:

> Here the dead, who will live eternally, our men who died in action, rise up against the living death, that is, against capital as an end in itself. While dispensing with all external ornament [and] using the means of steel romanticism, so to speak, Möller places the horrible grotesqueness of liberal world confusion before our eyes. The theater as attack, the theater as the tribunal of the world spirit![69]

Other critics put Möller's play on the same level as Shakespeare's *Merchant of Venice,* drawing a parallel between Rothschild and Shylock; in their view, both plays present "the tragedy of this race," but without falling into an anti-Semitic frenzy.[70]

From a purely literary and dramatic standpoint, Möller must be given credit for ability. The play is well constructed in the tradition of Shakespeare, and the dialogue is tight, concise, and quick-witted; it is by no means primitive propaganda, but for that reason is even more effective — and more dangerous.

Flat Land and Nordic Soul

It is obvious that, with all the harking back to *völkisch* roots, drama found a new subject matter, just as the novel did — except that up to 1938 "no definitive creator" had yet been found, as Wanderscheck complained.[71] Escape from the supposed fragmentation of the modern industrial age lay in flight into the myth of the people's rootedness in the German, Nordic earth. In the view of *völkisch* national circles, parliamentarianism, capitalism, and Marxism led away from the organic growth of the community of the people. But being a farmer means having a feeling for the organic interaction of all the forces in the "work as a whole," as the Reich leader of the farmers, Richard Walther Darré declared in his work *Das Bauerntum als Lebensquelle der nordischen Rasse* (The Peasantry as the Source of Life of the Nordic Race, 1929).[72] It was even presumptuously asserted that the German was a farmer by nature and that the concepts "German" and "rural" were identical.[73] What especially distinguishes farmers in the eyes of the Nazis is an intuitive understanding for natural, organic growth and decay and the fateful integration of the human being into this natural process. As a being rooted in the soil, the farmer is not mollycoddled and intellectualized as city dwellers are, but is open, straightforwardly natural, genuine in love and hate, and receptive to the fateful, magic forces of organic nature that include everything in eternal cycles. From such threads, numerous dramatists spin a mythological fabric in which earth, soil, and dirt clods assume a godly character. In Hans Frank's "dramatic poem" about the German man "Klaus Michel" (1925), a pilot who has crashed, even experiences an ecstatic, orgasmic union with the earth:

> Und hier der Aufprall
> war vielleicht
> das Schönste! Als die Erde in mich drang,
> aufjubelnd hab ich mich ihr hingereicht.
> . . .
> Ich werde
> lebendigen Leibes von der Erde

empfangen. Blut heißt hier Samen,
knie nieder! Bete! Amen . . . Amen . . .[74]

[And here the impact,
was perhaps
the best part! As the earth penetrated me,
jubilating, I reached into her.
. . .
I, my living body,
will be received
by the earth. Blood here is seed,
kneel down! Pray! Amen . . . Amen . . .]

Heavy, dark connectedness to the earth also runs through Friedrich Griese's peasant drama *Der Mensch, aus Erde gemacht* (The Human Being, Made of Earth, 1932), which in a prologue and five acts presents the fate of the peasant Biermann, his maid Lena, and his farm worker Konrad Godem. The drama begins with the prologue "after the decline of summer" in a cemetery. A conversation between two night spirits or goblins anticipates the dismal fate of the peasant Biermann. The actual action takes place in the Low German region on the Biermann farm, "long before our days." The timelessness emphasizes the fateful, gloomy character of the play, as do the words of the sexton at the beginning: "Time is a rushing wheel; woe unto them who are bound to the spokes."[75] Bierman is not only bound to the spokes of the wheel of fortune, but even dares to put his hand in. After the death of his first wife, he desires his maid Lena, but she is promised to the farm worker Konrad Godem. Fate and the law also stand on the stage in the figure of the mysterious Bailiff "of an indeterminate age and in ancestral garb" (7), who foretells Lena's future to her. The setting is nighttime; the moon glows green and bodes ill: "The air is poisonous, when the moon is as it is today. And the poison goes into the human being's blood and makes him completely ill" (11). Godem and Biermann come to blows over Lena; Godem has stolen money from Biermann and now wants to escape with Lena. Lena advises that he return the money, which is marked with crosses, but Godem views it as an act of fate: "It is a gift, Lena; there were voices and hands under the earth. You can see them and hear them; you must only believe in them" (12). The peasant Biermann has discovered the theft, which spells death, and wants to hand Godem over to the law, unless Lena yields to him, a broad, heavy, limping man in his late fifties. The pious sexton warns Biermann about lust of the flesh, but Biermann follows his dark urge: "God . . . put it in me as it is, and now he must see what I do with it . . . My body wants it that way; it demands what is its right, before it is knocked off the chair and under the table" (19).

To save Godem, Lena gives in to the extortive pressure from Biermann and becomes his wife. Godem leaves the farm. The juices rise in Biermann: "It is swamp time, rutting season; the blood festers and swells and makes blisters" (28). He does not even try to resist the urges of the flesh; just as are all creatures, he is, in his basic instincts, bound to the earth and to nature:

> I am a human being, you see, a human being made of dirt, of a dirt clod, as it says in the Bible. I must devour meat if I want to live and give my body what it demands. I can't change myself from what I am. I don't need any meat; I could also stuff dirt behind my teeth; I would chew it, and it would taste good. (32)

However, Biermann is not happy with satisfying his urges. The mysterious, unearthly Bailiff prophesizes misfortune: "You want to give the flesh its right? It will get its right, but not in the way you think right now" (34). Biermann wanders sleeplessly through the house, Lena becomes insane, and the spirit of Godem hovers over both of them; Biermann must acknowledge: "Something is there that is more powerful than the human being" (41). At the end of the play, Godem, who has been moving around restlessly, returns to find peace in the death sentence for his deed, Lena tries to drown herself, and Biermann hangs himself on the door beam.

In this strange play, which is not logically accessible, the people are not living characters, but are balls, tossed about by "demonic primal forces."[76] It shows human beings in their dark, gloomy restrictedness, but not as *völkisch*, healthy models, as Wanderscheck complains: "The drama is not a symbol of the rebirth of a completely creative country, nor does it show the humanity of rural values."[77] Still, he recognizes Griese's struggle for the "concept of blood and soil," but prefers Griese's peasant comedies, such as *Schafschur* (Sheep Shearing, 1944) or *Wind im Luch* (The Wind in the Bog, 1937) in which the gloom is presented "lightened by comedy."[78] Nevertheless, Griese's gloomy, demonic drama fits seamlessly into Nazi ideology in that, as Ketelsen explains, the author emphasizes the significance of the death experience as unification with cosmic forces in the National Socialist cult of the hero: "Heroic existence is thus in its deepest and actual meaning . . . existence to the death. Viewed from this perspective, Griese's Biermann is not a phenomenon on the periphery of the drama of the Third Reich."[79] Biermann also embodies something of the brutish primal force of Nietzsche's blond beast, which enjoyed considerable popularity with the Nazis.

At times, the lives of peasants and soldiers are connected. The fateful abandonment in Griese's *Der Mensch, aus Erde gemacht* is transformed into heroic warriors' spirit in the drama *Erde* (Earth, 1935) by Rudolf Ahlers, who reawakens themes of warriors and peasants according to old German, Nordic myth. In contrast to his war comrade Peter Wulf, who returns to the "swamp" of the big city, Michael Holt, "big, sinewy, [and] strong, a healthy breed of man with a touch of peasant, in a shabby officer's uniform,"[80] decides to take up the battle against the moor and to wrest away from it the soil to which he feels organically connected. From the National Socialist point of view, the high point for the German man has been reached: to stand as a peasant, struggling and fighting on German soil, productive and fruitful as an organic part of nature:

> Ich kenne nur die Erde hier. Wenn ich die
> Furchen ausziehe, dann wollen sie Saat. Genau
> So ist es mit — uns.[81]

> [I only know the earth here. When I plow the
> the furrows, they want seed. It is
> just the same with — us.]

Holt's first wife, rendered lame and infertile by an accident, yields to the "healthy vital instincts" of Holt and the maid Christin by committing suicide.

The myth of the free peasant, plowing furrows in the steaming German earth behind sturdy horses, to sow and harvest, encouraged the flight from an unloved reality taken over by technology. Return to an intrinsically German primal state was brought about by the reawakening of the myth of the Germanic Nordic people, the so-called "northern renaissance" that started with the idea "that the Germans, in terms of biology, intellect, and culture, belong exclusively to the Nordic-Germanic type."[82] In many works, Nordic myth blends with the myth of the peasantry: the warrior, farmer, German, and Northman melt together into a mystical oneness.

Nordic stories are not only treated in novels like Hans Friedrich Blunck's *Die Urvätersaga* (The Saga of the Forefathers, 1925), or Will Vesper's *Das harte Geschlecht* (The Harsh Family, 1931), but also found their way onto the stage, as in Curt Langenbeck's *Das Schwert* (The Sword, 1940), Otto Erler's *Thors Gast* (Thor's Guest, 1937), Gerhard Schumann's *Gundruns Tod* (Gundrun's Death, 1943), or Erich von Hartz's *Odrun* (1939). In the return to Nordic stories, it must, however, be taken into account that they are for the most part simply made up or substantially altered. As with other materials used for dramas, the Nazis, at the time of their seizure of power, found numerous works already in existence that were configured in their direction, for example, Eberhard König's drama *Wielant der Schmied* (Wielant, the Smith, written in 1906, premiere in 1921), which continues in the tradition of the Edda legend and was highly thought of and promoted by the Nazis.[83] These dramas generally cannot be considered either dramas à clef or historical plays without reference to the present. The closeness to the present is in any case evident from the "blood flow roaring down through the millennia," which intrinsically connects all real Nordic-Germanic Germans, as the Nazi ideologues maintained in their propaganda.[84]

Gerhard Schumann (1911–1995), who made a name for himself primarily as a producer of poetry, continues with his "tragedy of fate" *Gudruns Tod,* written in iambic pentameter in five classic acts, in the tradition of the Nordic-Viking *Kudrun* epic that existed around 1240, which he modifies, however, to fit his own purposes. Schumann's Hegelingen Queen Gudrun stands between Herwig, to whom she is engaged for reasons of state, and Hartmut, for whom fate has destined her. After Herwig's victory over Hartmut, she stabs herself next to Hartmut's body because she sees no way out of the conflict between the necessary engagement to Herwig and her fated connection to Hartmut. *Gundruns Tod* is a tragedy of fate about loyalty unto the death, as the Nazi ideologues demanded it. Through suicide, she remains true to herself, and loyalty is the force "die einzig / die Welt mit erznem Griff zusammenhält [that alone / Holds the world together with an iron grip]."[85] Gudrun has no choice; her death is predestined by fate. The unconditional submission of human beings to their fate prevails throughout the play. Its premiere on February 14, 1943, in Stettin, only two weeks after the tragedy of the German defeat of Stalingrad on January 31, 1943, certainly did not come at an inopportune time for the Nazis, especially not fateful lines such as: "What are we human beings, really? In one hour elevated to the stars and smashed to the ground. Nothing is certain. The walls must fall and everything that is constructed by human hand . . . is in an instant food for the flames."[86]

Reference to the contemporary world is also evident at other places in the drama: everyone swears "eternal loyalty" to Gudrun. Doubting voices that warn the Hegelingen citizens of the attack by their neighbors, because war only brings "suffering and blood and tears," are labeled treasonous, and the doubters are condemned to death:

> Aus Treue wächst allein der sichere Sieg.
> Und wenn ein Volk ums nackte Leben kämpft,
> Steht auf Verrat nur gnadenlos der Tod.[87]

> [Out of loyalty alone grows certain victory.
> And when a people fights for its naked life,
> For treason there is only death, without mercy.]

The war that the Hegelingen citizens are carrying on is like the cosmic fight for the survival of the people, analogous to the Nazi war against the "Huns" from the Soviet steppes:

> Die ganze Grenze steht in roten Flammen!
> Die wilden Horden aus den fernen Steppen,
> Schlitzäugig schwarz verschlagene Höllenbrut,
> Die nicht den Bauern auf dem Feld, die Frau
> Im Haus, das Kindlein in der Wiege schonen,

In Jahren stolzen Friedens auferbaut,

. . .

Wir werden sie, ein Blitz aus blauem Himmel,
Mit ungeheurem Schlag zu Boden schmettern.[88]

[The entire border stands in red flames!
The wild hordes from the distant steppes,
Slit-eyed, black haired, cunning hell's brood,
Who spare not the farmer in the field,
The woman in the house, the child in the cradle,
Built up in years of proud peace,

. . .

We will, a bolt out of the blue heavens,
Smash them to the ground, with a giant blow.]

In Schumann's play, the citizens of Hegelingen are victorious. The analogy to the Third Reich did not become reality.

With *Thors Gast*, Otto Erler (1872–1943) succeeded, in Wanderscheck's words, in producing "a stage work . . . that scarcely has an equal in the new dramatic literature. It is dedicated to German youth. Thysker, the German, who finds his way back to his family from another world, is a symbol for maintaining the legacy from ancestors and Germanic peoples."[89] In the fictional Nordic material, the monk Thysker, who is performing missionary work along with his companions, wants to convert Nordic heathens. However, everyone but Thysker dies in a storm. With a cross that he had wanted to take to the heathens, he escapes to the coast, where he is found by the "naïve, affectionate"[90] Germanic woman Thurid, is torn away from the Christian "religion of slaves," and is converted to the manly, heroic belief in the Germanic gods. Christ becomes Thor's guest, symbolically represented by the cross being built into the gate before the hall of Thor's high throne. Thurid is amazed to hear about the servile Christian religion in which men are called the servants of God and this God allows himself to be worshiped in stone buildings. In contrast, hers is a religion of proud and free individuals: "We are not Thor's servants; we are his friends and we worship him in the forest, where the sacred spring breaks out of the earth."[91] She especially asks Thysker to keep from her people that his God only suffered, without defending himself. Thurid has never heard of the hereafter; her religion finds fulfillment in the here and now. In Thurid's eyes, her God, who swings a hammer and unleashes weather, is in every way a decidedly more heroic and active God than Thysker's Christian God. Thysker is convinced and allows himself to be led back by Thurid to his Germanic primal belief from which he had been alienated by the "Christian-Jewish" doctrine "of southern lands." For Wanderscheck, Erler has created with this drama an exemplary didactic play: "In *Thors Gast*, the *völkisch* German drama has gained a theatrically effective didactic play."[92]

References to the immediate present can also be found in Curt Langen-beck's "tragic drama" *Das Schwert* (1940), although the play by no means represents pure Nazi propaganda, but instead was intended by Langenbeck to be a high-art play. The Germanic leader Gaiso finds himself in a fateful struggle for his people and living space when his brother Evruin accuses him of having provoked a war of aggression. Gaiso justifies his behavior with the argument that he could only escape the stranglehold of his enemies through battle in a pre-emptive strike:

> Du Narr! Die tödliche Gefahr erkennend, hab ich
> Den ersten scharfen Hieb gewagt zu unsrer Rettung.
>
> . . .
>
> Ich sah wie ihre Rüstung wuchs,
> Und ehe sie zu furchtbar wurde, packte ich zu.[93]
>
> [You fool! Recognizing the deadly danger, I
> I ventured the first blow for our deliverance.
>
> . . .
>
> I saw their weapons growing,
> And before they became too terrible, I struck.]

Gaiso did not push himself to accomplish this task, but was foreordained to do so by fate, or by Providence, as Hitler liked to call it. Fate also entangled him in tragic guilt because he had to have his defeatist brother Evruin mur-dered for the sake of the just cause of the people, a guilt that Gaiso can only atone for by suicide. Gaiso had to go through a long struggle to bring him-self to accomplish the difficult task:

> Wie mühsam und schweratmend ich aus tiefer Not
> Heraufgedrungen bin, bis meine Seele sah
> Und sich dem Ziel vermählte, das sich ihr enthüllte.[94]
>
> [How laboriously and with heavy breathing I rose up
> From below, in great distress, until my soul saw
> And wed the goal that was revealed to it.]

Gaiso realizes that he and his men have been chosen by fate to sustain the vital primal life force of the people in a world which has become base, threatens that life force, and is ruled by reason:

> Mitten in einer alten Welt, die dreist und gottlos
> Gemein geworden war, erhielt sich hier bei uns
> Ein gläubig brennendes Geschlecht, entschlossen und
> Berufen, in des Lebens strengbewegte Fülle
> Warmherzig einzusinken wieder, ahnungsvoll

Ergriffen und zu ritterlichem Dienst bereit
. . . Da
Wurde mir eingeschmiedet der Entschluß: zu schützen
Mit härtesten Waffen unsere Willigkeit und Jugend.
Kein Plan war das des eignen kleinen Hirns, auch nicht
Bezauberung durch brünstige Dämonen — Nein:
Natur war's, und aus ihr der göttliche Befehl![95]

[In the midst of an old world, grown brash and
Godlessly base, a devoutly burning clan survived
Here in our land, decisive and chosen,
To sink again warm-heartedly into
Life's strongly moving fullness, moved
By foreboding and ready for chivalrous service
. . . There
My resolve was forged: to protect
With fiercest weapons our willingness and youth.
No plan was it of my own small brain, nor
Magic spell of demons lustful in heat — No:
T'was nature, and from her the godly order!]

Evruin knows nothing of this, but his all-knowing, all-intuiting mother and
prophetess of fate, Awa, does. It is also she who hands the young Gerri Gaiso's
sword so that he can carry on the heroic battle. Gerri takes the sword, kisses
it, and swears to Awa to carry the final victory or to die in action:

Und nun, mit Ehrfurcht, Schwert, küß ich an dir das Blut
Des Helden, der sich selbst erschlug mit dir für uns.
Dir Mutter, die du alle Tapfren liebst, dir knie
Zu Füßen ich und schwöre, ins Gebet geborgen:
In Ehren siegen oder fallen wollen wir.[96]

[And now, with reverence, sword, I kiss on you the blood
Of the hero who slew himself with you for us.
At your feet, Mother, you who loves all the brave,
At your feet I kneel and swear, hidden in the prayer:
We shall carry the victory with honor, or fall.]

In the war year 1940, these allusions to the present were too clear to the
National Socialist culture politicians and the play was withdrawn from the
stage, but not from the book market.

The *Thingspiel*

In closing this chapter, reference must still be made to a special form of National Socialist theater: the *Thingspiel*. While the dramas treated to this point were all written for the existing conventional theater, the *Thingspiel* is a special dramatic form aspired to by the Nazis and requiring a specially created performance location in an open, natural setting. Art was to again become a cult and to flow from the natural spring of the people, as the Reich drama advisor Rainer Schlösser declared in a programmatic speech in 1935; *Thingplätze*, that is, the theaters for *Thingspiele*, were to become the "cult sites of the nation," and poets were to become real comrades of the people. According to Schlösser, who developed his conception of the *Thingspiel* in close collaboration with the dramatist Eberhard Wolfgang Möller, oratorio, pantomime, procession, and dance are elements of the *Thingspiel* for which they were striving, but they must be fused together by a *völkisch* national ideology and a dramatic form, using appropriate material to create a total work of art that is close to the people. As the medieval mystery plays for the Church, the *Thingspiele* were to provide mythical underpinnings for the new state: *"The longing is for a drama that intensifies historical events to create a mythical, universal, unambiguous reality beyond reality.* Only someone who knows this longing will be able to create the cultic people's drama of the future."[97] Any subject matter can be considered for these *Thingspiele*, as long as they are "placed in the context of the Nordic concept" and are "moved into the light of our genuine and just myth of blood and honor"; at least, that is what Schlösser wanted.[98]

The efforts of the *Thingspiel* movement were not that new — as was the case for everything in the Nazi movement. They could draw on the experience of the open-air theater movement in the twenties, as well as on other efforts seeking to get away from the picture-frame stage: plays of the youth movement, agitprop, the Catholic and Protestant amateur theater movement, mass plays of the labor movement, etc.[99] Ernst Wachler had already attempted to acquaint the people with *völkisch*, neo-pagan plays from German legends, tribes, and myths on his Open-Air Stage in Thale in the Harz mountains, which was founded in 1903.[100] In his book *Die inszenierte Volksgemeinschaft* (The Staged Community of the People),[101] Rainer Stommer follows the different phases and directions in the development of the *Thing* movement, from the "Reich Union for the Promotion of Open-Air Theater, Registered Association," founded on December 22, 1932, to the end of the official movement. The first business manager was Wilhelm Karl Gerst; in February of 1933, the writers' group still included prominent names from the Weimar period, such as Ödön von Horvath, Ernst Toller, and Carl Zuckmayer. Goebbels's Reich ministry for Propaganda recognized the value of the movement, and soon Goebbel's placed himself at the organization's head and made changes to suit his own purposes. Gerst, who came from the Catholic Theater Union, was removed in the course of development, and the writers' group changed in the direction of National Socialism. Otto Laubinger, the first president of the Reich Chamber of Theater (1933–1935), planned 400 *Thingplätze* for an audience capacity of up to 60,000. In 1934, the year of the *Thing* euphoria, twenty *Thingplätze* were under construction. Not all of them were finished because the *Thingspiel* movement waned around 1937, and the outbreak of war in 1939 practically ended the efforts. The largest and most important *Thing* stage was the Dietrich Eckart stage in Berlin, opened for the Olympic Games in 1936 and named after the pseudo-dramatist and friend of Hitler's. This stage hosts performances today under the name "Forest Stage" (*Waldbühne*); but is of course no longer called a *Thingspiel!*[102]

The *Thingspiel* movement produced plays like Richard Euringer's *Deutsche Passion* (1933), Kurt Heynicke's *Neurode, Spiel von deutscher Arbeit* (Neurode, Play About German Work, Halle *Thingplatz*, 1934), and *Der Weg ins Reich* (The Path to the Reich, 1935), and Kurt Egger's *Das Spiel von Job dem Deutschen* (The Play About Job the German, 1933) and *Das große Wandern: Ein Spiel vom ewigen deutschen Schicksal* (The Great Journey: A Play About the Eternal German Fate, 1934). The most significant of these *Thingspiele* is by Eberhard Wolfgang Möller, whose *Frankenburger Würfelspiel* (Frankenburg Dice Game) was selected by Goebbels as a culture program accompanying the Olympic Games for the ceremonial opening of the Dietrich Eckart Stage in 1936.

The *Frankenburger Würfelspiel* is one big trial in ten scenes, with a prologue and an epilogue; in it, seven judges sit in judgment upon Emperor Ferdinand II, Maximilian of Bavaria and his advisors and subordinates, as well as the Governor of Upper Austria, the Baron von Hebersdorf because they allowed the country to be devastated in the Thirty Years' War and abused the trust of the people. Court is held here according to the meaning of the term "*Thing*" taken over from the Germanic peoples; in Old German, the word designates a court proceeding of the people. Three prosecutors bring the action against Emperor Ferdinand, "the calamitous [ruler] of the House of Habsburg" "im Namen des Volkes von Oberösterreich, / im Namen dieser namenlos gequälten Bauern [in the name of the people of Upper Austria, / in the name of the namelessly tormented peasants]."[103] Because of their belief, the peasants must die at the behest of the emperor. The emperor, however, claims to have been misled by his advisors; all the others also cite the compulsion to obey orders — as did many Nazis after 1945.

The action takes place on a tri-level stage: the judges preside above, the prosecutors have their places with Ferdinand and his advisors in the middle, and below are Governor von Herbersdorf and the peasants. A prologue, presented "by a single narrator from the middle level of the stage," makes clear the parable character of the play; historical events past illustrate the present, and the audience is required to pass its own judgment:

> So nehmt das Spiel als Gleichnis, das verpflichtet.
> Zur Gegenwart wird die Vergangenheit.
> Die Richter stehn, doch euer Wille richtet,
> Und euer Mund verurteilt und verzeiht. (339)

> [So take the play as a parable that obligates.
> The past becomes the present.
> The judges stand, but your will judges,
> and your mouth condemns or pardons.]

A chorus accompanies the action; it has the function, at the high points in the scene, of filling the natural breaks in the play with lyrical observations about the deeper meaning of the whole (337). It is to "sing" its texts "after the manner of choruses in oratorios" (337). For example, the chorus makes the demand for a people that is prepared to fight:

> O hättet ihr Waffen, ihr Armen,
> ihr brauchtet nicht zu stehen
> und die Mächtigen um Erbarmen
> und Milde anzuflehn. (364–65)

> [Oh, had you but weapons, poor ones,
> you would not need to stand
> and plead with the powerful
> for mercy and mildness.]

The music accompanying the play is not to illustrate but is to have a "functional character" (337) with fanfares and alarm bells. To underscore the popular character, there are great processions of the people and riders: thus Herbersdorf has his riders come in to underline his, and the emperor's, power. On his order, the peasants also appear. Once more Herbersdorf demands submission from the thirty-six selected peasants who have appeared. Herbersdorf leaves the decision over life and death to the dice, and the peasants thus roll the dice for their lives. The losers are doomed to die but they know that they are dying as martyrs for future generations:

> Wenn man uns an die Kirchturmspitzen hängt,
> so werden wir Laternen sein, die noch
> den Enkeln in der Nacht des Zweifels leuchten.
> Wir werden Fahnen sein, die nie zerreißen,
> . . .
> Die Zukunft wird sich einst an uns entflammen. (371)

> [If we be hanged from the church spires' tips,
> we will be lanterns that still
> light the grandchildren's night of despair.
> We will be flags that never rend,
>   . . .
> The future will one day catch fire from us.]

The doomed peasants see themselves as a group of trusty followers in a time when no one can be relied upon:

> In dem Jahrhundert, das die Treu gebrochen
> gab es ein Fähnlein, das die Treue hielt. (371)

> [In the century when trust was broken
> a small group was there, which kept the faith.]

When Herbersdorf wants to move on with the executions, the crowd demands the doomed peasants back. The crowd becomes one people (*ein Volk*) that casts off the yoke of the tyrant:

> Gebt uns die Todgeweihten wieder her,
> die uns auf unserm Weg vorangezogen!
> Wir sind nicht Kinder und nicht Bettler mehr,
> wir sind ein neues Volk, ein neues Heer,
> und wehe denen, welche uns betrogen.
> Wir sind ein Wille, und wir sind ein Schrei,
> und kein Versprechen kann uns mehr entzweien.
> Wir wollen uns von aller Schinderei
> von allem Joch und aller Tyrannei
> in Gottes Namen endlich selbst befreien. (373)

> [Give back to us the doomed,
> who went before us on our way!
> No longer are we children, nor beggars;
> we are a new people, a new army,
> and woe to those who us betray.
> We are one will, and we are one cry,
> and no promise can again divide us.
> From all toil, from every yoke,
> and from all tyranny, we want finally
> In God's name to free ourselves.]

Thus Möller's play became the consecration of Hitler's seizure of power in 1933 and affirmation of the Nazi Reich in which the myth of the people and self-liberation was acted out before the crowd, and columns of Hitler Youth sang happily about the young people, ready for the storm with flags held high — as the text of a Hitler Youth song went. When Herbersdorf wants to intervene with force, a figure in black armor appears as *deus ex machina*, takes the dice, and forces the rulers to roll them.[104] All the rulers lose to the figure and are handed over to the judges, who condemn the disloyal and dishonorable servants of the people. An epilogue underlines the character of the play as the inaugural for the seed that sprouted after 1933: "Look: across the land and the bloody fields a new race is greening, invincible and great" (377), and invokes the law of the fittest: "The strong will eternally stride over the weak" (377).

Möller's play is based on a historical event that occurred in May of 1625 in Upper Austria. In the course of the Counter-Reformation Baron Herbersdorf attempted, as an emissary of Emperor Ferdinand II, to force the peasants to rejoin the Catholic faith. As a deterrent example, he had thirty-six peasants roll the dice for their lives; half of them were hanged. That led to the last Peasants War in which 4,000 to 7,000 peasants were killed. According to Möller's own statement, his dramatic models for his play were, "in addition to Orestes, Ludus de Antichristo, and a few mystery plays, Georg Kaiser's expressionist play *Die Bürger von Calais* (The Citizens of Calais) and Stravinsky's *Ödipus Rex* (Oedipus Rex).[105]

The premiere of the play took place on the Dietrich Eckart Stage on August 2, 1936, before 20,000 visitors, one day after the opening of the Olympic Games in the adjacent Olympic Stadium. The directors were Werner Pleister and Matthias Wiemann, who also played the role of the unknown black knight. The principal cast members were supplemented by 1,200 extras from the Reich Labor Service. The reaction of the critics varied. The Catholic journal *Germania* saw the play as an attack on the Catholic Church.[106] The National Socialist *Angriff* (Attack), on the other hand, spoke of a "miraculous hour in the history of the theater." The *Völkischer Beobachter* (Völkisch Observer) agreed: "Eberhard Wolfgang Möller, the boldest champion of the coming form among the creative spirits of the young generation, has mastered an unprecedented task."[107] But criticism also came from some National Socialist circles; for the Rosenberg group, the Christian tendencies of the play were too obvious.[108] After the premiere, the *Frankenburger Würfelspiel* was performed in numerous other *Thingplätze* and in conventional theaters.[109]

With this play, the high point, and at the same time the endpoint, of the *Thingspiel* movement was reached, although it continued to exist in a modified form, as Rainer Stommer has shown.[110] For a number of reasons, officials of the Nazi regime withdrew their support.[111] The *Thingspiel* movement, which was never uncontroversial, especially in the jurisdictional struggle between the Rosenberg office and the Reich Propaganda ministry, virtually disappeared from state theater planning after 1937, although "the *Thing-*

spiel, as political and cultural mass theater, represented the most important contribution that the National Socialists made to the artistic form of theater and literature."[112]

Summary

This section could only provide a brief look at the dramatic literature of the Third Reich. However, the attempt was made to present several basic categories, plays, and authors. The restriction to the "drama of National Socialism" could leave the impression that this genre dominated the stages from 1933 to 1945. But that was not at all the case. Even the most successful Nazi drama lagged behind light plays for entertainment and classic works. The most-performed representative of Nazi dramas, Hanns Johst, achieved a total of 1,337 performances from 1933 to 1938, while Bunje's *Etappenhase* (Base Wallah) was performed 2,837 times in the 1936–1937 season.[113] In his study of the programs of "five systematically selected provincial theaters" (Bielefeld, Dortmund, Ingolstadt, Coburg, and Karlsruhe), Konrad Dussel documents, for example, that not very much changed in the provinces after 1933 and that the proportion of light entertainment on the stage actually increased.[114] Therefore, there can hardly be discussion of a new, heroic theater that totally changed and dominated the stages after 1933. What Konrad Dussel establishes for the five theaters in his study probably also applies to other provincial stages and even to big city stages and Berlin. The concept of a heroic theater did thoroughly dominate the discussion in Nazi theater circles, especially in the Rosenberg office. But the actual development took a different course; the need for entertainment in the theater as well as in film increasingly gained ground, especially in difficult times. At the same time, it must be taken into consideration that even the plays for entertainment were by no means always free of ideology, as Rainer Stollmann has shown with the example of "invisible propaganda" in *Petermann fährt nach Madeira* (Petermann Travels to Madeira), the hit of the 1936–1937 season.[115]

The hope that "our theater" will again be "German-*völkisch* . . . in terms of national tradition and the German destiny, [and] Nordic-Germanic in terms of race," as Wolfgang Nufer put it in the *Deutsche Bühne* (German Stage), was not fulfilled — despite numerous official measures and instructions to theater directors.[116] A Dietrich Eckart Prize writing contest sponsored at the end of 1933 by the Reclam publishing house and the Propaganda ministry did bring in 800 entries, but not a single usable play. The results were similar for other writing contests and even for direct commissions.[117] Still, among the eleven plays that each reached 102 to 215 performances, out of 237 premieres in the 1936–1937 season, was Friedrich Bethge's play *Marsch der Veteranen,* which had stiff competition from comedies such as *Eintritt frei* (Free Entry) by Just Scheu and *Kämmerchen zu vermieten* (A Small Room to Let) by Leo Lenz.[118] Heinrich Zerkaulen, the author of the play *Jugend von Langemarck* discussed in this chapter, who was strongly promoted by the Nazis, had his greatest success with his comedy *Der Sprung aus dem Alltag* (Leap Out of the Everyday Routine), which premiered in 1935 and remained on the programs until 1944, when the majority of the population must have felt a strong desire to be able to leap out of the everyday routine.[119]

The Nazis did succeed, without any trouble, in driving out the great theater artists of the Weimar period such as Leopold Jesner, Georg Kaiser, Max Reinhardt, Erwin Piscator, Ernst Toller, Carl Zuckmayer, and so on, but not to replace them with members of their own ranks. The planned transformation did not occur; the theater programs remained menus for entertainment and "the domains of middle-class art theater."[120] The National Socialists, however, did not in any way reject the traditional function of the theater for education and entertainment. To the contrary, they conceded to it a certain usefulness as a release valve. Even Hitler was not at all opposed to theater as a diversion; as he said in 1938: "The performances must be an 'illusion' for the masses. The little man knows enough about the serious side of life."[121] For the educated public, the German dramatists of the classical period were available, especially Friedrich Schiller and Schiller's contemporary successors in the concept of theater as a moral institution sought to institute a German national theater.[122] Of course, the Party attempted also to recast the classical dramatists in their mold. On that subject, Hitler wrote in the *Völkischer Beobachter* of February 13, 1934: "It remained for National Socialism to give the true Friedrich Schiller to the German people for the first time and to show him to be what he really is: the predecessor of National Socialism."[123] Still, despite Hitler's declaration and many attempts, the Nazis never succeeded in real *Gleichschaltung* of the classical dramatists.[124]

After 1945, the plays discussed and their authors sank into oblivion. No attempt is being made here to revive them. Nevertheless, it is incumbent upon the literary historian to treat even the drama of the Third Reich as objectively as possible. In doing so, it is evident that many of the National Socialist dramatists were by no means without talent and were thoroughly capable of creating effective dramas that were more than shallow propaganda. Furthermore, as was emphasized at the beginning of the chapter, there was no uniform conception of National Socialist drama. The theater of the Third Reich was therefore considerably more varied than it appears to be at the first glance. From the standpoint of dramatic technique and artistry, however, Nazi drama, despite all the craftsman's skill, produced scarcely anything new — aside from a few exceptions, such as Möller — but instead reached almost exclusively into the past for earlier forms.

Notes

[1] Adolf Hitler, *Mein Kampf* (My Struggle), 17th edition of the popular edition (Munich: Eher Nachfolger, 1923), 283. The page citations in the text refer to this edition.

[2] Hermann Wanderscheck, *Deutsche Dramatik der Gegenwart* (German Drama of the Present) (Berlin: Bong, 1938), 7. The page citations in the text refer to this edition.

[3] Quoted in Wanderscheck, 26.

[4] See Uwe-K. Ketelsen, *Von heroischem Sein und völkischem Tod* (On Heroic Existence and *Völkisch* Death) (Bonn: Bouvier, 1970), 7–8.

[5] On that subject, see Boguslaw Drewniak, *Das Theater im NS Staat* (The Theater in the National Socialist State) (Düsseldorf: Droste Verlag, 1983), 13–41, chapter titled "Der Lenkungsapparat: Organisation, Ziele, Methoden" (The Control Apparatus: Organization, Goals, Methods).

[6] See Ketelsen, 7–8.

[7] Günther Rühle, ed., *Zeit und Theater: Diktatur und Exil 1933–1945* (Time and the Theater: Dictatorship and Exile, 1933–1945), volume 3 (Berlin: Propyläen, 1974), 27–28.

[8] See Drewniak, 42.

[9] Joachim C. Fest, *Hitler* (Frankfurt, Berlin, and Vienna: Ullstein-Propyläen, 1973), 708.

[10] Günther Rühle, *Zeit und Theater*, volume 3, 31.

[11] Hanns Johst, *Ich glaube: Bekenntnisse von Hanns Johst* (I Believe: Confessions of Hanns Johst) (Munich: Langen, 1928), 35–36.

[12] *Schlageter*, in *Zeit und Theater*, edited by Günther Rühle, volume 3, 115. The page citations in the text refer to this edition.

[13] Helmut Pfanner, *Hanns Johst* (The Hague and Paris: Mouton, 1970), 215–16.

[14] Günther Rühle, *Theater für die Republik 1917–1933* (Theater for the Republic, 1917–1933) (Frankfurt am Main: Fischer, 1967), 1159.

[15] Alfred Rosenberg, "Weltanschauung und Kunst" (Ideology and Art), in Alfred Rosenberg, *Gestaltung der Idee, Blut und Ehre, II. Band: Reden und Aufsätze 1932–1935* (Formation of the Idea, Blood and Honor, 2nd volume: Speeches and Essays), edited by Thilo von Trotha, 8th edition (Munich: Zentralverlag der NSDAP, 1938), 336.

[16] See *Mein Kampf,* 180–81.

[17] Quoted in Erwin Breßlein, *Völkisch-faschistoides und nationalsozialistisches Drama* (*Völkisch* Fascistoid and National Socialist Drama) (Frankfurt am Main: Haag + Herchen, 1980), 547.

[18] Quoted in Günther Rühle, *Zeit und Theater*, volume 3, 751–752. On the Langemarck theme, see also the essays of Uwe-K. Ketelsen, "'Die Jugend von Langemarck.' Ein poetisch-politisches Motiv der Zwischenkriegszeit" ("The Youth of Langemarck." A Poetic and Political Motif of the Period between the Wars), in *Mit uns zieht die neue Zeit — Der Mythos Jugend* (With Us Comes the New Era — The Myth of Youth), edited by Thomas Koebner, et al. (Frankfurt am Main: Suhrkamp, 1985), 68–96, and Herbert Lehnert, "Langemarck — historisch und symbolisch"

(Langemark — Historical and Symbolic), in *Orbis Litterarum* (The World of Literature), 42 (1987), 271–90.

[19] Quoted in Günther Rühle, *Zeit und Theater,* volume 3, 748–49. Franz von Papen (1879–1969) the last Chancellor of the Weimar Republic in 1932 before Hitler's appointment as Reich Chancellor in 1933 and served as Vice-Chancellor under him to 1934.

[20] *Jugend von Langemarck* (Youth of Langemarck), in *Zeit und Theater,* edited by Günther Rühle, volume 3, 156. The page citations in the text refer to this edition.

[21] See Günther Rühle, *Zeit und Theater,* volume 3, 749–50.

[22] See Friedrich Bethge, *Marsch der Veteranen* (March of the Veterans), in *Zeit und Theater,* edited by Günther Rühle, volume 3, 196. The page citations in the text refer to this edition.

[23] See Günther Rühle, *Zeit und Theater,* volume 3, 761.

[24] Quoted in Günther Rühle, *Zeit und Theater,* volume 3, 762.

[25] See Pfanner, 301.

[26] See Günther Rühle, *Zeit und Theater,* volume 3, 23.

[27] See Breßlein, 603.

[28] See Rainer Stollmann, "Theater im Dritten Reich" (Theater in the Third Reich), in *Leid der Worte: Panorama des literarischen Nationalsozialismus* (Suffering of Words: Panorama of Literary National Socialism), edited by Jörg Thunecke (Bonn: Bouvier, 1987), especially 72–74 and 76–79. Stollmann also finds this shift to historical material in the literature of the Inner Emigration and exile literature.

[29] Quoted in Breßlein, 447.

[30] See Wanderscheck, 20–21.

[31] See Wanderscheck, 21.

[32] See Breßlein, 452–57.

[33] Hanns Johst, *Propheten* (Prophets, 1922); Otto Bruder, *Luther, der Kämpfer* (Luther, the Fighter, 1933); Kurt Eggers, *Revolution um Luther* (Revolution About Luther, 1935); Karl Irmler, *Luthers Kampf und Sieg* (Luther's Battle and Victory, 1933); and Eberhard Wolfgang Möller, *Martin Luther oder die Höllische Reise* (Martin Luther or the Hellish Journey, 1933).

[34] Hans Hermann Wilhelm, *Ulrich von Hutten* (1934); Uli Klimsch, *Hutten* (1933); Hans Harrier, *Kampf um Ulrich von Huttens deutsche Sendung* (The Battle About Ulrich von Hutten's German Mission, 1936); Hans Hermann Wilhelm, *Ulrich von Hutten* (1934); Erich Bauer, *Laßt Hutten nicht verderben!* (Don't Let Hutten be Destroyed!, 1939); and Kurt Eggers, *Ulrich von Hutten* (1934)

[35] Paul Gurk, *Thomas Münzer* (1922); and Herbert Eulenberg, *Thomas Münzer oder das Trauerspiel des Bauernkriegs* (Thomas Münzer or the Tragedy of the Peasants War, 1932).

[36] Maximillian Böttcher, *Tauroggen: Ein Führerdrama* (Tauroggen: The Drama of a Leader, 1933); Paul Ernst, *Yorck* (1933, written in 1917); Hans Kyser, *Schicksal um Yorck* (Fate Surrounding Yorck, 1933); and Max Petzold, *Yorck* (1933).

[37] Joseph Buckhorn, *Heinrich von Kleist* (1935); Karl Faehler, *Die Tragödie Kleist* (The Kleist Tragedy, 1933); Hans Franck, *Kleist* (1933); Hans Heyk, *Kleist* (1933); and Uli Klimsch, *Kleists Tod* (Kleist's Death, 1933).

[38] Konrad Bürger, *Canossa* (1935); Paul Ernst, *Canossa* (1918); Erich von Hartz, *Kaiser Heinrich IV* (Emperor Henry IV, 1924); Erwin Guido Kolbenheyer, *Gregor und Heinrich* (Gregory and Henry, 1934); and Georg Schmückle, *Heinrich IV* (1940).

[39] Hans Rehbergs *Preußendramen* (Prussian Dramas, 1934–1937); Julius Bernhard, *Friedrich bei Leuthen* (Frederick at Leuthen, 1933); Hermann von Bötticher, *Friedrich der Große* (Frederick the Great, 2 parts, 1920 and 1922); Hermann Burte, *Katte* (1933); and Hans Christoph Kaergel, *Der Kurier des Königs* (The Courier of the King, 1942).

[40] Hans Friedrich Blunck, *Kampf um New York* (Battle for New York, 1938); and Curt Langenbeck, *Der Hochverräter* (The Man Who Committed High Treason, 1935).

[41] Walter Gilbricht, *Oliver Cromwells Sendung* (Oliver Cromwell's Mission, 1932); Erich Gower, *Cromwell* (1935); and Mirko Jelusich, *Cromwell* (1934).

[42] Hanns Johst, *Thomas Paine* (1927).

[43] Erwin Guido Kolbenheyer, *Gregor und Heinrich* (Gregory and Henry, 1934), in *Zeit und Theater,* edited by Günther Rühle, volume 3, 264. The page citations in the text refer to this edition.

[44] Kolbenheyer, "Heroische Leidenschaften" (Heroic Passions), in *Zeit und Theater,* edited by Günther Rühle, volume 3, 773.

[45] Quoted in Günther Rühle, *Zeit und Theater* (Time and the Theater), volume 3, 775.

[46] See Günther Rühle, *Zeit und Theater,* volume 3, 774–75.

[47] See Wanderscheck, 66.

[48] See Wanderscheck, 93.

[49] Curt Langenbeck, *Der Hochverräter* (The Man Who Committed High Treason, 1938), in *Zeit und Theater,* by Günther Rühle, volume 3, 381. The page citations in the text refer to this edition.

[50] See Günther Rühle, *Zeit und Theater,* volume 3, 801–02.

[51] See Günther Rühle, *Zeit und Theater,* volume 3, 803.

[52] See Günther Rühle, *Zeit und Theater,* volume 3, 805.

[53] See Günther Rühle, *Zeit und Theater,* volume 3, 806.

[54] See Wanderscheck, 153.

[55] See Wanderscheck, 153

[56] Quoted in Günther Rühle, *Zeit und Theater,* volume 3, 813.

[57] Quoted in Günther Rühle, *Zeit und Theater,* volume 3, 817.

[58] *Mein Kampf,* 286.

[59] Alfred Rosenberg, *Der Mythus des 20. Jahrhunderts* (The Myth of the Twentieth Century), 107,000th to 110,000th copies printed (Munich: Hoheneichen, 1937), 198.

[60] See Rosenberg, 198–99, and 293.

[61] Hans Rehberg, *Der siebenjährige Krieg* (The Seven Years War), in *Zeit und Theater,* edited by Günther Rühle, volume 3, 441. The page citations in the text refer to this edition.

[62] See Wanderscheck, 155.

[63] Quoted in *Zeit und Theater,* edited by Günther Rühle, volume 3, 817.

[64] See Wanderscheck, 108.

[65] See Wanderscheck, 109.

[66] Quoted in *Zeit und Theater,* edited by Günther Rühle, volume 3, 792.

[67] Eberhard Wolfgang Möller, *Rothschild siegt bei Waterloo* (Rothschild Wins at Waterloo) (Berlin: Langen-Müller, 1934), 6–7. The page citations in the text refer to this edition.

[68] See Wanderscheck, 110.

[69] Quoted in Wanderscheck, 110.

[70] See Wanderscheck, 111.

[71] See Wanderscheck, 239.

[72] Quoted in Breßlein, 261.

[73] See Breßlein, 262–63.

[74] Quoted in Breßlein, 264–65.

[75] Friedrich Griese, *Der Mensch, aus Erde gemacht* (The Human Being, Made of Earth) (Berlin: Bühnenvolksbund-Verlag, 1932), 7. The page citations in the text refer to this edition.

[76] Ketelsen, *Von heroischem Sein und völkischem Tod,* 263.

[77] See Wanderscheck, 241.

[78] See Wanderscheck, 240–41.

[79] See Ketelsen, 147–48.

[80] Quoted in Breßlein, 305.

[81] Quoted in Breßlein, 317.

[82] Franz Schonauer, *Deutsche Literatur im Dritten Reich* (German Literature in the Third Reich) (Olten and Freiburg in Breisgau: Walter-Verlag, 1961), 77.

[83] On that subject, see Breßlein, 53.

[84] Quoted in Breßlein, 93.

[85] Quoted in Breßlein, 115.

[86] Quoted in Breßlein, 105.

[87] Quoted in Breßlein, 119.

[88] Quoted in Breßlein, 120.

[89] See Wanderscheck, 74.

[90] See Ketelsen, *Von heroischem Sein,* 93.

[91] Quoted in Ketelsen, 94.

[92] See Wanderscheck, 74.

[93] Quoted in Ketelsen, 41.

[94] Quoted in Ketelsen, 242.

[95] Quoted in Ketelsen, 240.

[96] Quoted in Ketelsen, 350.

[97] Günther Rühle, *Zeit und Theater,* volume 3, 782.

[98] Günther Rühle, *Zeit und Theater,* volume 3, 783.

[99] On that subject, see Günther Rühle, *Zeit und Theater,* volume 3, 36, and Henning Eichberg, et al., *Massenspiele: NS-Thingspiel, Arbeiterweihespiel und olympisches Zeromoniell* (Mass Plays: National Socialist *Thingspiele,* Workers Initiation Plays, and Olympic Ceremonies) (Stuttgart-Bad Cannstatt: frommann-holzboog, 1977).

[100] See Eichberg, 22. Ernst Wachler, the author of the *Osning* (1914), the most influential *völkisch* novel of his time, dreamed of a Nordic renaissance, and in that way, as well as with his contributions to the mass plays, he lent significant support to National Socialist ideology. He died, racially persecuted, in 1944 in Theresienstadt Concentration Camp. On that subject, see George L. Mosse, *The Crisis of German Ideology* (New York: Grosset & Dunlap, 1964), 80–82.

[101] Subtitle, *Die "Thing-Bewegung" im Dritten Reich* (The "Thing Movement" in the Third Reich) (Marburg: Jonas, 1985).

[102] More on organization and *Thingplatz* construction, as well as the theory and history of the *Thingspiel* in H. Eichberg, et al., *Massenspiele* (Mass Plays, 1977), as well as in Stommer.

[103] Eberhard Wolfgang Möller, *Frankenburger Würfelspiel* (Frankenburg Dice Game), in *Zeit und Theater,* edited by Günther Rühle, volume 3, 342. The page citations in the text refer to this edition.

[104] According to Möller's intent, this highest judge was supposed to be the *Führer* Adolf Hitler, but the latter was already attending official Nazi spectacles that the *Thingspiel* could not, and was not supposed to, displace; reality had overtaken the theater; see Rainer Stollmann, "Theater im Dritten Reich," in *Leid der Worte: Panorama des literarischen Nationalsozialismus* (Suffering of Words: Panorama of Literary National Socialism), edited by Jörg Thunecke, 75.

[105] Günther Rühle, *Zeit und Theater,* volume 3, 785–86.

[106] See Eichberg, 51.

[107] Quoted in Eichberg, 51.

[108] See Eichberg, 51. For more reviews, also from abroad, see Eichberg, 51–52.

[109] On that subject, see Eichberg, 52. For the *Frankenburger Würfelspiel,* see also Eichberg in *Massenspiele,* 47–52, and Glen W. Gadberry, "Eberhard Wolfgang Möller's *Thingspiel Das Frankenburger Würfelspiel,*" in *Massenspiele,* edited by H. Eichberg, et al., 235–51. Gadberry sees in this play a moral core that goes beyond the "latent" National Socialism and therefore calls for a revival of Möller's *Thingspiel.*

[110] Rainer Stommer, 154–155. In this book, Stommer gives a detailed overview of the *Thing* movement, including the architecture of *Thingplätze,* the history of several of the *Thingplätze,* and a catalogue of all of the *Thingplätze* that were constructed.

[111] On that subject, see Günther Rühle, *Zeit und Theater,* volume 3, 40; Eichberg, 35–40, and Stommer, 154–155. The reasons included a lack of good plays, cost issues,

changes in personnel at the Propaganda ministry (promoter Otto Laubinger died, and was replaced by the less interested Franz Moraller, among others), weather conditions, acoustic problems, end of the struggle phase of the National Socialist movement, renewed respect after 1935 for inside theater, etc.; more can be read in Stommer.

[112] See Eichberg, 5.

[113] See Ketelsen, *Von heroischem Sein*, 14.

[114] Konrad Dussel, *Ein neues, ein heroisches Theater? Nationalsozialistische Theaterpolitik und ihre Auswirkungen* (A New, Heroic Theater? National Socialist Theater Policy and Its Effects) (Bonn: Bouvier, 1988).

[115] Stollmann, "Theater im Dritten Reich," 84.

[116] See Drewniak, 211.

[117] See Drewniak, 211–212.

[118] See Drewniak, 213.

[119] See Drewniak, 214.

[120] Ketelsen, *Völkisch-nationale und nationalsozialistische Literatur in Deutschland 1890–1945* (*Völkisch National and National Socialist Literature in Germany, 1890–1945*) (Stuttgart: Metzler, 1976), 88.

[121] Quoted in Drewniak, 44.

[122] On that subject, see Jutta Wardetsky, *Theaterpolitik im faschistischen Deutschland: Studien* (Theater Policies in Fascist Germany: Studies) (Berlin: Henschel, 1983), especially 69–79.

[123] Quoted in Joseph Wulf, *Literatur und Dichtung im Dritten Reich: Eine Dokumentation* (Literature and Poetry in the Third Reich: Documentation) (Frankfurt am Main: Ullstein, 1983), 391.

[124] Details on the reception of the classical writers in the Third Reich in Drewniak, 167–74, and Bernard Zeller, et al., eds., *Klassiker in finsteren Zeiten* (*Writers of German Classicism in Dark Times*) (Marbach: Deutsche Schiller Gesellschaft, 1983). On the reception of foreign dramas in Nazi Germany, see Drewniak, 244–81.

Agnes Miegel, some of whose poetry was characterized by fervent national socialist sentiments, and Heinrich Anacker, the "battle poet of the Second World War." Courtesy of Bundesarchiv, Koblenz.

6: National Socialist Poetry

The characteristic form for National Socialist poetry was the march song or community song that was derived from the folk song.[1] The Storm Trooper *Oberführer* Gerhard Schumann, one of the main representatives of Nazi poetry, recognized the simple folk song as the suitable vehicle in which "the primal sounds of the human German soul" could take on a "contemporary form." "Restrained toughness and trusting sincerity," as well as "leave-taking, separation, horror, staying the course, upswing, and victory" could be best expressed in this form, as Schumann explained in a speech about war poetry that he held in 1942 on the occasion of the "Pan-German and European Poets' Conference in Weimar."[2] Accordingly, the poetry of the Third Reich consisted mostly of purposeful occasional poetry with a direct political reference point, "political" being used in the broadest sense. However, as Gerhard Schumann proclaimed in his "lead article" in *SA-Mann* (Storm Trooper) in 1937, National Socialist poetry should be more than a Party program transferred into poetry:

> The National Socialist artist does not stop at the boundaries of the political in the narrow sense; in his treatment, he has to meld all the areas of existence; he has to pull back into himself and to generate from within himself *the whole of life;* he has to represent the harsh greatness of our heroic times as well as the stillness of the German landscape, the miracle of German humanity, the search of the German soul for God; [and] the personal as well as the general. For National Socialism in particular views the work of art not as the mechanical product of a collective, but as the organically grown fruit of a community.[3]

Schumann's statement provides a pretty good framework for National Socialist poetry that could also include the poetry of poets who did not produce pronounced National Socialist propaganda and who had little or nothing to do with National Socialism. Among National Socialist themes in the narrower sense are poems about the flag and *Führer*, drums and loyalty, belief and obedience, duty, honor and sacrifice, as well as blood, soil and fire. But poems about the German landscape, the German homeland, German history, and German people could also be used or called into service, even against the will or better judgment of the authors. Accordingly, this chapter will first introduce some of the themes and authors of National Socialist poetry in the narrow sense. Following that, the discussion will turn to a wide variety of authors, including Agnes Miegel, Gottfried Benn, Lulu von Strauß und Torney, and Josef Weinheber, who at least for some short period of time fell under the spell of the National Socialists. Their poetry, though, is a far cry from the purposeful occasional poetry of the National Socialists. The difference in quality between the two groups is in most cases substantial; Gottfried Benn and Josef Weinheber cannot be mentioned in the same breath with Heinrich Anacker and Gerhard Schumann. It should likewise be taken into consideration that authors such as Weinheber and Miegel were by no means as drenched in brown as Schumann and Anacker, and that only parts of their work belong in this chapter on Nazi poetry, while virtually the entire work of National Socialist bards such as Anacker and Schumann was under the influence of the swastika, at least until 1945.[4]

Themes and Authors of National Socialist Poetry

The poetry of the Third Reich calls upon and appeals to the so-called German soul of the people, as manifested in its "original form" in Dietrich Eckart's storm song, which ends with the cry "Germany awake!" Eckart (1868–1923) was considered "the first National Socialist poet,"[5] and his song a great prototype of National Socialist battle poetry. Eckart wrote one of the first of countless *Führer* poems:

> Die Herzen auf! Wer sehen will, der sieht!
> Die Kraft ist da, vor der die Nacht entflieht![6]
>
> [Hearts uplifted! Who wants to see will see!
> The strength is there, before the night does flee!]

For Eckart and his successors, Adolf Hitler was, after the defeat of 1918, the man who was going to lead Germany to new and wonderful times. In doing so, he would, like Albrecht Dürer's knight, have unspeakable difficulties to overcome, or so Heinrich Anacker claims in verse in his poem titled "Ritter, Tod und Teufel," which is based on the well-known Dürer picture:

> In Dürers Bild erkennen wir dich tief,
> du, den der Herr zum Führertum berief:
>
> Einsam, dem erzgeschienten Ritter gleich,
> begannst du deinen Ritt ins ferne Reich.
>
> Am Weg, der hart und steil und dornig war,
> lag hundertfältig lauernd die Gefahr.
>
> Und listiger Verführer suchten viel
> dich wegzulocken vom erkornen Ziel.

Du aber bleibst klar und unbeirrt,
kein Trugbild hat dir je den Sinn verwirrt.

Dein Blick, von einer innern Schau gebannt,
blieb streng zur deutschen Gralsburg hingewandt.

Unsichtbar zogen Tod und Teufel mit,
bis Kraft und Reinheit dir den Sieg erstritt![7]

[Deep in Dürer's picture we recognize you,
You whom the Lord called to leadership:

Solitary, like the iron-splinted knight,
You began your ride to the distant Reich.

On the way that was hard and steep, with thorns,
Danger lay lurking, hundredfold.

And cunning seducers often sought
To lure you from the chosen goal.

But you remained clear and steadfast,
Not ever did false images deceive your mind.

Your glance, held transfixed by an inner view,
Stayed turned, unswerving, to German Grail's castle.

Death and the devil rode along invisibly,
Until strength and purity made victory yours.]

Through the reference to Dürer and the Grail's castle ("Gralsburg"), Hitler becomes firmly anchored in German art, history, and mythology. His battle is presented in simplified form as the struggle between good and evil. Moreover, God is on his side, for the *Führer* is His chosen instrument. His path is marked out by an "inner view" and not determined by rational planning. This poem combines almost all of the National Socialist clichés that Ernst Loewy summarizes in catch words in the table of contents of his book *Literatur unterm Hakenkreuz* (Literature Under the Swastika), for example, "Defamed Reason," "Myths out of the Retort," "The 'Higher Order,'" "Belief in Authority," and "The Myth of Germany."[8]

The *Führer's* solitary struggle for Germany and the mystical founding of the Reich is celebrated in many other National Socialist poems, for example, in Gerhard Schumann's "Der Eine" (The One). In a parallel to the history from the Old Testament (Moses 2, 19, 16–25) of Moses's climb to the top of Mount Sinai, one of the central events in the history of the people of Israel, a parallel that sounds strange coming from a National Socialist poet,

"Der Eine" (The One) struggles, with his eyes bleeding, in a nocturnal battle on the mountain top, despairing, "until a command forced him to his knees." With whom he was struggling never becomes clear, but the poet is not concerned with rational explanations, but rather with mythical intuition. Instead of climbing down into the valley with Mosaic law tablets, "The One" descends with the "glowing fire of the chosen one around his head," frees the mass of people, and founds the Reich:

> Die Millionen beugten sich ihm schweigend,
> Erlöst. Der Himmel flammte morgenbleich.
> Die Sonne wuchs. Und mit ihr wuchs das Reich.[9]

> [The millions bowed down to him in silence,
> Saved. The heavens shot flames pale as morning.
> The sun grew. And with it grew the Reich.]

Thus, in the Schumann poem, the Reich is born of blood and fire through the chosen "One." Further questions are out of the question; the millions follow silently. The vivid images of flames and blood in this poem recall further key elements of National Socialist ideology evident in the countless solstice celebrations and the campfire romanticism of the Hitler Youth, where songs like "Flamme empor" (Flame rise upward) were a standard element. In his poem "Sonnenwende" (Solstice), Wolfgang Jünemann attempts to conjure up the purifying force of the blazing fire; only the first stanza will be quoted here:

> Lodernde Flammen, heilige Lohe,
> rauschend erstrahle, was immer auch drohe!
> Höher und höher! Aus Grauen und Nacht
> Ist endlich der Glaube ans Licht gebracht.[10]

> [Glowing flames, sacred blaze,
> Flare up, roaring, whatever threatens!
> Higher and higher! Out of horror and night
> Belief is finally brought to light.]

The swastika, too, is supposed to call fire and sun to mind. In Schummann's poem, "Deutschland" (Germany), Germany appears to his comrades and him as the "eternal fire that consumes us."[11] Flames and blood are connected to the *völkisch* idea and Home-to-the-Reich Movement in the poem "Grenzlandschwur" (Border Land Vow) by Heinrich Gutberlet:

> Volk will zu Volk, und Blut will zu Blut
> und Flamme will zur Flamme.
> Steig auf zum Himmel, heilige Glut,
> rausch auf vom Stamm zu Stamme.[12]

[Volk aspires to Volk, and blood,
to blood, and flame, to flame.
Rise up to the heavens, sacred fire,
Roar up from tribe to tribe!]

Blood is associated with the red of the swastika flag, which, in remembrance of the National Socialist "martyrs" from the Hitler putsch on November 9, 1923 — "in November many died in action" — becomes the "Blutfahne" (Blood Flag) in the poem by Wolfram Krupka. Here is the last stanza:

Die Fahne singt von Heldenmut.
Ihr Lied reckt uns zu neuer Tat.
Die Fahne singt von Heldenblut.
Ihr Lied weckt Leben: Saat um Saat.[13]

[The flag sings of heroes' courage.
Its song emboldens us to new deeds.
The flag sings of heroes' blood.
Its song awakens life: seed by seed.]

The flag is transfigured into a mythical-mystical symbol that waves before the entire nation in the Horst Wessel song "Die Fahne hoch" (Raise High the Flag) as the unofficial national anthem of the Nazis.[14] As does the *Führer*, the flag also inspires countless poets and poems, such as "Flaggenruf" (Call of the Flag) by Wolfgang Schwarz, "Wir hissen die Fahne" (We hoist the Flag) by Herbert Böhme, "Der Fahneneid" (The Oath on the Flag), by Heinrich Lersch or the two stanzas in "An die Fahne" (To the Flag) by Baldur von Schirach, the Reich Youth Leader of the German Reich, who also tried his hand at writing poetry. The last stanza of the latter poem is reproduced here:

Inbrunst und Wille bist du von uns allen.
Wer für dich fiel, zum Bild wird er in dir.
Du bist die Brücke zwischen dort und hier.
Heil denen, die in deinem Schatten fallen.[15]

[You are fervor and will for all of us.
He who fell for you turns to an image within.
You are the bridge between there and here.
Hail to those who fall in your shadow.]

Thus the central theme of death for the flag, *Führer*, and fatherland is addressed. The dead comrades from the "period of struggle" before 1933 are already mentioned in the Horst Wessel song; they join the march in spirit, like Wessel himself, or "Schlageter" in the poem by Hanns Johst, the author of the drama *Schlageter* (see the chapter on drama), in which the last stanza reads:

Wir stehn in seinem Zeichen
zu Pflicht und Dienst und Ziel
und schwören stets zu gleichen
ihm, der für Deutschland fiel:
Schlageter![16]

[We stand under his sign
in duty and service and goal
and swear always to be like
him who fell for Germany:
Schlageter!]

But even the dead of the First World War are called into action by the Nazis for their propaganda machine, especially the men who died in action at Langemarck. Poems in that vein were provided by Heinrich Zerkaulen ("Aus zieh ich meiner Jugend buntes Kleid [I Take Off the Many-Colored Dress of My Youth]"), Heinrich Lersch ("Soldatenabschied [Soldier's Good-bye]"), Herybert Menzel ("Junge Faust um heilige Fahne [Young Fist around the Sacred Flag]"), or Herbert Böhme, to mention just a few; Böhme's poem "Langemarck" ends as follows:

Sand weht über die Toten, doch die Erinnerung zeigt,
wie die Herzen einst lohten, ehe ihr Blick sich geneigt;
singt ein Lied über Gräbern ewiger Melodie:
Bleibe bei mir und lausche und vergesse sie nie,
Deutschland![17]

[Sand blows over the dead, but memory shows
how the hearts once glowed, before their glances expired;
sing a song of graves, the melody eternal:
Stay with me and listen and never forget them:
Germany!]

Even for Ernst Bertram, a professor of *Germanistik* in Cologne and at one time a friend of Thomas Mann, the path to people, homeland, light, and life leads through death:

Aber erst Gräber
schaffen Heimat,
erst unsere Toten
geben uns Licht.

Erst auf Hügeln
Klagende knien,
erst über Särgen
werdet ihr Volk.[18]

[But only graves
create a homeland;
only our dead
give us light.

Only when on hills
grieving souls kneel,
only coffins
forge one people.]

After the beginning of the Second World War, there would soon be ample opportunity for coffins. The folk song about the three lilies on the grave soon becomes reality for Heinrich Anacker in the poem "Drei Lilien" (Three Lilies):

Das Lied von den drei Lilien,
Wir sangen's vor Tag und Jahr —
Das Lied von den drei Lilien,
Nun ward es bitter wahr:

Vor Amiens liegt am Straßenrand
Ein frisches Soldatengrab;
Da bettete Kameradenhand
Den jungen Toten hinab.[19]

[The song of the three lilies,
we sang it a day, a year ago —
The song of the three lilies
Now bitterly came true.

Near Amiens at the roadside
A fresh soldier's grave is found,
There the hands of comrades
Laid the young dead man to rest below.]

In Heinrich Anacker's sonnet "Spuren des Kriegs" (Traces of War), little of the eagerness for war remains; on the contrary, a faint air of death and devastation wafts through the lines of the poem. The lightning war in the west also claimed many lives:

Hier brennen noch die Wunden ungekühlt,
Und viele Kreuze künden bittere Lücken,
Daß schauernd man den Hauch des Todes fühlt.[20]

[Here the wounds still burn, uncooled,
And so many crosses tell of bitter gaps,
That, shuddering, you feel the touch of death.]

In his volume of poems *Heimat und Front* (Homeland and Front) "from the fall of 1939," Anacker still celebrates the grandness of war, for example in the introductory poem "Aufbruch" (Beginning):

> Hoch in den Lüften dröhnt's von Motorengesang;
> Jagende Boote umdonnert der Brandungsklang.
> Hell wie die Sonne aus wolkenverhangener Nacht,
> Steigt aus den tobenden Wettern gigantischer Schlacht,
> Deutschland — dein Sieg![21]

> [High in the air the song of motors drones,
> The sound of the surf thunders around speeding boats.
> Bright like the sun from the cloud-enshrouded night,
> Rises from the raging storm of colossal battle,
> Germany — your victory!]

When the number of casualties rose immeasurably as the war progressed, poets attempted to find sense in the sacrifices and to urge the still living to hold the course. The rousing, heaven-storming beginning and attack have turned to elegiac grief and justification that appeals to the survivors to fulfill the legacy of the dead. In Karl Bröger's poem "Das Vermächtnis" (The Legacy), the dead are not gone but instead they speak to the living through nature:

> Alle lieben Brüder, die schon gefallen sind,
> reden aus Stein und Scholle, sprechen aus Wolke und Wind.

> [All the dear brothers who have already fallen
> speak out of stone and earth, speak out of clouds and wind.]

The voices of those killed in action are intended as an appeal and testament to the living not to give up but instead to carry on and to complete their work:

> Darum ist der toten Brüder letztes Gebot:
> "Halte das Werk am Leben, so ist kein Geopferter tot."[22]

> [The dead brother's last command is therefore:
> Keep the work alive, then no man sacrificed is dead!]

Even for Hans Carossa, the number of men killed in action is no cause for grief and lamentation, for the message of salvation even penetrates the sounds of battle:

> Der Himmel dröhnt von Tod. Die Erde blutet
> aus Wunden treuer Söhne Tag und Nacht.
> Weltende künden trauernde Propheten.
> Doch während Feinde dumpf ihr Schicksal suchen,
> Hörst du, mein Volk, durch Wahn und Wut noch Rufe
> Des Heils und glühst in Opfern auf . . .

. . .
Viel Blut, viel Blut muß in die Erde sinken;
nie wird sie sonst den Menschen heimatlich.[23]

[The heavens boom with death. The earth bleeds
from wounds of loyal sons, both day and night.
Grieving prophets pronounce the end of the world.
But while enemies dully seek their fate,
you hear, my people, through madness and rage, cries
of salvation, and blaze anew in sacrifice . . .
. . .
Much blood, much blood must sink into the earth;
Never will it otherwise be home to man.]

Poems from the First World War, like the following poem of Ina Seidel, are enlisted to justify the casualties of war for whose deaths no rational reason exists any more. In response to the question of the living about the meaning of the bloody sacrifices ("Für was, für was vergossen und vertan [For What, for What Spilled and Wasted]"), the war dead themselves speak at the end of Seidel's poem:

Beweint uns nicht, frag nicht nach dem Gewinn!
Wir sind der Strom, der sich ins Meer ergoß,
und ist kein Tropfen, der vergebens floß:
das Opfer ist des Opfers letzter Sinn.[24]

[Don't cry for us, don't ask about the gain!
We are the flood that poured into the sea.
and no drop is that flowed in vain:
Sacrifice is for the sacrifice's sake.]

The sound of the marching columns runs through numerous volumes of poetry, as everywhere in the "Magie der Viererreihe" (Magic of the Row of Four), which Anacker conjured up in a poem with the same title, became the leitmotiv of the movement. This magic brings everything under its spell and silences all questions and all thinking ("we scarcely ask"):

Das ist die harte Weihe,
die unsern Weg verschönt:
Magie der Viererreihe,
Wenn vorn die Trommel dröhnt![25]

[That is the hard induction,
which beautifies our path:
the magic of the row of four,
when the drum rolls out in front.]

The monotonous rhythm of marching, especially when accompanied by a drum, encourages placing everyone on the same level and enforces group solidarity; its "motoric suggestiveness" does not touch the intellect but mobilizes "deeper levels."[26] In a poem such as "Deutschland im Marschtritt" (Germany in March Step) by Herybert Menzel, the brisk cadence of an entire nation resounds through every line and every strophe, as in the last one here:

> Soldat! Soldat! So Tritt um Tritt
> Hört Deutschland, wie es stritt und litt!
> Hört Deutschland, wie es ewig zieht,
> Das beste Blut ins Heldenlied![27]

> [Soldier! Soldier! So step by step
> Hear Germany, how it marched and wept!
> Hear Germany, how it sweeps along,
> The best blood, into hero's song!]

Not only the marching, but also the interpretation of such a poem defies logical categories. Herybert Menzel and his brown-shirted compatriots knew very well about the "maelstrom of the collective," "which no one can escape," as he writes in the poem "Braune Kolonnen" (Brown Columns). The poem addresses a person who is still on the outside but will soon — as all of Germany — be absorbed into the brown-shirted columns because he will no longer be able to resist the singing and the fluttering flags:

> Da braun an braun Kolonnen ziehn,
> Ihr Marschtritt hämmert sich dir ein.
> Du weißt, du kannst nicht mehr entfliehn
> Du wirst doch morgen bei uns sein.

> [Endless brown columns pass by,
> Their march step hammers into you.
> You know you can escape no more;
> Tomorrow you will be with us.]

And where are they marching to?

> Die Straße führt zu Hitler hier,
> Der alle mit sich reißt![28]

> [The road leads to Hitler here,
> who carries everyone along!]

For fainter hearts and *Wandervogel* supporters, the rhythm of hiking afforded an opportunity for stimulating a sense of community, as Max Reuschle explains in his essay "Der Sinn des Gedichtes in unserer Zeit" (The Meaning of the Poem in Our Time):

> The lyric poem is very closely connected to journeying on foot. The person who is fulfilled by the primal experience of journeying on foot will, from the transformations of that activity which are part of the great cosmic cycle around us, fully realize and develop the poem whose seeds he holds within.[29]

The community talked about here is not that of the marching columns of men in brown or some other uniforms but rather one emerging from the feeling of organic involvement in the cosmic course of the world that is to act as a protective shield against the frazzling effects of the modern world and the threat posed by the "trivializing tendencies of a rational civilization." Such a poem, emanating from a "spirited fullness of life," is far removed from a "spiritless collective," but "close internally to the spirit of religious community and spiritual connection. This poem will be inspired by the love for the fertile earth and for the solitude of pristine nature — as well as for the cathedral towering over the city and for the sacredness of a mythical prehistory" (214–15). For Reuschle, the poem, as the "last respite of the basic element of poetic form — verse" (216), represents a bulwark against the "experiments and contortions of the naturalistic, the expressionistic, and the extremely objective directions." Reuschle closes his essay with a practical example intended to illustrate his theory of poetry:

> Ich trage in mir reine Flamme,
> Ich spüre dumpf und heiß mein Blut —
> Der Erde große Mutteramme
> Umschützt den Sturm, die Glut.
>
> Ich wachse aus den Erdenreichen
> Wie Baum und Blüte in den Raum —
> Ich kann nur Erdentsprossenem gleichen
> Und rühre an des Himmels Raum.
>
> [I carry in me pure flame,
> I feel my blood, heavy and hot —
> The earth's great mother-nurse
> Protects the storm, the fire.
>
> I grow out of the earthly realms,
> As trees and blossoms, into space —
> I can only resemble what sprouts from earth
> And touch on heaven's realm.]

This poem simultaneously serves as a good example for blood and soil mysticism so abundant in the poetry of the Third Reich. As Gerhard Schumann describes in his sonnet, which is typical for Nazi "Blu-Bo [blood and soil] poetry," the Reich grows out of the rootedness of German in the German soil. Here earth, blood, heaven and mother, seed and flag merge into a ghastly brown mass:

> Da bückte ich mich tief zur Erde nieder
> Und segnete die fruchtbare und sprach:
> Verloren, wie entwurzelt, lag ich brach,
> Ich komme heim, o Mutter, nimm mich wieder.
>
> Da wurde Strömung alten Blutes wach,
> Die in den dunklen Schächten schlief und schwieg,
> Erschauerte und wuchs und schwoll und stieg,
> Fuhr durch die Adern hin ein Flammenbach.
>
> Und aus des Herzens aufgerissnen Schollen
> Brach heiß das Blut und schäumte Frucht und Tat
> Wie Innen — Außen zueinander quollen!
>
> Und rot aufwehend, Fahne junger Saat,
> Schwang durch die Lüfte hin der Jubelleich.
> So wuchs aus Blut und Erde neu das Reich.[30]

> [There I bent down very low to the earth
> And blessed the fertile earth and spoke:
> Lost, as if uprooted, I lay fallow.
> I'm coming home, O mother, take me back.
>
> The flow of old blood then awakened
> Which slept and remained silent in the dark tunnels,
> Shivered and grew and swelled and rose,
> A stream of flames flowed through the veins.
>
> And from the heart's torn-open clods
> Hot blood broke, producing fruit and deed.
> How inside-outside surged to one another!
>
> Waving upward, red, the flag of young seed,
> The joyful lay quivered there through the air.
> Thus the Reich from blood and soil grew anew.]

Strictly occasional poetry accompanied the political events and the campaigns of the Second World War step by step, for example portrayed in the poetry volumes of Heinrich Anacker. In *Ein Volk — ein Reich — ein Führer*,

Gedichte um Österreichs Heimkehr (One People — One Reich — One Führer. Poems About Austria's Return Home), the poems describe the Austrians' tears of joy at their return home to the Reich and their thanks to the *Führer,* with the organ of Kufstein playing the Horst Wessel song; the ringing of the bells from Braunau and Leonding, the old home of the new *Führer;* and earth-breaking with a shovel by the *Führer* for the highway from Vienna to Munich, the "city of the Nazi movement." The volume *Heimat und Front, Gedichte aus dem Herbst 1939* (Homeland and Front, Poems From the Fall of 1939) praises the readiness of the homeland for the great war, the "return home of Danzig," the camaraderie of the front, the "silent determination," and the "sworn community." The sonnet "Friede des Führers" (Peace of the *Führer*) portrays Hitler as a courageous hero of peace; the blame for the war is pushed off on England in "England ist Schuld" (England is to Blame). Another sonnet ("Verdunkelte Stadt [Darkened City]") treats the blackouts during the bombing war. The volume *Bereitschaft und Aufbruch, Gedichte aus dem Kriegswinter 1940* (Readiness and Beginning. Poems From the Winter of War, 1940) describes the first battles and war heroes from the first weeks of the war, such as the battle for Narvik, the "steel wings" of the Air Force, the U-boat Captain Prien, "Frontweihnacht" (Front Christmas) and the "Weihnachtsglocken im Niemandsland" (Christmas Bells in No Man's Land). The volume *Über die Maas, über die Schelde und Rhein! Gedichte vom Feldzug im Westen* (Across the Maas, Across the Scheldt and Rhine! Poems of the Campaign in the West) accompanies the German soldiers from Flanders to Dunkirk, from Reims to Verdun, and into the forest of Compiègne where Hitler accepted the capitulation of France.

Poets in the Environment of National Socialism

Not all of the poetry of the Third Reich was insignificant, especially when it came from prominent poets who only lent the Nazis their pens for a short time, or who could be used by those in power for their own purposes. The latter course, though, was only possible if the works in question also already contained material suitable for the Nazi ideology. As Ketelsen showed in 1978, using the example of Weinheber, the poetry of National Socialism is not necessarily based on two premises, "pathetic rhyming" and the essential "connection to organized National Socialism."[31] The poets and poetesses in this section have little in common; they represent a wide variety of literary trends, from experimental expressionism to strictly formal Neo-Romanticism. What connects them — and that is what is of primary importance in this chapter — is only their more or less short-term sympathy with the ideology of National Socialism. Even lines from Stephan George's cycle *Das neue Reich* (The New Reich) fit well into the Nazi ideology, although the author himself wanted nothing to do with the brown-shirted men in power. However, his vision of

the new Reich, a great leader, bringer of order, and former of a sworn community of decent men, seemed to fit seamlessly into the Third Reich, as did
his view of the poet as the herald of a new age. The National Socialist Germanist Heinz Kindermann praises George as a poet who repeatedly added fuel
to "the sacred fire" and "with the true gesture of a visionary" conjured up
"the spirit of the future community of the people, our only salvation."[32] In
times of confusion, according to George, toughness is again necessary:

> Noch härtre pflugschar muß die scholle furchen
> Noch dickere nebel muß die luft bedräun . . .
>
> [Still harder plowshares must furrow the earth
> Still thicker mists must menace the air . . .]

On the ruins of the old and decayed a new race will arise:

> . . . Ihm wuchs schon heran
> unangetastet von dem geilen markt
> Von dünnem hirngeweb und giftgem flitter
> Gestählt im banne der verruchten jahre
> Ein jung geschlecht das wieder mensch und ding
> Mit echten maassen misst, . . .
> Das von sich spie was mürb und feig und lau
>
> [. . . In his care grew
> Untouched by the lewd marketplace
> By thin tissue of the brain and poisonous glitter
> Steeled in the course of the infamous years
> A young race that again measures man and thing
> With genuine measure, . . .
> That spits out what is rotting, craven, tepid]

This young and tough race will produce a leader that will found a new empire:

> Das aus geweihten träumen tun und dulden
> Den einzigen der hilft den Mann gebiert . . .
> Der sprengt die ketten fegt auf trümmerstätten
> Die ordnung, geißelt die verlaufnen heim
> Ins ewige recht wo großes wiederum groß ist
> Herr wiederum herr, zucht wiederum zucht, er heftet
> Das wahre sinnbild auf das völkische banner
> Er führt durch sturm und grausige signale
> Des frührots seiner treuen schar zum werk
> Des wachen tags und pflanzt das Neue Reich.[33]

[Which (the young race) brings forth from sacred dreams, acts and suffering
The only one who helps, bears man . . .
He breaks the chains, sweeps onto fields of ruins
Order, flogs the gone-astrays home
To eternal right where great is again great
Master again master, discipline again discipline, he clips
The true symbol to the *völkisch* banner
He leads through storm and ghastly signals
Of the red dawn his loyal troop to the work
Of awakened day, and plants the New Reich.]

The linguistic power of George's poem far surpasses that of Nazi poetry, but not in the ideological interpretation that the Nazis imposed upon it. Its influence on the leaders of the Third Reich is not to be underestimated, as Kindermann explains: "These visions of Stefan George sent out strong currents of national belief and had the effect of inspiring and giving direction to a number of today's leaders of the national uprising at decisive moments."[34] It is therefore not surprising that the new Culture Minister Bernhard Rust offered George a leadership position in the reorganized writers' academy. George refused; he did not deny the "ancestry of the new national movement," but he did point out that "the laws of the intellectual and of the political" are "very different." "George never distanced himself from the Nazis publicly";[35] he died on December 4, 1933, in exile in Switzerland.

Gottfried Benn, like Stefan George, was for many not only a brilliant poet but also a champion of fascism. Benn was never a member of the Party, but in contrast to George, he initially publicly declared his loyalty to the new powers-that-be. However, he soon realized his mistake. When he was himself denounced as "degenerate" by the Nazis because of his defense of expressionism and, in 1938, was excluded from the Reich Chamber of Writers, and his works banned, he had already been living for three years as a military physician in the "aristocratic form of exile" (Benn). In *Doppelleben* (Double Life), his autobiographical notebooks from 1950, he refers to his "illegal anti-fascist activity" when he illegally published a volume of poetry in 1943 which he financed on his own. He provides a sample from it, the poem "Monolog": ("Den Darm mit Rotz genährt, das Hirn mit Lügen — / erwählte Völker Narren eines Clowns . . . [The gut nourished with snot, the brain with lies — / chosen peoples, fools of a clown . . .]").[36] Here is not the place to go into detail about Benn's confessions of fascism or about the controversies that they provoked;[37] a few brief comments should be sufficient. Benn's public confessions of belief in the new state are not present in his poetry, although the anti-rational viewpoint contained there was very opportune for the Nazis, but rather in some of his essays, for example, *Der neue Staat und die Intellektuellen, Kunst und Macht* (The New State and the

Intellectuals, Art and Power), and his later explanation of his Nazi past in *Doppelleben* (Double Life). Benn's texts should be viewed in the context of a comprehensive critical review of the modern age, in which he initially viewed the new powers-that-be as allies. Benn suffered under the effects of "intellectual fragmentation" and the progressive cerebration of the human being; he longed for natural, archaic integration into a greater whole:

> O daß wir unsere Ururahnen wären.
> Ein Klümpchen Schleim in einem warmen Moor.
>
> . . .
>
> Schon ein Libellenkopf, ein Möwenflügel
> Wäre zu weit und litte schon zu sehr.[38]
>
> [O, were we but our most ancient ancestors.
> A little clump of slime out on a warm moor.
>
> . . .
>
> A dragonfly's head, a sea gull's wing
> Would be too complex and suffer already too much.]

Poems like "Verlorenes Ich" (Lost Self), "Ein Wort" (A Word), or "Gesänge I" (Singing I) are fitting poetic expressions of unspeakable isolation and abysmal cultural pessimism, from which National Socialism appeared to provide an escape. In *Der neue Staat und die Intellektuellen* (The New State and the Intellectuals), he accused intellectuals, among other things, of enthusiastically welcoming Marxism and

> of viewing the revolution of nationalism as immoral, dissolute, and directed against the meaning of history. . . . What an intellectual defect . . . not to see in it [the revolution] an anthropologically deeper value in its great feeling of willingness to sacrifice and its loss of self for the totality, the state, the race, the immanent, not [to see it] in its turning from economic concerns to the mythical, not [to see] all of this in it![39]

In response to a letter of the ballad writer Börries von Münchhausen, in which Münchhausen stated his belief that he discerned in Benn "Jewish characteristics," Benn reacted angrily and presented in *Lebensweg eines Intellektualisten* (Life Path of an Intellectual) his "proof of Aryanism":

> With regard to genealogy, I am descended on my father's side from a purely Aryan environment, and with regard to spiritual matters and breeding, from an environment in which Protestant theology has had its place for over a hundred years. . . . Into this hereditary environment my mother brought one-hundred-percent, never yet cross-bred Romanic blood. . . . A mixture resulted, but not mixed breeds, cross-breeding, but no bastards, [and] in any case an Aryan mixture resulted, one that has been legitimized frequently in Germany; it is the mixture of the French Protestant refugees: Fontane, Chamisso, [and] Du Bois-Reymond have proven it.[40]

In a response to the literary emigrants, Benn emphasizes that the "course of events in Germany it is not at all a matter of political shenanigans . . . but rather it is a matter of a new biological type; history mutates and a people wants to breed itself." So as not to be suspected of rationalism, he adds: "Of course the concept of the nature of the human being that underlies this breeding idea holds that the human being may be rational but is primarily mythical and deep."[41] Benn's later comments on his earlier texts can be read in *Doppelleben*, in which he concedes that he "today [would] no longer write" some of the passages in his earlier writings, especially in his response to the literary emigrants; "the writings are romantic, have an unpleasant energy, and are full of a kind of 'intoxication with fate.'" Furthermore, according to Benn in *Doppelleben* in 1950, his text is "less a plea for the National Socialist state than . . . for the right of a people to give itself a new way of life, and I was analyzing the method with which such a new way of life makes itself known and prevails over all rational and moral objections against it." For Benn, it was a matter of examining "how history moves," and this question was still of current interest to him in 1950.[42] Not everyone, however, was satisfied with Benn's explanations, to say the least.

The poets of the Göttingen circle surrounding Börries von Münchhausen (1874–1945), who was from the family of the "lying barons," were among the critics of the supposedly degenerate tendencies of the modern age. Münchhausen, who edited the *Göttinger Musenalmanach* (Göttingen Muses' Almanac) from 1897 to 1923, is considered the restorer of the German ballad, which was also cultivated by his friends Lulu von Strauß und Torney and Agnes Miegel. Münchhausen achieved great popularity with his ballads and songs of the homely earth and history, nobility and decline. His works such as *Balladen und ritterliche Lieder* (Ballads and Chivalric Songs, first in 1908) or *Das Herz im Harnisch: Neue Balladen und Lieder* (The Heart in Armor: New Ballads and Songs, first in 1911) went through numerous editions and were frequently set to music. In ballads and songs he sang of the Thirty Years War and Frederick the Great, the homeland and the nobility, but also "Das Buch Juda (The Book of Judah), which contains the following stanza in the "Mose" (Moses) ballad:

> Da ist uns ein König gekommen in Feuer und Geist,
> Da ist uns ein Führer gefunden, der Mose heißt,
> Ein Helfer hat sich erhoben, der hilft uns schnell,
> Jehovas Prophet ist erstanden in Israel![43]

> [A king has come to us here, in fire and spirit,
> A leader has been found for us whose name is Moses,
> A helper has risen, he helps us quickly;
> Jehovah's prophet has arisen in Israel.]

In the poem "Krieg" (War), Münchhausen uses images taken from nature to welcome war as the renewer and restorer of age-old traditional order:

Das ekle Unkraut, das aus heiligem Boden
Hoch über alle blonden Ähren stieg,
Kein Winter kanns aus deutscher Erde roden,
Nur einer pflügt so tief, das ist der Krieg!

Wenn dann des Krieges eisengraue Mähre
Den Pflug gerissen durch das träge Land,
Wiegt wieder sich des Kornes edle Ähre,
Wo vordem geil der gelbe Günsel stand,

Und in den Stapfen seiner mächtigen Hufe,
Eng an des Ackers Schollen angepreßt,
Baut wieder wohl mit lockend-süßem Rufe
Die Lerche ihr gesangumjubelt Nest.[44]

[The loathsome weeds that out of sacred earth
Rose high above all golden ears of grain,
From German soil no winter can uproot them,
One only plows so deep, and that is war!

When the iron-grey mare of war
Has torn the plow across the idle land,
The noble ears of grain again will sway,
Where long ago, lustful, yellow bugle stood.

And in the tracks of its mighty hooves,
Pressed tightly on the field's rough clods,
The lark with sweet, enticing calls again
Builds her nest, surrounded by rejoicing song.]

It is not surprising that this myth of battle and earth meshed so perfectly with National Socialist ideology. According to Langenbucher, "the best forces of German nature also live in the works of Münchhausen."[45] Münchhausen welcomed the seizure of power by the National Socialists, in whom he believed to have found the protectors and preservers of the "intellectual freedom of the world." In an essay in the *Das Börsenblatt für den deutschen Buchhandel* (The German Book Trade Gazette), he rebuked those who, with the rise of the Nazis, saw the coming sell-out of the German spirit: "The proud, powerful intellectual legacy of Germany, the world fame of the fatherland, the last and greatest stronghold of freedom in the world — would anyone believe that the Holy Third Reich would waste, squander, forfeit that!" Even if in the excessive enthusiasm for renewal some things get broken — so Münchhausen — you can't plane down wood without leaving shavings on the floor: "On the threshing floor of the world the wheat is once again being winnowed — what does it matter if in sweeping out the chaff a handful of grains get lost; the sacred harvest will still be saved!"[46] He realized his error too late and committed suicide in 1945.

Lulu von Strauß und Torney (1873–1956), who was closely associated with Börries von Münchhausen and Agnes Miegel through the *Göttinger Musenalmanach* celebrated her peasant, Low-German homeland in the Weser Mountains in poems, ballads, stories, and novels with titles such as *Bauernstolz: Novelle* (A Peasant's Pride: A Novella, 1901), *Der Judashof: Ein niederdeutscher Erbhof-Roman* (Farm of Judas: Novel About a Low-German Inherited Farm, 1937, new edition of *Judas*, 1911), *Erde der Väter: Gedichte* (Earth of the Fathers: Poems, 1936), or the complete edition of her ballads and poems with the title *Reif steht die Saat* (The Seed is Ripe, 1919, 1926, 1935, and 1940). It would be wrong to consider all the works that treated life in the country also to be predecessors of National Socialist blood and soil literature. Yet some works of Lulu Strauß und Torney fall into this category. Langenbucher places Strauß und Torney's peasant literature in a class with Löns's *Wehrwolf* (Werewolf) novel in her unsentimental portrayal of "hard, inner, fated reality."[47] In *Reif steht die Saat* (The Seed is Ripe), a group of poems focuses on the theme "Mutter Erde" (Mother Earth). In the main poem, "Mutter Erde" is praised as the beginning and end point of all life; the last of the three stanzas is below:

> Heil'ge Mutter, die die Müden hegt!
> Über meiner Qual und Wonne Streiten
> Magst du morgen deine Schollen breiten —
> Laß mich heut durch deinen Sommer schreiten
> Und so viel des süßen Rausches trinken,
> Als das Herz erträgt![48]

> [Holy Mother, who nurtures the weary!
> Over the struggle of my misery and bliss
> You may tomorrow spread your clods of earth —
> Today let me stride through your summer
> And drink as much of the sweet ecstasy
> As the heart can bear.]

The volume *Reif steht die Saat* ends with the dramatic poem "Sonnen-wende" (Solstice), which is to be performed outdoors with speakers representing the seasons, a chorus, and rhythmical movements. It closes with a solemn spoken song that sings the praises of the sun:

> Es loben dich Keim und Blüte, es reifen dir Saat und Frucht,
> Dich preist die Stimme der Wälder, und schimmernder Wolken Flucht,

Lebenschaffende Flamme, lodernder Schöpfer Geist,
Wir loben dich, Gott der Götter, der Sonne heißt!

[Bud and blossom laud you, seed and fruit ripen for you,
The voice of the forest praises you, and the flight of shimmering clouds,
....
Life-creating flame, blazing creator's spirit,
We praise you, god of gods, who's called the sun.]

Clear suggestions of the blood and soil mysticism invoked by the Nazis are
also evident in the poem "Väterheimat" (Homeland of the Fathers) from the
volume of poetry *Erde der Väter* (Earth of the Fathers, 1936) in which the
earth offers roots and a home to the restless blood:

Wandernde, Unrastvolle,
Treiben wir flüchtig hin,
Traum von Wurzel und Scholle
Liegt uns dunkel im Sinn, —
Und in drängender Welle,
Tief aus heiliger Quelle
Schwillt's zum Herzen und brennt,
Väter, vor eurer Schwelle:
Blut, das Erde erkennt![49]

[Wandering and restless
We drive fleetingly along,
A dream of roots and clods of earth
We hardly remember —
And in an urgent wave,
Deep, from the sacred source
It rises to the heart and burns,
Fathers, before your threshold:
Blood that recognizes earth!]

Strauß und Torney poems also found their way into volumes of poetry that
were put together by the high command of the *Wehrmacht* and were designed to strengthen the sense of mission of the German soldiers and their
belief in the people and the *Führer*. Here are a few lines from Strauß und
Torney's poem "Licht! Licht!" (Light! Light!) from the volume of collected
poems *Dem Führer: Worte deutscher Dichter* (To the Führer. Words of German Poets), which appeared in 1941:

Volk, glaube der Stimme der Finsternis nicht!
Hebe das Haupt, horch und spähe landein, —
siehst du nicht über den Äckern den grünen Schein,

siehst du nicht über den Bergen in Frühlingswehn
Morgenröten heiliger Zukunft stehn?

Ein Gestern versank, ein Heute erstand uns neu,
über den Trümmern steigt es strahlend und frei,
von schaffender Hand erbaut und schaffendem Geist,
das Heilige Haus, das da
Deutschland von Morgen
heißt![50]

[People, do not believe the voice of darkness!
Lift your head, listen and look inland —
don't you see across the fields the shining green,
don't you see across the mountains amidst spring breezes
the rosy dawn of a holy future?

A yesterday sank, a today arose for us anew,
It climbs above the ruins, radiant and free.
Built by a creating hand and a creating spirit
the Holy House, which there
is called
tomorrow's Germany!]

The poetess of the formerly German region in the east, Agnes Miegel (1879–1964) from Königberg, belongs in this chapter, at least with her volume of poems *Ostland* (1940, 1943). Like others, she also happened to be pulled into the realm of the National Socialists, who were able to make good use of her poetry for their drive to the east. She became a member of the National Socialist Women's Organization in 1937 and the NSDAP (the Nazi Party) in 1940. Anni Piorreck, in the chapter "The Great Error" of her apologetic Miegel biography (1967), *Agnes Miegel: Ihr Leben und ihre Dichtung* (Agnes Miegel: Her Life and Her Poetry), blames Miegel's affiliation with National Socialism on the "child-like innocence" of the poetess and the "indifference of the poet toward politics."[51] Miegel was inducted in May of 1933 into the "cleansed" Prussian Academy of Arts, Literature Section and was highly respected by the Nazis. For Piorreck, the poems in *Ostland* were a mistake, but even she cannot avoid admitting that "Agnes Miegel wrote them."[52] Of course for Piorreck, the *Ostland* poems are also formally poor and are an exception within Miegel's work, a view that probably requires thorough examination.

The *Ostland* volume, which includes once again several poems already published in earlier volumes, begins with a poem meant to be very personal, "An den Führer" (To the *Führer*), in which the aging Miegel expresses her reverence for the *Führer:*

Nicht mit der Jugend
Überschäumendem Jubel erlebt ich das Wunder
Deines Nahns.

[Not with youth's
Exuberance did I see the miracle
Of your drawing near.]

The revered *Führer* relieved her of her burden of "heavy memories" of "war and uprisings and the despair of dark days"; he wiped everything clean. Full of thanks, she places her poetic talent at the disposal of the *Führer* and the German people:

Übermächtig
Füllt mich demütiger Dank, daß ich dies erlebe,
Dir noch dienen kann, dienend den Deutschen
Mit der Gabe, die Gott mir verlieh!
....
Doch dies wäre
Höchste Erfüllung mir und Ehre der Ahnen:
Heilige Fackel, nie mehr weitergereichte,
Dir zu opfern![53]

[Overwhelmingly
Humble thanks fill me, that I am witnessing this,
Can still serve you, serving the Germans
With the gift that God gave me.
....
Still, it would be
The greatest fulfillment to me and honor to forebears:
To sacrifice to you,
The sacred torch, never more to be passed on.]

Piorreck attempts to lessen the embarrassing significance of this poem with the comment that it was a "commissioned poem."[54] Still, was such passion necessary for a poem of that sort? Piorreck herself writes at another point that Miegel had believed "in the *Führer*" "with her whole heart — trustingly and unconditionally, as was her nature."[55]

The following poems, "Hymne an Ostpreußen" (Hymn to East Prussia) and "Hindenburg" clearly supported the National Socialist drive to the east, especially in the historical context of the National Socialist period; the poems, given the clarity of their intent, did not require any reinterpretation by the Nazis. In "Hymne an Ostpreußen," an address to Borussia, the "genuine virgin and protective patroness of Prussia," describes in powerful words the land and its history filled with warriors, which, with the advent of the Third Reich, will be illuminated in new glory:

> Da erhebst Du Dein Haupt. Im klingenden Weststurm
> Grüßt das Zeichen am silbernen Flugzeug die Fahne
> Scharlachen flatternd vom Turm. Sie trägt in der weißen
> Scheibe das Kreuz, das einst der gotische Ahne
> Ritzte ins Schwert, das die zauberkundige, uralte
> Amme Dir wob in den Gürtel:
> Das heilige Zeichen
> Kreisenden Jahrs und sieghaft aufsteigender Sonne. (11–12)

> [Now you are raising your head. In the resounding storm in the west
> The symbol on the silvery airplane greets the flag
> Of scarlet, fluttering from the tower. It bears in the white
> Disk the cross which the Gothic ancestor once
> Etched on his sword, which the ancient nurse with knowledge
> Of magic wove into your belt:
> The sacred symbol
> Of the circling year and the triumphantly rising sun.]

In the poem "Hindenburg," the victor from Tannenberg is invoked, who, as one chosen by fate, freed the country from its misery. It need not be added that in Hitler a new savior has arisen, who, just as Hindenburg back then, will free the land; the historical context makes that implicit in the poem:

> Und ein verstörtes, zerquältes Land
> Griff aufatmend nach seiner mächtigem Hand
> Und lehnte sich wie ein Kind an seine Knie! (16)

> [And a distressed, tormented land
> Reached, breathing lighter, for his mighty hand
> And leaned, like a child, against his knee!]

In "Patrona Borussiae" (The Patroness of Borussia), the poetess implores the protective patroness Borussia for comfort and succor in difficult times and pleads of her: "Wir wollen heim. Führ uns sicher her! [We want to go home. Bring us safely there!]" (17). This plea is nothing more than a variant of the popular slogan of the time "Heim ins Reich" (Home to the Reich).

"Heimkehr des Kriegsgefangenen" (Return Home of the Prisoner of War), describes the return home, arduous yet full of anticipation, of a former prisoner of war, who, upon finally reaching his farm, finds nothing but a burned-out ruin. But instead of collapsing in shock, "the man strode erect down to his inheritance" (21), determined to fight a new battle. The call for return home echoes through the ballad, "Über die Weichsel drüben" (Across the Weichsel River There), which, written in 1920, recalls the happy settlement of the land and its devastation in the war against the Tartars and the Czars, and ends with the urgent cry to the German fatherland for help:

> Über die Weichsel drüben, Vaterland, höre uns an!
> Wir sinken, wie Pferd und Wagen versinken im Dünensand.
> Recke aus deine Hand
> Daß sie uns hält, die allein uns halten kann.
> Deutschland, heiliges Land,
> Vaterland! (24)

> [Over there, across the Weichsel, Fatherland, listen to us!
> We are sinking, as horse and wagon sink in dunes of sand.
> Reach out your hand
> That it holds us, as only it can hold us.
> Germany, Holy Land,
> Fatherland!]

In "Kopernikus" (Copernicus), Miegel commemorates one of the greatest sons of the contended borderland in the east. He, too, is brought home to the Reich and his Germanness is insistently invoked:

> Ich sprach zur Sonne: Steh still!
> Und ich bewegte die Erde.
> ....
> Aber ich frage Euch Völker in meiner Zunge:
> Warum im Kreis der Großen rechnet Ihr Fremden mich zu?
> ....
> Deutsch war Thorn, das mich trug.
> ....
> Ich sprach zur Sonne: Steh still!
> Und ich bewegte die Erde.
> Niklaus Köppernick, ich.
> Deutsche, ein Deutscher wie Ihr! (25–26)

> [I spoke to the sun: Stand still!
> And I moved the earth.
> ....
> But I ask you peoples in my tongue:
> Why, in the circle of greats, do you consider me foreign?
> ....
> Thorn was German, which bore me.
> ....
> I spoke to the sun: Stand still!
> And I moved the earth.

I, Niklaus Köppernick.
Germans, a German like you!

In the poems "Der Jahrestag. Gedenktag der Abstimmung" (Anniversary. Day in Remembrance of the Vote) and "Königsberg, 13. Juni 1924" (Könibgerg, June 13, 1924), Miegel remembers at a historical moment two significant dates from the history of East Prussia and its capital: the popular vote of July 11, 1920, prescribed by the Treaty of Versailles, in which 97.8 percent of the East Prussians decided in favor of Germany, and the unification of Altstadt, Kneiphof, and Löbenicht in 1724 by the Prussian King Friedrich Wilhelm I to form the city of Danzig.

The "Holy Homeland, which God gave me to be my mother," praised in the poem "Heilige Heimat" (Holy Homeland), was bought at a high price, as Miegel describes in the poem "Kriegergräber" (Warriors' Graves). As in the poem by Ernst Bertram quoted earlier, for Miegel, too, only graves provide a home:

> Siehe, sie liegen
> Weitgezogener Wachtring rings um die Erde
> Die sie fallend mit ihrem Blute tränkten,
> Bruder und Feind, ausruhend vom niemals ruhenden
> Kampf um das Ostland. (37)

> [See, they lie
> A widely drawn guard ring around the earth,
> Which they soaked with their blood as they fell,
> Brother and enemy, resting from the never-resting
> Battle for the *Ostland*.]

This *Ostland* is destined to be the battlefield of peoples, where the best sacrifice their lives to make possible a new life for new generations, in an eternal cycle:

> Wo er die Besten erwählt, zu opfern den Brüdern
> Blut und Leben, damit wieder aus ihnen
> Beste wenden den Pflug und zu nährendem Acker
> Wandeln das Schlachtfeld! (38)

> [Where he chooses the best, to lay down for their brothers
> Blood and life, that again of them
> The best wield the plow, and of the battlefield
> Make a life-giving field.]

"Nachtgespräch. Memelland 1935" (Night Conversation. Memelland, 1935) laments, in a dialogue among a chorus, women's voices, men's voices, and the East Prussian Baroque poet Simon Dach, the loss of the Memelland that went to Lithuania after the First World War. "Sonnwendreigen. Danzig 1939" (Solstice Roundels. Danzig, 1939) celebrates the return home of Danzig to the Reich, and the poem "Viktoria" (Victory), encourages the pursuit of new victories:

> Schutzgeist unseres Volkes, strahlende Jungfrau,
> Du im Licht auffahrende Siegsgöttin,
> Zieh uns voran! (47)

> [Protective spirit of our people, radiant virgin,
> You goddess of victory, ascending to the light,
> Go before us!]

Miegel's final poem in *Ostland*, "An Deutschlands Jugend" (To Germany's Youth), accompanied the outbreak of the Second World War with an appeal to the newly united pan-German community of the people to stand ready:

> Wir stehn, wir Deutsche,
> Volk das zu Volk fand, folgend dem Ruf des Führers,
> Stehen zum erstenmal, nicht Gatten und Brüder
> Nur allein, wir stehen, Frauen und Kinder,
> Alle im Kampf und stehn gefaßten Herzens,
> Auf uns zu nehmen wie sie die Schrecken des Krieges:
> Feuer und Nacht und Not und grausames Sterben,
> Wie es das Schicksal bestimmt. (49)

> [We stand here, we Germans,
> People that became a people, following the call of the *Führer,*
> We are here for the first time, not spouse and brother
> Not alone, we stand here, women and children,
> Altogether in battle, and we are ready
> To take on, as they did, the horrors of war:
> Fire and night and want and terrible death,
> As fate has decided.]

Miegel's National Socialist poetry in *Ostland* may be considerably more impressive poetically than the rhyming of other Nazi poets quoted earlier, but her ideological orientation is no different. After the war, Agnes Miegel recognized her error and lost both her audience and any connection to German postwar literature. All of her works should not be judged, as was here necessarily the case, only from the perspective of National Socialism and as a result be relegated to oblivion. At the same time, however, her National Socialist past likewise should not simply be passed over in silence, as is the practice of refugees from her East Prussian homeland who are tending her and their traditions.[56]

Ina Seidel's (1885–1974) themes of romanticized connectedness to the earth, cults of the mother and ancestors, willingness to make sacrifices, and reverence for the Prussians were very opportune for the culture policies of the National Socialists. According to Helmut Langenbucher, "the most important . . . of the forces in the works of Ina Seidel" is "the idea of the eternal-motherly and fulfillment of the laws of life that are conditioned by blood and heredity and determine the fate of human beings."[57] These themes run through her main work, the novel *Das Wunschkind* (The Wish Child, 1930), which takes place in the Napoleonic period, but also through her poetry. For example, the connectedness of the farmer to the earth is portrayed vividly in the poem "Der Pflüger" (The Plowsman):

> Mit wuchtigen Knien,
> Von Krähen umschrien,
> Im Dunst seiner Pferde,
> Die Fäuste am Sterz —
> Samt Pflugschar und Rossen
> Selbst bodenentquollen,
> Stampft er jetzt die Schollen
> Und zwingt die Erde
> Sein reißendes Erz.
>
> Die Brache umbrechen,
> Heißt Kräfte lossprechen,
> Die Erde braucht Hände,
> Zu lösen ihr Herz.
> Mann, Pflugschar und Rosse:
> Von Erde genommen,
> Zur Erde gekommen,
> Gestalt aus Gelände
> Im dampfenden März.[58]
>
> [With strongly built knees,
> Surrounded by screeching crows,
> In mist from his horses,
> His fists on plowtails —
> With plowshare and horses
> Himself sprung out of earth,
> He stamps now the dirt clods
> And his tearing iron
> Forces the earth.

To turn fallow land
Means forces set free,
Earth has need of hands
To unloose its heart.
Man, plowshare, and horse:
Taken from earth,
Returned to earth,
Figure rising from landscape
In steaming March.]

In its archaizing myth of the earth, the poem is reminiscent of Griese's drama *Der Mensch, aus Erde gemacht* (The Human Being, Made of Earth) (see the chapter on drama). Her poem "Lichtdom" (Cathedral of Light), on the other hand, rises to the bright heights and surrounds the *Führer* with the aura of mysticism, produced by flags and torches, which unreservedly pulls people along:

In Gold und Scharlach, feierlich mit Schweigen,
Ziehn die Standarten vor dem Führer auf.
Wer will das Haupt nicht überwältigt neigen?
Wer hebt den Blick nicht voll Vertrauen auf?
Ist dieser Dom, erbaut aus klarem Feuer,
Nicht mehr als eine Burg aus Stahl und Stein,
Und muß er nicht ein Heiligtum, uns teuer,
Ewigen Deutschtums neues Sinnbild sein?[59]

[In gold and scarlet, solemnly in silence,
the standards parade before the *Führer*.
Who does not, overwhelmed, want to bow his head?
Who does not, trustfully, lift up his gaze?
Is not this cathedral, built of clear fire,
more than a fortress of steel and stone,
and should not it be a temple, dear to us,
a new emblem of Germanness eternal?]

After the war, Ina Seidel recognized her error and condemned her blind idealism: "That person did not want victory but instead peace based on the invincibility of German arms and the preservation of the German right of self-determination. And after that, the *idiot* dreamed, the *inner* cleansing was supposed to come. I was one of those idiots."[60]

The Viennese writer Josef Weinheber (1892–1945) placed himself completely in the service of the National Socialists and paid the price for that in 1945 with his complete breakdown and suicide.[61] He shared with National Socialism a hierarchical, heroic, irrational ideology, which was probably expressed in its most unadulterated form in his "Heroische Trilogie" (Heroic Trilogy).[62] It was not least of all gratitude that bound Weinheber to the Nazis, who discovered him after he had worked for over twenty years in seclusion. He commented in his "Speech at the Pan-German Writer's Congress" in Weimar on October 29, 1939: "For twenty-two years I stood at my writing desk in the darkness of aimless, despairing, frustrating artistic activity. I have National Socialism to thank for the fact that today I have reached the people to an almost unbelievable extent, given the difficulty of the work. It was National Socialism that finally again reopened *that* exchange between *high* poetry and the people."[63] In a world that he viewed as formless and chaotic, Weinheber attempted to hold onto classic forms such as the hymn, the ode, and the sonnet, which he handled masterfully. As he explained in his "Ceremonial Speech of Thanks on the Occasion of Being Awarded the Honorary Doctorate of Philosophy at the University of Vienna on March 18, 1942," he had in our time reintroduced the sonnet cycle into German poetry.[64] He had illustrated this with examples such as the fourteen formally perfect sonnets "Von der Kunst und dem Künstler" (Of Art and Artists) at the beginning of the volume of poetry *Späte Krone;* these sonnets, which use Michelangelo's sonnet to Victoria Colonna as a model, define his conception of art in verse form.[65] German forms from Hölderlin, Horace, Michelangelo, and Pindar are among his models, but also free verse and quatrains.

His literary antagonists include Erich Maria Remarque and, unlike Benn, expressionism:

> Many of us writers [he is referring to those present at the Weimar Writers' Congress] have, with gnashing of the teeth and much time lost, gone through the chaos of the sell-out of the German language that almost cost the people their intellectual life. . . . Today the files are closed on Remarque's *All Quiet on the Western Front.* The evil, devious, far-reaching effects of this book, which have as their aim the destruction of the German essence, have been compensated. (Weimar speech, 113 and 119)

In his "Ceremonial Speech of Thanks upon Being Awarded the Mozart Prize of the Goethe Foundation of the University of Marburg on April 30, 1936," he takes a stand against expressionism and its "language-destroying" features, which he seeks to counter with his linguistic artistry:

> For my feelings about art, so closely tied to formal knowledge and skill, it would be senseless not to make use of these preexisting forms, which *have to* be of use, like the shape of the circle for the wheel, and to go up against nothingness without any presuppositions at all, as expressionism actually did, bringing about dissolution not only of forms but also of the language itself and its inherent laws, in order in that way to make the question of the meaning and value of art a problem once again. Standing hostilely to one side, I watched decay set in, and it was just those crimes against language in that era that made me consciously a defender of the word, an "epigone," if you will.[66]

Weinheber also objects equally strongly to strictly occasional poetry and to l'art pour l'art. In his opinion, poetry should be an organic element of the body of the people:

> Ah, the biological function of *poetry*, of which Kolbenheyer says that it is really a life force, cannot be denied even when, as in the preceding epoch, the sub-human is triumphant. . . . Today we know again what poetry and poets are there for. The people are calling us. The people are asking us. It is up to us to bring order to perhaps still muffled forces, to lead the spirits. Dignity, bravery, nobility, and sacrifice: It is up to us to take these big words, in an exemplary and convincing manner, into the people's midst. For it is precisely because the people and the poet are in the process of finding their way back together that poetry has again become a moral force and a moral challenge. (113)

For Weinheber, the German language was holy like a god; it resides in the unfathomable depths of the German people, as he describes in the "Hymnus auf die deutsche Sprache" (Hymn to the German Language):

> O wie raunt, lebt, atmet in deinem Laut
> der tiefe Gott, dein Herr, unsre Seel,
> die da ist das Schicksal der Welt.
> Du des Erhabenen
> starres Antlitz,
> mildes Auge des Traumes,
> eherne Schwertfaust!
> ....
> Du unverbraucht wie dein Volk!
> Du tief wie dein Volk!
> Du schwer und spröde wie dein Volk!
> Du wie dein Volk niemals beendet![67]

> [O, how in your sound murmurs, lives, breathes
> the deep god, your lord, our soul,
> which is the fate of the world.
> You, rigid visage
> of the sublime,
> mild eye of dream,
> iron sword's fist!
> ....
> You, unspoiled like your people!
> You, deep like your people!
> You, heavy and brittle like your people!
> You, like your people, never ending!]

According to Weinheber, poets are again to become the intellectual and moral leaders of the people in the sense of Hölderlin, to whom he refers in his Weimar speech. Poets are "the megaphone of the people, but through our mouths the gods speak!" (103). Poetry is thus surrounded by a mystical, mysterious aura "where reason falls silent and the visionary begins" (102). It was not clear to Weinheber that he was only being used and misused as a signboard for the Nazis. Accordingly, he served the regime with *Führer* poems and other works that are not among his best, such as the following *Führer* poem only the first stanza of which is quoted here:

> Deutschlands Genius, Deutschlands Herz und Haupt,
> Ehre Deutschlands, ihm solang' geraubt.
> Macht des Schwerts, daran die Erde glaubt.[68]

> [Germany's genius, Germany's heart and head,
> Germany's honor, denied for so long,
> Sword's power, in which the earth believes.]

In the war year 1940, Weinheber made his contribution to the war effort with a poem cycle on "Die deutschen Tugenden im Kriege" (The German Virtues in War). The twelve poems, each consisting of twelve lines with rhymed couplets, praise "bravery, chivalrous behavior, the comradely spirit, loyalty, manliness, perseverance, moderation, willingness to go into action, strength in suffering, unselfishness, and trust in God." The cycle is introduced with the following "prologue":

> Jedwedes Volk, das leben will,
> braucht Tucht und Zucht, nicht Tand und Spiel.
> Das eine fault vor Überfluß,
> das andre kämpft, sein' Not ist Muß.
> Weil wir nun alle, Mann, Weib, Kind,
> Soldaten, nur Soldaten sind,
> beschwört der Sänger — bis zum Sieg! —
> die deutschen Tugenden im Krieg.
> Wir haben sie, noch ungetrübt:
> Er nennt nur, was ihr bluthaft übt.
> Ihr schweigt davon, denn Würd und Ehr
> bedarf der großen Wort nicht mehr.
> Und Ehr und Würde sind zuletzt
> der Born, der alle Ausfahrt netzt.
> Fahr aus, gut's Schwert, dir selb zu Ruhm;
> Der Deutschen Art heißt: Heldentum.[69]

[Any people that wants to live
needs diligence and discipline, not trifles and games.
One people rots from excess,
the other fights, his need, a must,
Because we all now, man, woman, child,
are soldiers, only soldiers,
the singer calls for — until victory! —
the German virtues in war.
We have them, still unalloyed:
He only says what you do by blood.
You speak not of it, for dignity, honor
Have need no more of high-flown words.
And dignity and honor are in the end
the font that splashes every departure.
Depart, good sword, for your own glory;
The name of German nature is: heroism.]

Weinheber was also ready to celebrate the hero's death in his poetry. In November of 1940, Weinheber's hymns "Den Gefallenen" (To the Fallen) appeared on fine deckle-edged paper in Gothic script as a special printing from the volume of poems *Späte Krone* (1936); in these hymns, Weinheber immortalizes those who died but continued to live in the "people's stream of blood":

Dies erst genügt — und keine andre
Tröstung für uns oder euch reicht der gewaltige Engel,
als daß in der ewigen,
in der Seele des Volkes ihr
unvergänglich beschlossen seid!
In Millionen Herzkammern rauscht euer Blut,
rauscht groß euer Leiden nach, rauscht
eure Unsterblichkeit.
Alles Fleisch, es ist wie Gras,
und der Berühmten Ruhm ist das kurze Licht eines Namens.
Euer Ruhm ist des Volkes
Treue zumVolk.
Denn eines Volkes Gräber sind nicht seine Trauer allein,
eines Volkes Gefallenen
sind eines Volkes Stolz,
und eines Volkes Stolz, dieser höchste, gebiert
wieder die Welt.[70]

[This is enough — and no other
comfort is offered us or you by the mighty angel,
but that you are immutably

sealed in the eternal
soul of the people!
In millions of heart chambers your blood roars.
loudly your suffering echoes, roars
your immortality.
All flesh, it is like grass,
and the fame of the famous is the brief light of a name.
Your fame is the people's
loyalty to the people.
For a people's graves are not its grief alone,
a people's fallen,
a people's pride,
and a people's pride, this highest, gives birth to
the world anew.]

The point of this chapter was not to rebuke poets such as Benn, Weinheber, Miegel, and Seidel for their Nazi pasts, even if in the framework of this chapter the emphasis has been placed on their entanglement in the net of National Socialism, but to examine a segment of literary history. At the same time, the texts by the authors cited that lent support to National Socialism, as different from each other as they are, were very possibly, because of the status of their authors or the artistic quality of the texts, far more effective than the primitive rhyming of some of the above-named National Socialist poets.

Notes

[1] On that subject, see Alexander von Bormann, "Das nationalsozialistische Gemeinschaftslied" (The National Socialist Community Song), in *Die deutsche Literatur im Dritten Reich* (German Literature in the Third Reich), edited by Horst Denkler and Karl Prümm (Stuttgart: Reclam, 1976), 256–280.

[2] Gerhard Schumman, *Ruf und Berufung: Aufsätze und Reden* (Call and Calling: Essays and Speeches) (Munich: Langen/Müller, 1943), 51,

[3] Schumman, *Ruf und Berufung* (Call and Calling), 13.

[4] The exceptions are several love poems by Schumann, for example, in the volume of poems *Bewährung* (Proof of Valor) (Munich: Langen/Müller, 1940), although there, too, National Socialist vocabulary shows through.

[5] Helmut Langenbucher, *Volkhafte Dichtung der Zeit* (People's Literature of the Time), 6th edition (Berlin: Junker und Dünnhaupt, 1941), 606.

[6] "Adolf Hitler zum Geburtstag" (For Adolf Hitler's Birthday), in *Rufe in das Reich: Die heldische Dichtung von Langemarck bis zur Gegenwart* (Calls into the Reich: Heroic Poetry from Langemarck up to the Present), edited by Herbert Böhme (Berlin: Verlag Junge Generation, 1934), 117.

[7] *Rufe in das Reich,* 124. On the subject of "Knight, Death, and Devil," see also the picture by Hubert Lanzinger that shows Hitler in knight's armor, but with his visor pushed up. Lanzinger's picture was part of the exhibit "German Art," which was mounted in 1937 in Munich in contrast to the so-called "degenerate art."

[8] See Ernst Loewy, *Literatur unterm Hakenkreuz: Das Dritte Reich und seine Dichtung* (Literature Under the Swastika: The Third Reich and Its Literature) (Frankfurt: Fischer, 1987).

[9] *Rufe in das Reich,* 120. The parallels to the people of Israel can be carried further. The God of the Israelites also appears, cloaked in fire, on Mount Sinai (II Moses 19:18); he also goes in front of the Israelites on their way out of slavery to Egypt, "during the day as a pillar of clouds . . . and at night as a pillar of fire" (II Moses 13:21).

[10] *Rufe in das Reich,* 80.

[11] Gerhard Schumann, *Die Lieder vom Reich* (Songs from the Reich) (Munich: Langen/Müller, 1935), 33.

[12] *Rufe in das Reich,* 86. This poem is one of the many "ethnic German wake-up calls" that Gutberlet signed as author. The last two lines of this poem read: "We want to go home to the motherland, to which we pledge our loyalty." According to Gutberlet's statement, "'Feuerspruch (Fire Poem)' became the national anthem of the Germans in Poland," *Rufe in das Reich,* 372.

[13] *Rufe in das Reich,* 340.

[14] See the Hitler Youth song "Unsere Fahne flattert uns voran" (Our Flag Flutters Before Us).

[15] *Rufe in das Reich,* 343.

[16] *Rufe in das Reich,* 348.

[17] *Rufe in das Reich,* 16.

[18] *Rufe in das Reich,* 17.

[19] Heinrich Anacker, *Über die Maas, über die Schelde und Rhein! Gedichte vom Feldzug im Westen* (Across the Maas, across the Scheldt and Rhine! Poems of the Campaign in the West) (Munich: Zentralverlag der NSDAP, Franz Eher Nachfolger, 1942), 19.

[20] Anacker, *Über die Maas,* 58.

[21] Heinrich Anacker, *Heimat und Front: Gedichte aus dem Herbst 1939* (Homeland and Front: Poems from the Fall of 1939) (Munich: Zentralverlag der NSDAP, Franz Eher Nachfolger, 1940), 5.

[22] In Karl Bröger, *Sturz und Erhebung* (Fall and Rise) (Jena: Diederichs, 1943), quoted in Loewy, 183.

[23] In *Die Ernte der Gegenwart: Deutsche Lyrik von heute* (The Harvest of the Present. German Poetry of Today), edited by Will Vesper, 3rd edition (Ebenhausen near Munich: Langewiesche-Brandt, 1943), quoted in Loewy, 181–182.

[24] In *Die Ernte der Gegenwart* (The Harvest of the Present), quoted in Loewy, 182–83.

[25] Heinrich Anacker, *S.A.-Gedichte* (SA Poems) (Munich: Franz Eher Nachfolger, 1933), quoted in Albrecht Schöne, *Über politische Lyrik im 20. Jahrhundert* (On Political Poetry in the Twentieth Century) (Göttingen: Vandenhoeck & Ruprecht, 1965), 65.

[26] Albrecht Schöne, 21–22.

[27] Herybert Menzel, *Gedichte der Kameradschaft* (Poems of Comradeship) (Hamburg: Hanseatische Verlagsanstalt, 1936), quoted in Schöne, 64. Wolf Biermann wrote the contrafactum to this Nazi poem in his anti-military song "Soldat Soldat" (Soldier, Soldier), in *Mit Marx- und Engelszungen* (With Marx's and Engels's Tongues) (Berlin: Wagenbach, 1968), 36.

[28] Herybert Menzel, *Im Marschtritt der SA* (In the March Step of the SA) (Berlin, 1933), quoted in Schöne, 65.

[29] Max Reuschle, "Der Sinn des Gedichtes in unserer Zeit" (The Meaning of the Poem in Our Time), in *Des deutschen Dichters Sendung in der Gegenwart,* edited by Heinz Kindermann (The Mission of the German Poet in the Present) (Leipzig: Reclam, 1933), 213. The page citations in the text refer to this edition.

[30] Gerhard Schumann, *Lieder vom Reich,* 16.

[31] Uwe-K. Ketelsen, "Nationalsozialismus und Drittes Reich" (National Socialism and the Third Reich), in *Geschichte der politischen Lyrik in Deutschland* (History of Political Poetry in Germany), edited by Walter Hinderer (Stuttgart: Reclam, 1978), 306.

[32] Heinz Kindermann in his epilogue to *Des deutschen Dichters Sendung in der Gegenwart,* edited by Heinz Kindermann, 271.

[33] Quoted in Stefan George, *Das neue Reich* (The New Reich) (Düsseldorf: Küpper, 1964), 38–39 (Reprint of volume 9 of the complete edition of 1928).

[34] See Kindermann, 271.

[35] See Michael Winkler, *Stefan George* (Stuttgart: Metzler, 1970), 61–62.

[36] Gottfried Benn, *Autobiographische Schriften* (Autobiographical Writings), in *Gesammelte Werke in acht Bänden* (Collected Works in Eight Volumes), volume 8, edited by Dieter Wellershoff (Wiesbaden: Limes, 1960), 1975.

[37] On that subject, see for example the relevant texts in *Über Gottfried Benn: Kritische Stimmen 1912–1956* (On Gottfried Benn: Critical Voices, 1912–1956), edited by Bruno Hillebrand (Frankfurt am Main: S. Fischer, 1987).

[38] Gottfried Benn, *Gedichte* (Poems), in *Gesammelte Werke in acht Bänden,* volume 3, edited by Dieter Wellershoff (Wiesbaden: Limes, 1960), 25. Benn's criticism of the modern age was shared by many others and was not limited to Germany. See Benn's 1934 speech on Marinetti.

[39] Quoted in Loewy, 52–53.

[40] Benn, *Gesammelte Werke,* volume 8, 1889–91

[41] Quoted in Loewy, 84.

[42] Benn, *Gesammelte Werke,* volume 8, 1946.

[43] Börries von Münchhausen, *Das Herz im Harnisch: Neue Balladen und Lieder* (The Heart in Armor: New Ballads and Songs), 36,000th to 38,000th copies printed (Stuttgart and Berlin: Deutsche Verlagsanstalt, 1911 and 1935), 114.

[44] Münchhausen, 144.

[45] Helmut Langenbucher, *Volkhafte Dichtung der Zeit,* 418.

[46] Quoted in Loewy, 250.

[47] See Langenbucher, 237.

[48] Lulu von Strauß und Torney, *Reif steht die Saat* (The Seed is Ripe) (Jena: Diederichs, 1926), 155.

[49] Quoted in Loewy, 118.

[50] Quoted in Loewy, 146–47.

[51] Anni Piorreck, *Agnes Miegel: Ihr Leben und ihre Dichtung* (Agnes Miegel: Her Life and Her Poetry) (Düsseldorf: Diederichs, 1967), 185.

[52] See Piorreck, 190.

[53] Agnes Miegel, *Ostland* (Jena: Diederichs, 1940 and 1943), 5–6. The page citations in the text refer to this edition.

[54] See Piorreck, 208.

[55] See Piorreck, 188.

[56] On that subject, see Godele von der Decken, *Emanzipation auf Abwegen: Frauenkultur und Frauenliteratur im Umkreis des Nationalsozialismus* (Emancipation on the Wrong Track: Women's Culture and Women's Literature in the National Socialist Environment) (Frankfurt am Main: Athenäum, 1988), 268–69. There are also further references here to women authors and National Socialism.

[57] See Langenbucher, 137.

[58] Quoted in Loewy, 118.

[59] Quoted in Loewy, 283.

[60] Ina Seidel, *Aus den schwarzen Wachstumsheften: Monologe, Notizen, Fragmente* (From the Black Growth Notebooks: Monologues, Notes, Fragments) (Stuttgart, 1980). Quoted in Godele von der Decken, 271.

[61] On the quite complex relationship of Weinheber to National Socialism and existential philosophy as the answer to the modern awareness of crises, see among others Jeanette Lee Atkinson, "Joseph Weinheber: Sänger des Austrofaschismus?" (Joseph Weinheber: The Singer of Austrian Fascism?), in *Leid der Worte: Panorama des literarischen Nationalsozialismus* (Suffering of Words: Panorama of Literary National Socialism), edited by Jörg Thunecke (Bonn: Bouvier, 1987), 403–19.

[62] In Josef Weinheber, *Adel und Untergang* (Nobility and Decline), 6th edition (Vienna and Leipzig: Luser, 1934), 46–73.

[63] Josef Weinheber, *Kleine Prosa* (Small Prose Works), in *Sämtliche Werke* (Complete Works), volume 4, edited by Josef Nadler and Hedwig Weinheber (Salzburg: Otto Müller Verlag, 1954), 116. The page citations in the text refer to this edition.

[64] Weinheber, *Sämtliche Werke*, volume 4, 127.

[65] Josef Weinheber, *Späte Krone: Gedichte* (Late Crown: Poems) (Munich: Langen/Müller, 1936), 9–24. In his ceremonial speech of thanks for being awarded his honorary doctorate at the University of Vienna, Weinheber provides further comments regarding the sonnet cycle: "Just as the sonnet consists of fourteen lines, so, too, the sonnet cycle consists of fourteen sonnets. A fifteenth, so-called master sonnet closes the series. The last line of each sonnet is at the same time the first line of the next sonnet, and the fourteenth sonnet ends with the beginning line of the first sonnet. The master sonnet consists of the fourteen beginning, or ending, lines

of the preceding sonnets" (127). This is only one example of the great importance Weinheber attached to polished artistic structure. The volume *Späte Krone* closes with a sonnet cycle, "An die Nacht" (To the Night).

[66] Josef Weinheber, *Sämtliche Werke,* volume 4, 99.

[67] Josef Weinheber, from "Hymnus auf die deutsche Sprache" (Hymn to the German Language), in *Adel und Untergang,* 99.

[68] Quoted in Loewy, 284.

[69] Josef Weinheber, *Sämtliche Werke,* volume 4, 697.

[70] Quoted in *Späte Krone,* 65–66. In "The Legacy. A Handwritten Series of 'Books of the Rose,' written by Professor Dr. Otto Hurm, Vienna, in November, 1940, for Wilhelm Langewiesche-Brandt Publishers, Ebenhausen near Munich"; this poem is divided into two poems.

Ferdinand Marian in the title role of *Jud Süß*.
Marian's good ("Aryan") looks and his popularity almost
turned the Nazi view of the ugly Jew on its head.
Photo courtesy of Deutsches Filminstitut-DIF, Frankfurt.

7: Film in the Third Reich

IN RECENT YEARS no other area of the cultural life within the Third Reich has received more attention than film, especially in the United States where a number of books on film in the Third Reich have been published since the mid-nineties. These studies complement earlier works by Francis Courtade and Pierre Cadars (1972), David Stewart Hull (1969), Siegfried Kracauer (1947), Stephen Lowry (1991), David Welch (1983), and Karsten Witte (1976 and later), to name only a few. These also include books by Eric Rentschler (*The Ministry of Illusion*, 1996), Linda Schulte-Sasse (*Entertaining the Third Reich*, 1996), Sabine Hake (*Popular Cinema of the Third Reich*, 2001), Mary-Elizabeth O'Brien (*Nazi Cinema as Enchantment: The Politics of Entertainment in the Third Reich*, 2003), and a special edition of *New German Critique* (no. 74, Spring-Summer 1998) with articles by Anton Kaes, Klaus Kreimeier, Stephen Lowry, Patrice Petro, Karsten Witte, and others.[1] As Patrice Petro suggests, the reason for this increase in scholarly inquiry into films of the Third Reich may be connected with the recent turn of historians to everyday life under Fascism for which, in her opinion, films from that period provide excellent examples: "Indeed, what better place than cinema to find traces of the choices, emotions, and coping mechanisms of ordinary Germans?"[2] These recent books on film in the Third Reich[3] dispel the notion that movies made in the Third Reich were nothing but propaganda and provide a better understanding of films made between 1933 and 1945 with detailed analyses of a variety of films, including a large number of films made mostly for entertainment. To what extent these films also contain elements of propaganda remains a matter of contention and depends largely on the viewers: if they want to find propaganda in them, they will find it; if they don't, they will not. There is no question, however, that it was a deliberate policy of "film minister" Goebbels to provide entertainment for the masses, especially during hard times. The lack of obvious Nazi propaganda in the majority of films from the Nazi period also explains that some of the movies from that time remain popular to this day. The end of the Third Reich in 1945 was not such a deep watershed in the film industry as it was in politics and history, nor was 1933, for film in the Third Reich continued some traditions from film in the Weimar Republic.

The Nazis, in particular Josef Goebbels, the minister for propaganda, recognized quite early what propaganda opportunities the media of radio and film afforded them. The American film critic Eric Rentschler even views the entire Nazi state as a huge cinematographic event — "a sustained cinematographic event."[4] With the "radio receivers for the people" (*Volksempfänger*) and the motion picture theaters, the Nazis could reach far larger and broader audiences than with literature and theater. Fritz Hippler, the director of the film section in Goebbel's Propaganda ministry and the Reich film advisor, pointed out the emotional, mass psychological effects of film from Hitler's viewpoint: "Compared to the other arts, film, because of the inherent characteristic that its effects are primarily optical and emotional, i.e., not intellectual, has particularly powerful and long-lasting effects in terms of mass psychology and propaganda."[5] To attain this goal, it was felt that film could not be left to individual producers and directors, or *"Spielleiter"* (acting directors), as they were to be called from now on in "correct" German instead of *"Regisseure,"*[6] who might still harbor liberal views. As in all other areas, film was also to be guided by the state, *gleichgeschaltet,* and controlled by a central chamber: the Reich Chamber of Film. "If a state claims the right to teach a child his numbers and ABC's, then how much greater is the right of the state to all the means and possibilities that could be used for education and guidance of the people. Besides the press and radio, one of these means is film."[7] Looking back from 1940, Karl Melzer points out the success of the measures that were taken in 1933: "Film producers, film artists, film distributors, and film theater owners who are brought together in the Reich Chamber for Film have overcome dangerous liberal thinking . . ., with some sacrifices. Their professional views conform today to the ideology expected of all members by the National Socialist state."[8] Among the "sacrifices" were the many film artists who had to leave the Reich for political reasons, such as Fritz Kortner or Fritz Lang, although Goebbels offered the latter the directorship of the Film Section in his Propaganda ministry despite Lang's Jewish ancestry.[9] Even with the loss of noted artists, an adequate number of directors and actors remained — often trained by Max Reinhardt, for example, Veit Harlan — to produce films of good artistic quality. Many others are named here: Emil Jannings, Heinrich George, Werner Hinz, Paul Hörbiger, Hans Albers, Werner Krauss, Erich Ponto, Ilse Werner, Marianne Hoppe, Hilde Krahl, Kristina Söderbaum, Grete Weiser, Paula Wessely, and Zarah Leander. The technical equipment was excellent; it compared favorably to that in Hollywood.[10]

Josef Goebbels, the newly appointed minister for Popular Enlightenment and Propaganda, established a provisional Reich Film Chamber (*Reichsfilmkammer* — RFK) on July 14, 1933, before the establishment of the Reich Chamber of Culture (*Reichskulturkammer* — RKK) on September 22, 1933; the RFK became one of seven chambers (the others were devoted to fine arts, literature, music, press, radio, and theater). Individuals in all branches of the film industry had to be members, providing effective control over who worked on films in the Third Reich, although Goebbels could make special exemptions. Generally, Jews and other "undesirable elements" need not apply. Always the careful tactician, Goebbels initially refrained from nationalization of the film industry to maintain a resemblance of normalcy while the regime was not yet in firm control — despite pressures from the radical right to do so, including from Alfred Rosenberg's *Kampfbund für deutsche Kultur* (Fighting League for German Culture). But with the establishment of the Filmkreditbank (FKB) in June of 1933 to help the debt-ridden film industry, his influence steadily increased, often behind the scenes. According to David Welch the FKB was initially "inaugurated to assist the small independent producer; however, by 1936 it was financing over 73 percent of all German feature films."[11]

Beginning in February of 1934, the Reich Cinema Law provided Goebbels with a "legal" basis to extend his powers of censorship through the so-called pre-censorship undertaken by the propaganda ministry's Reich Film Director, who was obligated to follow all of Goebbels's wishes. The law of 1934 replaced the law of 1920 that had regulated films in the Weimar Republic. The actual examination of films was delegated to a censorship office with branches in Berlin and Munich. The censorship office awarded rating points that helped in obtaining financial support. On Goebbels's orders negative criticism of films was replaced by descriptive reviews, especially after his ban of art criticism in November of 1936. In 1936–1937, Goebbels took advantage of the precarious financial situation of the two major film companies to take over Ufa and Tobis from the Hugenberg concern. His agent Dr. Max Winkler created a trust company, Kaution Treuhand GmbH, to act as majority shareholder. Later, other film companies were added, for example, Bavaria and Terra, as well as Wien-Film after the *Anschluß* and Prag Film after the occupation of Czechoslovakia. Although the state now had a controlling interest in these companies, they were referred to as only indirectly state-controlled, presumably to give the appearance that the Nazi state, unlike the Soviet Union, supported private enterprise. In January of 1942 a giant holding company, Ufa-Film GmbH (called Ufi), was created to control the entire German film industry and its branches in occupied countries. With the creation of the Reich film directorate to control all the political affairs of the film industry and the installation of Fritz Hippler, the head of the film section in the propaganda ministry, as its first head, Goebbels's control mechanisms over the film industry were complete.

Goebbels's personal interest in film was more than fleeting: both Goebbels and Hitler were avid film buffs. In a speech on March 28, 1933, Goebbels referred to many evenings spent "with the Reich Chancellor in the cinema, after the nerve-racking struggles of the day, and found relaxation" in that form of entertainment.[12] Until he had his own projection room in the new Reich Chancellery, Hitler had a screen and projector set up to watch his favorite movies, such as *Quax der Bruchpilot* (Quax, the Crash-Happy Pilot) and *Die Feuerzangenbowle* (The Punch Bowl), both starring his favorite actor, the comedian Heinz Rühmann. But foreign films also fascinated him, notably Walt Disney's cartoons, a number of them given to him by his loyal servant Goebbels for Christmas. Hitler went to great lengths to obtain some of the films: "The cartoon fairy-tale *Snow White and the Seven Dwarfs* had to be shipped from the USA via a circuitous route" (Moeller, 133). Between 1935 and 1939, when he stopped watching feature films and switched to news reels, Hitler saw a large number of German and foreign films that, in his judgment, ranged from "excellent" to "utter rubbish" (Moeller, 132). Occasionally Hitler intervened in the area of censorship without, of course, going through the usual channels; a critical word from the *Führer* was enough for Goebbels to ban a film.

Of the two, Hitler and Goebbels, the latter was unquestionably the greater "expert" when it came to judging films — after all, he had a doctorate in literature and considered himself a writer. Until the outbreak of the war in 1939 (and 1941 with the USA), he greatly admired American, French, and Russian films. For him, the great model to be emulated by the Nazi-controlled film industry was Serge Eisenstein's *Battleship Potemkin*, which couched propaganda in highly artistic form, as he noted in his diary of June 30, 1928: "In the evening we saw *Potemkin.* I have to say that this film is fabulously made. With quite magnificent crowd scenes. Technical and landscape details of succinct power. And the hard-hitting slogans are formulated so skillfully that it is impossible to contradict them. That is what is actually dangerous about this film" (quoted after Moeller, 27). He was so impressed that after coming to power he demanded that the German film industry produce a "National Socialist *Potemkin*" (Moeller, 27). Even during the war with the Soviet Union, he admired Soviet documentary war propaganda. As he wrote in his diary on March 24, 1942, about *Retreat at Klin:* "Bolsheviks had hit the nail on the head in propaganda terms" (Moeller, 35).

Goebbels also admired American films such as Greta Garbo's *Grand Hotel, Anna Karenina,* and *Maria Walevska* and, mostly for political reasons, films aimed at social reforms made during Roosevelt's New Deal era. On May 27, 1939, for example, he noted in his diary about Frank Capra's film *Mr. Deeds Goes to Town:* "Very high American standard with Cooper. Magnificently done, wonderfully tendentious, excellently acted. I am most enthusiastic" (Moeller, 33). Another American film he greatly admired was *Gone with the Wind*. He screened it numerous times and recommended it as a model for German film people: "You have to see it more than once. We should take it as an example" (Goebbels's diary of July 30, 1940; Moeller, 34). It is no surprise that he wanted to make the German film industry rival that of Hollywood.

Another film Goebbels recommended as a model was Fritz Lang's film *Die Nibelungen* (The Nibelungs) as he noted in his diary entry of November

4, 1929: "A pinnacle of German achievement. I am more deeply moved by this grandiose depiction of German power, greatness and beauty" (Moeller, 26). For other films made by Jewish directors, on the other hand, he had nothing but contempt. The screening of the Polish-Yiddish film *The Dybbuk* lead to violent anti-Semitic outbursts in his diary entry of February 18, 1942, that is, at the onset of the "final solution": "This film is intended as Jewish propaganda. It seems so anti-Semitic that one can only be amazed how little the Jews know about themselves and how unclear they are about what is repellent to a non-Jewish person and what not. When watching this film it is suddenly clear once more that the Jewish race is the most dangerous to populate the globe, and that one may not permit oneself mercy or indulgence when dealing with them. This rabble must be eradicated root and branch; otherwise it is not possible to bring peace to the world" (Moeller, 35).

The films produced within the Third Reich treated themes similar to those of the novel and the drama: battle, war, heroism and martyrdom, blood and soil, German mythology and history, anti-Semitism, and anti-Bolshevism. As Kracauer remarks, the way for the film of the Third Reich had already been prepared before Hitler's seizure of power by films with authoritarian tendencies that place great individuals as rebels, leaders, or war heroes in the spotlight, such as Erich Waschneck's *Drei Mädels im Boot* (Three Girls in a Boat, 1932), Gustav Ucicky's submarine film *Morgenrot* (Dawn, 1933), or the mountain films of Arnold Franck, Leni Riefenstahl, and Luis Trenker.[13] However, just as in the novel and drama, films were mainly for entertainment, not for propaganda. Film in the Third Reich was effective more because of its entertainment value and its use of familiar structures than because of its propaganda.[14] This fact explains the popularity that films of the Third Reich still enjoy today.[15] Of course elements of propaganda also slipped in, but pure entertainment and propaganda are not always easy to distinguish from one another. According to Rentschler, more swastikas and arms extended in the Hitler salute turned up in the Hollywood films of the forties than in films from the Third Reich. Propaganda films such as *Jud Süß* (Jew Süß) and *Triumph des Willens* (Triumph of the Will) were the exceptions, not the rule.

Creating illusions was more important than trite propaganda. Accordingly, Rentschler's book on film in the Third Reich has the significant title *The Ministry of Illusion;* film in the Third Reich spread more illusions than fear: "Films in the Third Reich emanated from a Ministry of Illusion, not a Ministry of Fear."[16] Of a total production of 1,350 films in the Third Reich, 1,200 were primarily, although not entirely, entertainment films.[17] According to Rentschler, 941 of the 1,094 "feature films" in the Third Reich were "unpolitical"; of them, 123 were mysteries, 295 melodramas and biographies, and 523 comedies and musicals, that is, "cheerful" films.[18] Film schedules show that as the political and military situation of the Third Reich grew increasingly worse the proportion of propaganda films markedly declined compared to entertainment films.[19] The Nazis were keenly aware that the population needed diversion in these difficult times and promoted entertainment films for that purpose. In October of 1941, Propaganda Minister Goebbels declared: "In a time when the entire nation is weighed down with such heavy cares and burdens entertainment is also of special value for national policy."[20] Particularly worth mentioning in this context are the musical comedies of Zarah Leander and Marika Rökk with titles such as *Die große Liebe* (The Great Love, 1942), known above all for the song "I know that a miracle will happen sometime," sung by Leander in her sexy, sonorous voice, and *Die Frau meiner Träume* (The Woman of My Dreams, 1944) in which Rökk created *the* hit of the Third Reich with the song "At Night a Person Doesn't Like to be Alone."

As statistical tables show, ticket sales, gross receipts, and attendance in film theaters rose steadily from 1933 to 1943, from 244.9 million tickets sold in 1933/1934 to 1.1 billion tickets sold in 1943 with a slight decline in 1944. The average attendance rose from 4.7 visits per year in 1933/1934 to 14.4 in 1943.[21] There were a number of overtly political films reflecting the political situation, for example *Ich klage an* (I Accuse) during the euthanasia campaign in 1941, blatantly anti-Semitic films such as *Der ewige Jude* (The Eternal Jew, 1940*), Jud Süß* (1940), and *Die Rothschilds* (The Rothschilds, 1940), or the films of perseverance (*Durchhaltefilme*) in 1944–1945 such as *Kolberg* (1945), one of the most expensive films made in the Third Reich, and *Die Degenhardts* (The Degenhardts, 1944), modeled after the American film *Mrs. Miniver* (1942), about a Lübeck family during the bombing raids on that city. Churchill supposedly said that the film *Mrs. Miniver,* portraying an English family during the war, "is worth more than six divisions" (Moeller, 117). Goebbels was attracted to this film by its anti-German "propaganda slant that is tremendously subtle and effective," and he recommended a German propaganda film with an anti-British/American slant after this American film. However, from 1942 on the production of light entertainment films increased dramatically and overtly political films "could officially make up 20 percent of production at the most" (Moeller, 114).

Film in the Third Reich will be illustrated in the following pages with three paradigmatic examples, two political films and one entertainment film. *Hitlerjunge Quex* (Hitler Youth Quex) and *Jud Süß* are among the most striking examples of the film *of* the Third Reich, and *Münchhausen,* of film *within* the Third Reich. My discussion of these films is based primarily on the standard works on film within the Third Reich by the Frenchmen Francis Courtade and Pierre Cadars and by the Americans Eric Rentschler and Linda Schulte-Sasse.

The first real Nazi film was *Hitlerjunge Quex* (1933), which was based on Karl Aloys Schenzinger's novel by the same name and is treated extensively in the chapter on the novel. The director was Hans Steinhoff, who up to that point had been known primarily for entertainment films, but who had already had his National Socialist Party card in his pocket for several years. Heinrich George played the father, and Berta Drews, the mother of Heini Völker, called Quex, who was played in the film by Hermann Speelmans. The formal world premiere of this Ufa film was held in September of 1933 in Munich with the *Führer* in attendance. The *Reichsfilmblatt* (Reich Film Gazette) of September 16, 1933, reported among other things the following:

> As the last picture faded at the premiere of the film, the Hitler youth and the Hitler girl stood on the large stage like two small wanderers in a big world and saluted the *Führer* with raised arms. He, however, stepped forward and thanked them likewise and looked down with a kindly smile at the two actors and spokespersons for the great German Hitler Youth. . . . The salute of the *Führer* was for the steadfastness of a spirit that stands by the fatherland for better or worse and that repeatedly springs forth unobtrusively from the depths of the film.[22]

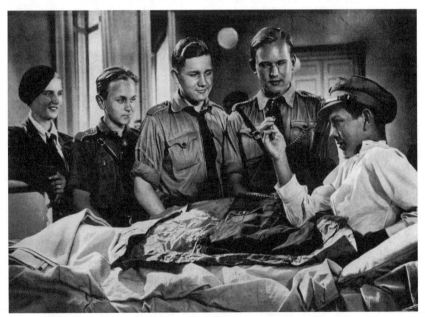

Hitlerjunge Quex: Quex's friends visit him in the hospital.
Courtesy of Deutsches Filminstitut-DIF, Frankfurt.

The tone of the program was set with Bruckner's symphony in F major and a "captivating speech by the Reich Youth Leader" Baldur von Schirach.[23] Ideology aside, Courtade and Cadars consider this film "a kind of masterpiece of Nazi film," especially as it borrows artistic elements from the Soviet propaganda film and German realism (*Kuhle Wampe* [Empty Belly], *M*, or *Die Dreigroschenoper* [The Three Penny Opera]).[24] The intention to recruit communists for National Socialism is even more evident than in the novel, as a central scene of the film that is not contained in the novel makes clear.[25] Films that had similar themes but were less successful were *SA-Mann Brand* (SA Man Brand) and *Hans Westmar,* as well as *Blutendes Deutschland* (Bleeding Germany).

Hitlerjunge Quex: Quex must choose between his
father (Heinrich George) and his new friend.
Courtesy of Deutsches Filminstitut-DIF, Frankfurt.

As did the novel, the film also shows the transformation of the printer's apprentice Heini Völker from a young communist to a Hitler youth. The name "Völker" already indicates that the main character in this drama of transformation is not an individualist but rather a type that is to serve as the model for an entire generation of young people. The film shows that the Party transcends family ties and leads to a true community of the people that replaces the communist class struggle. The settings that create the structure are the fair and the German forest. The fair represents disorder, sensual pleasure, and lack of discipline; it is the world of the young communists that Heini leaves behind. The German forest in which Heini spies a Hitler Youth troop stands for the order, discipline, and organic unity that Heini embraces.[26] The circular carousel, on which the sensuous communist girl Gerda attempts to seduce Heini into sexual adventures, is a metaphor for Communism, which turns in circles and leads nowhere, while the straight line of the Hitler Youth column stands for National Socialism, which leads in the direction of a better future.[27]

Karl-Heinz Huber evidences just how influential this film was in his book *Jugend unterm Hakenkreuz* (Youth Under the Swastika, 1982) in which Bernhard K., who was ten years old in 1933, reports in retrospect what an overwhelming effect the film had on him. His friend and he were enthusiastic about the Hitler Youth and were filled with disgust for the disorderly Communists.[28] As Linda Schulte-Sasse explains in her book *Entertaining the Third Reich* (1996), Father Völker also undergoes a transformation from an international Communist to a National Socialist, although the focus of the story is the conversion of his son.[29] The film thus encompasses the two most important target groups of Nazi propaganda at the beginning of the Third Reich: youth and the working class. As it turned out, the Nazis were quite successful in both groups.

Of the anti-Semitic films of the Third Reich, *Jud Süß* (1940) is the best known and the most effective, even if not the only one, as the film titles *Die Rothschilds* (1940), based on the drama *Rothschild siegt bei Waterloo* (Rothschild is Victorious at Waterloo) by Eberhard Wolfgang Möller (see the chapter on drama), or *Der ewige Jude* (1940) indicate. After the war, no film of the Nazi era was as disputed and controversial as *Jud Süß*. From the artistic and technical standpoint, it is the best and the commercially most successful of these films. The half-Jew Joseph Süß Oppenheimer was the son of the Baron von Heyersdorff and his Jewish wife, the daughter of a Jewish cantor from Frankfurt. He became the financial advisor of the Duke of Württemberg from 1733–1737, and was taken to court by his enemies after the duke's death and sentenced to death. In the film, the duke is shown as an oppressor of the people as a result of the intrigues and under the influence of the Jew Süß, squeezing the last penny out of his subjects with new taxes, opening the city of Stuttgart to Jews, and as the film suggests, giving the rats free rein.

Süß uses his position of power to commit his worst sin against German blood; he seduces the Aryan girl Dorothea Sturm and drives her to suicide. In contrast to the natives of Württemberg, Süß has no home; his home is the world. In the trial against him, he protests that he had only done his duty. After his death, the Jews are again driven out of Stuttgart; Stuttgart becomes "cleansed of Jews." The film closes with the admonition to future generations to learn from the bad experiences of the citizens of Stuttgart with Jews, and to treat the Jews accordingly and drive them out. Süß appears to be an urbane and assimilated Jew: however, the film seeks to show the true face behind the mask. Whether without a beard and assimilated or with a beard and caftan, they are all the same: mendacious and power-hungry. The film avails itself of all the anti-Semitic clichés — the Jew as greedy for money, rootless, and sexually perverse — but in a quite complex manner, as Schulte-Sasse demonstrates in detail.[30]

Jud Süß: Süss (Ferdinand Marian) and his friend and "advisor" Rabbi Loew (Werner Krauss). In Nazi propaganda all Jews were the same, whether in courtly attire or in traditional Jewish garb. Consequently, Krauss played all the major Jewish characters in the film besides Süss. Courtesy of Deutsches Filminstitut-DIF, Frankfurt.

Jud Süß was the most successful film of the 1939–1940 film season; by 1943, it had been seen by 20.3 million people.[31] Contributing to the success of the film, the (Aryan) cast of stars, in particular, Ferdinand Marian in the title role of Jew Süß, who enjoyed great popularity with women.[32] It also helped that the film connected to familiar models like the middle-class tragedy and American historical film biographies, and even to well-known villains from horror films of the Weimar Republic such as *Nosferatu, Mabuse,* or Bram Stoker's *Dracula.*[33] The material was reworked a number of times:

in 1827 in a novella by Wilhelm Hauff, in 1925 in a novel by Lion Feuchtwanger, and in 1934 in a pro-Semitic film by Lothar Mendes. Under the
direction of Veit Harlan and according to instructions of Goebbels, *Jud Süß*
became an anti-Semitic propaganda work that contributed more after 1945
to the undoing of almost all the participants than any of their other films.[34]

After the world premiere in Venice, one critic wrote, among other
things: "A historical example of Jewry's ability to sneak again and again into
German lands."[35] For the *Völkischer Beobachter* (Völkisch Observer), *Jud Süß*
was an example that "stands terribly for the whole."[36] The dramatist Eberhard Wolfgang Möller collaborated on the script; the main roles were played
by Ferdinand Marian (Süß), Heinrich George (the Duke of Württemberg),
Werner Krauss (Rabbi Loew, Lévy, Isaac), and Kristina Söderbaum
(Dorothea Sturm). The film contributed substantially to the spread of anti-
Semitism. After seeing the film, youths held hunts for Jews.[37] The film
helped prepare the way for the "final solution" and was "always shown to
the 'Aryan' population when 'resettlement' to the extermination camps was
ahead, . . . in order to stir up the 'Aryan' population of the particular country against the Jews."[38] Himmler made showings obligatory for all military,
SS, and police units.[39]

Jud Süß: Süss (Ferdinand Marian) shortly before his public execution
for his "crimes." Courtesy of Deutsches Filminstitut-DIF,
Frankfurt.

The film *Münchhausen* was probably the biggest, most expensive, and most successful film spectacle in the Third Reich. This film stood at the center of the ceremonies for the 25th Anniversary of Ufa; it premiered on March 5, 1943, in the Berlin Ufa Palace, three days after a heavy bombing attack on the Reich capital. On February 18, 1943, shortly after the decisive defeat of the German armed forces in Stalingrad, Goebbels held his notorious speech on total war ("Do you want total war"); with *Münchhausen,* Goebbels wanted the total film. Cost was not a factor; Goebbels wanted his film in color and with a technical set-up that could compete with any Hollywood film. The production costs ran about RM 6.5 million; by the end of the Third Reich, 25 million tickets had been sold.[40] The story derives from the well-known tall tales of Baron von Münchhausen, which were to a great extent known to the public from schoolbooks. A cast of stars with the popular Hans Albers in the title role contributed considerably to the success of the film.

Münchhausen: In Saint Petersburg, Münchhausen (Hans Albers) has an affair with Czarina Catherine the Great (Brigitte Horney). Courtesy of Deutsches Filminstitut-DIF, Frankfurt.

The script was by one Bertold Bürger, the cover name for the banned Erich Kästner, who had been prohibited from publishing. The pseudonym was cleverly chosen, since it recalled the exiled dramatist Bertolt Brecht (B. B.) and Gottfried August Bürger (1747–1794) to whom the folk tale is attributed. The first seventeen adventurous stories about Hieronymous Karl Friedrich Baron von Münchhausen (1720–1797) appeared from 1791 to 1793 in the "Vademecum for Merry People." The bon vivant Rudolf Erich Raspe, who had fled from his creditors to England, translated the stories into

English in 1785; Bürger then retranslated them from English into German and in the course of time supplemented them with new stories. The stories from the genre of the tall tale, which was widely distributed in the Baroque era such as *Horribilicribifax* by Gryphius and *Schelmuffski* by Reuter, were popular nationally and internationally. In 1838–1839 Immermann wrote his satirical novel *Münchhausen* "against the swindling spirit of the times."[41] Dramas from Lienhard and Eulenberg followed, as did "Stories from History" in which Börries von Münchhausen in 1934 recounts the life of his ancestor. As Rentschler demonstrates, the "lying baron" also has a solid place in the international history film from Georges Méliès's *Les Aventures de Baron de Münchhausen* (The Adventures of Baron Münchhausen) of 1911 to Terry Gilliam's *The Adventures of Baron Munchhausen* (1988).[42]

Münchhausen: Baron Münchhausen rides the cannonball.
Courtesy of Deutsches Filminstitut-DIF, Frankfurt.

The film begins in the twentieth century with a Rococo costume ball but proceeds to detailed flashbacks in which Baron Münchhausen, the host of the ball, relates the adventures of the legendary Baron von Münchhausen from the eighteenth century. The Baron and his servant Christian accompany Prince Anton Ulrich von Brunswick to the court of the Czarina Catherine II in Saint Petersburg. Münchhausen has an affair with her, has a duel with the jealous Prince Potemkin, and receives a magic ring that makes him invisible and immortal from the magician Cagliostro, played in the film by Ferdinand Marian, the actor who played Jew Süß. Riding on a canon ball, Münchhausen manages to go from St. Petersburg to the palace of Sultan Abdul Hamid in Constantinople; from there he escapes with the Princess Isabella d'Este to Venice, where he meets the legendary Casanova. Pursued by the Inquisition and the vengeful brother of the princess, he gets away in a balloon and lands on the moon, where he is not particularly comfortable. He returns to earth and to the embrace of his wife, who has grown old.

The special position of the film *Münchhausen* is not only attributable to its high costs and great success. It is one of the few films of the imagination in the Third Reich, and, in contrast to other prudish films of the time, it radiates sensuous sexuality. Kästner's script contains many barbs aimed at the Third Reich, for example, the remark that not only the Baron's clock but also the times themselves are broken. Nevertheless, Rentschler considers the film eminently political, since it glorifies not only the machinery of war, Christian's gun with a range of 110 miles and Münchhausen's cannon ball, but also Aryan heroes.[43] Linda Schulte-Sasse is considerably more reserved, and rightly so, emphasizing the entertainment value of the film, which goes beyond space and time and thus rivets the viewers. For them, Münchhausen is not the vehicle for an idea; he has no mission and moves almost completely in his private sphere. As a permanent traveler, he even has an affinity to the "rootless" Jew Süß; both are individualists in the Reich of mass movements.[44] The connection to *Jud Süß* becomes even more apparent through the character of the magician Cagliostro. The conflict between hatred for and fascination with the "Jew" is especially clearly expressed in the Münchhausen-Cagliostro relationship.[45] The popularity of the film is based not least of all on that fact, but certainly not always to the joy of the Nazis.

Whether or not *Münchhausen* and other entertainment films in the Third Reich also contain propaganda, however subliminal, depends largely on the viewer. In any case, not each and every thing that reached the public in the Third Reich must be seen exclusively through political glasses, particularly in retrospect over fifty years later. Contemporary witnesses such as the German Jews Victor Klemperer and Inge Deutschkron, who survived the Third Reich within Germany (Klemperer protected by his "Aryan" wife; Deutschkron in the underground), truly cannot be accused of having sympathy with the Nazis, but even they could not discover any propaganda in a great number of films. Both of them just loved to go to the cinema, as long as they were still allowed to; Inge Deutschkron even attended "illegally" and without a Jewish star after the cinema prohibition for Jews had been imposed. Victor Klemperer noted in his diary on March 20, 1933: "I like so much to be at the cinema; it carries me away."[46] On May 30, 1938, he saw *Habenera* and noted on the following day: "Yesterday the *Habenera* with Zarah Leander, downright frighteningly good."[47] The last films that he was still able to see in 1938 "were the circus film *Fahrendes Volk* (Traveling People) and the film *Die vier Gesellen* (The Four Journeymen), which was equally valuable as literature and for its acting."[48] Klemperer was never allowed to see *Münchhausen*. Inge Deutschkron, on the other hand, slipped out of her hiding place and went illegally to this film, noting retrospectively on the matter in her book *Ich trug den gelben Stern* (I Wore the Yellow Star): "I even managed to talk my mother into going to cultural events, which at that time were at a very high level, as the Nazis spared no expenses financially for cultural activities in order to keep the population in the 'mood.' I still remember many of them today. Among those was the beautiful ballet from *Die Fledermaus* (The Bat) in the Berlin Opera, a gala production performed every New Year's, or even Hans Albers's unforgettable role of Münchhausen in the film by the same name, which was produced at great expense for the 25th anniversary of Ufa."[49]

A few days after the attempt on Hitler's life on July 20, 1944, the dramatist and Reich culture senator Friedrich Bethge offered his drama *Marsch der Veteranen* (March of the Veterans) (see the chapter on drama) to the Reich film director for filming. Because Germany was engaged in war against the United States — the Allies were already in France — Bethge wanted to move the action back to America:

> However, I consider that the time is now here to come out with the March of the Veterans as a big film, but not set back in Napoleonic Russia as it was in my drama back then for artistically compelling reasons, and not in the post-war Germany of, let's say, 1919–20, but rather in the country and the time where the idea for the drama originated, namely, Washington in 1932. I can think of few film subjects that show the mendacity of "civilized" America more convincingly and at the same time put before the eyes of the whole world what the treatment of the American participants in the war by their own fatherland was like back then and that it would presumably not be much different at the end of this war, and probably not in England either.[50]

The film was never made.

Hans Zöberlein, who is treated in the chapter on the novel, also turns up in the film annals of the Third Reich; he reworked his novel *Der Glaube an Deutschland* (Belief in Germany, 1931), which was highly praised by

Hitler, for the film *Stosstrupp 1917* (Combat Patrol 1917), which was publicized as "the most powerful and rousing German war film."[51] According to Kracauer, this film was the answer of the Nazis to Georg Wilhelm Pabst's pacifistic anti-war film *Westfront 1918* (Western Front, 1918, 1930).[52] The *Völkischer Beobachter* wrote about the premiere of the film, which Hitler attended, in February of 1934 in the Ufa palace with the following words, among others: "Here in this film the unknown front-line soldier sees himself, the genuine, uncomplicated warrior for Germany, as he was and will be, and here he is filled with the memory of the greatness of his accomplishment, the accomplishment of which he was capable, and always has been, if properly led."[53] Also in 1934, the anti-Bolshevik film about the volunteer corps, *Um die Menschenrechte* (About Human Rights), with a script by Zöberlein, was released.

Among the historical films, films about the Prussian King Friedrich II, also called the Great or the Only, are especially numerous; from his likeness, the *Führer* gained new strength when bad news left him depressed.[54] Even before the seizure of power by Hitler on January 30, 1933, several right-oriented films about Friedrich had appeared, usually with Otto Gebühr in the title role, for example, Gustav Ucicky's *Das Flötenkonzert von Sanssouci* (The Flute Concert at Sanssouci, 1930), Friedrich Zelnick's *Barbarina, die Tänzerin von Sanssouci* (Barbarina, the Dancer of Sanssouci, 1932), and Carl Froehlich's *Der Choral von Leuthen* (The Choral of Leuthen, 1933). These and similar films glorified the person of the leader who intuitively makes the right decision in solitary greatness.[55] Hans Steinhoff, the director of *Hitlerjunge Quex*, and Veit Harlan joined in with *Der alte und der junge König* (The Old and the Young Kings, 1935) and *Der grosse König* (The Great King, 1942). Both films featured a prominent cast: Emil Jannings as the old King Friedrich Wilhelm I and Werner Hinz as his son, the young King Friedrich II; Otto Gebühr as the great King Friedrich II, Kristina Söderbaum as Luise, and in other roles, Gustav Fröhlich, Paul Henkels, Elisabeth Flickenschildt, and Hilde Körber. Themes running through these films are the leader principle and absolute obedience. The Prussian stories also include the film *Das Fräulein von Barnhelm* (The Young Lady from Barnhelm, 1940). With this "free filmic interpretation" of "Lessing's prototype" (*Minna von Barnhelm*), the director Hans Schweikart, who became director of the Munich Kammerspiele after the war, sought to claim the German classic writer for the Third Reich.[56]

When the retreat on all fronts seemed unstoppable and defeat was already evident, the attempt was made to tap the last reserves of resistance with a film on staying the course, *Kolberg*. The film was supposed to show "that a people united at home and at the front overcomes any enemy."[57] The film is based on the resistance of the port city of Kolberg (near Danzig) against the Napoleonic troops, but it interprets the facts quite generously in the direction of the necessary slogans on staying the course. The film, made by Veit Harlan, with

Heinrich George in the main role as Mayor Nettelbeck, was flown to the French city of La Rochelle, encircled by the Allies, for the premiere on January 30, 1945. The film, however, no longer had much effect; La Rochelle surrendered a few days later. The city of Kolberg was already occupied by Soviet troops. Just what significance the Nazis attached to the subject of the film is evident from the costs: no costs were spared in production, and it became the most expensive film in the history of German film.[58]

One of the best-known filmmakers from the era of the Third Reich was unquestionably Leni Riefenstahl, who was born in 1902 in Berlin. She began as an actress but soon produced her own films. Her first film as a producer, in which she also played the main role, was *Das blaue Licht* (The Blue Light), a symbolic legend from the Dolomites. Hitler was so impressed by this film that he commissioned her to film the Nuremberg Party Congress of 1933, the "Party Congress of Victory." The film appeared with the title *Sieg des Glaubens* (Victory of Belief) and was officially distributed by Goebbels's Propaganda ministry. After the premiere of the film in Berlin's "Ufa Palace next to the Zoo," the assembled Nazi dignitaries, led by Adolf Hitler, sang the "Horst Wessel song." As Courtade and Cadars show, the speeches of the *Führer* in the film were "so successful and so many supporters had gathered in the surrounding streets that the police and bodyguards had their hands full holding back the fanatic crowd. Hitler had to leave the hall through a side door."[59]

However, her film *Triumph des Willens* about the Party Congress of 1934, as Hitler sat firmly in the saddle after having "cleansed the Party," and *Olympia,* about the 1936 Olympic Games, became more famous. Both films were ordered by the Party and were made with its support and at huge expense. *Triumph des Willens* was rated "especially commendable in terms of state policy and artistry." On May 1, 1935, Goebbels honored the film with the "National Film Prize" and praised it with the words: "It elevated the hard rhythm of this great era to the eminently artistic; it is monumental, shaken throughout by the pace of the marching formations, steely in its view, and steeped in artistic passion."[60] The 1938 film *Olympia,* actually, two films: *Fest der Völker* (Festival of the People) and *Fest der Schönheit* (Festival of Beauty), attained artistic mastery and international success. However, it was unquestionably also part of Nazi propaganda: "The film work was quite obviously also drawn into the gigantic propaganda effort. Leni Riefenstahl did not make a film about the Olympic Games but about Olympic Germany."[61] She always emphasized the non-political nature of the film on the Olympics and used the argument that her film was recognized by the Olympic Committee as the official Olympic film and was honored with a certificate and a gold medal.[62]

Notes

[1] For more literature on film in the Third Reich consult the bibliography in this book and those mentioned in the text. Rentschler, in particular, provides fifty-five pages of bibliography on film and filmmakers in the Third Reich; see Eric Rentschler, *The Ministry of Illusion: Nazi Cinema and its Afterlife* (Cambridge, MA, and London: Harvard UP, 1996).

[2] Patrice Petro, "Nazi Cinema at the Intersection of the Classical and the Popular," in *New German Critique*, 74 (Spring-Summer 1998), 42.

[3] I prefer this terminology to the term "Nazi film," which suggests that all films from this period are propaganda films.

[4] Eric Rentschler, *The Ministry of Illusion: Nazi Cinema and its Afterlife*, 1.

[5] See Francis Courtade and Pierre Cadars, *Geschichte des Films im Dritten Reich* (The History of Film in the Third Reich) (Munich: Hanser, 1975), 9.

[6] See Courtade and Cadars, 10.

[7] Quoted in Joseph Wulf, *Theater und Film im Dritten Reich* (Theater and Film in the Third Reich) (Frankfurt am Main, Berlin, and Vienna: Ullstein, 1983), 320.

[8] Quoted in Wulf, 321.

[9] See Courtade and Cadars, 22.

[10] See Courtade and Cadars, 31. Ulrich Gregor's observation that "when Hitler and the National Socialists took over, the German film industry became as still as a graveyard" is simply not borne out by the facts. See Ulrich Gregor, "Film in Berlin," translated from German by Marguerite Mounier, in *Berlin 1910–1933*, edited by Eberhard Roters (Secaucus, NJ: Wellfleet Press, 1982), 206.

[11] David Welch, *Propaganda and the German Cinema, 1933–1945* (Oxford: Oxford UP, 1983), 15.

[12] Quoted in Felix Moeller, *The Film Minister: Goebbels and the Cinema in the "Third Reich,"* with a foreword by Volker Schlöndorff, translated from the German by Michael Robinson (Stuttgart and London: Edition Axel Menges, 2000), 132.

[13] See Siegfried Kracauer, *From Caligari to Hitler* (Princeton: Princeton UP, 1947), 256–60; 269–70. Kracauer probably goes too far when he has all of German film culminate in fascism: "Self-appointed Caligaris hypnotized innumerable Cesares into murder. Raving Mabuses committed fantastic crimes with impunity, and mad Ivans devised unheard-of tortures. Along with this unholy procession, many motifs known from the screen turned into actual events" (272).

[14] Linda Schulte-Sasse, *Entertaining the Third Reich* (Durham & London: Duke UP, 1996), 1–16.

[15] See Rentschler, 3–7; Schulte-Sasse, 12–13.

[16] See Rentschler, 7.

[17] See Courtade and Cadars, 223.

[18] See Rentschler, 7.

[19] See Gerd Albrecht, *Nationalsozialistische Filmpolitik* (National Socialist Film Policies) (Stuttgart: Ferdinand Enke Verlag, 1969), 371–95.

[20] Quoted in Courtade and Cadars, 222.

[21] David Welch, *Propaganda and the German Cinema, 1933–1945*, 31 and 35.

[22] Quoted in Wulf, 401.

[23] See Wulf, 401.

[24] See Courtade and Cadars, 43 and 46.

[25] On that subject, see Erwin Leiser, *Deutschland erwache: Propaganda im Film des Dritten Reiches* (Germany Awake: Propaganda in the Film of the Third Reich) (Reinbek: Rowohlt, 1968), 31–35.

[26] See Rentschler, 62.

[27] See Schulte-Sasse, 263–265. See, on the other hand, the statement of the contemporary Austrian painter Friedensreich Hundertwasser: "The straight line is immoral."

[28] Karl-Heinz Huber, *Jugend unterm Hakenkreuz* (Youth Under the Swastika) (Berlin: Ullstein, 1982), 19.

[29] See Schulte-Sasse, 259–262.

[30] See Schulte-Sasse, 67–89.

[31] See Rentschler, 154.

[32] Schulte-Sasse points out correctly that the cliché of the ugly Jew breaks down here, and in fact is turned on its head (80–81).

[33] See Rentschler, 150 and 155–157. Also Schulte-Sasse, 47–91, and on Dracula in particular, 62–64. Schulte-Sasse especially points to the vampire-like, bloodsucker motif; the anti-Semites often described the Jews as "blood-suckers," including in Hitler's *Mein Kampf* (My Struggle). On the other hand, the thesis posited in various quarters that the anti-feminism in *Jud Süß* (Jew Süß) is just as central as the anti-Semitism seems to me at the very least exaggerated; such an assertion amounts in the final analysis to diminishing the pervasive anti-Semitism of the film (on that subject, see Schulte-Sasse, 56–57).

[34] On that subject, see Courtade and Cadars, 184–93.

[35] Quoted in Wulf, 448.

[36] Quoted in Leiser, 73.

[37] See David Stewart Hull, *Film in the Third Reich* (Berkeley and Los Angeles: U of California P, 1969), 169.

[38] See Wulf, 6.

[39] See Hull, 170. On that subject, see also Leiser, 73. For Jud Süß, see also Linda Schulte-Sasse, "The Jew as Other Under National Socialism: Veit Harlan's Jud Süß," in *The German Quarterly* 61, 1 (Winter, 1988): 22–49.

[40] See Rentschler, 193–213.

[41] Gero von Wilpert, *Sachwörterbuch der Literatur* (Dictionary for Literature), 4th edition (Stuttgart: Kröner, 1964), 443.

[42] See Rentschler, 194.

[43] "It enacts the heroic myth central to Aryan self-fashioning," Rentschler, 196.

[44] See Schulte-Sasse, 307.

[45] See Schulte-Sasse, 309.

[46] Victor Klemperer, *Ich will Zeugnis ablegen bis zum letzten: Tagebücher 1931–1941* (I Shall Bear Witness to the End: Diaries, 1931–1941), edited by V. Walter Nowojoski in association with Hadwig Klemperer (Berlin: Aufbau, 1995), 13.

[47] See Klemperer, 396.

[48] See Klemperer, 441, entry of December 6, 1938.

[49] Inge Deutschkron, *Ich trug den gelben Stern* (I Wore the Yellow Star), 15th edition (Stuttgart: dtv, 1998), 59.

[50] Quoted in Wulf, 415.

[51] See Courtade and Cadars, 120.

[52] See Kracauer, 235.

[53] Quoted in Courtade and Cadars, 122.

[54] See Courtade and Cadars, 68.

[55] On that subject, see Kracauer, 266–69.

[56] On that subject, see Karsten Witte, "Major Tellheim nimmt Minna von Barnhelm in Dienst oder Wie der Nazifilm mit Klassikern mobil machte" (Major Tellheim Takes Minna von Barnhelm into Service, or How Nazi Film Mobilized Using the Classic Writers), in *Neue Rundschau* (New Review), 96, 1 (1985), 158–73.

[57] So said Goebbels in a letter to the director Veit Harlan, quoted in Courtade and Cadars, 217.

[58] See Courtade and Cadars, 219.

[59] See Courtade and Cadars, 56.

[60] See Courtade and Cadars, 61. Leni Riefenstahl reports on the work for this film in her book *Hinter den Kulissen des Reichsparteifilms* (Behind the Curtains of the Reich Party Congress Film) (Munich: Franz Eher Nachfolger, 1935).

[61] See Courtade and Cadars, 62–63. Riefenstahl later tried to downplay the propaganda content in her films; on that subject, see Riefenstahl interview with *Cahiers du Cinéma* (Cinema Notebooks), 170 (1965); Courtade and Cadars, 57 and 59; Leni Riefenstahl's *Memoiren* (Memoirs) (Munich: Knaus, 1987), and Fritz J Raddatz's discussion of this book in *Die Zeit* (The Times), No. 42 (October 16, 1987).

[62] See Hull, 135.

Ernst Wiechert, who spent several months in Buchenwald
concentration camp in 1938.
Courtesy of Bundesarchiv, Koblenz.

8: Non-National Socialist and Anti-National Socialist Literature

THIS CHAPTER WILL introduce the literature that did not serve the goals and the propaganda of the National Socialists and was not expressly recommended by the Rosenberg Office or the Reich Chamber of Writers. Most of the works treated in this chapter belong to the categories of "undesirable" or even "prohibited" literature. That includes the literature of the Inner Emigration and the literature of open and hidden resistance.

Inner Emigration

The literature of the Inner Emigration is the most extensive. The concept of Inner Emigration is controversial and has not been clearly defined. The dispute between the "outer emigrant" Thomas Mann and "inner emigrants" such as Otto Flake, Walter von Molo, and especially Frank Thiess on the question of who had the worst lot to contend with will not be discussed here, as it contributes little to elucidation of the facts.[1] It is certain that there were severe communication problems between the two groups of emigrants, as neither would or could understand the problems of the other. Thus, Ernst Wiechert wrote in his memoirs *Jahre und Zeiten* (Years and Times), which he composed immediately after the war:

> I understand that it is hard for the victors to imagine the life of the outcasts in those years and to make a fair judgment. Erika Mann said in a disparaging manner in the *New York Herald Tribune* that after my release from the camp I had become an "obedient boy." But I do not know whether Erika Mann, if she had just been released from a German camp, would not have become an "obedient girl." And if she knows anything about what it is like to have listened every night long for seven years to every car that drove down the street, and to reach for the pistol to see if it is cocked. I do not know if she learned that in Switzerland or in California, and I would not wish that on her, either. I only wish that she would realize that the life in the column of the newspaper is very different from what we led every night for seven years.[2]

In attempting to define Inner Emigration, Reinhold Grimm rightly points out the "the phenomenon as such is not clearly delimited as a concept" (Grimm, 48). He therefore suggests a "sliding scale" "that extends from active resistance to passive refusal. . . . A person who was not writing as a fascist was still not necessarily writing as a non-fascist or even an anti-fascist. Only an opposing position that was recognizable deserves the name Inner Emigration" (Grimm, 48). In an article that appeared in 1970 in the *Weimarer Beiträge,* Wolfgang Brekle includes in the Inner Emigration those writers who "were not influenced by the Nazi ideology, wrote humanistic works, and did not allow themselves to be *gleichgeschaltet* by fascist policies."[3] In his book *Schriftsteller im antifaschistischen Widerstand 1933–1945 in Deutschland* (Authors in the Anti-Fascist Resistance from 1933 to 1945 in Germany), which was published in 1985, he limits the concept to "non-fascist literature," which he differentiated from anti-fascist literature.[4] However, as Brekle acknowledges (Brekle, 18), this separation does not hold up in every case, as under the dictatorial conditions of the Third Reich even refusal and hidden opposition presented in the "slave language had to be counted as resistance."

According to Werner Bergengruen, there was no work of opponents of Nazism who had remained in the country

> that was not affected by that era. Even those of my novellas which were written in the infamous twelve years and in which to all appearances nothing about the terrible events of the time was touched upon did not deny the years in which they were written, even if only in the fact that an attempt was made to present an opposing image by which the era could be measured.[5]

In an autobiographical sketch from 1947, Bergengruen points out the difficulties associated with writing the truth under fascism and the resulting problems for future generations in understanding anti-fascist works created under these conditions and the coded language used in them:

> It is impossible for anyone who is not familiar with a system of terror and censorship of the National Socialist type [and] who has grown up taking for granted the enjoyment of freedom of speech and of the written word, to understand the technique of allusions with cue words, the technique of indirect but clear expression. It is impossible for such a person to understand the more and more refined art of writing — but also of reading — between the lines.[6]

On the other hand, it was precisely the indirect "slave language," with its tendency to ambiguity that favored misunderstandings, failures to understand, and intentional distortions. Thus it was possible for the Nazi paper *Völkischer Beobacher* (Völkisch Observer) to write of Bergengruen's novel *Der Großtyrann und das Gericht* (The Great Tyrant and the Court) that it "is *the Führer* novel of the renaissance period!"[7] Other critics attempt to avoid the concept of Inner Emigration completely and propose instead the category of "The Other Germany," in which they also include exile literature.[8] In view of the dispute between "outer" and "inner" emigrants and the questionable behavior of some "inner" emigrants toward National Socialism, for example, Gottfried Benn, Ernst Jünger, and Frank Thiess, this concept also remains controversial.

It is certain, however, that the concept Inner Emigration did not first appear after 1945 as a defense for those who had remained at home, but was already used by numerous authors in the thirties, for example, by Frank Thiess and Klaus Mann.[9] Under the title Inner Emigration, Stefan Andres described his emigration into fascist Italy in 1937 because he was in opposition to the Nazis and had a half-Jewish wife; he thus remained "in the German police area" until "the front . . . moved between me and those police mentioned." As he is uncertain whether the concept of "emigrant" also applies to him under these special circumstances ("I do not know specifically at all whether I was one, an authentic, genuine emigrant"), he includes his life under the fascists in the concept of Inner Emigration.[10] Franz Schonauer is very skeptical about Inner Emigration, not only because Gottfried Benn and Ernst Jünger also claim the term for themselves, that is, authors who at least for a time supported the Nazi ideology — either directly or through their works — but because he viewed it purely and simply as an unproductive escape into edifying idylls: "The idealistic and apolitical attitude of the German middle class, which was what made National Socialism possible in the first place, did not, because of the terrible situation that it had helped to conjure up, find its way out of its unproductive 'inwardness.'"[11] Despite the problems and the indistinct delimitation, the concepts Inner Emigration, non-National Socialist and anti-National Socialist literature, as well as resistance literature will nevertheless be retained in this chapter. Only individual analyses, which are attempted in this chapter on the basis of examples, can provide a more specific definition. The Inner Emigrants are not at all a homogeneous group. They come from all parts of Germany and from a wide variety of social classes; they represent different ideologies and literary genres. Nature poets stand next to writers of historical novels and novels critical of the times; military-aristocratic views assert themselves in concert with Christian-social positions. The following pages present several examples for the literature of the Inner Emigration.

Werner Bergengruen's novel *Der Großtyrann und das Gericht* appeared in 1935. The author had already encountered the main motif of the novel in 1926 in the form of a fairy tale in which a sultan ordered his vizier "to solve a puzzling murder within three days or else his head would be placed at his feet."[12] Writing began in 1929 with the prologue and the first three chapters. Other parts were produced in 1931; "the largest portion of the book was written in 1933 and 1934" (174). As Bergengruen explained retrospectively in his *Schreibtischerinnerungen* (Writing Desk Memoirs, 1961), awareness of the relevance of the plot caused him to devote his "entire energy to the Great Tyrant" (174). He sensed that after 1933 "the action of the novel planned" would have an "uncanny, terrible relevance" (174).

An entire nation asks itself questions which I planned to have the characters in my book ask. The ease with which the powerless and threatened were seduced was evident everywhere. All human freedom was abolished, everyone was threatened, and almost all participants in power succumbed to the temptation of wanting to be God's equal. I found myself in a state of despair and outrage about everything that was happening before my eyes and burning anxiety about what we would have to expect from the immediate future. Now it became self-evident that my book had to seek answers not only to constantly nagging human questions but also to the concrete questions of the German present. And now certain features became sharper in a much different manner from what had originally been my intent. (174–75)

In retrospect, Bergengruen asserts convincingly that his novel *Der Großtyrann und das Gericht* has to be viewed in the context of the Third Reich; Bergengruen even designates it a "battle document."[13] The Nazis considered Bergengruen, as a convinced Christian, "politically unreliable" and "related to Jews"; he was unable to produce any proof of Aryan ancestry for his wife.[14]

The plot of the novel centers around a case of murder: in the palace garden of the Great Tyrant, the agent Fra Agostino has been murdered and the Great Tyrant's head of secret services, Nespoli, must find the murderer in three days or lose his head. The place of action is Cassano, a mythical Italian city-state at the time of the Renaissance. The hunt for the murderer leads to self-incrimination and to suspicions being raised by everyone about everyone else: "Brother spies on brother and is ready to sell him . . . Everything that was bound [has] been loosed."[15] At the end, it turns out that none of the many suspects committed the murder but instead that none other than the Great Tyrant saw himself forced to secretly eliminate the traitor Fra Augustino for reasons of state, as court proceedings would bring state secrets to light (314). In the novel, however, it is not the Great Tyrant that is accused but rather the fickle nature of human beings who allow themselves to be seduced so easily by a dictator. The prologue already clearly indicates the main theme of the novel: "This book will report about the temptations of the powerful and the ease with which the powerless and threatened are seduced." Of course, the Great Tyrant does not get off entirely unscathed; he is accused of arrogance and of wanting to be the equal of God: "You alone, however, have sinned by striving to elevate yourself above what is human and wanting to be God's equal. . . . That is the accusation that is being made against you here. And now you know, Majesty, that you are before the court, even if not before ours" (318–19).

The Great Tyrant has often been compared to Hitler and parallels can indeed be found. The Great Tyrant is the unrestricted ruler who also speaks of "Providence"; he is an upstart who pushes the old families aside (62). He loves functional buildings (62), has "an especially great desire to build," and wants to erect a monument to himself with buildings because he has no children. He prefers to withdraw to an isolated hunting cabin in the mountains (122) and surrounds himself with many flatterers (232). However, in contrast to the brown dictator, he is wise and submits to the judgment against him. Bergengruen, asked many times about these parallels, sharply rejects the comparison: "The question cited has always annoyed me, and I have considered it offensive to my hero. . . . The dangers of power and the great temptations of the powerful must be shown very specifically with a man of intellect and statesmanship, not with a criminal fool who belonged to the dirtiest dregs of humanity. And how would I have gotten it into my head that a Hitler could undergo a spiritual transformation and, deeply affected, place himself before the court of his own conscience?"[16] Bergengruen considers another question much more important, namely, the question of how this book could be published during the Third Reich at all. In his answer, Bergengruen points to the publisher, the aligned (*gleichgeschaltet*) Hanseatic Publishing House in Hamburg, which the Nazis did not find suspicious, and the courageous attitude of the conservative and anti-Nazi director of the publishing house, Benno Ziegler (181). When the book appeared in the fall of 1935, it was immediately "understood" by anybody "who had not been infected by the brown plague or who was only affected by a mild partial infection" (181).

It also demonstrated, however, how two-edged the sword of the slave language was, for "the seriously infected [. . .] read and praised [the book] without an inkling that judgment was being passed here on everything that they themselves embodied and at the same time viewed in the light of divine transfiguration" (181). Even the "main mouthpiece of tyranny, the *Völkischer Beobachter*, . . . wrote literally 'This is *the Führer* novel of the renaissance period!'" (182).[17] In 1936, a year after the appearance of the book, the chief ideologue of the National Socialists, Alfred Rosenberg, of all people, expressed his "thorough appreciation" of the book (185). Even a dramatization of the book was under discussion and was prevented by the author himself (182). The editor-in-chief "of a large, widely distributed newspaper," to whom Bergengruen had offered the manuscript for prepublication, understood the explosiveness of the novel very well, for he demanded that the title be simply "The Temptation" and the designation "Great Tyrant" be completely avoided; all allusions to the tyrant's childless state and desire to build as well as "all statements about politics, power, reasons of state, administration of justice . . . [are] to be ruthlessly eliminated as distracting digressions" (183–84). For Bergengruen, the double effect of his novel remained a "mystery"; he could only explain it by way of the isolation from the people in which the Nazis lived (186). Not until 1941–1942 came attacks on the novel and calls for its prohibition, primarily from the Rosenberg Office, but without any echo from the Propaganda Ministry (188–91).

Looking back today, it is hard to imagine that readers in the Third Reich, when reading certain passages, did not have to think of the political and historical environment in which they lived. In a conversation between Diomedes, a young idealist, and the Great Tyrant about the judicial system, the Great Tyrant maintains that he is "the source of law in this state and its environs, and thus the master of its interpretation." To that, Diomedes replies, as a warning:

> If it [justice] should begin to follow a course based on considerations . . . of what for a few seconds seems beneficial to a human community or form of government, it could find itself in the position of knowingly imposing wrong instead of right; for under some circumstances, justice may be better served with an unjust decision than with a just one. (194–95)

Who does not have to think here of the distortions of justice in the Third Reich in which law was what worked to the advantage of the state? In a discussion between Diomedes and the Great Tyrant about power, people, and will, the Great Tyrant maintains that he was born to power and embodied the unconscious will of the people:

> Thus, I am the hidden will of the people. . . . Tell me, Diomedes, why does an individual seize power and why does he rule? . . . First, because he was born to it and no man can fail to do what he was by nature created for. Thus, for his own sake. But secondly, for the sake of those ruled, in that the ruler . . . is a person who more clearly recognizes the will of the people to be ruled than they do themselves. (237)

How often did Hitler, too, make these claims about himself; such a view is an essential element of the *Führer* cult. One last example: A dubious character named Rettichkopf (Radish Head) believes, in extortive and totally insane blindness induced by power, to have the whole world in his hand:

> Whether I proceed in this manner or that, [make] this decision or that, determines the course of fate of this or that number of people who are among the most distinguished of the city, and even their offsprings! Yes, perhaps of an entire community. Or even the entire earth! Of the world! (167)

In contrast to the voices of praise, Wolfgang Emmerich, in his article "Die Literatur des antifaschistischen Widerstands" (The Literature of Anti-Fascist Resistance), in 1976 criticizes Bergengruen's novel, which in Emmerich's opinion does not lead to resistance, but away from it:

> One may mistrust the language of Bergengruen, which is archaizing, priestly, and pompous over long stretches; one may doubt whether an Upper Italian Renaissance tyrannic state can provide the appropriate

social and historical model to attack in disguise the fascist system of rule; crucial is the *Catholic basic structure,* in the literal sense, of the novel, the plot of which falls into the scheme of temptation — guilt — sacrifice — regret — mercy and punishment (as an act of God) and which has no place in active resistance.[18]

Bergengruen's satirical poems and spoonerisms, on the other hand, are clearly resistance literature; numerous copies of these poems, which were written between 1933 and 1939, circulated anonymously through the population. Here are two examples:

Ende, Schwätzer, endlich deine miesen
Reden! Adolf? Ja, ich meine diesen.

[Finally stop, you windbag, your lousy
Speeches! Adolf? Yes, that's the one.]

Rassenabgott deiner Rindermasse,
Oberhornochs deiner Minderrasse,
Taugst fürwahr zum Strohbrandschürer fein.
Führer, sprich: wo ist dein Führerschein?[19]

[Racial idol of your cattle-masses,
Super horned-ox of your lesser race,
Good indeed as a straw fire stoker fine,
Führer, speak: where is your *Führer's* (a pun, leader's or driver's) permit?]

Opposition to the National Socialist regime is also evident in some poems from Bergengruen's volumes of poetry *Der ewige Kaiser* (The Eternal Emperor, 1937), which appeared anonymously in Graz and was banned in 1938 after the *Anschluß* and *Dies Irae* (Day of Anger), written in summer of 1944 and published in 1945. In the volume of poetry *Dies Irae,* Bergengruen treats, in light of defeat, the theme of guilt and atonement for crimes committed. In the poem "Die Lüge" (The Lie), he asks in well-crafted hexameters about the moral and emotional damage caused by Nazi rule:

Wo ist das Volk, das dies schadlos an seiner Seele ertrüge?
Jahre und Jahre war unsere tägliche Nahrung die Lüge.
Festlich hoben sie an, bekränzten Maschinen und Pflüge,
Sprachen von Freiheit und Brot, und alles, alles war Lüge.[20]

[Where is the people that could without harm to its soul bear this?
Year in and year out our daily sustenance was a lie.
Festively they began, machines and plows adorned with wreaths,
Spoke of freedom and bread, and all of it, all was a lie.]

In the longer poem "In dieser Zeit" (In These Times), however, Bergengruen does not call upon the people for active resistance; instead, he appeals to their steadfastness to remain intact and endure in these times of general betrayal and persecution:

> Inmitten eurer eignen Wände
> seid ihr Verfolgte und verhöhnt.
> Wer aber ausharrt bis ans Ende,
> wird überwesentlich gekrönt.

> [In the confines of your own walls
> you are persecuted and mocked.
> But he who endures until the end,
> will be crowned over and beyond.]

In the twelfth year of Nazi rule, the Christian poet Bergengruen, in the last poem of the cycle *Dies Irae,* "An die Völker der Erde" (To the Peoples of the Earth), does not, mindful of his own guilt, condemn all Germans, for "no one saw the suffering. . . . Through the blare of the fanfares, calls of celebration, and the ringing of bells, only He [God] heard the cries of those being tortured, the sighs of fear, and the groaning."

In an attempt to find sense in what is apparently senseless, Bergengruen views the catastrophe as punishment for the world's falling away from God, for which the Germans — at least that is how the "we" of the poem is to be interpreted — have suffered on behalf of everyone.

> Völker der Welt, die der Ordnung des Schöpfers entglitt,
> Völker, wir litten für eure Verschuldung mit.
> ....
> Völker der Welt, der Abfall war allen gemein.
> Gott hat jedem gesetzt, des Bruders Hüter zu sein.

> [Peoples of the world, which slipped from the creator's order,
> Peoples, we also suffered for your guilt.
> ....
> Peoples of the world, the falling away was shared by all.
> God gave each the task of being his brother's keeper.]

Other peoples, according to Bergengruen, saw the world go up in flames and did nothing to stop it:

> Alles Schrecknis geschah vor euren Ohren und Blicken,
> und nur ein Kleines war es, den frühen Brand zu ersticken.
> ....
> Sicher meintet ihr euch hinter Meeren und schirmendem Walle
> und vergaßt das Geheimnis: was einen trifft, das trifft alle.

[All the horrors unfolded in front of your ears and eyes,
and only a small thing was it to smother the early fire.
....
Safe you thought yourselves behind oceans and shielding ramparts
and you forgot the secret: what strikes just one, strikes all.]

Everyone felt safe until the demon broke forth from his borders, attacked the world, and also brought immeasurable calamity to others. Now that the time of judgment has come, Bergengruen not only appeals to the peoples of the world to remember their own omissions but also reminds them that they were not tempted and therefore cannot know how they would have conducted themselves:

Völker der Erde, ihr haltet Gericht.
Völker der Erde, vergeßt dieses Eine nicht:
Immer am lautesten hat sich der Unversuchte entrüstet,
Immer der Ungeprüfte mit seiner Stärke gebrüstet.

[Peoples of the earth, you are holding court.
Peoples of the earth, do not forget this one thing:
Always loudest was the indignation of the one not tempted,
Always did the one not tested boast of his might.]

With guilt, Bergengruen means moral guilt, guilt before God, before whose judgment seat everyone must appear and take responsibility for himself:

Völker der Welt, der Ruf des Gerichtes gilt uns allen.
Alle verklagt das gemeinsam Verrat'ne, gemeinsame Entweihte.

[Peoples of the world, the call of the court applies to us all.
All are charged with the commonly betrayed, the commonly profaned.]

The world, which has become disjointed and has been punished by God, will be made right by changing its ways and doing penance: "Peoples, hear with us all the divine: metanoeite!" With the last word, the poet is referring to the sermon of John (Matthew 3:2), which in this way calls for penance (literally: "Change your ways"). This poem in particular inflamed criticism of the Christian attitude toward resistance, as the Christian opposition reacted to Nazi crimes only with passive toleration and calls for penance. Thus, the Swiss writer Max Frisch decisively rejected this poem's dispersion of concrete guilt into the general guilt of all mankind.[21] For Wolfgang Brekle, the limits of Bergengruen's opposition to fascism are especially clear in the volume of poems *Dies Irae:* "Mythicizing war, [remaining] ignorant of the social and economic root causes of fascism and the war, considering the defeat of Hitler Germany to be the absolute end, welcoming the end as a 'day of heavenly judgment,' [and] hoping for salvation from divine forces." Like Frisch, Brekle considers the clouding of the guilt question problematic "because he [Bergengruen] claims that everyone is guilty," especially in the poem "Wer will die Reinen von den Schuldigen scheiden?" (Who Wants to Separate the Pure from the Guilty?).[22]

Bartolomé de Las Casas (1474–1566), whose father came with Columbus to the New World, fought passionately, as a Spanish Dominican missionary in the New World, at that time New India, against the cruelty with which the Spanish colonizers treated the native population. Reinhold Schneider reworked this material in the novel *Las Casas vor Karl V.* (Las Casas Before Charles V), which appeared in 1938 as a further result of Schneider's intensive preoccupation with the Iberian world. As Schneider writes in his autobiographic work *Die Zeit in uns* (The Time in Us), he wanted to use this novel to protest against the persecution of the Jews by the National Socialists: "While working on *Inselreich* [Island Empire, Schneider's travel book about England, published in 1936] I realized that the story of Las Casas afforded me the opportunity to protest against the persecution of the Jews."[23] However, he was likewise interested in the problem of guilt, with which all of Christendom had burdened itself during the colonization of the New World: "At the same time, I was gripped by the old theme of the guilt of Europe [and] of Christianity for the world, the tragedy of colonization" (*Die Zeit in uns* [The Time in Us], 111). Because of its dual intent and the coded presentation, the novel could miss its goal but it could also be published. Nevertheless, there can be little doubt about the anti-fascist interpretation of many passages in the novel, and many people understood the message after its publication in 1938. After reading the book, the anti-fascist Jochen Klepper wrote in 1938 to his friend Reinhold Schneider:

> In this book from the 16th century the dispute about the race problems and tragedies of the 20th century and of our decade are very often evident — and that [is the case] in the most moving parts. How the present has taught us to read sources.[24]

For good reason Schneider, whose writings and sonnets were distributed illegally, belonged to the "undesirable" and disliked authors in the Third Reich. Court proceedings for high treason were even initiated against him in 1945; only the end of the war saved him. Despite all that, his book *Las Casas vor Karl V.,* was reprinted in the years 1940 and 1941, until he did not receive any more paper allotments for his writings.

The novel *Las Casas vor Karl V.* begins in the port of Veracruz, where Father Las Casas boards a ship so that he can, after his return to Spain, make an appeal to Charles V on behalf of the mistreated Indios. During the stormy crossing, Las Casas saves the ship through prayer and by expertly taking over the helm. In the long weeks of the journey, the Spanish knight Bernardino de Lares, shaken by feverish dreams, attempts to relieve his conscience by telling Las Casas about his shameful past as a conquistador. The terrible atrocities, committed in the name of an imperialistic "Christian" ideology, are described in the process in considerable detail, for example, the description of the "easiest way to get gold": "We set the villages on fire, then burn the people, and the gold is left, just as in smelting."[25]

Having arrived in Spain, Las Casas goes to Valladolid in order to debate with the legal scholar Gineés de Sepulveda about the treatment of the Indios in the New World before Charles V. As in Bergengruen's *Der Großtyrann*, the issues here are power and law. Las Casas would like to convert the Indios "by means of belief alone" (166), without regard for any interests of state; his fellow Dominican brothers in Haiti and Cuba back then had "opened his eyes to the majesty of law and the terrible abuse that it suffered" (167). Las Casas wants to put forward his belief in law just now "because the Spanish people are in danger of selling their souls to secular powers" (167). Sepulveda, on the other hand, places the state and the interests of the state above "eternal law." In Sepulveda's eyes, law is what works to the state's advantage; the end justifies the means. He claims that "whatever contributes to the stability of the state is good" (208). In his book "On the Just Reasons for War Against the Indios," he provides proof "from pre-Christian times, that is, from the Old Testament . . . about the potential right of a people to rule over another people" (178). He is only concerned with preserving the rights of the Spanish government in the conquered areas. Las Casas, on the other hand, is seeking a complete change in the power relationships in New India; to him, "wars of conquest" are "illegal, tyrannical, [and] hellish" (208). He reports the extermination of entire peoples and other criminal atrocities of the Spanish: "I saw all of that, and I couldn't do anything but make the sign of the cross in the air over mountains of bodies" (228). Las Casas requests that Charles V give the Indios their freedom. His plea for law and justice culminates in the vision of a great court that will come over the whole country: "Guilt has already become part of our life; all warnings are in vain. Spain has failed to recognize its hour" (238). He does not want to play the role of a prophet, but his God forces him to prophesy future calamity:

> And still . . . it is true that the court will come over this land! For anyone who fails to carry out the highest order will incur the greatest guilt. . . .
> For that reason God is right when He destroys this country's reputation.
> For terrible crimes there is now a terrible punishment. (239)

What prophetic words in 1938, which many understood; "Spanish" or "Spain" need only be replaced with "German" or "Germany" to see what Schneider intended with his book.

The book ends on an optimistic note: Charles V hears Las Casas, promises to give the Indios their freedom and to send Las Casas back to the New World as a bishop, although doubts remain about Las Casas's plans being put into effect. With his attack on dictatorial tyranny, Schneider by no means advocates a democratic alternative to fascism. The King is acknowledged as a just and legitimate prince, indeed, is even exonerated because he supposedly knew nothing of the atrocities of his subjects: "How could a king order what is against the law on which his rule is based? . . . That happened because the noble King Ferdinand was lied to in the most shameful possible way by the admirals . . . and by his own advisors" (223).[26]

In his study *Deutsche Literatur im Dritten Reich* (German Literature in the Third Reich), which was written with "polemical and didactic intent," even Franz Schonauer, who was quite skeptical about the Inner Emigration, concedes that, of all the works of the "Inner Emigration, *Las Casas vor Karl V.*" could be "most clearly interpreted as resistance to an unjust power."[27] As Günter Wirth documents,[28] Schneider follows the historical events surrounding Las Casas quite accurately, except for the debate with Sepulveda that is central to his work. Throughout history up to the most recent times, Las Casas has been considered a champion of equality and human rights for all peoples. Thus, Las Casas's work inspired the Netherlands in their struggle for freedom against the Spanish; Herder, in his "Briefe zu Beförderung der Menschheit" (Letters for the Advancement of Humanity), granted him an important place; the theologians of freedom in Latin America in our day refer to Las Casas; and in 1966 Hans Magnus Enzensberger arranged for a new edition of Las Casas's "Kurzgefaßtem Bericht" (Concise Report).

Stefan Andres, like Reinhold Schneider, a Christian-Catholic opponent of National Socialism and after 1945 one of the spokesmen for what he calls "other Germany" in his speeches and essays, collected in *Der Dichter in dieser Zeit* (The Poet in These Times), participated in the same manner as Schneider and Bergengruen in camouflaged resistance to the Nazis with his story *El Greco malt den Großinquisitor* (El Greco Paints the Grand Inquisitor). In this story there are also clear parallels between the tyranny of the Inquisition and the rule of terror of National Socialism. In the story, the painter of foreign ancestry, El Greco, actually Domenicos Theodokopolos from Crete, is ordered to go from his place of residence, Toledo, to the Grand Inquisitor in Seville in order to paint a portrait of him. Filled with fear, El Greco sets out; he has not always been submissive to the powers-that-be, and his pictures have not always conformed to the norm: "Your style of painting, compared to Juan del Mudo's, has to be called — very . . . foreign."[29] He is afraid of making unthinking statements, and therefore "examines his internal world, not to see whether it is good, but to see whether it is closed off and sealed" (7). But he only succeeds partially in accomplishing that end. In a conversation with the chaplain, who takes him to the Grand Inquisitor, he calls the leader of the people to account: "The people can never be called schismatic; it is the priests, the shepherds — who set up boundaries and tear them down!" (8).

Visions of the Inquisitor's victims plague him; he curses his "craving for fame, which drove him out of the free air of Venice into the sphere of influence of the Escorial" (11). He remembers his last meeting with the Grand Inquisitor, on the occasion of the unveiling of "his painting of the martyrdom of St. Mauritius," in which a snake extends to the nameplate of the painter. This snake, as El Greco explains to the Cardinal Inquisitor, represents evil; his name is supposed "to prevent the entry" of evil "into the picture" (10). In the picture of the Cardinal he no longer needs a viper under his picture; the viper is the object of the picture in the person of the Cardinal and is warded of by the image on the canvas itself. Like the books of the Inner Emigration, and of hidden resistance, El Greco's pictures are a declaration and legacy to the future: "I make my declaration in pictures" (14). In an empire of lies, he wants to gain acceptance for the truth, despite the warning of his friend and physician Cazalla: "All necks turn to all sides, like screws, trying to pay attention; all backs are bent; all dreams are filled with the dancing of flames. If we want to live, we learn to lie" (15). El Greco also dismisses any thought of exile, too, as enticing as it may seem (15).

Before leaving for Seville, El Greco and his physician Cazalla complain about the terrible times in the empire: "The entire Spanish Empire has gout: the king, the army, [and] the fleet — they have all become stiff, swollen, [and] unmovable. What a powerful disease he thought, that can cause the death of an entire age" (12). News of the death of King Philipp affords El Greco an opportunity to observe that no ruler is irreplaceable:

> It is getting to be time for everyone who knows that the earth is not the center of the universe to no longer allow any one person to be the center of human beings. We have a different center. And that is why the country breathes easy at the death of a ruler, even one more bearable than Philipp — it is something ungirding and a disarming, the expectation of something unbelievable that will swell the loins of the empire. (12)[30]

Fortified internally, El Greco appears before the Cardinal and paints the truth, as he sees it, and not according to the wishes of the Cardinal. He paints, "as God orders me to through truthfulness. . . . According to that truthfulness which the Lord expressed when he put himself into the image of lightning which lights up from its beginning to its end and reveals everything that is hidden" (21). Instead of "advent violet" he paints the biretta of the Cardinal "blood red," his face, pale, his collar and his surplice, white, and the background, dark. The colors black, white, and red invoke death, and they are also the colors of the Third Reich; the red points of the biretta are also reminiscent of the bloody victims of the swastika. The Cardinal understands what El Greco means with his picture: "You mean the Holy Church with this picture!" (21–22). The latter confirms this courageously: "It has become a bloody fire, Your Eminence!" (22). He confesses to his friend Cazalla: "You know, it is futile to kill the Inquisitors. What we can do is record the visages of these proscribers of Christ" (28). Like cutting open a piece of rotten fruit, El Greco wants, with his pictures, to cut "through the middle of the world, yes, I want to do that, and Nino [the Cardinal] should notice what the General Inquisitor looks like inside" (34). The Grand Inquisitor sees through the painter, but he pays him a princely sum. El Greco returns to Toledo, but the flames at the stakes continue to burn. Andres seems to say that the artist can depict the truth in the hope that others will recognize it but does not have the means to act on it. Despite the involved narrative form, the plot brings out several very clear passages containing criticism of the system.

Ernst Jünger's novel *Auf den Marmorklippen* (On the Marble Cliffs), which appeared in 1939 and was reprinted most recently in 1980, has often been interpreted as a resistance novel, criticizing the primitive practices of the Nazis from a conservative, elitist standpoint. That certainly applies to a large extent; however, in the epilogue to the Ullstein edition of 1980, Jünger demonstrates a certain aversion to the concept "resistance" and emphasizes that "this shoe fits on various feet."[31]

In this novel, Jünger was more concerned with "an allegory of a feeling for life" than with resistance. However, numerous contemporaries, for example Ernst Schnabel or Heinrich Böll, saw in Jünger's work "a gigantic *roman à clef* relating to the Third Reich."[32] In the novel, the battle is transferred from the realistic realm of *In Stahlgewittern* (In Storms of Steel) to the elemental and mythical; the novel takes place in an exotic landscape at an indefinite time and has as its theme the collapse of an advanced culture. A bloodthirsty "Head Forester" from "Campagne," the "swamps and dark chasms out of which bloody tyranny threatens" (35), harries the land of peaceable and spiritual people, the land of "Marina." The first early signs of calamity were "not recognized"; the first messengers of force were not brought before a court. "Therefore dark consultants blossomed who protected injustice from the courts, and in the small port bars the conspirators openly took root" (39). Violence spread, supported by inferior bards who hammered out iambic poetry of "hate and revenge." The Head Forester did not proceed without skill in eliminating all resistance on the way to seizing power: "In this area in particular the Head Forester had a masterful characteristic: he administered fear in small doses that he gradually increased and that were intended to disable the resistance" (45). As a result, "terror began to rule completely and assumed the mask of order" (47). At the center of the cruel Head Forester's empire stands the "oppressor's cabin at Köppelsbleek" (87). Köppelsbleek is an empire of violence and death, "the cellars over which the proud castles of tyranny rise . . .: horribly stinking caves in which dubious gangs condemned for all eternity amuse themselves by terribly violating human dignity and human freedom. Then the Muses fall silent, and the truth begins to flicker, like a lantern in foul weather air" (85). The cities of Marina go up in flames, and over the broken remnants "waved the standard of the Head Forester, the red boar's head" (134). Biedenhorn, a mercenary leader for the Head Forester, especially enjoyed torturing writers and intellectuals: "He was now filled very openly with delight that the writers, verse-makers, and philosophers were now in for a hiding" (34).

The novel can be read as an exact parable of Hitler's rise to power and his violent rule, including concentration camps; and it was understood by many in that way when it appeared, as Jünger's afterword in 1972 attests. In its generality, however, the novel also applies to other violent systems, for example, to Bolshevism, as Jünger also indicates in his afterword: "Shortly after the war there were rumors of illegal printings in Ukraine and Lithuania" (14). The Nazis, who viewed themselves as the bulwark of western civilization against Bolshevik barbarism probably understood the novel in that context; otherwise they certainly would have prevented its publication. The influence of Nietzsche's legacy is clearly evident in the novel, especially Nietzsche's *Zarathustra*. In the depths resides the vulgar; in the crevices of the marble cliffs, the cultural world in its solitariness. What connects this novel to *In Stahlgewittern* is the conservative ideology that is apparent primarily in the emphasis on the role of fate and in the glorification of battle and cruelty — however, in contrast to the sober language of the early work, in George-like aesthetic, mythical, exaggerated form. As the narrator sees the fire at the mysterious town of "Köppelsbleek" and the heads of the princes on stakes, he is seized by a "shudder deep inside":

> Here it became clear to me what I had often doubted: there were still noble people among us in whose hearts the knowledge of great order still was alive and was affirmed. And just as the shining example prompts us to follow, I swear to myself before this head in all of the future ahead that I would rather fall alone with the free than walk in triumph with slaves. (119–20)

Of the horrors of bloody battle, he perceives only the beauty in destruction: "Of all the horrors of annihilation, only the golden shimmer rose to the marble cliffs. Thus, foreign worlds blaze up in the beauty of destruction, bringing pleasure to the eye" (125). The echo of *In Stahlgewittern* is even clearer in the following passage: "The human order resembles the cosmos in that it must plunge into fire in order to be reborn anew" (55). The storms of steel of the First World War were for Jünger such a time. In the end, however, the quotation is not referring to any real situations, but as Ralf Schnell explains, to "conformance to natural law and thus to the timelessness of social catastrophes," the return of which is "inevitable."[33] But whether Jünger's mythical stylization of horror amounts to his "exculpation from Nazi crimes," as Schnell claims, remains highly doubtful.[34]

Ernst Wiechert's story "Der weiße Büffel. Oder von der grossen Gerechtigkeit" (The White Buffalo. Or the Great Justice, written in 1937, first published in 1946) also deals with truth, law, and justice in a world ruled by tyrants. An East Prussian by birth, Ernst Wiechert (1887–1950) was initially not far removed from conservative, nationalistic thinking, which in the beginning gained him sympathetic support from the National Socialists. In his novel *Der Totenwolf* (The Wolf of the Dead, 1924), the focus was still on the glorification of naked violence. By 1937, however, when Wiechert wrote the story in question, that had very basically changed; the "Weißer Büffel" can in fact be viewed as a retraction of *Der Totenwolf*. Wiechert publicly read from the "Weißer Büffel" in several cities, Bonn, Essen, and Cologne, on a reading tour through the Rhineland in 1937; the audience, and the authorities as well, understood the indirectly stated critical allusions to the Third Reich all too well.[35] A reading that was planned for February of 1938 in Basel was consequently not approved, nor was the printing of the story. In May of 1938, Wiechert was taken to the Munich police prison, and seven weeks later to Buchenwald Concentration Camp, from which he was released on August 30, 1938, with the warning from the Reich propaganda minister "that he would be put back in the camp for the slightest reason, but then 'for life and with the aim of destroying him physically.'"[36] He wrote down his experiences in the concentration camp in *Der Totenwald: Ein Bericht* (The Forest of the Dead: A Report) a year after his release. This report, along with his other writings, he buried in his garden until its first publication in 1945.

The fairy-tale-like story "Der weiße Büffel. Oder von der grossen Gerechtigkeit" takes place at an indeterminate time in an indeterminate locale in a mythical India. Vasudeva, the main character, experiences the violent invasion of his home village by predatory tax collectors and from that point on seeks, with his companions, to repay force with force: "The law ceased being over them as something peaceful. They themselves were the law, and from now on blood was no longer something to be shied away from."[37] However, no amount of power and bloody battles can cover up the feelings of emptiness; he realizes "that he had erred" (574). A holy man enlightens him: "He who holds power and riches in his hands . . . does not walk with any less of a burden. And he, who carries blood on them, must bear the greatest burden of all" (574). He returns to his village and devotes himself under the strong influence of his mother to the task of helping bring about justice with peaceful means.

When the king's horsemen beat to death an old man's buffalo that was blocking their way, Vasudeva goes to the tyrannical King Murduk to demand justice from him, symbolically represented by a "white buffalo with golden horns." On the way to Murduk he refuses to fall on his knees like the other people before the King's golden mask, which hangs everywhere. For that reason, he is thrown in chains and taken to the ruler. The latter believes "that power withers and decays if the sword becomes dull or if justice seeks to stand up to power. For him life knows only two possibilities: with the sword or under the sword" (600–601). He therefore uses every possible means, including torture and corruption, to make Vasudeva bow before him. But Vasudeva stands firm in his passive resistance, for he knows that only in that way can he be victorious over power and bring about justice:

> All those whom you know worship you, at least with their foreheads, which rest in the dust, and with their lips, which can tell any lie. But I don't worship you, not even with my forehead and my lips. And from that you see how impotent you are. You cannot force me; you can only kill me. But you will cry over my corpse, for then you will have burned the bridge and you will always know, with every heartbeat, that a man once lived before whom you were a beggar. (606)

Murduk feels that his power is threatened by the passive resistance of one individual; he feels that Vasudeva's example will set a precedent:

> Your deed, it is flying on wings across the land. A thousand heads are lifting, like animals in cages when the bolt rattles. A thousand lips are whispering tonight around the lonely fire. A thousand hands are feeling for the dagger at the hip. Your hand has aimed for my heart, and for such a hand there is only repentance or death. (608)

Murduk wants to buy Vasudeva with the promise that he will send a "hundred white buffaloes with golden horns" if Vasudeva will worship him, for "it is only safe . . . when *everyone* worships" (610). Vasudeva does not allow himself to be deterred from his straight path even when Murduk orders Vasudeva's mother to die by fire. The story ends with Vasudeva's death, but he remains the victor. The King renounces power and the world finds inner peace; justice has triumphed by the sacrifice of an honorable man: a "caravan of justice," consisting of fifty pairs of white buffaloes with golden horns, travels through the land.

"This report does not seek to be anything but the introduction to the great symphony of death that will be written sometime by people more qualified than I."[38] So begins the prologue of Wiechert's report *Der Totenwald*. "People more qualified" such as Ellie Wiesel or Primo Levi have in the meantime recorded their experiences with the brutal murder machine of the Third Reich, Bruno Apitz even from the Buchenwald camp in particular.[39] However, Wiechert's report remains a lasting and shocking record documenting the cruelties that human beings are capable of inflicting on other human beings. At the same time, it is a song of high praise to the humanity of some of his fellow prisoners, without whom Wiechert would not have survived.

Der Totenwald, an autobiographical report, is written in the third person; "the assumed name of the person acting and suffering in these notebooks" is Johannes.[40] Johannes first describes his mental state before the arrest. He has tried to comfort fellow human beings in need, but he is plagued by feelings of guilt because "he had deigned to give a reluctant 'Yes,'" when an "unbending attitude would have required a 'No.'" Pastor Niemöller's being dragged off to the concentration camp was for him the turning point and the spur to act; he composed a protest letter to the authorities. In it, he emphasized that he was acting as an individual from a sense of ethical and moral responsibility, and was not a conspirator: "Neither was he a conspirator nor had he ever taken up with anyone who was intent on subverting order" (208). The consequences of his actions were completely clear to him: arrest and incarceration. Being arrested, the jail routine, the cellmates, other prisoners, guards, and other helpers of the system are described in detail and reflected upon. After six weeks of police detention, Johannes is transported to Buchenwald Concentration Camp, while being ogled by the curious population, for the prison transports were apparently a macabre form of entertainment.

Johannes's cellmate in the police prison had already described to him the horrors of the camp, but the reality exceeded the power of his imagination. SS troops received the prisoners at the Weimar railroad station and made clear to them "that upon any attempt to escape or the slightest insubordination they would immediately be 'shot down,' that they had to point their 'snouts' straight ahead, [and] that these 'swine' would get their rough edges knocked off" (256). Then the police car went up the Ettersberg, "the same mountain from which Goethe, with Charlotte von Stein, had looked out over the Thuringian landscape and where now, behind the electric wire entanglements, the camp awaited them" (257). In the camp, they first had to stand for two hours in a hot barracks. Older prisoners fell unconscious to the floor. The guards screamed, "Let the swine lie," and no one touched them. The deputy camp commander, Harmann, a minister's son, pulled out a Jew "with a well-known name" who was over seventy (258), and promised "to really give it to this old Jewish pig" (258). Johannes saw everything and "did not want to overlook anything or forget anything. It seemed to him that he had come here in order at some time to bear witness before a court that he did not know yet and before which every word would be weighed" (259). He describes the geography of the camp, the tops of the beech trees in front of the blue sky, and the screams of the persons being tortured. And the work at the quarry:

> The situation was that a large part of the Jewish [camp] population, and among them the weakest and the most debilitated, had been driven together, so that they could be finished off as easily as possible. Here stood the most brutal sentries, the most brutal non-commissioned officers, [and] the most brutal foremen. Here the seventy-year-old man, who only

still tottered like a shadow, got the same load on his shoulders as the seventeen-year-old, and if he collapsed three times, then the load was placed on him a fourth time, and when he remained lying on the ground, then he was "mutinying," and mutiny was punishable by death.

The Jews in the camp in particular "were only vermin, which were stomped to death" (271). Johannes himself did not work in the quarry but he saw "the long procession of the damned climb out of the depths and up the hill. . . . He saw the bent figures, skeletons with ghostly arms and legs, covered with sores, colored by coagulated blood" (274). Johannes is ashamed for his people, a people, "among whom Goethe lived," a people that is now producing such brutal acts, the sight of which makes Johannes go rigid. It is a world without God: "Johannes saw all of that, while the empty, ice-cold feeling inside him grew and grew, . . . The sun shone all right, and the clouds went by over them. But it was no longer God's sun and they were no longer God's clouds. God had died" (275).

Johannes was lucky; he was put in Block 17 for political prisoners, the "model of a comradely community" (277). Among the prisoners, he experienced exemplary human greatness and goodness, personified by fellow prisoners such as "Father Hermann," "Father Kilb," Walter Husemann, and especially his "lifesaver," Josef Bissel, without whom he would have "gone up the chimney" (278). But besides human greatness, Johannes also found among the prisoners examples of corruption, apathy, spiritual emptiness, and narrow-minded dogmatism, the latter especially in Jehovah's Witnesses, socialists, and communists, who reminded him vividly of Gottfried Keller's righteous comb makers. "He considered all ideology a disaster and he could only see hope, if he still had any, in 'education of the human race.'" However, he admired the endurance and stubbornness of these ideologues. Moreover, it was the communists in particular, such as Josef Bissel, who were closest to Johannes on a human level. But Johannes differentiates neatly between the communist and the human being; "Anyone who had helped him in the camp had done so not as a communist but as a human being who had preserved his sense of right and dignity, in contrast to those who defiled that sense" (310).

Shortly before his release, Johannes was granted special privileges. He received letters containing money and permission to have his books sent for the camp library. In the person of the camp library administrator, Walter Husemann, "he gained a lasting friendship, one that brought him very great happiness" (317). Husemann, too, was a communist and had been arrested as an active resistance fighter; he was released four weeks after Johannes and was executed in 1943 as a member of the resistance group *"Rote Kapelle"* (Red Orchestra). Johannes left the camp, and his physical wounds scarred over, but not his spiritual wounds: "No skin would grow over [them], from time, from forgetting, or from growing indifference. . . . The wounds that Johannes took away with him were not only his own wounds, not only those of the thousands that he left back here, indeed, not only those of his people. All of humanity had been violated" (325–26).

As the example of Bergengruen has already shown, opposition to the Nazi Reich was expressed not only in prose, but in poetry as well. Because of their brevity, poems in particular were considerably better suited for surreptitious distribution in the underground than longer prose. Thus, Reinhold Schneider wrote from Paris at the beginning of 1939 to his friend in Berlin, Jochen Klepper: "I am no longer thinking of big books, only of the most powerful symbols possible."[41] As Theodor Ziolkowski[42] and before him Charles Hoffmann[43] already established, many authors of the Inner Emigration used the sonnet form, in order to assert themselves with form against the chaos, or as Reinhold Schneider puts it in the last tercet of a sonnet on the sonnet form:

> So wird das Leben doch in Form gezwungen
> Und muß, von einem fremden Glanz erhellt,
> Unwiderruflich enden als Sonett. (192)
>
> [Thus life is pressed into a form
> And must, brightened by a foreign sheen,
> End irreversibly as a sonnet.]

For many authors, the "un-German" form of the sonnet was already an act of opposition. While most of the Nazi bards spurned the sonnet form in favor of the march song, authors in opposition to Nazi rule wrote sonnets and sonnet collections, for example Reinhold Schneider, Rudolf Hagelstange ("Venezianisches Credo [Venetian Credo]"), Georg Britting ("Die Begegnung [The Encounter]"), Albrecht Haushofer ("Moabiter Sonette [Moabit Sonnet]"), Hans von Hülsen ("Gerichtstag [Judgment Day]"), Wolfgang Petzet ("Die Sonette des Satans [The Sonnet of Satan]"), Wilhelm Tidemann (Sonette eines Deutschen [Sonnet of a German]"), Marie Louise Kaschnitz, Wolf von Nebelschütz, and others.[44] Numerous sonnets that were written in the era of the Third Reich could only be published after 1945. Many of them circulated in the underground — for example, many of the sonnets of Reinhold Schneider — where they provided comfort and hope: "They penetrated the prisons and camps; they were found among the final belongings of the men who had died in action; they were passed from hand to hand in the bomb shelters of the big cities."[45]

Reinhold Schneider wrote around 200 sonnets from 1933 to 1945, only a few of which, for example, *Die Sonette* (1939, Insel Publishers) could be published during the Third Reich. Like his prose, Schneider's poetry is based on Christian, specifically Catholic, morality. For Schneider the Nazis are only part of a greater evil intended as punishment for modern man's distance from God; like Bergengruen, Schneider seeks with his works to make an appeal for contemplation and a change in people's ways, not for active resistance. The "Reich des Wahnsinns" (Reich of Madness) can only be overcome by turning to the cross of Christ, as the following sonnet, written in 1937, says:

> Nun baut der Wahn die tönernen Paläste
> Und läßt sein Zeichen in die Straßen rammen;
> Er treibt das blind verwirrte Volk zusammen
> Vom Lärm zum Lärme und von Fest zu Feste.
>
> Schon reißt der höllische Schwarm verruchter Gäste
> Die Letzten mit, die besserer Art entstammen.
> Und tanzend in des Hasses grellen Flammen,
> Entweihn sie noch der Toten arme Reste.
>
> Jetzt ist die Zeit, das Kreuz des Herrn zu lieben
> Und auszufüllen jeden unsrer Tage
> Mit Opfer und Verzicht und heißen Bitten.
>
> Es wird das Wahnreich über Nacht zerstieben
> Und furchtbar treffen uns des Richters Frage,
> Ob Stund' um Stunde wir sein Reich erstritten. (109)
>
> [Now the madness builds palaces of clay
> And has its symbols rammed into the streets;
> It herds together blindly confused people
> From noise to noise and event to event.
>
> The hellish swarm of wicked guests already drags
> Along the last, who are born of better ways,
> And dancing in the garish flames of hate,
> They desecrate even the dead's last traces.
>
> Now is the time to embrace the cross of the Lord
> And to spend each of our every day
> With sacrifice, forbearance, and fervid pleas.
>
> Overnight the Reich of madness will dissipate,
> And terribly will the Judge's question strike us,
> Whether in each hour we battled for His kingdom.]

In the sonnet "Der Antichrist" (The Antichrist), Schneider portrays Adolf Hitler as the Antichrist who through deception gains control of the people and is even praised by artists:

> Er wird sich kleiden in des Herrn Gestalt . . .
> Und übers Volk erlangen die Gewalt . . .
> Die Künstler und die Weisen mit ihm zechen,
> Um den sein Lob aus Künstlermunde hallt.
>
> [He will cloak himself in the Lord's own form . . .
> And over the people attain control . . .
> The artists and wise men carouse with him,
> 'Round him resounds his praise from artists' mouths.]

However, he is shattered by the "lightning bolt from on high" and will be pitched back into the darkness "whence he originally came" (26).

Rudolf Hagelstange (1912–1984), who is to be considered basically a postwar writer, was a soldier in France and Italy from 1940–1945 and was one of the many members of the German army who carried Reinhold Schneider's sonnets in his field pack. As a soldier in Italy in 1944, he wrote the sonnets of *Venezianisches Credo* (Venetian Credo), 155 copies of which "were printed for the first time in April of 1945 . . . on the hand press of the Officina Bodini in Verona";[46] the copies were distributed illegally, for the most part in army circles.[47] The model for the "Venezianisches Credo" was Rilke's "Sonnets to Orpheus" and Reinhold Schneider's sonnets, as Hagelstange revealed in 1952 in the essay "Die Form als erste Entscheidung" (The Form as the First Decision).[48] The theme of this sonnet cycle was, much as for Schneider, "overcoming transient chaos by contemplation of the powers of human beings that are beyond and outside of time" (38). To Hagelstange, sonnets seemed to be the poetic form best suited for this purpose, for "their strict form . . . is already an external manifestation of the aversion to formlessness, the will to new law" (38). Hagelstange also points out the astonishing number of sonnets that were written in the last years of the war: "The sonnet, created in opposition to the demon, became a downright fashionable form of resistance" (38).

Similar to Bertolt Brecht in the poem "An die Nachgeborenen" (To Future Generations) ("Was sind das für Zeiten, wo / Ein Gespräch über Bäume fast ein Verbrechen ist" [What kind of times are these, when / A discussion of trees is almost a crime]), Hagelstange questions right in the first sonnet of the collection the justification for poetry in the face of horrors:

> Wie kann man singen, wenn aus allen Kehlen
> der Angstschrei und die Klage bricht . . . (9)
>
> [How can one sing, when from every throat
> the cry of fear and the lament break forth . . .]

The horrors are described in several sonnets:

> Denn was geschieht ist maßlos. Und Entsetzen
> wölkt wie Gewitter über jedem Nacken.
> Es jagt der Tod mit flammenden Schabracken
> durch Tag und Nacht, und seine Hufe fetzen,
> was Werk und Leben heißt, zu tausend Stücken. (37)

> [For what is happening is without measure. And fright
> runs shivers like a storm down the back of every neck.
> Death gallops in pursuit, with flaming mares,
> through day and night, and his hooves tear and shred
> to a thousand pieces what is called work and life.]

Other sonnets are an appeal for contemplation of inner values and the expression of hope, as the last sonnet of the collection shows:

> Der Feige weihe sich dem Untergange,
> der Narr dem Taumel und der Knecht dem Raube.
> Mir aber, unzerstörbar, brennt der Glaube
> an einen neuen Tag. (42)

> [The coward would dedicate himself to the fall,
> the fool to giddiness, and the servant to theft.
> But for me belief burns indestructibly,
> Belief in a new day.]

According to Hagelstange, only the pure will be able to survive injustice unsullied and to help justice return to its accustomed place:

> Denn dies ist alles: Reinen Sinnes streben
> und reiner Hände reines Werk zu tun
>
> ....
>
> Das Recht wird mächtig, und den reinen Händen
> gelingts, das Werk des Menschen zu vollenden. (30)

> [For this is everything: to strive with pure mind
> and to accomplish pure work with pure hands.
>
> ....
>
> Justice grows powerful, and the pure hands
> succeed in perfecting the work of man.]

The late works of Oskar Loerke will serve as the final example for Inner Emigration. For Elisabeth Langgässer, Oskar Loerke (1884–1941) was "a major witness for Inner Emigration."[49] When the National Socialists came to power, Loerke was, in the course of *Gleichschaltung,* removed as the

Secretary of the Section for Literature of the Prussian Academy of the Arts, but remained a member and even signed a loyalty oath of eighty-eight writers for Hitler in October of 1933. This act is only comprehensible with knowledge of the particular circumstances under which Loerke affixed his signature. Loerke was at that time a reader at the Fischer publishing house and was induced by Fischer to sign so that the upper-middle-class Jewish publishing house did not get into even greater difficulties.[50] Loerke did not get over his having given his consent to sign or the chicaneries that he was exposed to under the Nazis; he suffered from heart attacks and depressions that brought about his death in 1941. In his diary, published after the war by his friend Hermann Kasack, he documented his loathing for the regime and his own spiritual agonies; he applied the designation "years of calamity" to the entries from 1933–1934. It is the diary of a person in despair. Thus Loerke remarked on February 19, 1933: "I am standing between the terrorists of the right and of the left. Possibly I must perish. My nerves can't take it any more. Grief, at having to face terrible consequences without having done or even having known the slightest thing."[51] Previous friends no longer answer, such as Hermann Stehr, who is conforming to the new line. Loerke's professional possibilities become more and more limited: "I am too old and too sick to cut stones. And then my being slowly murdered. If the publishing house is finished, my work is down the drain" (308–9). He lives more and more in the past "with the great old wise men and poets and musicians, as if living with our ancestors" (287). Life has lost any meaning for him: "At an earlier time, life had meaning, because it was life . . . Now it has no meaning because it is no longer life" (337). Loerke could have adapted, like many of his previous friends, but that is alien to him, for "a crime does not cease being a crime just because it has been made law. Rather, it is then widely acknowledged and its distribution a thousand times over is assured. Accordingly: when a hundred thousand people lie and only one tells the truth, then only one person tells the truth' and the majority of a hundred-thousand times as many tells lies against him" (336–37). Toward the end, the entries become increasingly brief: "February 28, 1939: The disgrace. Finally expelled from middle-class respectability" (339). A short two years later, Loerke died in Berlin.

With Wilhelm Lehmann, Loerke was one of the best-known nature poets of the twenties; his poetry was completely apolitical. After 1933, he continued to write nature poetry but politics also pushed their way into his verses. He, like Brecht, would also rather continue writing about trees:

> Doch wenn sich freche Bruten Schicksal nennen,
> Mußt du, mein Haß, des Schicksals Schicksal werden.[52]
>
> [But when insolent brutes call themselves fate,
> You must, my hatred, become the fate of fate.]

The late poem "Zum Abschluß meiner sieben Gedichtbände" (At the Conclusion of My Seven Volumes of Poetry) says in retrospect:

> Nun geh, mein Siebenbuch, gesellt
> Den Trümmern, dem Gerölle;
> Begonnen in der lieben Welt
> Vollendet in der Hölle. (622)

> [Now go, my seven books, join
> The rubble, and the debris;
> Started in the kindly world,
> Completed in hell.]

Numerous poems chastise the Nazi government in coded form. For example, the poem "Genesungsheim" (Convalescent Home) appeared in 1934 in the volume of poems *Der Silberdistelwald* (The Silver Thistle Forest). The poem was nothing if not clear:

> Was schlug man diesen zum Krüppel?
> Er dachte hinter der Stirn:
> Da öffnete ihm der Knüppel
> Den Schädel, und Hirn war nur Hirn.

> Warum haben Jauche-Humpen
> Dort jenen die Augen verbrannt?
> Sie haben einen Lumpen
> Einen Lumpen genannt.

> Warum schweigt dieser im Knebel?
> Weil sein Gewissen schrie!
> Wes Kopf sprang zum Reiche der Nebel?
> Dessen Gurgel vor Ekel spie! (440)

> [Why was this man beaten 'til crippled?
> He thought behind his forehead:
> Then the cudgel opened for him
> His skull, and his brain was only a brain.

> Why then did the slop tankards
> Burn the eyes of those persons there?
> They called a scoundrel
> A scoundrel.

> Why is this gagged man silent?
> Because his conscience screamed!
> Who is it whose head burst to the realm of the mists?
> He, whose gorge revolted with disgust.]

The poem "Die Spötter der Hilflosen" (Those Who Mock the Helpless), which was written in July of 1940, expresses Loerke's great personal despair:

> Die Alb-Lawinen rollen
> Auf mich herab von allen Seiten.
> Und meine Freunde wollen,
> Ich solle dennoch vorwärts schreiten. (573)

> [Nightmarish avalanches roar
> Down on me from every side.
> And my friends insist that I
> Should all the same move forward.]

In Loerke pessimism predominates, but sometimes a glimmer of hope is also evident when thinking of the demise of the Nazi Reich and faith in the power of poetry, as in "Vermächtnis" (Legacy), which was composed in 1940:

> Jedwedes blutgefügte Reich
> Sinkt ein, dem Maulwürfhügel gleich.
> Jedwedes lichtgeborene Wort
> Wirkt durch das Dunkel fort und fort. (614)

> [Every blood-based empire
> sinks into the earth, like the mole's hill.
> Every word brought forth by light
> Shines on and on through the darkness.]

Loerke's resistance to National Socialism was purely passive; he was not a man of action but of the art of words. In the poem "Wehrlos" (Defenseless), he illustrates the problems of the passive Inner Emigration:[53]

> Wir sahen zu und haben nichts verteidigt
> Es toste ein Gewitter und wir schwiegen,
> Als führen wir mitsamt in einem Nachen,
> Oh, wären wir trotzem doch ausgestiegen!
> Und unverziehen bleibt uns unser Lachen. (588)

> [We watched and defended nothing.
> A storm raged and we stayed silent,
> As if we rode together in one boat.
> Oh, if only we had still climbed out!
> And unforgiven we remain for our laughter.]

In addition to the authors and works treated here in detail there are countless others who can only be mentioned selectively and briefly. In these cases, their non-National-Socialist or anti-National-Socialist attitudes are determined by their works, their personal behavior, or both. Besides Ernst

Jünger, Walter von Molo and Friedrich Reck-Malleczewen criticized the Nazis from a conservative, aristocratic perspective. Von Molo (1880–1958), one of the founders of the German PEN Club (1919) and president of the Poetry Section of the Prussian Academy of the Arts from 1928 to 1930, and defamed by the Nazis as un-German, Marxist, liberal, and pacifistic, moved back from Berlin to Murnau in Upper Bavaria after the seizure of power. Ignoring everyday politics, he took the road of the Inner Emigration, which he defended after 1945 against exile authors, particularly Thomas Mann.[54] Friedrich Reck-Malleczewen (1884–1945), who came from an East Prussian landowner's family, expressed his rejection of the Nazis in his *Tagebuch eines Verzweifelten* (Diary of a Man in Despair), which was written between 1936 and 1944 and published in 1947 and 1981. His novel *Bockelson: Geschichte eines Massenwahns* (Bockelson. A Story of Mass Insanity) appeared in 1937; in it, Reck lashes out against the Nazi mass insanity of the twentieth century by depicting the Anabaptist mass insanity of the sixteenth century. In 1944, Reck was arrested and sent to Dachau concentration camp; one of his fellow-citizens had denounced him to the Gestapo. He died in Dachau on February 16, 1945.[55]

The Christian, Protestant writer Jochen Klepper (1903–1942) also became a victim of Nazi tyranny. In 1937, he was excluded from the Reich Chamber of Writers and thus silenced. His main work, the novel *Der Vater* (The Father), a description of the life of the Prussian King Friedrich Wilhelm I, was thoroughly saturated with Christian thought; it could only be published in 1937 because the Nazis misunderstood it as the glorification of a great leader. In December of 1942, he committed suicide with his Jewish wife and his Jewish stepdaughter Renate because both women were threatened with deportation.

Richarda Huch (1864–1947), "the leading woman of Germany" (Thomas Mann) displayed a courageous personal attitude when in the spring of 1933 she announced her resignation from the Prussian Academy of the Arts in a letter to the president of that organization. That letter said, among other things: "What the present government prescribes as the national way of thinking is not my [idea of] Germanness. I consider the centralization, the coercion, the brutal methods, the defamation of people who think differently, [and] the boastful self-praise to be un-German and disastrous."[56] In the same letter, she also stood up for Alfred Döblin and against the "Jew-baiting." Her three volume *Deutsche Geschichte* (German History, 1934) brought Huch directly in conflict with the Nazis. In 1937 the authoress was charged under the 1937 "law against treachery" because she supported Käthe Kollwitz and her "degenerate" art; but the Nazis settled for placing her on the list of undesirable authors.

Not every prominent author exhibited such civil courage. Gerhart Hauptmann (1862–1946), for example, expressed his opposition to fascism privately but did not take a decisive stand against it in public and showed himself willing to accept many compromises. His *Atrides* tetralogy consisting of *Iphigenie in Aulis, Agamemnons Tod* (Agamemnon's Death), *Elektra,* and *Iphigenie in Delphi,* all pervaded with dark tragedy, is frequently interpreted as criticism of Nazi barbarism, but others see in it only a further example demonstrating the lack of freedom and the restricted existence of human beings, which run through Hauptmann's works from the beginning on. Hans Carossa (1878–1956) also vacillated between opposition and adaptation. In 1933, he refused an appointment to the Writers' Academy, section 3, of the newly reorganized Prussian Academy of the Arts, but he accepted the Goethe Prize of the City of Frankfurt am Main in 1938, the San Remo Prize in fascist Italy in 1939, and the presidency of the Nazi "European Union of Writers" in 1941. In his *Lebensbericht* (Report of His Life), which appeared in 1951 in the Insel Publishers in Wiesbaden with the title *Ungleiche Welten* (Unequal Worlds) and is very much worth reading, Carossa speaks of the powerlessness of humanistic poets to oppose violence, but also of the support that they afford countless fellow human beings with their poetry: "Every truly free, deeply human word that was ventured within the state built on violence, every real artistic creation that was formed in the shadow of the Secret Police according to genuinely internal laws was pure fortification and an irreplaceable comfort for the well-meaning souls of those years" (81). Carossa also read the writers of German classicism, most especially Goethe, with this in mind: "Once again it was Goethe from whom encouragement and guidance came. The writer needed only to read a few pages from *Wilhelm Meister* or certain passages from *Iphigenie* or *Faust* to learn that he had a place and a voice in an invisible but powerful empire in which all the *Gauleiter* and top regional leaders had lost their power to give orders" (82). Carossa also professed his belief in the humanizing force of Goethe in his speech on the "Wirkung Goethes in der Gegenwart" (Effect of Goethe in the Present), which he presented on June 8, 1938, before the Goethe Society in Weimar (Leipzig: Insel, 1938 and 1944). In the speech, he called for "forbearance and tolerance, as well as for renunciation of force" (28), thereby joining the "ranks of those for whom all the countries and oceans of the world would not be enough if the realm of the spirit and the heart remained unconquered" (34).

An especially tragic case of Inner Emigration was the fate of Elisabeth Langgässer (1899–1950). In 1933, she had cast her vote for the Nazis, but in 1936 she was excluded from the Reich Chamber of Writers by those same Nazis and was banned from writing because she was half Jewish. After 1936, she could no longer publish in the Reich; the volume *Rettung am Rhein* (Rescue on the Rhine), consisting of three stories, was published in 1938 by Otto Müller Publishers in Austria, which had not yet been occupied. Only her "Aryan" husband Wilhelm Hoffmann saved her from the concentration camp. Things went worse for her daughter Cordelia from a previous relationship; Cordelia was classified as a full Jew (her father was Jewish) by the Nazis and deported to Auschwitz. Cordelia survived; in 1986 her memoir *Gebranntes Kind sucht Feuer* (Burned Child Seeks Fire) was published in the Federal Republic under her married name Cordelia Edvardson.[57] Regarding the accusation that her mother did not spend enough time taking care of her daughter and the subject of guilt and atonement in general, she said in the magazine of the *Frankfurter Allgemeine Zeitung:*

> What was most important (in *Gebranntes Kind sucht Feuer*) was the identification with the victims, and see my mother as a victim, too. I find it unbelievable that the question is repeatedly asked: "How could your mother abandon you?" People try to unload their own guilt onto other people. The question is never asked: How could we create such a system and allow a mother to be faced with such a terrible conflict?" My mother was a victim.[58]

Langgässer was one of the very few Inner Emigrants whose drawers did not prove to be empty after 1945. Under the most difficult conditions such as threat to her person as a half Jew, the fate of her daughter Cordelia, and bombing attacks on Berlin, she worked from 1937 to 1945 on her great novel and main work *Das unauslöschliche Siegel* (The Indelible Seal), which appeared in 1947, in the same year as her volume of poems *Der Laubmann und die Rose* (Laubmann and the Rose), which had also been written in the Nazi period. In 1949 Langgässer wrote about the evolution of the novel:

> What fear I endured for that enormously thick manuscript. Because of the persecution, only the original existed, and I carried it with me everywhere. In the air raid shelter during the nightly bombings I tied it to my skirt; I was carrying it next to my body when the house collapsed around us; after the victory it was in a suitcase through which the Russians ran their bayonets. Our last hoarded sugar flowed out, [and] my underwear was stabbed, but all those thrusts missed the manuscript![59]

Together with Hermann Kasack's novel *Die Stadt hinter dem Strom* (The City Behind the River), *Das unauslöschliche Siegel* was one of the most significant German publications of the years immediately after the war. In the fall of 1947, Langässer, at the first German writers' congress after the war, delivered a paper on "Schriftsteller unter der Hitler-Diktatur" (Writers in the Hitler Dictatorship). In the paper, she called it a blessing that she had already been thrown out of the Reich Chamber of Writers at an early date because for that reason she had never been tempted "to make a pact with this rabble." She insisted that inner and outer emigrants were of equal value and had equal rights, as both shared a common intellectual home and language, which was to be kept pure. She warns of withdrawing to the ivory tower and acknowledges only the nature poetry of Loerke and Lehmann as an alternative to Nazi-tinged literature or escape into detachment. After the misuse of language by National Socialism, she recommends to writers that they should remain silent for a time:

> We shouldn't believe that new wine can be put in old bottles — neither in those of 1933 or in those of 1923! But more than anything else, the language should be given a period of rest and silence. Every field must recover and with the alternation of root crops and wheat mature into its intended purpose. What that purpose might be, no one can say yet today.[60]

Among the authors banned by the Nazis were also the former expressionist and Alsatian Otto Flake (1880–1963), Mecklenburg native Hans Fallada (1893–1947), and Dresden native Erich Kästner (1899–1974), whose socially critical works were burned on the stake in 1933 and, according to the "Black Lists" in the trade paper *Börsenblatt,* were "to be unconditionally eradicated, . . . everything — except Emil."[61] The middle-class leftist Flake did not get any more paper to print his works, and Hans Fallada, the chronicler of the little man toward the end of the Weimar Republic (*Kleiner Mann, was nun?* [Little Man, What Now?], 1932), was judged negatively by the official critics of the Third Reich. His novel of the inflationary period *Wolf unter Wölfen* (Wolf Among Wolves) was allowed to be published in 1937 and was even to be made into a film, but was attacked in 1938 in the *Bücherkunde* (Bibliography) as the "confusion of an unbridled imagination" of an author against whose "shoddy literary compositions the strongest possible objection" should be raised.[62]

Frank Thiess (1890–1977) in particular was the spokesperson of the inner emigrants after 1945, although his position during the Third Reich is not uncontroversial; for example, he was never, in contrast to numerous other colleagues, excluded from the Reich Chamber of Writers. In 1941, he published *Das Reich der Dämonen* (The Empire of Demons), a historical work about the Hellenic, Roman, and Byzantine states; he gave it the significant subtitle, "The Novel of a Thousand Years," which many people believed was an allusion to the "Thousand-Year Reich." The book was quickly out of print and placed under a review ban. In this work there are a few critical allusions, most of which were, however, added in the new edition after the war.[63] His "Novel of a Sea Battle" between Russia and Japan, *Tsushima,* was even published as an "edition for the army" (Grimm, 45), although Thiess intended in both novels "to oppose the madness of supposed statesmanship," as he wrote after the war in *Jahre des Unheils: Fragmente erlebter Geschichte* (Years of Calamity: Fragments of History Witnessed).[64] In his memoirs, Thiess claims to have created *Tsushima,* read by many during the war as a heroic epic, as an anti-war book. He sees *Das Reich der Dämonen* (The Reich of Demons), on the other hand, as "my historically rendered attempt to move the character Diocletian so close to the present that anyone who did not have his eyes closed would have to see what I wanted to say there" (133).[65] In an attempt at justification in his essay "Zur Frage der Mitschuld" (On the Question of Shared Guilt, 144–50), Thiess points out the defenselessness of the individual "in a state of absolute power" (146). He sees the "core of shared responsibility" in the fact that the individual "did not allow himself to commit suicide in the false spirit of heroism," as did the Scholl sisters or the Christians at Diocletian's time, to whom Thiess refers. In his opinion, "the meaning of resistance did not lie in the excessiveness of rushing out into total self-destruction . . ., it could lie in holding onto the thought of salvation" (149–50).

Resistance Literature

Opposition to National Socialism did not only come from the Christian, religious side — Gertrud von le Fort and Rudolf Alexander Schröder should be included among the representatives mentioned above — but also from writers of the left. In the case of the latter, however, opposition was not internalized but instead manifested itself as hidden or open resistance. After the seizure of power, the communist Union of Proletarian Revolutionary Writers, which was founded at the end of the twenties, continued exerting influence in the underground until its destruction in 1935. Short poems in folksy doggerel were best suited for the illegal battle; reproduced and circulated with primitive means, they were publicly evident, pasted on walls. For the underground battle, Johannes R. Becher had already given his advice before his emigration in 1932: "Use doggerel! Exploit Wilhelm Busch for your cause!" and had himself provided an example:

> Ich komme heut als Wandgedicht
> Das zu euch von den Wänden spricht.
> Klebt mich so an die Wände hin
> Daß ich auch gut zu lesen bin.
>
> ....
>
> Nehmt meinen Spruch von Mund zu Mund
> Geh er und tu sich allen kund.[66]
>
> [Today I come as a wall poem
> That speaks to you from the walls.
> Do stick me to the wall out there
> So that I am easy to read.
>
> ....
>
> Take what I say: from mouth to mouth
> It should go and let everyone know.]

Both upright citizens and the police found leaflets, wall sayings, and reconstituted children's prayers, for example:

> Lieber Gott, mach' mich blind,
> Daß ich alles herrlich find.

> Lieber Gott, mach' mich taub,
> Daß ich an den Schwindel glaub.

> Lieber Gott, mach' mich stumm,
> Daß ich nicht nach Dachau kumm.

> [Dear God, make me blind,
> So that I find it all great.

> Dear God, make me deaf,
> So that I fall for the hoax.

> Dear God, make me mute,
> So that I don't go to Dachau.]

The combination of the three characteristics constituted the perfect Nazi follower:

> Mach mich blind, stumm, taub zugleich,
> Daß ich paß' ins Dritte Reich!

> [Make me blind, deaf, and dumb alike,
> So that I fit into the Third Reich!]

The well-known children's song about the ladybug suddenly becomes:

> Maikäfer fliege,
> Der Vater fiel im Kriege.

> Die Mutter starb den Bombentod
> Und alle Kinder leiden Not.[67]

> [Ladybug, fly away,
> The father fell in battle,
> The mother died a bombing death
> And all the children suffer need.]

Camouflaged writings were smuggled from abroad into Germany, for example, the Brecht essay "Fünf Schwierigkeiten beim Schreiben der Wahrheit" (Five Difficulties in Writing the Truth), disguised as "Satzungen des Reichsverbandes Deutscher Schriftsteller" (Bylaws of the Reich Association of Writers) or "Praktischer Wegweiser für erste Hilfe" (Practical Guide for First Aid). Excepts from Ludwig Renn's novel *Krieg* (War) circulated as *Der*

Frontsoldat (The Front-Line Soldier) by the Nazi author Werner Beumel-burg. Behind one edition of the score of "The Beautiful Blue Danube. Waltzes by Johann Strauß, Opus 314" socialist fighting songs were hidden. Indeed, even Reclam editions of the writers of German classicism disguised resistance literature, for example, an anti-fascist montage of quotations from Schiller's *Wilhelm Tell* or an anti-fascist parody of heroes from the *Nibelun-genlied* (Song of the Nibelungen) in an inexpensive popular edition.[68]

The noteworthy accomplishment of the Berlin group of the Union of Pro-letarian Revolutionary Writers was the publication of the underground newspa-per *Stich und Hieb* (Cut and Thrust), which appeared from August of 1933 until the arrest of the members of the group in the middle of 1935.[69] In this newspa-per, produced in tiny format so that it fit into a matchbox, the worker-writer Jan Petersen (actually Hans Schwalm, 1906–1969) also published, under the pseu-donym Halm, his story "Unsere Straße" (Our Street), which was the basis for his diary novel *Unsere Straße*. The novel was written in Germany in 1933–1934, taken out of the Reich and abroad for publication, then from there smuggled back into Germany and distributed illegally. In the novel, Petersen describes the anti-fascist struggle of a communist resistance group in Berlin.[70] At the center is the struggle between the communists and the National Socialists for the Wall Street in Berlin-Charlottenburg, which becomes the symbol of resistance in general. In the fighting, the SA man Maikowski is shot to death by his own men, but a communist is hanged for the deed. The Nazis win the struggle, and the street is renamed Maikowski Street. Petersen documents in his novel the heroic resistance, but also the miserable situation of the workers in Berlin around 1933–1934, as well as the difficulties, failures, and errors in the anti-fascist struggle. The Nazi terror on the streets and in the camps is described in detail, including the torture and murder of the writer Erich Mühsam in Brandenburg Concentration Camp. Fear, Nazi terror, and unemployment caused many workers to cross over to the Nazis. In order to strengthen the anti-fascist strug-gle, Petersen also pleads in the novel for a coalition with the social democrats, who were reviled among the communists in the beginning as "social fascists." The novel is narrated in the first person and includes leaflets, Nazi speeches, eyewitness reports, and newspaper articles. Jan Petersen, who makes use of a great deal of autobiographical material in the novel, was hunted without success by the Nazis; after a dramatic appearance at the First International Writers' Congress for the Defense of Culture in Paris in June of 1935, he remained in exile in France, in Switzerland, and in England.[71]

In contrast to *Unsere Straße*, the novel *Der Deutsche von Bayencourt* (The German from Bayencourt) by Adam Kuckhoff could still be published in Germany in 1937 (first as a pre-publication in the liberal, middle-class *Kölner Zeitung*, then as a book), as it was favored at that time by the state as "literature of understanding."[72] Kuckhoff was a Germanist with a doctor-ate; his experiences included a study of the young Schiller, editing an edition of Büchner's works, thus a Büchner expert, a theater man as the Director of the Frankfurt Artists' Theater and the first dramatic advisor of the State Theater in Berlin, a journalist as the editor of *Die Tat* (The Deed), and an active resistance fighter in the "Rote Kapelle."[73] The novel was actually planned as a trilogy; however, volumes two and three could not be written. His resistance activities and the Nazi hangmen left Kuckhoff no time for that; "Adam Kuckhoff, too, is an author of unwritten works . . ."[74] who died at the hands of the Nazis.

The novel is based on a newspaper ad and on Kuckhoff's play *Rufendes Land* (Calling Land), written in 1915, printed by Fischer as *Der Deutsche von Bayencourt,* and performed in 1918. Adam Kuckhoff, a manufacturer's son from Aachen (1887–1943), establishes the main themes of the novel through the main character, the German-French farmer Bernard Sommer: the German-French relationship, nationalism, homeland, war, and social classes. The novel is set in the village of Bayencourt near Amiens. Sommer, who came from the Rhineland near Aachen, found a new home there over twenty years ago but is brutally driven out of it at the beginning of the war by the chauvinism of the population. When he hides a cut-off German patrol at his house, his fate is sealed; he is brought before a French court-martial, convicted as a traitor, and immediately executed. Marcel, Sommer's pacifist son, condemns the general enthusiasm about the war; Barnabas, Sommer's hired hand, condemns the class divisions. Marcel serves at the beginning of the war as a French soldier. Shortly before he moves out from Amiens, the father and son have a heart-to-heart talk in which the son, to the alarm of his father, condemns all the warmongering politics of the politicians and the profiteering on all sides associated with the war:

> For what coalesced in him found expression in passionate outbursts . . .
> a single accusation . . . against each and every person: the statesmen,
> the professional police, the profiteers, large and small, the press, the
> war industry, the parties, the representatives of the people, the govern-
> ments, [and] not least of all, the people who have tolerated these politi-
> cians, these profiteers, these parties, these representatives of the people,
> [and] these governments.[75]

Behind the accusations is "the real matter: the boundless horror of this war" (98). To the response of the father that an entire people rising up is really a great event, the son replies that the other side thinks so, too, and that the catastrophe of the war results from feelings being whipped up on both sides. As a good, if only naturalized, Frenchman, father Sommer is not against the war, but even he sees no difference between a hero's death and an "ordinary" death: "That was just death again, this time a hero's death on the battle field; it leaves [us] very empty and pitiful, like every other [death]" (111).

The hired man Barnabas, a revolutionary and socialist, is a good worker, but he does not keep his opinions to himself when Sommer expects him to defend his homeland. The war is for him a war of the people of property; the losers are always the little people: "Under the Germans we will have just as much and just as little to eat and to slave as under the French" (243). For Barnabas, only the people of property can defend "their land"; love of the homeland is in his mind only something for the property-owning class. Wars are in his opinion waged out of stupidity and meanness and against common sense, and he suggests that war be declared against "other things." What Barnabas does not say makes the context clear: Barnabas means war against social injustice. Sommer senses that "here is the enemy, the real one, who cannot be satisfied with any peace" (246). At the end Sommer loses every home, the one inside and the one outside. He was a German who had found his home in France, but the war and chauvinism left him no place to survive.

Careful reading makes clear that *Der Deutsche von Bayencourt* is not a national peasant novel in which a German is moved by his feelings to follow the call of his people, but rather an anti-war novel in the service of understanding among peoples, here the Germans and the French. On account of its coded language, the novel was actually misunderstood, as commendatory reviews in the *Völkischer Beobachter* and the *Nationalsozialistische Monatshefte* (National Socialist Monthly) show.[76] For the reviewer of the *Völkischer Beobachter,* Sommer followed "the voice of his blood" in deed when he offered the German soldiers protection.[77] The novel was even to be made into a film, but Kuckhoff refused to give his permission. "What initially may appear to be a concession to the blood and soil ideology, reveals itself upon closer examination to be the opposite."[78] For Wolfgang Emmerich, "Kuckhoff's historical *roman a clef*" is "at the same time an exemplary *regional novel*" comparable to Anna Seghers's *Das siebte Kreuz* (The Seventh Cross)[79] and a counter-version to the National Socialist regional novel. The initial approval of Kuckhoff by the National Socialist press quickly changed into hatred and persecution; Adam Kuckhoff, together with Harro Schulze-Boysen, Arvid and Mildred Harnack, and many others, was executed in 1943 in Berlin-Plötzensee. In his novel *Die Ästhetik des Widerstands* (The Aesthetics of Resistance), Peter Weiss created a lasting memorial to Adam Kuckhoff and the martyrs of the Harnack-Schulze-Boysen group.[80] For example, Peter Weiss describes, among other things, how Kuckhoff is marched to his execution, standing tall: "Kuckhoff strode after her [Anna Krauss]; his forehead formed a broad arch in his thin hair, and his huge dark eyes dominated his face, on which his mouth was now only a crooked line; spots and stripes covered the stocky body in the baggy trousers; his skin seemed to hang down in shreds, but his bearing was that of a prophet" (233).

Two other members of the "Rote Kapelle" will be discussed here; despite the Nazi hangmen they survived: Werner Krauss and Günther Weisenborn. The well-known specialist in romance languages and literatures, Werner Krauss

(1900–1976), who was a professor at Marburg and Leipzig, wrote his anti-fascist resistance novel, *PLN: Die Passionen der halykonischen Seele* (ZIP Code: The Passions of the Halyconian Soul), in 1943 and the beginning of 1944 in Berlin-Plötzensee prison "as well as in the Berlin-Buch . . . and Fort Zinna-Torgau army prisons," with his hands tied part of the time, and expecting death.[81] As Krauss comments in the introduction, this novel deals with "the attempt of a condemned man to come to terms with his experience of Germany. The constraints of the circumstances, however, require representation in code." The novel was smuggled "out of their shared cell" by Alfred Kothe, a young fellow prisoner, in the form of "pieces of paper written quickly in cramped writing," but not until 1946 could a small edition be published in Frankfurt am Main and in 1948 in the Soviet zone of occupied Germany.[82]

At the center of the episodic action is the conscientious, if indecisive and naïve minister of Postal Affairs, Aloys, Knight of Schnipfmeier, who develops from a representative of German inwardness and a tool of the Halyconian powers-that-be to a member of the resistance. The action takes place in the seventh year of a world war waged by the Great Halyconian Empire: "Millions of bloody victims were mourned without tears, and their memory died in a heart that had turned to stone" (9). Cultivation of Halyconian inwardness is now also a thing of the past:

> Crippled by pressure growing from the inside outward into the inestimable, in daily view of its horribly maimed cities, surrounded by the early signs of an apocalyptic nemesis, this people saw itself betrayed by endlessly accumulated crimes, which were often only tolerated or hidden from it, betrayed in its last hope of bringing about the rebirth of its world in the quiet spaces of the soul. (10)

At this time, a bureaucratic act excites the people: the introduction of the postal code by the minister of the Post, Aloys, Knight of Schnipfmeier, philatelist and soulful human being. For that purpose, extensive regulations are issued; according to Article 23, violations are to be draconically punished; according to Article 78, verdicts take effect "three minutes after announcement of the verdict." The order is signed ("sig.") by "Mufti I, Grand Ruler of the Pan-Halyconian Superior and Extended Empire" and Tassilo von Spitzfelder, Second Deputy Personnel Chief and Duly Authorized Commissioner in Office C II a j for Accelerated Creation of Justice" (14). As a result of the official measure, the post office succeeds in improving the delivery of mail items, for example, news and bundles of clothing to the survivors of people who have been executed, or the information sheet C II 857, "What every Halyconian must know!" (48). On this information sheet, nine paragraphs of the Halyconian basic rights are listed, for example:

1. Every Halyconian has the unrestricted right to remove oxygen from the air, day and night, free of charge.

2. Supplementary Article 175 III f of the State Constitution declares the Halyconic nation a reproductive society. Sexual intercourse between not more than two persons of adult age and different gender inside and outside marriage remains without penalty, if the actions undertaken with mutual consent were verifiably performed for the purpose of maintaining and increasing the stock of the race.

7. Every Halyconian can achieve spiritual nobility through work. (49)

This satirical attack on the bureaucracy and racial doctrine of National Socialism is followed by an attack on the German drive for feeling and inwardness: "9. Every Halyconian is authorized to conduct within himself a moral inner life and in the process to maintain, in a culturally creative manner, the customary values of feelings, personality formation, and character strengthening" (49).

A further great deed of Schnipfmeier and his subordinate, Baron von Geishaber, was the foundation of a "Relief Organization for Alleviating the Fates of Unmarried Post Office Officials' Daughters (ROAFUPOOD)" (60) — in a clear and mocking allusion to such National Socialist organizations as the "Bund deutscher Mädel (BdM)" (League of German Girls), "Glaube und Schönheit" (Faith and Beauty), "Kraft durch Freude (KdF)" (Strength through Joy), or the "Winterhilfswerk (WHW)" (Winter Relief Agency). For the benefit of the relief organization, the philatelist Schnipfmeier issues a series of stamps that, "depending upon the ranking of the values," represents "a whole series of living things . . . in order to seek out, in the entire realm of nature, the blessings of a well-rounded family life" (74). Thus, for example, "mother love through thick and thin" is represented by "the jumping kangaroo with two joey faces peering curiously out of her pouch" (74). For his creations, Schnipfmeier receives commendatory telegrams from high places, wishing him well, for example, from Mufti, "the Grand Ruler of the Pan-Halyconian People," in a perfect imitation of the *Führer* tone: "Esteemed Knight von Schnipfmeier! To my best wishes for a fruitful development of ROAFUPOOD, I add my warm-hearted recognition, and that of the Pan-Halyconian people, for your accomplishments in building this colossal office" (75). Air Marshal Oleander (i.e., Göring) joins in and emphasizes that "your kangaroo stamps in particular" have been "well received by my air force" (76). Nor can Koben, the "State Minister for the Dissemination of Truth and Optimism" (i.e., Goebbels) restrain his appreciation for works of art:

> Esteemed von Schnipfmeier! You have taken inspiration of the most valuable kind from the inexhaustible well-spring of Halyconian art in order to bring the life-seeking forces of the nation in fruitful contact with the blessings of sunny family happiness. Your accomplishments already belong today to the eternal history of our people, which can no longer be imagined without you. (76)

The sciences, too, in the person of "Professor Eugen Widehopf, ethnologist and ethnopsychologist," from the "Museum for Applied Ethnopsychology, the Study of Races, and Associated Fields," give voice to their own views on the stamp series, as the author Krauss notes in a biting satire on the so-called "scientific orientation" of the Third Reich. Professor Widehopf emphasizes above all else the significance of the kangaroo, which for him becomes the "symbol of a world order." In contrast to a New Zealand stamp series, which shows the kangaroo comfortably squatting in a resting position, "the kangaroo . . . in the Halyconian representation" is "caught at the height of its performance capability. We see the animal even before it touches the ground, beginning its gliding flight to earth, after the pleasure of maximal exertion" (79). The Pan-Halyconian kangaroo embodies the concentrated will to perform and

A final determined effort. . . . The kangaroo has thus become, through its bold act of spirit, a symbol of a new, more just and better world order led by Pan-Halyconia, and from today on, although the kangaroo is not native to our forests and meadows, it belongs to us in the same sense that Shakespeare, through the act of a translator who is a kindred spirit, may find his place in the amiably receptive ranks of Halyconian classic writers . . . (80)

At the height of his power, however, Schnipfmeier exhibits, in the eyes of the men in power, suspicious weaknesses. In his naïve inwardness and his infinite need to make people happy, he goes into the central hall of the main post office and makes the customers happy with free postage, until the central hall is transformed into exuberant pandemonium. The contact with a real, unregulated community of people does him so much good that he then carries the mail, as a simple postman, to the poorest sectors of the city. In the process, he is attacked by dogs, bundled into an ambulance, and transported through the demolished city in a confused mixture of dream and reality:

Then he propped himself up and looked with his full gaze at the scenes dancing by, ghostlike, scenes of a city lying completely in ruins. From time to time, one could hear the typical sound of walls collapsing, like that of a locomotive letting off steam. At some distance, timed fuses exploded. A gunshot directly grazed the roof of the vehicle, which raced on at the highest RPM. Through the middle of the debris, one could see the emergence of new roads, rolled flat by heavy tanks. (119)

The ruined landscape of the big city — Berlin is meant — becomes the symbol for the collapse of the national German culture of the soul: "Here and there one could see in the mass of debris a long pole extending upward; at its end the shreds of a half-burned sheet fluttered. Some ruins were marked with hand-painted signs: "Harsh Weather Palace, Crazy Peace Villa, Trash Heap Guesthouse, etc." (119). Hunger and the need for housing, but also genuine popular humor were reflected in other inscriptions, for example, *"Brick flour is distributed here without charge. Sunny private home in an airy location for rent, available immediately, reasonable price"* (119). German Romanticism blossoms in a grotesque form in the ruins:

> Chamber pots with winter-hardened plants crowned the exposed foundation walls at regular intervals, like amphorae from the time of the Empire. From a hacked out bed, freshly planted ivy climbed up crumbling facades. From time to time, a croaking or hoarse cooing betrayed the first preparations of the owls, lifting their wings for night flight. Larger animals had also found shelter in the burned-out ruins. (120)

These animals were the survivors of the bombing of the zoological garden, after which the city was afflicted by a pack of hungry exotic animals. The population could not be moved, however, even by this terrible bombing, to ask what the causes of this catastrophe might be, but instead put up with it and remained in a strange state of unreality:

> If the government initially issued words of heroic determination for the still surviving inhabitants of the ruins, the idyllic inclination of the Halyconian person, who will still find a blue flower[83] in every abyss, was soon left completely undisturbed. This characteristic of making the best of horror gave the state the certainty that, in the future as well, during even more difficult trials, the nation would not have the capacity to be shaken into a dangerous state of wakefulness. (122)

Schnipfmeier's situation becomes even more precarious after a cabinet ministers' meeting. The minister of police in particular attacks his invention of the postal code. The postal code had given rise to discussions among the people; but — as the minister of police, who with his rimless glasses resembles Himmler, comments — "discussions have always been the beginning of the end of any organically formed society" (153). Indeed, the slogans of the minister of the post office encouraging use of the postal code had even produced destructive counter-slogans. Next to warnings such as "Anyone who loots will be shot" and slogans of the minister of the post office, such as "Just don't forget the postal code / To spare the Post Office misery's load," counter slogans soon appeared on the walls of the ruins, such as "The zip code number, dear public, / Just makes the mailman lazy and dumb" (154). In the view of the minister of police, the authority of the state is being completely undermined by wall slogans such as "The zip code number, the slogan as well / With the state together can go to hell!" (155). Schnipfmeier leaves the meeting a broken man and finds his way to the cellar of the resistance organization called the "Catacomb Society," also called the "Union for Unswerving Joy of Life," which had already cast an eye on him for an extended period. The leader of this society is a pilot officer and a member of the general staff, behind whom can be recognized, thinly disguised, the air force officer Harro Schulze-Boysen of the resistance group "Rote Kapelle," who was executed in December of 1942. The attempt is made to convince the religiously bound Schnipfmeier that "a power which repudiates God's justice, . . . has removed the basis of its own mission" and "the power without a basis" has "forfeited any claim to obedience" (173). Schnipfmeier is beset with greater and greater conflicts of conscience and finally ends up as an inmate in prison. When a member who can no longer stand the torture betrays the Catacomb Society, the police break it up, and Schnipfmeier's connection to it becomes known.

The last part of the novel takes place in the police prison in which Schnipfmeier at first desperately endeavors to keep his human identity — the attempt is being made to convince him that he is Haffermann — but then gives up, refuses food, and already in a delirium and near death, is dragged during a night of bombing into a prison vehicle by a raiding squad and is presumably taken to be shot. In the last part, all irony is abandoned in the terrible narrative present. If in the novel Schnipfmeier was an agglomeration of different persons and characteristics, now Schnipfmeier-Haffermann recedes behind the convicted prisoner Werner Krauss: "Haffermann was locked in an empty single cell and lived, like hundreds of thousands of prisoners live in Pan-Halyconia" (345–46). Seldom has a prison cell been drawn by an inmate with such stylistic brilliance:

> The dull light from above, which was divided by the grill and fell down through the frosted pane onto the bare walls, was still too bright to hide the out-of-date prison equipment, which was geared to the bare necessities of existence. Even the huge width of the cot, which almost filled up the entire cell, ceaselessly anticipated the thought of martyrdom which made the nights seem endless. Nothing belongs to you. Even these meager fragments of a neglected household are only lent contributions whose whereabouts and condition are constantly monitored. All the paths are closed to you, but all the paths lead to you and you must tremble in constant readiness. Your condition can become more critical by the hour, and what seems unbearable to you today, flows together with the happy dream of lost freedom tomorrow. You are no longer a human being, but only a stored piece of human life, artificially preserved for an unknown purpose or misuse. (350)

This picaresque novel is full of digressions and flashes of thought that often make it difficult to even recognize the red thread of the plot. Thus the meeting of Detective Superintendent Krummnagel with the real people in his investigation of Farmer Meier in the postal code for Neudorf (of which there are thirty-five) takes up a great deal of space without having any direct connection to the adventures of Schnipfmeier. On his odyssey, however, Krummnagel does ascertain that the people scarcely bother with him and do practically everything that is prohibited. The Krummnagel episode gives Krauss an opportunity to illuminate satirically the blood and soil mysticism of the Nazis using an expert report of the "Office for Folklore, Peasant Customs, and Old-Halyconian Prehistory" (225) and reference to "the famous standard work of the Chief Curator Dr. Dr. Pfannenlecker ("pan licker") entitled 'Swine Slaughtering on St. Martin's Day in Old-Halyconian Folk Mythology'" (226). The extensive description of Schnipfmeier's engagement to a senior post office official, her kidnapping, and Schnipfmeier's wanderings in the destroyed city, when he ends up in a nightclub playing the drums, also goes beyond the scope even of a loose narrative sequence. According to Brekle, this novel represents "the amalgamation of the *roman à clef*, the picaresque novel, the grotesque tale, and the satire, joined by an intense delight in inventing stories and permeated with Marxist social perceptions."[84] As literary models for the novel, the Romance literature expert Krauss drew on Cervantes (*Don Quixote*), Grimmelshausen (*Simplicissimus*), Rabelais, and the modern French novel, but also on Kafka.[85]

Brecht's erstwhile collaborator, the writer Günter Weisenborn, also belonged to the "Rote Kapelle," but to camouflage himself in the Third Reich he only published mostly "harmless" literature, such as his drama *Die Neuberin* (Mrs. Neuber, appeared in 1935 under the pseudonyms Christian Munk = Weisenborn and E. Förster = Eberhard Kleindorff), or the novels *Das Mädchen von Fanö* (The Girl from Fanö, 1935) and *Die Furie* (The Fury, 1937), which of course also contained hidden references to the present. In jail he wrote anti-fascist poems, among them "Moabiter Notturno" (Moabit Nocturne), drafts of the anti-capitalist drama *Babel*, and the resistance drama *Die Illegalen* (The Illegals), in which Weisenborn portrayed in literature the last days of the "Rote Kapelle" (written in 1945, appeared in 1946). In a poem composed in 1940, "Leben der Illegalen (The Life of the Illegals), Weisenborn characterized resistance work as follows:

> Von Angst umflackert und von Haß umschrien,
> Von Mordlust und von Bränden rot umloht,
> Mußt du gefährlich deine Straße ziehn.
> Führt sie aus dieser Hölle in den Tod?
> Einst hieß man Hölle sie, jetzt heißt sie Welt![86]

> [Ringed by flickering fear and screaming hate,
> Ringed by murd'rous lust and by fires blazing red,
> You must dangerously walk down your road.
> Does it lead out of this hell into death?
> Long ago called hell, now it is called the world!]

That is certainly not great poetry, but it portrays powerfully the dangerous position of the individual in the resistance against Hitler.

Literature from Camps, Ghettos, and Prisons

The *Moabiter Sonette* (Moabit Sonnets) of Albrecht Haushofer are undoubtedly among the best known works from Nazi prisons and camps today. These sonnets were not written for the anti-fascist struggle but rather as a poetic diary of experiences and reflections in the face of death. Haushofer was from the outset against Hitler and early on belonged to the Kreisau circle of the conservative resistance around Count Helmut James von Moltke; Haushofer was arrested after the failed assassination attempt on Hitler of July 20, 1944, taken to the Moabit prison in Lehrter Street, and shot to death a few days before the end of the war. In the hands of the dead man, his brother found a notebook with seventy-nine sonnets, which were published in 1946. Albrecht Haushofer, the son of the well-known conservative geopolitician Karl Haushofer (Rudolf Heß, the deputy of the *Führer*, was a friend of the family), was from 1940 on a professor of political geography and geopolitics in Berlin. Before the sonnets, he had already written a few plays, such as *Scipio* (1934), *Sulla* (1938), *Augustus* (1939), *Chinesische Legende* (Chinese Legend, posthumously in 1949), and *Die Makedonen* (The Macedonians, unpublished), in which he criticized his times in code.[87]

In the sonnets, Haushofer once again roams through the fields of his extensive humanistic education and his extended travels. The sonnets are his personal expression of hope and despair. Hope rises in contemplation of the remaining humanistic values, as in the sonnet "Die Großen Toten" (The Great Dead):

> Ein Kant, ein Bach, ein Goethe werden zeugen
> noch lange für zerstörtes Volk und Land,
> auch wenn die Menge nie den Sinn verstand.[88]

> [A Kant, a Bach, a Goethe will for long
> bear witness still for a ruined land and people,
> even if the multitude never understood their meaning.] (94–95)

In the sonnet "Rattenzug" (Rat Trek), Hitler and his supporters are compared to a procession of rats that decimates and drags along everything:

> Ein Heer von grauen Ratten frißt im Land.
> Sie nähern sich dem Strom in wildem Drängen.
> Voraus ein Pfeifer, der mit irren Klängen
> zu wunderlichen Zuckungen sie band.
>
> ....
>
> was zögern wollte, wurde mitgerissen,
> was widerstrebte, blindlings totgebissen —

[An army of gray rats is eating up the country.
They're getting near the river in their frantic push.
In the lead a piper, whose erratic tunes
Have bound them in this odd, spasmodic drive.
....
Any that lingered were simply torn along,
any resisting, blindly bitten to death.] (82–83)

At the end, however, the whole wild pack plunges into the sea and drowns:

ein schriller Pfiff — ein gellendes Gekreisch:
Der irre Laut ersäuft im Stromgebraus . . .
die Ratten treiben tot ins Meer hinaus . . .

[a shrill whistle — a piercing shriek, a screeching:
The crazy sound goes under in the roar of the river . . .
The rats drift on out to the ocean, dead, . . .] (82–83)

Despair overcomes Haushofer because of his hopeless situation in prison, certain death before his eyes. He does have time in his cell to dream, but the "Dienstgeklirr der Schlüssel" (Clinking of the Keys) pulls him back into harsh reality:

Dann weiß ich, aus den Träumen aufgestört,
wie einer fühlt in seinen letzten Stunden,
der an ein ruderloses Boot gebunden,
den Fall des Niagara tosen hört.

[Then I know, disturbed out of my dreams,
how a man would feel in his last hours
who has been bound to a rudderless boat
and hears the roaring of Niagara Falls.]
("Zeit" [Time], 160–61)

But worse are the feelings of guilt that plague him. Although he did considerably more against the Nazi regime than the majority of his contemporaries and fellow citizens, he judges himself harshly for not having warned of the Nazis earlier and more forcefully. He feels innocent under the laws on earth, but not so before his inner moral judge:

Ich trage leicht an dem, was das Gericht
mir Schuld benennen wird: an Plan und Sorgen.
Verbrecher wär' ich, hätt' ich für das Morgen
des Volkes nicht geplant aus eigner Pflicht.

Doch schuldig bin ich anders als ihr denkt,
ich mußte früher meine Pflicht erkennen,

ich mußte schärfer Unheil Unheil nennen —
mein Urteil hab ich viel zu lang gelenkt . . .

Ich klage mich in meinem Herzen an:
Ich habe mein Gewissen lang betrogen,
ich hab mich selbst und andere belogen —

ich kannte früh des Jammers ganze Bahn —
ich hab gewarnt — nicht hart genug und klar!
Und heute weiß ich, was ich schuldig war . . .

[I bear lightly that of which the Court
will call me guilty: the planning and the caring.
Criminal I would have been had I not planned
as my own duty for the people's morrow.

Yet I am guilty otherwise than you think,
I should have recognized my duty sooner,
more sharply named disaster as disaster —
I withheld my judgment much too long.

In my heart I do accuse myself:
for long I deceived my conscience,
I lied to myself and to others —

Early on I knew the whole range of misery —
I gave warning — not loud enough and clear!
Today I know what I was guilty of . . .]
("Schuld" [Guilt], 78–79)

In "Kassandro" (Cassandro) he complains about the futility of his warnings; no one would listen to him. Now it is too late; despite all the reports of victory, the catastrophe can no longer be staved off:

Mit vollen Segeln jagten sie das Boot
im Sturm hinein in klippenreiche Sunde,
mit Jubelton verfrühter Siegeskunde —

[Full sail into the storm they drove the boat,
into the strait of perilous cliffs, too soon
Proclaiming jubilant news of victory.] (120–21)

But the failed assassination attempt on Hitler on July 20, 1944, has also been the undoing of the resistance:

Nun scheitern sie — und wir. In letzter Not
versuchter Griff zum Steuer ist mißlungen. —
Jetzt warten wir, bis uns die See verschlungen.

[Now they are smashing up — and we. It failed,
that desperate last grasping of the helm.
Now we are waiting, till the sea has swallowed us.]
("Kassandro [Cassandro]," 120–21)

What remains is rubble and ashes ("Verhängnis [Doom]"). The cultural
world of the Occident, which is invoked once more in the sonnets, will go
under: "In Schutt und Staub ist Babylon versunken, / . . . auch unser ganzes
Erbe sind Ruinen/ . . . Wir sind die Letzten" ["In dust and rubble Babylon
went down / . . . and our entire inheritance is in ruins / . . . We are the
last"] ("Das Erbe [Heritage]," 96–97). And yet, complete destruction is
necessary to prevent a new stab-in-the-back legend:

> Das Ende wittern selbst erprobte Toren.
> Doch kann der Krieg nicht enden dieses Mal,
> bis kein Gefreiter mehr, kein General
> behaupten darf, er wäre nicht verloren.
>
> . . .
>
> Der Wahn allein war Herr in diesem Land.
> In Leichenfeldern schließt sein stolzer Lauf,
> und Elend, unermeßbar, steigt herauf.
> ("Dem Ende zu" [Toward the End], 108)

[Even well-tested madmen scent the end.
And yet the war cannot be over this time
until no corporal any more, no general
dares declare that it has not been lost.

Madness alone ruled over this country.
Its proud run finishes in fields of corpses,
And misery, immeasurable, rises up.]
("Dem Ende zu" [Nearing the End], 108–9)

Other sonnets deal with home, family, important cultural sites ("Mem-
phis") and cultural works ("Bhagavadgita"), great humanists ("Boethius"
and "Beethoven"), book-burning, and every-day life in prison. In his bare
cell, Haushofer feels connectedness to countless predecessors ("In Fesseln
[In Fetters]") and the impending death by the German rope or the Anglo-
American bombers ("Silvestersegen [New Year's Eve Blessing]" and "Bom-
benregen [Rain of Bombs]").

The Moabit sonnets, even though not always artistically successful, are
lasting testimony to the time of terror, a memorial to the dead, and a warning obligation to the living, especially in the last terzet of "Silvestersegen"
(New Year's Eve Blessing):

> Das alte China kannte die Gefahr.
> Es bannte schon das Pulver, weil darin
> Versuchung lag zu groß für Menschensinn.
>
> [Ancient China recognized the danger.
> It banned gunpowder early, because therein
> temptation lay too great for human minds.] (24–25)

A large number of the texts that were written in the fascist camps and survived were published in 1960 in the collection *An den Wind geschrieben* (Written to the Wind) edited by Manfred Schlösser, with a motto by Oscar Loerke. In the collection, many unknown authors have their say; for example, Ruth K. Klüger, who was born in 1931 in Vienna and today lives and works as a Germanist in the United States, initially with the name Ruth K. Angress and then again as Ruth Klüger. In one of her poems she described the chimney of the crematorium in Auschwitz Concentration Camp in 1944, as the prisoners saw it daily before their eyes:

> Täglich hinter den Baracken
> Seh' ich Rauch und Feuer stehn,
> Jude, beuge deinen Nacken,
> Keiner hier kann dem entgehn.[89]
> . . .
>
> [Daily behind the barracks
> I see smoke and fire stand,
> Jew, bend down your head,
> No one here can escape it.
> . . .]

Ruth Klüger survived; but her father and brother were murdered. In 1992 she published her memories from the concentration camp Theresienstadt in her book *Weiter leben* translated into English in 2001 as *Still Alive: A Holocaust Girlhood Remembered*.

Numerous other poems by authors, such as Gertrud Kantorowics, Franz Heitgres, Hasso Grabner, or Johannes Aufricht, describe the atrocities of the SS and the kapos, concentration camp guards drawn from inmates, in the ghettos and the concentration camps. Among the most powerful are the Dachau poems of Edgar Kupfer-Koberwitz and the cantos of Hermann Adler.[90] For example, the poem "Ein Pole" (A Pole) by Edgar Kupfer-Koberwitz describes in every horrible detail the death of a prisoner who was brutally beaten to death at morning roll call; here is only the first stanza:

> Was ist geschehen — wem hat man geschlagen
> Die Faust ins Gesicht und in den Magen —
> Wen hat man getreten wie ein Vieh,
> Daß er so laut und so gräßlich schrie? —[91]

> [What has happened — who has been beaten,
> The fist in the face and in the stomach —
> Who has been kicked like an animal,
> That he screams so loudly, so terribly? —]

There are voices of despair and fear, but also of hope, especially in the case of Christian poets such as the Protestant pastor Dietrich Bonhoeffer, who was murdered in Flossenbürg Concentration Camp shortly before the end of the war on April 9, 1944. The last stanza of the poem "Von den guten Mächten" (The Forces of Good), which was smuggled out of the notorious Gestapo prison in Berlin's Prinz-Albrecht-Straße by a guard and buried in his garden, and thus survived the war, is filled with faith in God:

> Von guten Mächten wunderbar geborgen,
> erwarten wir getrost, was kommen mag.
> Gott ist mit uns am Abend und am Morgen
> und ganz gewiß an jedem neuen Tag.[92]

> [By forces of good wonderfully protected,
> we await, hopefully, whatever comes.
> God is with us, at night, in the morning
> and most certainly on every new day.]

Others wrangle with their fate, accuse, or resort to open resistance, like the Zionist Hermann Adler, who participated actively in the uprising in the Warsaw Ghetto.[93] His poem "Hände der Schwächsten, sie werden zu Stahl" (Hands of the Weakest, They Become Steel) describes the heroic, if futile uprising in lines such as:

> Flattert ihr Fahnen der Freiheit, im sterbenden Warschauer Ghetto,
> denn der Versklavteste fühlt sich nun als Sterbender frei.[94]

> [Wave, you flags of freedom, in the dying Warsaw ghetto,
> For the most enslaved, as he's dying, now feels free.]

Schneider, Bergengruen, and other Christian poets seek to place blame for the catastrophe on man's falling away from God. Adler is considerably more direct, and in his bitterness, accuses all Germans of being involved in the rise of Hitler and the persecution of the Jews. Indeed, not even the English are exonerated from guilt, as they wanted to deny the Jews their homeland in Palestine:

Alle sind schuldig; alle! Nicht nur, die
aufgehetzt ein Volk zu Tode stiessen;
schuldig sind auch jene, welche den, der schrie,
nicht ins eigene Land der Väter ließen![95] (86)

[All are guilty; all! Not only those who,
inflamed, shoved a people to its death;
guilty are they, too, who did not let him,
who screamed, into his forefathers' own land.]

Prophetically and full of sarcasm, Adler predicts in the poem "Schuldlose Heimat der Dichter und Denker" (Guiltless Homeland of Poets and Thinkers) that after the inevitable end every one of the Nazis will reject all guilt and deny having known anything:

Jeder, der heute die Augen verschliesst, um das Blut nicht zu sehen,
spricht einst ganz wahr, wenn er lügt, dass er nichts wusste und sah.
Alle, die heute in Deutschland die Mörder noch feiern, erklären
morgen dann würdig, das Volk Deutschlands sei schuldlos wie stets.[96]

[Everyone who today closes his eyes so as not to see the blood,
speaks the truth for once when he lies that he knew, and saw, nothing.
All, who today in Germany still praise the murderers, tomorrow
will say, haughtily: Germany's people are guiltless as always.]

"Todesfuge" (Death Fugue), the best-known and most accomplished poem on life in the camps of annihilation, was written in 1945. Its author, Paul Celan, was born in 1920 to German-speaking Jewish parents in Czernowitz in Bukovina (Romania); he lost his parents in German concentration camps in Ukraine. After the invasion by German and Romanian troops, he personally spent time in the Czernowitz Ghetto and in labor camps, where he wrote some of his poetry, for example, the following poem from 1943:

Es fällt nun, Mutter, Schnee in der Ukraine:
Des Heilands Kreuz aus tausend Körnchen Kummer . . .
Von meiner Träne hier erreicht dich keine;
von frühern Winken nur ein stolzer, stummer . . .[97]

[Now snow is falling, Mother, in the Ukraine:
The Savior's cross of a thousand grains of sorrow . . .
Of my tears here none will reach you;
of earlier signs only a proud one, mute . . .]

Or the poem "Gemurmel der Toten" (Murmuring of the Dead), in which Celan has the murdered people speak and beg the worms for mercy:

Unsere Augenhöhlen sind klar
Von Käferlichtern erhellt.
Mit Lehm, mit verfilztem
Baun wir fort an der Welt.

. . .

[The sockets of our eyes are clearly
lit up with beetle lights.
With clay, with matted stuff
We continue to build the world.]

The poetess Rose Ausländer, actually Rosalie Beatrice Scherzer, was a native of the same town as Celan; she was born in 1901 in Czernowitz, then still Austria, and survived there during the ghetto years of 1941–1944. Her friendship with Celan dates from that period. After the war, she immigrated to the United States, after having already lived there from 1921 to 1931, but was not comfortable there and returned to Düsseldorf, Germany, in 1965, where she found respite in a home of the Jewish community. In the ghetto, Ausländer wrote many poems, "in which she on one hand mirrored the situation in the ghetto and on the other sketched ideal conditions."[98] The poem "Geisterweg" (Path of Ghosts) expresses fear and threatening danger:

Giftige Geister lauern am Weg.
Wir gehen schräg
um sie nicht zu berühren.

Wir stehn vor versiegelten Türen.

Es war unser Haus, es war
unser Garten mit feingekämmten Haar.
Es war Mutterduft, es war.

Wir kehren um, gehn schräg
den giftschwarzen Weg
ins Ghetto. (163)

[Poisonous ghosts lurk on the path.
We tread obliquely
So as not to touch them.

We stand before tightly sealed doors.

It was our house; it was
our garden with finely combed hair.
It was mother's scent, it was.

We turn back, tread obliquely
the poison-black path
to the ghetto.]

The color black relates the poem to Celan's "Todesfuge" (Death Fugue); in both poems black stands for death. As Michael Moll explains, the word "black" also recalls historical Jewish pogroms, when the Jews were accused in the Middle Ages of having caused the "black death" by poisoning wells.[99] The memory of this historical persecution also dominates Ausländer's poem "Angst I" (Fear I), through an allusion to these wells:

Die Brunnen lassen uns nicht schlafen,
wir lauschen bis auf ihren Grund.
Wer sind die Stimmen, die uns strafen?
Und wer ihr Mund?

[The wells will not let us sleep,
We listen down to their depths.
Who are the voices that punish us?
And who their mouth?]

A poet who retained the spirit to fight against fascism and for a more just world even when incarcerated in a concentration camp was the Austrian Jura Soyfer. He had become known in Vienna in the thirties as a writer of socialist battle poems and plays for small art theaters who in his art combined Raimund and Nestroy with Marx and Brecht.[100] The Marxist and Jew Soyfer had long been a thorn in the side of the fascists in Austria and Germany because he mocked them with poems such as "Reformiertes Kirchenlied" (Reformed Hymn), "Heil Hitler!" "Kraft durch Freude" (Strength Through Joy), "Wahlen im Dritten Reich" (Elections in the Third Reich), or "Rassische Liebesballade" (Racial Love Ballad), most of which appeared in Vienna's *Arbeiter-Zeitung* (Worker's Newspaper). Here, as an example, is the beginning of the "Rassische Liebesballade" (Racial Love Ballad), which appropriates the well known song "Es waren zwei Königskinder" (There Were Two King's Children), and first appeared in the *Arbeiter-Zeitung* on August 19, 1933:

Es waren zwei Nazikinder,
Die hatten einander so lieb,
Sie konnten zusammen nicht kommen,
Denn sie war ein ostischer Typ.

Ihr Schädel nämlich war rundlich,
Ihr Busen hingegen oval,
(Statt umgekehrt) — rassenkundlich
War dieses Weib ein Skandal.

Sein Haupthaar war siegfriedisch,
Sein Auge preußischblau:
Kein Partner für die negroidisch —
Mongolisch gemixte Frau.
. . . (126–27)

[There once were two Nazi children
they loved each other dearly.
They could not get together.
For she was an eastern type.

Her skull was decidedly round,
Her bosom in contrast oval,
(Not the reverse) — in racial terms
The woman was just a scandal.

His head of hair was Siegfried-like;
His eyes were Prussian blue:
Not a partner for the negroid —
Mongolian mixed-blood lass.]

Obviously Soyfer was high on the wanted list of the Nazis. In attempting after
the annexation of Austria in 1938 to escape across the Austrian border into
Switzerland on skis, he was caught and transported via the police prisons in
Feldkirch and Innsbruck to Dachau and Buchenwald, where he became infected
with typhoid while working carrying bodies and died on February 16, 1939, at
the age of 26. His well-known "Dachaulied" (Dachau Song), set to music by
his fellow prisoner Herbert Zipper, is a testimonial to Soyfer's optimism and will
to fight, unbroken to the end. The poem portrays the sad situation of the prisoners, but uses in its refrain the cynical Nazi slogan over the gate, "Arbeit macht
frei" (Work sets you free), as a call to his comrades in the camps to resist:

Stacheldraht, mit Tod geladen,
Ist um unsere Welt gespannt.
Drauf ein Himmel ohne Gnaden
Sendet Frost und Sonnenbrand.
Fern von uns sind alle Freuden,
Fern die Heimat und die Fraun
Wenn wir stumm zur Arbeit schreiten,
Tausende im Morgengraun,
Doch wir haben die Losung von Dachau gelernt,
Und wir wurden stahlhart dabei.
Bleib ein Mensch, Kamerad,
Sei ein Mann, Kamerad,
Mach ganze Arbeit, pack an, Kamerad:

Denn Arbeit, denn Arbeit macht frei,
Denn Arbeit, denn Arbeit macht frei!

[Barbed wire, with the charge of death,
Is wrapped around our world.
Above a heaven without mercy
Sends forth frost and burning rays.
Far from us are all the pleasures,
Far the homeland and the women,
When in silence we stride to work,
Thousands in the breaking daylight.
Still, we have learned the motto of Dachau,
And with that we grew hard as steel,
Stay a human, comrade,
Be a man, comrade,
Do your work well, get going, comrade:
For work, for work sets you free,
For work, for work sets you free.]

The last stanza promises the reward of endurance with the prospect of freedom and a new world in which all comrades are needed:

Einst wird die Sirene künden:
Auf zum letzten Zählappell!
Draußen dann, wo wir uns finden,
Bist du, Kamerad zur Stell.
Hell wird uns die Freiheit lachen,
Schaffen heißt's mit großem Mut.
Und die Arbeit, die wir machen,
Diese Arbeit, die wird gut.
Denn wir haben die Losung von Dachau gelernt,
. . . (245–46)

[The siren one day will announce:
On to the last roll call!
Out there then, where we are standing,
You, comrade, will be present.
Freedom will smile brightly at us.
Let us work with great courage,
And the labor that we do,
That work, it will be good.
For we have learned the motto of Dachau,
. . .]

The Writers of German Classicism as Resistance Fighters

Resistance came not only from contemporary authors, but also from the writers of past generations, as, for example, Schiller illustrates. Schiller was in fact the preferred writer of Classicism for the Nazis — from 1933 to 1941 he was one of the most performed classic writers[101] — but parts of his works caused demonstrations by the opposition. In 1933 at a production of *Don Carlos* in the Bremen State Theater, such a storm of applause broke out after Marquis Posa's request to King Philip II, "Give me freedom of thought" (3, 10), that the performance had to be stopped on order of the police. Similar events occurred in numerous other cities, for example, in 1937 at a production of the play in Berlin directed by Heinz Hilpert, which Goebbels and the Reich drama advisor Rainer Schlösser personally attended. German emigrants, such as Bertolt Brecht, Lion Feuchtwanger, and Thomas Mann, followed these protest demonstrations in the Reich with great interest, since they provided evidence of opposition to the hated Nazis. In a speech in New York, Thomas Mann commented (with some irony?) on these protest actions as follows: "These protests, being so political, are by no means without danger; they are so touching because here a people is using the words of a poet, in a manner of speaking, to save its intellectual honor before the world and to make known that it does not want to be a slave." The Nazi press in Germany took the public to task and accused it of lacking the ability to think politically.[102]

Schiller's *Wilhelm Tell* belonged from the beginning to the patriotic inventory of National Socialism, especially the Rütli oath. The play also served to propagate the family policies that the National Socialists had adopted. But that soon changed. In 1941, all performances of *Tell* were prohibited on the order of the *Führer*, as was its treatment in school instruction. It had become clear to the Nazis that *Tell* was a revolutionary drama that was directed against a repressive, dictatorial system and glorified tyrannicide. Furthermore, bringing ostensibly German territories "home" to the Reich directly conflicted with the ideology of *Tell*, as in that drama exactly the opposite is praised. Thus, Schiller was transformed almost overnight from a nominal supporter to a state enemy of the Nazis.[103]

The Beginnings of German Postwar Literature

In the shadow of the Third Reich, German postwar literature also emerged in the works of Rose Ausländer, Johannes Bobrowski, Paul Celan, Günter Eich, Albrecht Goes, Peter Huchel, Marie Luise Kaschnitz, Wolfgang Koeppen, and Karl Krolow, to mention only a few, whose literary beginnings extend back into this period.[104] Even the Swiss writer Max Frisch was already known in Germany in the thirties for his prose works *Jürg Reinhart: Eine sommerliche Schicksalsfahrt* (Jürg Reinhart: A Summery Journey of Fate, 1934) and *Antwort aus der Stille* (Answer from the Silence, 1937). During the Third Reich, Günter Eich (1907–1972) published individual poems in *Das Innere Reich* (The Inner Realm), *Die Dame* (The Lady), and *Die Koralle* (The Coral).[105] Most of his radio plays were broadcast from October of 1933 to May of 1940 by "Radio Germany" in the series put together by Eich and Martin Raschke called "Monthly Images of Königswusterhausen's Country Messenger." In his study of Günter Eich's life and works between 1933 and 1945, *Career at the Cost of Compromise,* the American Glenn Cuomo records a total of 160 radio texts in which Eich was involved, only eight of which are entirely preserved, and only two more exist as fragments. According to Cuomo, Eich, in his radio texts, came dangerously close to the National Socialist blood and soil ideology.[106] More than a third of the poems in Eich's *Abgelegene Gehöfte* (Out-of-the-Way Farms) were already written during the Third Reich. Wolfgang Koeppen's first novel *Eine unglückliche Liebe* (An Unhappy Love) was published in 1934 by Cassirer Publishers; a second novel *Die Mauer schwankt* (The Wall Teeters) followed in 1935, and was re-issued three years later with the heroic-sounding title, *Die Pflicht* (Duty).[107] Peter Huchel (1903–1982) was initially even promoted by National Socialist organizations. He published poems in journals such as *Das Innere Reich* (The Inner Realm), *Die Dame* (The Lady), and *Die Koralle* (The Coral), and in anthologies, and he went before the public with radio plays and readings. Johannes Bobrowski began in 1944 with the publication of several odes to Russia in the *Inneres Reich* (Inner Realm). "In the last years of the war . . . fifty poems and several dozen articles" by Karl Krolow appeared "in the press, and he seldom had to make compromises with National Socialist ideology."[108] The Swabian pastor Albrecht Goes (1908–2000) was also able to publish his Anacreontic poems without any difficulty in the volumes *Der Hirte* (The Shepherd, 1934), *Heimat ist gut* (Home Is Good, 1935), and *Der Nachbar* (The Neighbor, 1940).

Notes

[1] On this subject, see among others J. F. G. Grosser, ed., *Die große Kontoverse: Ein Briefwechsel um Deutschland* (The Great Controversy: A Correspondence About German) (Hamburg: Nagel, 1963); Ralf Schnell, *Literarische Innere Emigration 1933–1945* (Literary Inner Emigration, 1933–1945) (Stuttgart: Metzler, 1976), 1–5 and 169–70; and Reinhold Grimm, "Innere Emigration als Lebensform" (Inner Emigration as a Way of Life), in *Exil und Innere Emigration* (Exile and Inner Emigration), edited by Reinhold Grimm and Jost Hermand (Frankfurt am Main: Athenäum, 1972), 35–58. The debate ignited on the basis of a sentence in Thomas Mann's open letter of October 12, 1945, in which Mann claimed that all the books

that had appeared in Germany from 1933 to 1945 would always have an "air of blood and ignominy" about them (Grosser, 31).

[2] Ernst Wiechert, *Jahre und Zeiten: Erinnerungen* (Years and Times: Memoirs), in *Sämtliche Werke in Zehn Bänden* (Complete Works in Ten Volumes), volume 9 (Vienna: Desch, 1957), 687–88.

[3] Wolfgang Brekle, "Die antifaschistische Literatur in Deutschland" (The Anti-Fascist Literature in Germany), in *Weimarer Beiträge* (Weimar Essays), 11, 6 (1970), 71.

[4] Wolfgang Brekle, *Schriftsteller im antifaschistischen Widerstand 1933–1945 in Deutschland* (Authors in the Anti-Fascist Resistance from 1933 to 1945 in Germany) (Berlin and Weimar: Aufbau, 1985), 36. Further discussion of the concept and an overview of the state of research can also be found in Ralf Schnell, *Literarische Innere Emigration 1933–1945*, and in *Flight of Fantasy: New Perspectives on Inner Emigration in German Literature, 1933–1945*, edited by Neil H. Donahue and Doris Kirchner (New York: Berghahn Publishers, 2003).

[5] Werner Bergengruen, *Schreibtischerinnerungen* (Writing Desk Memoirs) (Zurich: Arche, 1961; licensed edition in Germany by Nymphenburg Verlagshandlung), 176.

[6] Werner Bergengruen, *Dichtergehäuse: Aus den autobiographischen Aufzeichnungen* (Poet's Cabinet: From the Autobiographical Notebooks), edited by Charlotte Bergengruen (Zurich: Arche, 1966), 141–42.

[7] Quoted in Bergengruen, *Schreibtischerinnerungen*, 182.

[8] On that subject, see Wolfgang Brekle, *Schriftsteller im antifaschistischen Widerstand*, 32–36, and Schnell, 6–7.

[9] On that subject, see Grimm, 42; Brekle, *Schriftsteller im antifaschistischen Widerstand*, 32–36; and Schnell, 1–5.

[10] Stefan Andres, "Innere Emigration" (Inner Emigration), in Stefan Andres, *Der Dichter in dieser Zeit: Reden und Aufsätze* (The Poet in These Times: Speeches and Essays) (Munich: Piper, 1974), 57.

[11] Franz Schonauer, *Deutsche Literatur im Dritten Reich: Versuch einer Darstellung in polemisch-didaktischer Absicht* (German Literature in the Third Reich: Attempt at Representation with Polemical and Didactic Intent) (Olten und Freiburg m. Breisgau: Walter, 1961), 127.

[12] Bergengruen, *Schreibtischerinnerungen*, 161.

[13] *Schreibtischerinnerungen*, 160–61. That may be exaggerated but one should not immediately go to the opposite extreme as does Wolfgang Brekle, who estimates that the "anti-fascist content of the novel is slight"; see Wolfgang Brekle, *Schriftsteller im antifaschistischen Widerstand*, 180.

[14] On that subject, see Joseph Wulf, *Literatur und Dichtung im Dritten Reich: Eine Dokumentation* (Literature and Poetry in the Third Reich: Documentation) (Frankfurt am Main: Ullstein, 1983), 518–19. The "Overall Assessment" (reprinted there) of the leadership of the *Ortsgruppe* of Munich-Solln, Bergengruen's home community, says, among other things: "Bergengruen is probably not politically reliable. Even though he hangs a swastika flag in his window when there is reason to do so, or gladly contributes when collections are taken up, his attitude otherwise nevertheless gives cause for him to be viewed as politically unreliable. Neither he nor his wife and child are members of

a Nazi organization. The German greeting 'Heil Hitler' is not used either by him or by his family, even if he now and then lifts his hand a bit. Nor does he subscribe to the National Socialist press, at least as far as is known. His attitude is probably attributable to the fact that he or his wife may be related to Jews."

[15] Quoted in Werner Bergengruen, *Der Großtyrann und das Gericht* (The Great Tyrant and the Court) Munich: Nymphenburger Verlagshandlung, 1951), 228. The page citations in the text refer to this edition.

[16] *Schreibtischerinnerungen*, 180. The subsequent page citations in the text refer to this edition.

[17] On the problem of historical distance, see Ralf Schnell, *Literarische Innere Emigration 1933–1945*, 100–101.

[18] In *Deutsche Literatur im Dritten Reich: Themen — Traditionen — Wirkungen* (German Literature in the Third Reich: Themes — Traditions — Effects), edited by Horst Denkler and Karl Prümm (Stuttgart: Reclam, 1976), 449–50.

[19] See Brekle, *Schriftsteller im antifaschistischen Widerstand*, 168.

[20] Werner Bergengruen, *Dies Irae* (Day of Anger) (Munich: Zinnen-Verlag Kurt Desch, no date [1945]), 7. The page citations in the text refer to this edition.

[21] See Max Frisch, "Stimmen eines anderen Deutschlands? Zu den Zeugnissen von Wiechert und Bergengruen" (Voices of a Different Germany? On the Testimonials of Wiechert and Bergengruen), in *Neue Schweizer Rundschau* (*New Swiss Review*), 13 (1945–46), 537–47. Quoted in Charles Wesley Hoffmann, "Opposition Poetry in Nazi Germany, 1933–1945" (Dissertation, University of Illinois, 1956), 60 and 80.

[22] See Brekle, *Schriftsteller im antifaschistischen Widerstand*, 175–76.

[23] Reinhold Schneider, *Zwei autobiographische Werke: Verhüllter Tag; Winter in Wien* (Two Autobiographical Works: Enshrouded Day; Winter in Vienna), in *Gesammelte Werke* (Collected Works), volume 10: *Die Zeit in uns* (The Time in Us), edited by Edwin Maria Landau (Frankfurt am Main: Insel, 1978), 111.

[24] Quoted in Wolfgang Brekle, *Schriftsteller im antifaschistischen Widerstand*, 161.

[25] Reinhold Schneider, *Las Casas vor Karl V.* (Las Casas Before Charles V), in *Gesammelte Werke* (Collected Works), volume 3: *Der Große Verzicht* (The Great Renunciation), edited by Edwin Maria Landau (Frankfurt am Main: Insel, 1978), 155.

[26] On that subject, see also Ralf Schnell, *Literarische Innere Emigration*, 132–33.

[27] Franz Schonauer, *Deutsche Literatur im Dritten Reich*, 152.

[28] Günter Wirth, "Eine Stimme für die Gleichberechtigung der Völker. Reinhold Schneider: 'Las Casas vor Karl V. Szenen aus der Konquistadorenzeit'" (A Voice for the Equality of the Peoples. Reinhold Schneider: "Las Casas Before Charles V. Scenes from the Time of the Conquistadors"), in *Erfahrung Nazideutschland: Romane in Deutschland 1933–1945: Analysen* (The Experience of Nazi Germany: Novels in Germany, 1933–1945: Analyses), edited by Sigrid Bock und Manfred Hahn (Berlin: Aufbau, 1987), 298–334.

[29] Stefan Andres, *El Greco malt den Großinquisitor* (El Greco Paints the Grand Inquisitor), in Stefan Andres, *Novellen und Erzählungen* (Novellas and Stories) (Munich: Piper, 1962), 8. The page citations in the text refer to this edition.

[30] The parallels to Brecht's *Galileo* are obvious; Brecht's play also referred, in the form of alienation and historicizing, to the National Socialist present.

[31] Ernst Jünger, *Auf den Marmorklippen* (On the Marble Cliffs) (Frankfurt am Main: Ullstein, 1980), 141. The page citations in the text refer to this edition. The first edition appeared in 1939.

[32] See Hans Dieter Schäfer, "Die nichtfaschistische Literatur der 'jungen Generation' im nationalsozialistischen Deutschland" (Non-fascist Literature of the "Young Generation" in National Socialist Germany), in *Deutsche Literatur im Dritten Reich*, edited by Horst Denkler and Karl Prümm, 472.

[33] See Schnell, 142.

[34] See Schnell, 142.

[35] See Guido Reiner, *Ernst Wiechert im Dritten Reich: Eine Dokumentation* (Ernst Wiechert in the Third Reich: Documentation) (Paris: Self-Published, 1974), 89–90.

[36] Ernst Wiechert, *Der Totenwald* (The Forest of the Dead), in *Sämtliche Werke in zehn Bänden* (Complete Works in Ten Volumes), volume 9 (Vienna: Desch, 1957), 327. The page citations in the text refer to this edition.

[37] Ernst Wiechert, "Der weiße Büffel. Oder von der grossen Gerechtigkeit" (The White Buffalo. Or the Great Justice), in *Sämtliche Werke in zehn Bänden*, volume 6 (Vienna: Desch, 1957), 572. The page citations in the text refer to this edition.

[38] Ernst Wiechert, *Der Totenwald*, 199. The diary form, according to Hans Dieter Schäfer, became "the central genre for the 'Inner Emigration': it came closest to the penchant for the private, and confessional, but also for the sketch and for the witty remark," see Hans Dieter Schäfer, "Die nichtfaschistische Literatur der 'jungen Generation,'" 468.

[39] See his novel *Nackt unter Wölfen* (Naked Among Wolves) (Halle: Mitteldeutscher Verlag, 1958).

[40] Johannes, or John, was known to be Jesus's favorite disciple. But Johannes also refers to the Swiss writer Max Picard, to whom Wiechert dedicated his book of remembrance *Jahre und Zeiten* with great reverence. There he writes of Picard on pages 668–69: "He was a prophet, . . . He was like John on Patmos. . . . But for me in those years of decision (the time of his arrest), the most unforgettable thing was those flashing blue eyes. They kept me on my path. They protected me from error and from any fear."

[41] Reinhold Schneider, *Lyrik* (Poetry), selection and foreword by Christoph Perels, in *Gesammelte Werke* (Collected Works), volume 5, edited by Edwin Maria Landau (Frankfurt am Main: Insel, 1981). The page citations in the text refer to this edition.

[42] Theodor Ziolkowski, "Form als Protest. Das Sonett in der Literatur des Exils und der Inneren Emigration" (Form as Protest. The Sonnet in the Literature of Exile and the Inner Emigration), in *Exil und Innere Emigration*, Reinhold Grimm and Jost Hermand, 153–72.

[43] See Charles Wesley Hoffmann, 103.

[44] See Ziolkowski, 157.

[45] Ingo Zimmermann, *Reinhold Schneider: Weg eines Schriftstellers* (Reinhold Schneider: Path of a Writer) (Berlin: Union Verlag, 1982), 136.

[46] Afterword to Rudolf Hagelstange, *Venezianisches Credo* (Venetian Credo) (Munich: Insel, 1946). The page citations in the text refer to this edition.

[47] See *De Profundis: Deutsche Lyrik in dieser Zeit, Eine Anthologie aus zwölf Jahren* (De Profundis: German Poetry in These Times: An Anthology from Twelve Years), edited by Gunter Groll (Munich: Desch, 1946), 134.

[48] Rudolf Hagelstange, "Die Form als erste Entscheidung" (The Form as the First Decision), in *Mein Gedicht ist mein Messer: Lyriker zu ihren Gedichten* (My Poem is My Knife: Poets on Their Poems), edited by Hans Bender (Munich: List, 1964), 38. The page citations in the text refer to this edition. Hagelstange's essay appeared the first time in *Ballade vom verschütteten Leben* (Ballad of Spilled Life) (Frankfurt am Main: Insel, 1952).

[49] *Klassiker in finsteren Zeiten* (Writers of German Classicism in Dark Times), volume 2, edited by Bernhard Zeller et al. (Marbach: Deutsche Schillergesellschaft, 1983), 205.

[50] See Brekle, *Schriftsteller im antifaschistischen Widerstand*, 191.

[51] Oskar Loerke, *Die Tagebücher 1903–1939* (*The Diaries, 1903–1939*), edited by Hermann Kasack (Heidelberg and Darmstadt: Schneider, 1956), 261. The page citations in the text refer to this edition.

[52] Oskar Loerke, *Die Gedichte* (The Poems), edited by Peter Suhrkamp (Frankfurt am Main: Suhrkamp, 1958), 638 ("Das edle Ross [The Noble Horse]"). The page citations in the text refer to this edition.

[53] With regard to these problems, see Theo Elm's exemplary interpretation of Loerke's poem "Das Auge des Todes" (The Eye of Death) from the volume of poems *Der Wald der Welt* (The Forest of the World), which appeared in 1936; Theo Elm, "Aufklärung als Widerstand. Oskar Loerke's poem 'Das Auge des Todes'" (Education as Resistance. Oskar Loerke's poem "The Eye of Death" [1934]), in *Oskar Loerke: Marbacher Kolloquium 1984* (*Oskar Loerke: Marbach Colloquium, 1984*), edited by Reinhard Tgahrt (Mainz: Hase & Koehler, 1986), 89–105. The friend and kindred spirit of Loerke, the nature poet Wilhelm Lehmann, can only be mentioned here. Lehmann sent his first volume of poetry, *Antwort des Schweigens* (Answer of Silence, 1935), to Loerke with the dedication "Greetings Out of Despair," see Loerke's *Tagebücher 1903–1939*, 320 (September 29, 1935).

[54] On that subject, see Walter von Molo, *Zwischen Tag und Traum: Reden und Aufsätze, 1930* (Between Day and Dream: Speeches and Essays, 1930), new edition in 1950, and J. F. G. Grosser, ed., *Die grosse Kontroverse*.

[55] See also Karl-Heinz Schoeps, "Conservative Opposition: Friedrich Reck-Ralleczewen's Antifascist Novel *Bockelson: A History of Mass Hysteria*," in *Flight of Fantasy: New Perspectives on Inner Emigration in German Literature, 1933–1945* (New York: Berghahn, 2003), in print.

[56] See Joseph Wulf, *Literatur und Dichtung im Dritten Reich*, 27.

[57] Cordelia Edvardson, *Gebranntes Kind sucht Feuer* (Burned Child Seeks Fire), translated from Swedish by Anna Liese Kornitzky (Munich and Vienna, 1986). The Swedish original title was *Bränt barn söker sig till elden* (1984). An English translation appeared in 1997: *Burned Child Seeks Fire: A Memoir*, translated by Joel Agee (Boston: Beacon Press, 1997).

[58] Quoted in Karlheinz Müller, *Elisabeth Langgässer: Eine biographische Skizze* (Elisabeth Langgässer: A Biographical Sketch) (Darmstadt: Gesellschaft Hessischer Literaturfreunde, 1990), 69.

[59] Quoted in Müller, *Langgässer*, 72–73.

[60] Quoted and summarized in Müller, *Langgässer*, 76–77. Langgässer's speech originally appeared in *Ost und West* (*East and West*), 4 (1947).

[61] See Wulf, 65.

[62] *Erfahrung Nazideutschland: Romane in Deutschland 1933–1945: Analysen*, edited by Sigrid Bock and Manfred Hahn, 125.

[63] See Reinhold Grimm, "Innere Emigration als Lebensform," 43.

[64] Frank Thiess, *Jahre des Unheils: Fragmente erlebter Geschichte* (Year of Calamity: Fragments of Experienced History) (Vienna: Zsolnay, 1972), 100. The page citations in the text are to this edition.

[65] Diocletian, 284–305 A.D., was the creator of an authoritarian, coercive state and initiator of a renewed and intensified persecution of Christians.

[66] Quoted in Florian Vaßen, "'Das illegale Wort.' Literatur und Literaturverhältnisse des Bundes proletarisch-revolutionärer Schriftsteller nach 1933 (Literature and Literary Circumstances of the Union of Proletarian Revolutionary Writers After 1933," in *Kunst und Kultur im deutschen Faschismus* (Art and Culture in German Fascism), edited by Ralf Schnell (Stuttgart: Metzler, 1978), 293.

[67] All quoted in Brekle, *Schriftsteller im antifaschistischen Widerstand*, 46–47.

[68] See Wolfgang Emmerich, "Die Literatur des antifaschistischen Widerstandes" (The Literature of the Anti-Fascist Resistance), in *Die deutsche Literatur im Dritten Reich*, edited by Horst Denkler and Karl Prümm, 438.

[69] On that subject, see Brekle, *Schriftsteller im antifaschistischen Widerstand*, 47–53 and Vaßen, 294–300.

[70] On that subject, see Sigrid Bock, "Arbeiterkorrespondenten und -schriftsteller bewähren sich. Jan Petersen: *Unsere Straße*" (Worker-Correspondents and Worker-Writers Prove Themselves. Jan Petersen: Our Street), in *Erfahrung Nazideutschland*, 44–98.

[71] See Brekle, *Schriftsteller im antifaschistischen Widerstand*, 61–68. Sigrid Bock provides an extensive interpretation of the novel in her article "Arbeiterkorrespondenten und -schriftsteller bewähren sich" (Worker-Correspondents and Worker-Writers Prove Themselves), in *Erfahrung Nazideutschland* (The Experience of Nazi Germany), edited by Sigrid Bock and Manfred Hahn, 44–98.

[72] See Sigrid Bock, "Kämpfer vor dem Sieg. Adam Kuckhoff: *Der Deutsche von Bayencourt*" (Fighter Before Victory. Adam Kuckhoff: The German from Bayencourt), in *Erfahrung Nazideutschland*, edited by Sigrid Bock and Manfred Hahn, 183.

[73] According to Gilles Perrault, Kuckhoff was one of the three supporting pillars, together with Harro Schulze-Boysen and Arvid Harnack, of the Berlin group of the "Rote Kapelle" (Red Orchestra); of the three men, Kuckhoff was "the most remarkable." Kuckhoff's last play, *Till Eulenspiegel*, served as the key for decoding secret messages of the "Rote Kapelle," see Gilles Perrault, *L'orchestre rouge* (The Red

Orchestra) (Paris: Fayars, 1967), 383–84. The resistance organization was called "Rote Kapelle" by the Nazis because of their pro-Soviet views.

[74] See Sigrid Bock, "Kämpfer vor dem Sieg," 181.

[75] Adam Kuckhoff, *Der Deutsche von Bayencourt* (The German from Bayencourt) (Berlin: Rowohlt, 1937), 96. The page citations in the text refer to this edition.

[76] See Brekle, *Schriftsteller im antifaschistischen Widerstand*, 105.

[77] See Sigrid Bock, "Kämpfer vor dem Sieg," 186.

[78] According to Wolfgang Emmerich, "Die Literatur des antifaschistischen Widerstandes," 448.

[79] See Emmerich, 448.

[80] See Peter Weiss, *Die Ästhetik des Widerstands* (The Aesthetics of Resistance), volume 3 (Frankfurt am Main: Suhrkamp, 1981), especially 190–91. Weiss's first-person narrator Hans Coppi was a member of the "Rote Kapelle." Peter Weiss criticizes the insignificant response granted to Kuckhoff: Coppi also finds in Kuckhoff a writer — "whose poetry and novels will not pass into the history of literature" (202). After the Second World War, only a few works of Kuckhoff were published, among them, *Adam Kuckhoff zum Gedenken: Novellen, Gedichte, Briefe* (In Memory of Adam Kuckhoff: Novellas, Poems, Letters), edited and introduced by Greta Kuckhoff (Berlin: Aufbau, 1946). In 1985 in Kuckhoff's hometown, an edition of his selected works appeared with the title *Fröhlich bestehen, Adam Kuckhoff: Prosa, Lyrik, Dramatik* (Happily Exist: Adam Kuckhoff: Prose, Poetry, Drama) (Aachen: Alano, 1985) with an introduction by Werner Jung. On the "Rote Kapelle" and other resistance movements, see also *Der lautlose Aufstand: Bericht über die Widerstandsbewegung des deutschen Volkes 1933–1945* (The Soundless Revolution: Report on the Resistance Movement of the German People, 1933–1945), edited by Günther Weisenborn (Hamburg: Rowohlt, 1953).

[81] Werner Krauss, *PLN: Die Passionen der halykonischen Seele* (ZIP Code: The Passions of the Halyconian Soul) (Frankfurt am Main: Klostermann, 1946), Introduction. The page citations in the text refer to this edition. For other works of Werner Krauss and information about Werner Krauss as a person, see among others, Werner Krauss, *Grundprobleme der Literaturwissenschaft* (Fundamental Problems of the Study of Literature) (Reinbeck: Rohwohlt, 1968), and Werner Krauss, *Literaturtheorie, Philosophie, und Politik* (Literary Theory, Philosophy, and Politics), edited by Manfred Naumann (Berlin and Weimar: Aufbau, 1984). PLN stands for "Postleitzahl" (ZIP code), Halyconia for a despotic regime that is not appropriate to its time according to Brekle evoked by oriental titles such as mufti, or caliph, or the names Halys (Kizil) and Konya (Iconium), a river and city in Turkey. See Brekle, *Schriftsteller im antifaschistischen Widerstand*, 110.

[82] The novel remained almost unknown until a second, revised edition with an afterword by Peter Härtling was published in 1983 by Klostermann in Frankfurt am Main.

[83] The *"Blaue Blume"* (Blue Flower) was first used by Novalis (Friedrich von Hardenberg, 1772–1801) in his novel *Heinrich von Ofterdingen* (published posthumously in 1802) as a symbol for longing and became a symbol for German Romanticism itself.

[84] See Brekle, *Schriftsteller im antifaschistischen Widerstand*, 120. Copies of the novel are difficult to find today; further details can be read in Brekle.

[85] See Brekle, *Schriftsteller im antifaschistischen Widerstand*, 121.

[86] Quoted in *An den Wind geschrieben: Lyrik der Freiheit 1933–1945* (Written to the Wind: Poetry of Freedom, 1933–1945), edited by Manfred Schlösser (Darmstadt: Agora, 1960; 2nd edition, 1961), 237.

[87] On Haushofer, see among others, Brekle, *Schriftsteller im antifaschistischen Widerstand*, 226–27, and Charles H. Hoffmann, 116–17.

[88] Quoted in the German-English edition of the *Moabit Sonnets*, translated by M. D. Herter Norton (London and New York: Norton, 1978), 94. The page citations in the text refer to this edition.

[89] *An den Wind geschrieben* (Written to the Wind), 121. In 1992, Ruth Klüger published her highly respected memoir *Weiter leben: eine Jugend* (Live On: A Youth) (Göttingen: Hallstein, 1992), translated as *Still Alive: A Holocaust Girlhood Remembered* (New York: Feminist Press at the City University of New York: 2001).

[90] Herman Adler, *Gesänge aus der Stadt des Todes* (Songs from the City of Death) (Zurich and New York, 1945), and Edgar Kupfer-Koberwitz, *Kette der Tage: Gedichte aus Dachau* (Chain of Days. Poems from Dachau) (Stuttgart and Calw, 1947), quoted in Charles W. Hoffmann, 248–49.

[91] Quoted in Michael Moll, *Lyrik in einer entmenschten Welt: Interpretationsversuche zu deutschsprachigen Gedichten aus nationalsozialistischen Gefängnissen, Ghettos und KZ's* (Poetry in a Dehumanized World: Attempts at Interpretation of Poems from National Socialist Prisons, Ghettos, and Concentration Camps) (Frankfurt am Main: R. G. Fischer, 1988), XI.

[92] *An den Wind geschrieben*, 267

[93] Hermann Adler, who was born in 1911 in Diosek, Pressburg, and raised in Nuremberg, was put in the Wilna Ghetto in 1941, and was liberated from Bergen-Belsen Concentration Camp in 1945.

[94] Quoted in Hoffmann, 253.

[95] "Wir hoffen auf Freude" (We Hope for Joy), in Hoffmann, 263.

[96] Quoted in Hoffmann, 264.

[97] Quoted in Moll from appendix I. The following poem also from that source, see appendix II.

[98] Helmut Braunn in his introduction to Rose Ausländer, *Die Erde war ein atlasweißes Feld: Gedichte 1927–1956* (The World was a Satin-White Field: Poems, 1927–1956) (Frankfurt am Main: Fischer, 1985), 10. The page citations in the text refer to this edition.

[99] See Moll, 195.

[100] On that subject, see Horst Jarka's introduction to Jura Soyfer, *Das Gesamtwerk* (The Complete Works) (Vienna: Europa Verlag, 1980), 26. The pages citations in the text refer to this edition. On Soyfer, see also Peter Langmann, *Sozialismus und Literatur — Jura Soyfer: Studien zu einem österreichischen Schriftsteller der Zwischenkriegszeit* (Socialism and Literatur — Jura Soyfer: Studies of an Austrian Writer of the Period Between the Wars) (Frankfurt am Main: Hain Meisenheim, 1986).

[101] *Klassiker in Finsteren Zeiten* (Writers of German Classicism in Dark Times), volume 1, edited by Bernhard Zeller et al., 409.

[102] See Zeller, *Klassiker*, volume 2, 410–12.

[103] See Zeller, *Klassiker*, volume 2, 421–22.

[104] On the non-fascist authors of the younger generation who began writing toward the end of the Weimar Republic and in the Third Reich, see Hans Dieter Schäfer's anthology *Am Rande der Nacht: Moderne Klassik im Dritten Reich* (On the Edge of Night: Modern Classics in the Third Reich) (Frankfurt am Main: Ullstein, 1984), which includes works of Johannes Bobrowski, Wolfgang Borchert, Heimito von Doderer, Günter Eich, Peter Huchel, Frido Lampe, Horst Lange, and Hermann Lenz, as well as Hans Dieter Schäfer's essay, "Die nichtfaschistische Literatur der 'jungen Generation' im nationalsozialistischen Deutschland" (Non-fascist Literature of the 'Young Generation' in National Socialist Germany), in *Deutsche Literatur im Dritten Reich*, edited by Horst Denkler and Karl Prümm, 459–503. This article appeared in 1981, in a slightly revised form in Hans Dieter Schäfer, *Das gespaltene Bewußtsein: Deutsche Kultur und Lebenswirklichkeit 1933–1945* (Divided Consciousness: German Culture and the Reality of Life, 1933–1945) (Munich: Hanser, 1981), 7–54.

[105] Publication in the literary showpiece journal *Das Innere Reich* (The Inner Realm) by no means meant sympathy with the Nazi regime; this journal was far too "Janus-headed" for that, as Horst Denkler demonstrates in his essay "Janusköpfig. Zur ideologischen Physiognomie der Zeitschrift *Das Innere Reich* (1934–1944)" (Janus-headed. On the Ideological Physiognomy of the Journal *The Inner Realm* (1934–1944)); see *Deutsche Literatur im Dritten Reich*, edited by Horst Denkler and Karl Prümm, 382–405.

[106] See Glenn Cuomo, *Career at the Cost of Compromise: Günter Eich's Life and Work in the Years 1933–1945* (Amsterdam and Atlanta: Rodopi, 1989), 44–45.

[107] See Schäfer, "Die nichtfaschistische Literatur," 462. On Koeppen's novel *Die Mauer schwankt* (The Wall Teeters), see Simone Barck, "Ein junger Schriftsteller im dritten Reich. Wolfgang Koeppen: *Die Mauer Schwankt* (A Young Writer in the Third Reich: Wolfgang Koeppen: The Wall Teeters), in Bock and Hahn, 9–43.

[108] See Schäfer, "Die nichtfaschistische Literatur," 462.

9: Closing Comments

NEITHER THE LITERATURE of the Third Reich nor the literature of the Inner Emigration or the resistance played an essential role after the war in building a new literature in the occupation zones and the two German states that followed. Still, 1945 was not the absolute zero hour; especially in the Federal Republic, numerous leading representatives of National Socialist literature happily went on publishing, some of them even in the same spirit as before, for example, Erwin Guido Kolbenheyer.[1] Others switched over to harmless topics, such as Hans Friedrich Blunck with his *Neue Märchen* (New Fairy Tales, 1951), Edwin Erich Dwinger with *Das Glück der Erde* (Happiness on Earth, 1957), a "Reitbrevier für Pferdefreunde" (Riding Guide for Horse Lovers), Hanns Johst with his novel *Gesegnete Vergänglichkeit* (Blessed Transitoriness, 1955), or Gerhard Schumann's "thoughtful, cheerful verses" of the *Stachel-Beeren-Auslese* (Gooseberry Selection; *Stachel* also means stinger, 1960), in which, for example, he gives the reader the following advice:

> Einfach nicht ärgern!
> Ärger geht auf die Galle.
> Die Fröhlichen sind die Stärkern
> In jedem Falle.[2]

> (Just don't be annoyed!
> Annoyance raises the bile.
> Happy people are the stronger ones
> In any case!)

The inner emigrants could have their unprinted works published, but in doing so had little response. Authors such as Reinhold Schneider got into new difficulties when they objected to the failure to deal with the National Socialist past and the rearmament of Germany. Reinhold Schneider, highly respected immediately after the war, fell into disfavor at the beginning of the fifties because he criticized the restorative policies of Adenauer. Schneider was denounced as a communist and withdrew for a second time into inner emigration.[3]

The new literary scene in the young Federal Republic was largely determined by the Gruppe 47; in the German Democratic Republic, it was for the most part the returnees from emigration, such as Johannes R. Becher, Bertolt Brecht, Anna Seghers, and Friedrich Wolf, who set the tone, if not without difficulties with the narrow-minded functionaries.

Much of the literature presented in this volume strikes today's reader as a fossil from times past but it is part and parcel of German cultural and literary history. Knowledge of this literature and the circumstances in which it was written should also be understood as a step towards overcoming the past and can thus be a shield against repeating it. Wolfgang Wippermann's remark about the study of history applies at least to the same extent to the study of literature and the history of literature: "Hitler has been dead for over forty years, but the history and ideology associated with his name are by no means past history that has been 'overcome.'"[4]

Notes

[1] On his seventy-fifth birthday, Hermann Burte congratulated him for being a man who does not crawl to the cross; see Ernst Loewy, *Literatur unterm Hakenkreuz* (Literature Under the Swastika), 317.

[2] Gerhard Schumann, *Stachel-Beeren-Auslese* (Gooseberry Selection) (Stuttgart: Silberburg, 1960), 91.

[3] On that subject, see the chapter "Der 'Fall Reinhold Schneider'" (The "Reinhold Schneider Case"), in *Reinhold Schneider: Weg eines Schriftstellers* (Reinhold Schneider: The Path of a Writer), edited by Ingo Zimmermann (Berlin: Union, 1982), 142–70.

[4] Wolfgang Wippermann, ed., *Kontroversen um Hitler* (Controversies About Hitler), edited by Wolfgang Wippermann (Frankfurt am Main: Suhrkamp, 1986), 92.

Biographical and Bibliographical List of Authors

THE AUTHORS LISTED represent a selection that is intended to introduce some of the most important authors of fascist and non-fascist literature in the Third Reich and at the same time to also include some of the authors who could only be treated very briefly in the text, or not at all. Authors whose main body of work did not fall in the period of the Third Reich (for example, Rose Ausländer, Paul Celan, Günter Eich, Paul Ernst, Ricarda Huch, among others) are not represented in this list. The dates were taken for the most part from relevant literature lexicons, such as Kunisch, Lennartz, von Wilpert, from the *Literatur Lexikon* (Literature Lexicon) edited by Walter Killy, and from the *Biographisches Lexikon zum Dritten Reich* (Biographical Lexicon of the Third Reich) edited by Hermann Weiß (Frankfurt am Main: Fischer, 1998). Works written after 1945 are not considered.

List of Abbreviations

Aut	Autobiography	O	Oratoria
Biog	Biography	P	Poems
C	Correspondence	Rep	Reportage
Cb	Children's book	Rp	Radio play
Co	Comedy	S, Ss	Story (Stories), Novella(s)
Cp	Choral Play		
Di	Diary	Se	Sermons
Dr	Drama	Sg	Songs
Ep	Epic	Sk	Sketch
Es	Essay(s)	Sp	Speech
F	Fairy tales	T	Tragedy
Fi	Film script	Tb	Travel book, Travel report
L	Lecture		
Le	Letters	W	Writings, Reports
N	Novel		

Alverdes, Paul

May 6, 1897, Strasbourg–January 28, 1979, Munich. Father: Prussian officer. Member of the *Wandervogel* movement. War volunteer at 17 years old; in 1915, a serious injury to his pharynx. Studied law, *Germanistik,* and art history in Munich and Jena; Ph.D. in 1921 with a dissertation on "The Mystical Eros in the Religious Poetry of Pietism." After 1922, a freelance writer in Munich, especially of stories and radio plays, often with war themes, and after 1945, of many children's fairy tales. From 1934 to 1944, editor of the conservative journal *Das Innere Reich* (The Interior Realm) together with K. B. von Mechow. First great success: *Die Pfeiferstube* (The Whistlers' Room) (S, 1929) is set in a hospital room with a German wounded in the pharynx; dedicated to Hans Carossa.

Works: *Kilian* (S, 1922), *Die Nördlichen* (P, 1922), *Die ewige Weihnacht* (Dr, 1922), *Die feindlichen Brüder* (T, 1923), *Die Flucht* (Ss, 1924; as Rp, 1936), *Reinhold im Dienst* (S; *Reinhold oder die Verwundeten,* Ss, 1931), *Die Freiwilligen* (Rp, 1934), *Das Zwiegesicht* (S, 1937), *Das Männlein Mittenzwei* (F, 1937), *Das Schlaftürlein* (F, 1938), *Das Winterlager* (Rp, 1934), *Gespräch über Goethes Harzreise im Winter* (Es, 1938), *Dank und Dienst* (Es, 1939), *Dem Andenken Mozarts* (Sp, 1941), *Jette im Wald* (S, 1942).

Anacker, Heinrich

January 29, 1901, Aarau (Switzerland)–January 14, 1971, Wasserburg on the Bodensee. Of "German-Swiss" and Thuringian ancestry. *Abitur* (final and comprehensive examination at the end of high school [Gymnasium]) in Aarau; lectures on the history of literature in Zurich and Vienna. Member of the NSDAP from April of 1924. Activities as a merchant in the twenties. From 1933 on, a freelance writer in Berlin. Member of the Reich Culture Senate. From 1921 on, writer of poems: political poetry in the National Socialist spirit, fighting songs, glorification of war, homeland, and the front, also nature and love poetry. Shared the Dietrich Eckart Prize in 1934 for the Choral Play *SA ruft ins Volk* (SA Calls to the People) with Adolf Weber; received the art prize of the NSDAP in 1936 for his complete works. When denazified, ranked as "less incriminated."

Works: *Klinge, kleines Frühlingslied* (P, 1921), *Werdezeit* (P, 1922), *Auf Wanderwegen* (P, 1923), *Sonne* (P, 1925), *Ebbe und Flut* (P, 1927), *Bunter Reigen* (P, 1930), *SA-Gedichte: Die Trommel* (P, 1931), *Gedichte der deutschen Erhebung: Die Fanfare* (P, 1933), *Einkehr* (P, 1934), *SA ruft ins Volk* (Cp, 1935, with Adolf Weber), *Der Aufbau* (P, 1935), *Kämpfen und Siegen* (P, 1936), *Lieder aus Stille und Stürmen* (P, 1937), *Wir wachsen in das Reich hinein* (P, 1937), *Gedichte um Österreichs Heimkehr: Ein Volk — Ein Reich — Ein Führer* (P, 1938), *Heimat und Front: Gedichte aus dem Herbst*

1939 (P, 1940), *Gedichte aus dem Kriegswinter 1940: Bereitschaft und Aufbruch* (P, 1940), *Über die Maas, über Schelde und Rhein! Gedichte vom Feldzug im Westen* (P, 1942).

Andres, Stefan

June 26, 1906, Breitweis on the Mosel–June 29, 1970, Rome. Father: miller. Childhood defined by the village and the Catholic Church. Began monastery school in 1917; 1926–1928, novitiate in a Capuchin monastery; career goal, Catholic priest. But left the monastery and studied *Germanistik* in Cologne, Jena, and Berlin. Writer. From 1937 to 1949, lived in Positano with his wife and children, in 1950 in Unkel on the Rhine, and in Rome from 1961 until his death in 1970. In 1933 awarded the Prize of the Abraham Lincoln Foundation, in 1948 the Rhine Literature Prize, in 1952 the Rhineland-Palatinate Literature Prize, in 1954 the Grand Art Prize of North Rhine-Westphalia for Literature, in 1957 the Dramatist Prize of the City of Oldenburg. In the 1950's, Stefan Andres was one of the most-read authors. Often as disguised biography, stories center around the farmer's home and the time he spends near the Mediterranean; joy with the world, religious search for truth; conventional narrative form.

Works: *Das Märchen im Liebfrauendom* (F, 1928), *Bruder Luzifer* (N, 1933), *Eberhard im Kontrapunkt* (N, 1933), *Die Löwenkanzel* (P, 1933), *Die unsichtbare Mauer* (N, 1934), *Der ewige Strom* (O, P, 1935), *El Greco malt den Großinquisitor* (S, 1936), *Vom heiligen Pfäfflein Domenico* (S, 1936), *Utz, der Nachfahr* (S, 1936), *Moselländische Novellen* (Ss, 1937), *Schwarze Strahlen* (Dr, 1938), *Der Mann von Asteri* (N, 1939), *Das Grab des Neides* (Ss, 1940), "Der olympische Frieden" (S, 1940), *Der gefrorene Dionysos* (S, 1942), *Wir sind Utopia* (S, 1943), *Italiener* (Es, 1943), *Wirtshaus zur weiten Welt* (Ss, 1943), *Das goldene Gitter* (S, 1943).

Berens, Josefa (Berens-Totenohl)

March 30, 1891, Grevenstein in the Sauerland–June 6, 1969, Meschede. Father: blacksmith. Was an elementary school teacher for ten years in the Weserland, then in Düsseldorf, where she was also active as a painter. From 1923 on, a freelance writer and painter in Höxter, Totenohl on the Lenne, and Gleierbrück. Her first novel, *Der Fehmhof*, written in Totenohl, brought her success and the addition to her name. A member of the Hoffmann von Fallersleben Society. Received the Westphalian Literature Prize in 1936. Representative of blood-and-soil literature.

Works: *Der Femhof* (N, 1934), *Frau Magdalena* (N, 1935) — both novels were reprinted in 1958 as *Die Leute vom Femhof, Das schlafende Brot* (P, 1936), *Die Frau als Schöpferin und Erhalterin des Volkstums* (Sp, 1938), *Einer Sippe Gesicht* (Ep, 1941), *Der Fels* (N, 1942), *Im Moor* (N, 1944).

Bergengruen, Werner

September 16, 1892, Riga–September 4, 1964, Baden-Baden. Father: physician. Studied law, history, and *Germanistik* in Marburg, Munich, and Berlin. Served in the First World War and in the battles in the Baltic States. Journalist, then freelance writer in Berlin from 1927 to 1936, in Solln near Munich from 1936 to 1942, in Achenkirch, Tirol from 1942 to 1946, in Zurich from 1946 to 1958), and finally in Baden-Baden. In 1936 converted to Catholicism. Was considered "politically unreliable" in the Third Reich and was excluded from the Reich Chamber of Literature in 1937, as the Nazis did not consider him suitable "to work on the construction of German culture with publications" (Joseph Wulf, *Literatur im Dritten Reich,* 518). He belonged to the "undesirable" authors whose works were usually ranked "negative" in Rosenberg's annual gazette of expert reports. Prose that is perfect in form and exemplary novels; historic themes and travel reports.

Works: *Das Gesetz des Atum* (N, 1923), *Das große Alkahest* (N, 1926; retitled *Der Starost,* 1938), *Das Kaiserreich in Trümmern* (N, 1927), *Herzog Karl der Kühne* (N, 1930, revised 1943), *Der goldene Griffel* (N, 1931), *Baedeker des Herzens* (Tb, 1932), *Die Feuerprobe* (S, 1933), *Der Großtyrann und das Gericht* (N, 1935), *Die Schnur um den Hals* (Ss, 1935), *Die Rose von Jericho* (P, 1936), *Die drei Falken* (S, 1937), *Der ewige Kaiser* (P, 1937), *Der Tod von Reval* (Ss, 1939), *Am Himmel wie auf Erden* (N, 1940), *Der spanische Rosenstock* (S, 1941), *Das Hornunger Heimweh* (N, 1942), *Schatzgräbergeschichte* (S, 1942), *Dies Irae* (P, 1945).

Bethge, Friedrich

May 24, 1891, Berlin–September 17, 1963, Bad Homburg vor der Höhe. Son of a teacher from an East Prussian family of pastors. Officer in the First World War, then a city official in Berlin. In January of 1919, participated in putting down the Spartacus uprising in Berlin for which he received the Schlageter Badge in 1935. From 1935–1945, Member of the Reich Culture Senate and general director of the stages in Frankfurt am Main. Placed in a prisoner-of-war camp in 1945. "Bethke is considered the 'front-line soldier' among the dramatists of the Third Reich" (Rühle).

Works: *Pfarr Peder* (Dr, 1922), *Pierre und Jeanette* (S, 1926; retitled *Das triumphierende Herz,* 1937), *Reims* (Dr, 1929), *Die Blutprobe* (Co, 1931), *Marsch der Veteranen* (Dr, 1934), *Heinrich von Plauen* (Dr, 1938), *Rebellion um Preußen* (T, 1939), *Anke von Skoepen* (Dr, 1940), *Copernicus* (Dr, 1944).

Beumelburg, Werner

February 19, 1899, Traben-Trarbach on the Mosel–March 9, 1963, Würzburg. Father: pastor. War volunteer and officer in the First World War.

Studied political science at Cologne University; 1921–1926 editor in Düsseldorf and Berlin. From 1926 a freelance writer. In the Third Reich, editor at the Writers' Academy, member of the Legion Condor, and major in the air force in the Second World War. Predominantly a storywriter and a journalist. Received the Art Prize of the *Gau* West Mark in 1937. Main themes are war, comradeship, and the Reich idea.

Works: *Douamont* (W, 1925), *Ypern* (W, 1925), *Flandern 1917* (W, 1927), *Sperrfeuer um Deutschland* (N, 1928), *Gruppe Bosemüller* (N, 1929), *Deutschland in Ketten: Von Versailles bis zum Youngplan* (N, 1931), *Bismarck gründet das Reich* (N, 1932), *Bismarck greift zum Steuer* (N, 1932), *Wilhelm II. und Bülow* (W, 1932), *Das eherne Gesetz* (N, 1934), *Friedrich II. von Hohenstaufen* (W, 1934), *Preußische Novelle* (S, 1935), *Kaiser und Herzog* (N, 1936), *Mont Royal* (N, 1936), *Reich und Rom* (N, 1937), *Der König und die Kaiserin* (N, 1937), *Kampf um Spanien: Die Geschichte der Legion Condor* (W, 1939).

Billinger, Richard

July 2, 1890, St. Marienkirchen in Upper Austria–June 7, 1965, in Linz on the Danube. Father: farmer; raised by the Jesuits. A seaman for a short time in Kiel. Studied philosophy in Kiel, Innsbruck, and Vienna. Freelance writer in Berlin, Munich, and Niederpöcking on Lake Starnberg. Received the Writers' Prize of the City of Vienna in 1924, and the Kleist Prize in 1932. Honorarium for life from the Upper Austrian state. Dramatist, especially material about the peasantry; also a poet and storywriter, with his glorification of the *Volkstum* close to the Nazis.

Works: *Über die Äcker* (P, 1923), *Das Perchtenspiel* (Dr, 1928), *Die Asche des Fegefeuers: Eine Dorfkindheit* (Aut, N, 1931), *Rosse, Rauhnacht* (2 Dr, 1931), *Spiel vom Knechte, Reise nach Ursprung* (2 Dr, 1932), *Lob des Landes* (Dr, 1933), *Das Verlöbnis* (Dr, 1933), *Der Pfeil im Wappen* (P, 1933), *Das Schutzengelhaus* (N, 1934, 1937, 1944), *Leben aus Gottes Hand* (N, 1935), *Die Hexe von Passau* (Dr, 1935), *Nachtwache* (Sg and P, 1935, 1943), *Der Gigant* (Dr, 1937), *Das verschenkte Leben* (N, 1937, 1942), *Am hohen Meer* (Dr, 1939), *Holder Morgen* (Sg and P, 1942, 1943), *Paracelsus, Ein Salzburger Festspiel* (Dr, 1943), *Das Spiel von Erasmus Grasser* (1943).

Binding, Rudolf Georg

August 13, 1867, Basel–August 4, 1938, Starnberg. Father: professor of criminal law in Leipzig. Spent his youth in Freiburg in Breisgau, Strasbourg, Leipzig, and Frankfurt am Main. Studied law in Tübingen and Heidelberg without completing his studies, then studied medicine in Berlin. Involved in horse breeding and was a successful jockey. 1910 on in Buchschlag (Hessia) and was mayor there. Served in the First World War as a cavalry captain.

Began his activities as a writer after a trip to Greece in 1909. Strict form in his poetry and the prose of his novels, determined by the traditions of the nineteenth century. Themes: individuals in extraordinary situations facing conflicts and having to prove themselves, aristocrats, national consciousness, and war as a manly test of mettle.

Works: *Legenden der Zeit* (Ss, 1909), *Die Geige* (Ss, 1911), *Opfergang* (S, 1912), *Gedichte aus dem Kriege* (P, 1913), *Der Wingult* (Ss, 1921), *Stolz und Trauer* (P, 1922), *Aus dem Kriege* (C and Di, 1924), *Tage* (P, 1924), *Erlebtes Leben* (Aut, 1928), *Rufe und Reden* (Es, 1928), *Moselfahrt aus Liebeskummer* (Ss, 1932), *Das Heiligtum der Pferde* (Ss, 1935), *Wir fordern Reims zur Übergabe auf* (Ss, 1935), *Die Spiegelgespräche* (Es, 1935), *Die Geliebten* (P, 1935), *Waffenbrüder* (S, 1935), *Der Durchlöcherte* (Ss, 1936), *Sieg des Herzens* (P, 1937 and 1950), *Die Perle* (Ss, 1938), *Natur und Kunst* (Es, 1939), *Von der Kraft deutschen Worts als Ausdruck der Nation* (Sp, 1938), *Von Freiheit und Vaterland* (Di, 1939), *Ad se ipsum* (Di, 1939), *Dies war das Maß* (Ss and Di, 1939).

Blunck, Hans Friedrich

September 3, 1888, Altona–April 25, 1961, Hamburg. Teacher's son. Studied law in Kiel and Heidelberg, received a doctorate in law, member of the youth movement, officer in the First World War, then a finance official, and in 1920 a *Regierungsrat* in Hamburg. From 1925–1928, syndic of the University of Hamburg, then a freelance writer. Travels to America, Africa, Mediterranean countries, the Balkans. From 1933–1935, President of the Reich Chamber of Literature. Member of the Reich Culture Senate and the Senate of the Academy of Literature. Received the Goethe Medal in 1938, the Ring of Honor of the German Language Association, and the Wartburg Poet's Rose. Categorized as a "sympathizer" when denazified in 1949; fined DM 10,000. Lived on his estate, Mölenhoff near Grebin in Holstein and in Hamburg-Großflottbeck. National *völkisch* poet, dramatist, and storywriter. Representative of the "Northern Renaissance." In 1950, attempted to justify himself as an "anti-fascist on the chair of the Chamber of Literature."

Works: *Nordmark* (P, 1912), *Stelling Rotkinnsohn* (N, 1923; retitled *Werdendes Volk*, 1934), *Märchen von der Niederelbe* (F, 1922–30), *Kampf der Gestirne* (N, 1926), *Gewalt über das Feuer* (N, 1928; retitled *Die Urvätersaga*, 1934), *Volkswende* (N, 1930), *Über allem das Reich!* (Sp, 1930), *Niederdeutsche Märchen* (1934), *Der einsame König* (N, 1936), *König Geiserich* (S, 1936), *Deutsche Heldensagen* (1938), *Wolter von Plettenberg, Deutschordensmeister in Livland* (N, 1938), *Kampf um Neuyork* (Dr, 1938; reprinted as a novel, 1951), *Die Sage vom Reich* (Ep, 2 volumes, 1940–43), *Von Tieren und sonderbaren Käuzen* (S, 1943).

Brehm, Bruno

July 23, 1892, Laibach, Krain–June 5, 1974, Alt-Aussee, Salzkammergut. Father: Austrian imperial officer. Officer in 1913, wounded and then in Russian prisoner-of-war camp (acquaintance with Dwinger). Studied art history in Göteburg, Stockholm, and Vienna, Ph.D., professor's assistant at the University of Vienna. Worked in the publishing business, and then from 1927 on as a freelance writer. National Socialist, editor of the Journal *Der getreue Eckart*. After the *Anschluß*, councilman for the City of Vienna, in 1941 on president of the Vienna Culture Chamber. Ordinance officer in the Second World War, interned in 1945. Awarded the State Prize in 1939, Nordgau Culture Prize of the City of Amberg in 1958, and the Art Prize of the Sudeten Germans in 1963. Representative of the Pan-German concept who enthusiastically celebrated the *Anschluß*. Author of cheerful, as well as fateful novels.

Works: *Der lachende Gott* (N, 1928; retitled *Der fremde Gott*, 1948), *Susanne und Marie* (N, 1929; retitled *Auf Wiedersehen, Susanne,* 1939), *Ein Graf spielt Theater* (N, 1930; retitled *Ein Schloß in Böhmen*, 1942), novel trilogy on the First World War: *Apis und Este* (So fing es an) (1931), *Das war das Ende* (Von Brest Litowsk bis Versailles) (1932), *Weder Kaiser noch König* (Der Untergang der Habsburg Monarchie) (1933; revised and retitled *Die Throne stürzen,* 1951), *Heimat ist Arbeit* (S, 1934), *Die größere Heimat* (S, 1934), *Die schrecklichen Pferde* (N, 1934; retitled *Die sieghaften Pferde,* 1956), *Zu früh und zu spät* (historical fiction on the wars of liberation, 1936), *Die weiße Adlerfeder* (Ss, 1937), *Glückliches Österreich* (W, 1938), *Die Grenze geht mitten durch das Herz* (S, 1938), *Tag der Erfüllung* (Sp and Di, 28 entries, 1939; in it, among other works, "Über die Tapferkeit — Brevier für junge Deutsche"), *Im Großdeutschen Reich* (W, 1940), *Deutsche Haltung vor Fremden — Ein Kameradenwort an unsere Soldaten* (W, 1940), *Die sanfte Gewalt* (N, 1940).

Britting, Georg

February 17, 1891, Regensburg–April 27, 1964, Munich. Son of a city technical official. Studied in Regensburg. War volunteer from 1914 to 1918, company commander. Seriously wounded in 1918. After 1920, freelance writer in Munich. Editorial activities, including journal, collection of selected Möricke poems, and a poetry anthology. Numerous trips through Europe and Africa. After the First World War, followed late expressionism; co-editor of the journal *Die Sichel* (1919–1921). Novellas and poetry strongly influenced by G. Heym. Image of a world ruled by tragedy and demons; demonization of the world of objects. Prose with mythical and magical undertones. Awarded the Literature Prize of the City of Munich in 1936.

Works: *Der Mann im Mond* (Dr, 1920), *Der verlachte Hiob* (S, 1921), *Das Storchenfest* (Dr, 1921–1922), *Michael und das Fräulein* (S, 1927), *Paula und Bianca* (Dr, 1928), *Gedichte* (P, 1930), *Lebenslauf eines dicken Mannes, der Hamlet hieß* (Ep, 1932), *Die kleine Welt am Strom* (S, 1933), *Das treue Eheweib* (S, 1933), *Die Feldschlacht: Das Waldhorn* (Ss, 1934), *Der irdische Tag* (P, 1935), *Der bekränzte Weiher* (S, 1937), *Das gerettete Bild* (S, 1938), *Rabe, Roß und Hahn* (P, 1939), *Jugend an der Donau* (S, 1940), *Der alte Mond* (S, 1941), *Der Schneckenweg* (S, 1941), *Lob des Weines* (P, 1944, expanded in 1947, expanded in 1950).

Burte, Hermann (Hermann Strübe)

February 15, 1879, Maulburg, Baden–March 21, 1960, Lörrach. Father: the Alemannian poet Friedrich Strübe. Studied at the Academy of Arts in Karlsruhe. Was a painter in Oxford, London, and Paris from 1904 to 1908, then a painter and writer in Lörrach. Received the Kleist Prize in 1912 for *Wiltfeber, der ewige Deutsche,* an honorary Ph.D. from the University of Freiburg in Breisgau in 1924, the Schiller Prize in 1927, the Hebel Prize in 1936, the Pan-German Dialect Prize in 1938, the Goethe Medal in 1939, the Scheffel Ring in 1944, the Poet's Ring of the German Culture Works in 1953, and the Jean Paul Medal in 1957. Poet, dramatist, and storywriter subscribing to a *völkisch*-Germanic ideology. Nazi supporter.

Works: *Wiltfeber, der ewige Deutsche* (N, 1912), *Die Flügelspielerin* (P, 1913), *Herzog Utz* (Dr, 1913), *Katte* (Dr, 1914), *Madlee* (Alemmanian P, 1923), *Krist vor Gericht* (Dr, 1930), *Ursula* (P, 1930), *Warbeck* (Dr, 1935), *Anker am Rhein* (P, 1937), *Das unsichtbare Bild* (Nibelungen Dr, 1941), *Deutsche Sendung des Wortes und der Letter* (L, 1942), *Hebel, Scheffel, und die Gegenwart* (L, 1942), *Sieben Reden* (Sp, 1943), *Das Schloß Dürande* (Libretto based on Eichendorff, music by O. Schoeck, 1943), *H. B. gegen John Masefield* (German answer to English verse, 1944).

Carossa, Hans

December 15, 1887, Bad Tölz–September 12, 1956, Rittsteig near Passau. Father: country doctor. Starting in 1888 attended the humanistic Gymnasium in Landhut, *Abitur* (final examination at Gymnasium [high school]) in 1897. Studied medicine in Munich, Würzburg, and Leipzig. Received his degree in medicine in 1903. General practitioner and cardiopulmonary specialist in several Bavarian cities, including his father's practice in Passau. Beginnings of his literary activities before the First World War; acquaintance of Hofmannsthal and Rilke. Served in the First World War as a battalion physician; was slightly wounded and spent time in the hospital. After the First World War, a writer-physician again; after 1929, a freelance writer in Passau. Literary lecture tours. Attempted in his poems and in his (largely autobiographical) prose to emphasize the timeless validity of humanistic ideals. Moved away from the contexts of contemporary history. Models were especially Goethe and Stifter. During the National Socialist period, inner emigrant and involuntary representative of National Socialist culture policies. Received the Gottfried Keller Prize in 1931, refused an invitation to join the Prussian Academy of Writers in 1933, and received the Goethe Prize of the City of Frankfurt in 1938. In 1941 became the president of a European writers' association. At the end of April, 1945, Carossa implored the Lord Mayor of Passau not to defend the city and was in consequence sentenced to death in absentia by the SS *Gauleiter*. After the Second World War, continued his activities as a writer.

Works: *Stella Mystica* (P, 1907), *Gedichte* (P, 1910), *Doktor Bürgers Ende* (N, 1913), *Die Flucht* (P, 1916), *Ostern* (P, 1920), *Eine Kindheit* (S, 1922), *Rumänisches Tagebuch* (Di, 1924), *Verwandlungen einer Jugend* (Aut, 1928), *Der Arzt Gion* (N, 1931), *Führung und Geleit* (Aut, 1933), *Worte über Goethe* (Sp, 1936), *Geheimnisse des reifen Lebens* (Aut and S, 1936), *Wirkungen Goethes in der Gegenwart* (Sp, 1938), *Das Jahr der schönen Täuschungen* (Aut, 1941).

Claudius, Hermann

October 24, 1878, Langenfelde (Holstein)–September 8, 1980, Grönwohld bei Trittau. Father: train trackmaster. Great-grandson of Matthias Claudius. Elementary school teacher from 1904 to 1934; early retirement because of a traffic accident that left him hearing impaired. Claudius was initially close in his thinking to the social democrats and wrote social poems about the big city in Low German (*Mank Muern*). But mainly wrote simple folk-song-like poems, stories, and novels with strong ties to the homeland. The naïve, pious tone and intellectual simplicity, in some cases nationalistically glorifying world war, were well received by the Nazis. Became a member of the Prussian Academy of Literature in 1933 and a member of the Erfurt Academy of Sciences for the Common Good. Made famous by the poem "Wenn wir schreiten Seit an Seit."

Works: *Mank Muern* (P, 1912), *Hörst du nicht den Eisenschritt* (P, 1914), *Lieder der Unruhe* (Sg, 1920), *Licht* (Dr, 1920), *Hamborger Kinnerbok* (Cb and P, 1920), *Brücke in der Zeit* (P, 1922), *Das Silberschiff* (N, 1923), *Bodderlicker set di* (P, 1924), *Heimkehr: Lieder von Gott, Ehe, und Armut* (Sg, 1925), *Meister Bertram van Mynden* (N, 1927), *Menschheitswille* (Dr, 1927), *Rumpelstilzchen* (Dr, 1928), *Speeldeel für Jungs un Deerns* (Dr, 1930), *Armantje* (N, 1934), *Wie ich den lieben Gott suchte* (N, 1935), *Daß dein Herz fest sei* (P, 1935), *Und weiter wachsen Gott und Welt* (P, 1936), *Mein Vetter Emil* (N, 1938), *Matthias Claudius* (Biog, 1938), *Jeden Morgen geht die Sonne auf* (P, 1938), *Zuhause* (P, 1940), *Deutsche Sonette* (P, 1942), *Aldebaran* (P, 1944).

Dinter, Artur

June 27, 1876, Mülhausen, Alsace–May 21, 1948, Offenburg, Baden. Father: senior customs inspector. Studied natural science and philosophy; doctorates in philosophy and natural sciences. Director of the botanical school gardens in Strasbourg; in 1904, senior teacher in Constantinople. Producer for a number of theaters, including the Schiller Theater in Berlin. In 1908 founded the "Society of German Stage Writers." Soldier from 1914 to 1918. After 1924, a representative of the NSDAP in the Thuringian *Landtag*. After 1928, editor of the monthly publication *Geistchristentum*, the journal of the "Aryan" "German People's Church" that Dinter founded in 1927 but was outlawed in 1937. Fell into disfavor and was expelled from the Party. The fifteenth edition of his anti-Semitic book *Sünde wider das Blut* (1917) appeared in 1921, and more than 250,000 copies of the book had been printed by 1934. Dramas, novels, and treatises.

Works: *Reinhard* (Dr, 1900), *D' Schmuggler* (Co, 1903), *Der Dämon* (Dr, 1906), *Prüfung* (Co, 1909), *Die schöne Erzieherin* (Co, 1909), *Goethe, Chamberlain, Brentano und die Rassenfrage* (W, 1916), "Die Verjudung der deutschen Schaubühne" (W, 1916), "Lichtstrahlen aus dem Talmud" (Le, 1919), *Die Sünde wider den Geist* (N, 1921), *Die Sünde wider die Liebe* (N, 1922), *Ursprung, Ziel und Weg der deutschvölkischen Freiheitsbewegung* (W, 1924), *Unser Ziel* (W, 1934), *War Jesu Jude?* (W, 1934), *Das Glaubensbekenntnis der deutschen Volkskirche* (W, 1935).

Dwinger, Edwin Erich

April 23, 1898, Kiel–December 17, 1981, Gmund on the Tegernsee. Father: naval officer. Mother: Russian. Volunteered for the eastern front at sixteen, was wounded, and was put in a Russian prisoner-of-war camp; escaped, took part in the battles of Koltshak's White Russian army against the Bolsheviks, was taken prisoner again, and escaped again. Returned home in 1921, and became a farmer in Tanneck near Weiler. Later he was the owner of the estate and riding school at Hedwigshof near Seeg, Allgäu. In the Spanish civil war, he fought on Franco's side. In the Second World War, he was an SS *Obersturmführer* at the eastern front. In 1933, became a member of the Prussian Academy of Arts, Poetry Section. Received the Dietrich Eckart Prize in 1935. Was a member of the Reich Culture Senate; was a national revolutionary and militant anti-communist. Journalistic novels about the war and prison camps based on his own experience.

Works: *Das große Grab: Sibirischer Roman* (N, 1920), *Korsakoff, Die Geschichte eines Heimatlosen* (N, 1926; retitled Hanka, 1952), *Das letzte Opfer* (N, 1928), *Die Armee hinter Stacheldraht. Das Sibirische Tagebuch* (Di, 1929 and 1950), *Zwischen Weiß und Rot: Die russische Tragödie 1919–1920* (N, 1930),

Wir rufen Deutschland: Heimkehr und Vermächtnis (N, 1932), *Die Namenlosen* (Dr, 1934), *Der letzte Traum. Eine deutsche Tragödie* (Dr, 1934), *Wo ist Deutschland* (Dr, 1934), *Die letzten Reiter* (N, 1935 and 1953), *Und Gott schweigt . . .? Bericht und Aufruf* (W, 1936), *Ein Erbhof im Algäu* (W, 1937), *Spanische Silhouetten: Tagebuch einer Frontreise* (Di, 1937), *Auf halbem Wege* (N, 1939), *Der Tod in Polen: Der volksdeutsche Passion* (W, 1940), *Panzerführer: Tagebuchblätter vom Frankreichfeldzug* (Di, 1941), *Wiedersehen mit Sowjetrußland: Tagebuch vom Ostfeldzug* (Di, 1942).

Eggers, Kurt

November 10, 1904, Berlin–August 12, 1943, killed in action near Bjelograd. Studied Lutheran theology, then became a National Socialist. Was considered the "most revolutionary poet" of the Hitler movement. In 1934, became the head of broadcasting of Middle-German Radio in Leipzig, then in Berlin. During the war, was *Obersturmbannführer* of the Waffen SS.

Works: *Das Spiel von Job dem Deutschen* (Dr, 1933), *Annaberg* (Dr, 1933), *Ulrich von Hutten* (Dr, 1933), *Deutsche Gedichte* (1934), *Das große Wandern* (*Thingspiel*, 1934), *Die wundersame Weite* (N, 1934), *Hutten: Roman eines Deutschen* (N, 1934), *Deutsches Bekenntnis* (P and Es, 1934), *Sturmsignale: Revolutionäre Sprechchöre* (Cp, 1934), *Tagebuch einer frohen Fahrt* (Di, 1934), *Revolution um Luther* (Dr, 1935), *Rom gegen Reich: Ein Kapitel deutscher Geschichte um Bismarck* (W, 1935), *Vom mutigen Leben und tapferen Sterben* (Es, 1935), *Herz im Osten, Roman Li Taipes des Dichters* (N, 1935), *Schicksalsbrüder: Gedichte und Gesänge* (P, 1935), *Die Bauern vor Meissen: Ein Spiel um das Jahr 1790* (Dr, 1936), *Die Geburt des Jahrtausends* (Es, 1936), *Tausend Jahre Kalkeldütt* (N, 1936), *Schüsse bei Krupp: Ein Spiel aus deutscher Dämmerung* (Dr, 1937), *Der Berg der Rebellen* (N, 1937), *Der deutsche Dämon* (P, 1937), *Das Kreuz der Freiheit* (Dr, 1937), *Der junge Hutten* (1938), *Die Heimat der Starken* (Es, 1938), *Feuer über Deutschland: Eine Huttenballade* (P, 1939), *Der Tanz aus der Reihe* (N, 1939), *Von Kampf und Krieg* (W, 1940), *Kamerad: Gedichte eines Soldaten* (P, 1940), *Der Gerechte* (Dr, 1940), *Der Krieg des Kriegers: Gedanken im Felde* (W, 1942), *Des Reiches Herrlichkeit* (P, 1943).

Euringer, Richard

April 4, 1891, Augsburg–August 29, 1953, Essen. Father: physician. Studied music. Pilot in the First World War; piloted a German expeditionary corps to the Sinai front in Syria in 1916. From 1917 to the end of the war, head of Bavarian Pilot School 4 in Lechfeld. After the war, studied art history and economics, then became a woodcutter, river driver, laborer, publisher's employee, and bank trainee in Stadtlohn, Westphalia. After 1933, became the head of the city library in Essen, and after 1936, a freelance writer in Asental near Salzuflen. Reich Culture Senator of the NSDAP. Dramatist, storywriter, radio play author, "dark" poet (von Wilpert), and cultural politician.

Works: *Der neue Midas* (Dr, 1920), *Das Kreuz im Kreise* (N, 1921), *Vagel Bunt* (Ss, 1923), *Fliegerschule 4* (N, 1929), *Die Arbeitslosen* (N, 1930), *Deutsche Passion* (Rp, 1933), *Dietrich Eckart: Leben eines deutschen Dichters* (Biog, 1935), *Die Fürsten fallen* (N, 1935), *Deutsche Mythe* (W, 1935), *Totentanz* (Dr, 1935), *Chronik einer deutschen Wandlung 1925–1935* (W, 1936), *Fahrten, Fernen, Landschaften* (Tb, 1936), *Die Gedichte* (P, 1937), *Vortrupp "Pascha"* (N, 1938), *Zug durch die Wüste* (N, 1938), *Die letzte Mühle* (S, 1939), *Der Seraster* (Biog, 1939), *Als Flieger in zwei Kriegen: Erlebnisse* (W, 1941), *Aphorismen* (1943).

Ewers, Hanns Heinz

November 3, 1871, Düsseldorf–June 12, 1943, Berlin. Father: painter. Studied law in Berlin, Geneva, and Bonn, and received his doctorate in law in 1894. *Referendar* in Neuß, Düsseldorf, and Saarbrücken. Freelance writer after 1897. In the cabaret "Überbrettl" from 1900 to 1901. World travels; interned in the U.S. from 1914 to 1921 because of his nationalistic war books. Early member of the NSDAP. With a commission from Hitler, wrote the Horst Wessel novel in 1932; the film based on the book was not released. In 1934, his books were banned and seized, ostensibly because of the occult, erotic-perverse influence of E. T. A. Hoffmann and Edgar Allan Poe.

Works: *Der gekreuzigte Tannhäuser* (S, 1901), *Die Macht der Liebe* (Dr, 1902), *E. A. Poe* (S, 1906), *Das Grauen* (Ss, 1908), *Die Bessessenen* (Ss, 1909), *Der Zauberlehrling* (N, 1909), *Grotesken* (W, 1910), *Alraune* (N, 1911, in 1922, the 238,000th copy printed), *Indien und ich* (Tb, 1911), *Vampir* (N, 1921), *Nachtmahr* (Ss, 1922), *Reiter in deutscher Nacht* (N, 1932), *Horst Wessel* (N, 1932), *Die schönsten Hände der Welt* (Ss, 1943).

Fallada, Hans (Rudolf Ditzen)

July 21, 1893, Greifswald–February 5, 1947, East Berlin. Father: regional court magistrate. After failing school, held a variety of occupations, including work on different estates in Saxony, Mecklenburg, West Prussia, and Silesia. Alcoholic and morphine addict; several stays in rehabilitation programs. Prison sentences in 1923 and 1926 for embezzlement. In 1929 married Anna Margarethe Issel. With his earnings from the successful novel *Kleiner Mann, was nun?* (1932), purchased a rural estate in Mecklenburg. After 1945, mayor of Feldberg for four months, then through mediation of Johannes R. Becher, freelance employee of the East German paper *Tägliche Rundschau*. As a representative of the new objectivity at the end of the Weimar Republic, one of the most popular authors; precise images of society. For the most part judged negatively by the Third Reich. Erects a memorial to the resistance movement among the workers with the novel *Jeder stirbt für sich allein* (1947).

Works: *Der junge Goedeschall* (N, 1920), *Anton und Gerda* (N, 1923), *Bauern, Bonzen und Bomben* (N, 1931), *Wer einmal aus dem Blechnapf frißt* (N, 1934), *Wir hatten mal ein Kind* (N, 1934), *Altes Herz geht auf die Reise* (N, 1936), *Wolf unter Wölfen* (N, 1937), *Der eiserne Gustav* (N, 1938), *Geschichten aus der Murkelei* (F, 1938), *Kleiner Mann, großer Mann — alles vertauscht* (N, 1940), *Der ungeliebte Mann* (N, 1940), *Damals bei uns daheim* (Aut, 1943).

Flake, Otto (Leo F. Kotta)

October 29, 1880, Metz–November 10, 1963, Baden-Baden. Studied *Germanistik,* philosophy, and art history in Strassbourg. In the First World War, worked with the political section of the army in Brussels. Traveled through Russia, England, and France. In 1927, expelled from Italy because of his sympathies with South Tyrol. Moved to Baden-Baden in 1928. Advocate for his Alsatian homeland, reconciliation of France and Germany, and European understanding (1924 essay collection *Zum guten Europäer*). Rejected by the Nazis because he represented individualistic and liberal European ideas, published in the *Weltbühne,* and because his second wife was half Jewish. "Of the great German storywriters of the first half of the century, . . . [he has been] the least researched" (*Neues Handbuch der deutschsprachigen Gegenwartsliteratur seit 1945,* 331). Storywriter, essayist, cultural philosopher, and culture critic.

Works: *Schritt für Schritt* (N, 1912), *Freitagskind* (N, 1913; 1928 as *Eine Kindheit*), *Horns Ring* (N, 1916), *Die Stadt des Hirns* (N, 1919), *Nein und Ja* (N, 1920), *Die moralische Idee* (Es, 1921), *Die Unvollendbarkeit der Welt* (Es, 1923), *Sommerroman* (N, 1927), *Es ist Zeit* (N, 1929), *Montijo oder die Suche nach der Nation* (N, 1931), *Hortense* (N, 1933), *Badische Chronik 1; Die junge Monthiver* (N, 1934). 2: *Anselm und Verena* (N, 1935), *Die Töchter Noras* (N, 1934), *Türkenlouis* (Bio, 1937), *Personen und Persönchen* (N, 1938), *Große Dramen des Barock* (Es, 1939), *Das Quintett* (N, 1943).

Flex, Walter

July 6, 1887, Eisenach–October 15, 1917, Oesel Island (killed in action). Father: Gymnasium teacher. In 1906 to 1910, studied *Germanistik* and history in Strasbourg and Erlangen; in 1910, received his Ph.D. Tutor for the Bismarck family in Varzin and Friedrichsruh. War volunteer and officer. Fatherland-oriented, idealistic poet of the First World War and storywriter of the war volunteer generation. Strong influence of the youth movement. A million copies of his war report *Wanderer zwischen beiden Welten* (1917) were printed. In the Third Reich, was considered the model of willingness to sacrifice and readiness to fight for the people and the fatherland.

Works: *Demetrius* (T, 1909), *Im Wechsel* (P, 1910), *Klaus von Bismarck* (T, 1913), *Zwölf Bismarcks* (Ss, 1913), *Das Volk in Eisen: Kriegsgesänge eines Kriegsfreiwilligen* (P, 1914), *Vom großen Abendmahl* (P, 1915), *Sonne und Schild* (P, 1915), *Im Felde zwischen Nacht und Tag* (P, 1917), *Wallensteins Antlitz* (Ss, 1918), *Wolf Eschenlohr* (N fragment, 1919), *Lothar* (Dr, 1920).

Frenssen, Gustav

October 19, 1863, Barlt, Holstein–April 11, 1945, Barlt. Father: cabinet-maker. Studied Lutheran theology in Tübingen, Berlin, and Kiel. From 1890 to 1902, pastor in Hennstedt and Hemme. After resigning from office because he rejected church dogma, he became a freelance writer in Meldorf, Blankensee, and Barlt. A national liberal in the Weimar Republic,; after 1932, National Socialist (without a Party membership book). After 1933, member of the German Academy of Literature. In 1933, received the Wilhelm Raabe Prize, and in 1938, the Goethe Medal for Art and Science. Received an honorary Ph.D. in theology in 1933. *Völkisch* German story-writer who combined northern myth with anti-Semitism and saw in Christianity a form of the Germanic master race.

Works: *Die Sandgräfin* (N, 1896), *Die drei Getreuen* (N, 1898), *Dorfpredigten* (Se, 1899–1902), *Jörn Uhl* (N, 1902), *Das Heimatfest* (Dr, 1903), *Hilligenlei* (N, 1905), *Das Leben des Heilandes* (W, 1907), *Bismarck* (Ep, 1914), *Der Pastor von Poggsee* (N, 1921), *Meino der Prahler* (N, 1933), *Von Saat und Ernte: Ein Buch vom Bauernleben* (W, 1933), *Geert Brügge* (Dr, 1934), *Die Witwe von Husum* (S, 1935), *Der Glaube der Nordmark* (W, 1936), *Der Weg unseres Volkes* (W, 1938), *Prinz Wilhelm* (Dr, 1938), *Lebensbericht* (Aut, 1940), *Der Landvogt von Sylt* (S, 1943).

Griese, Friedrich

October 2, 1890, Lehsten near Waren, Mecklenburg–June 1, 1975, Lübeck. Father: small farmer. Attended the teachers' seminar, teacher in Strahlendorf near Parchim and Kiel. From 1915 to 1916, war volunteer. Returned in 1935 as a freelance writer to his own farm near Parchim, Mecklenburg. Imprisoned in Neu-Strelitz prison in 1945/46, escaped in 1947 to Velgen near Uelzen. Moved to Lübeck in 1935. In 1934, a member of the Academy of Literature, and received the Lessing Prize of the City of Hamburg. In 1936, received the John Brinkman Prize, and in 1964, the Mecklenburg Culture Prize of the Mecklenburg *Heimat* Association. Influence of Hamsun; mythicizing and glorification of the "blood and soil aspects" of the farmer's life.

Works: *Feuer* (N, 1921), *Ur: Eine deutsche Passion* (N, 1922), *Das Korn rauscht* (Ss, 1923), *Die letzte Garbe* (Ss, 1927), *Der ewige Acker* (N, 1930), *Der Herzog* (N, 1931), *Mensch, aus Erde gemacht* (Dr, 1932), *Der Saatgang* (Ss, 1932), *Der Ruf der Erde* (S, 1933), *Das letzte Gesicht* (N, 1934), *Mein Leben: Von der Kraft der Landschaft* (Aut, 1934), *Der Ruf des Schicksals* (Ss, 1934), *Bäume im Wind* (N, 1937), *Das Kind des Torfmachers* (S, 1937), *Wind im Luch* (Co, 1937), *Fritz Reuter* (Bio, 1938), *Der heimliche König* (Dr, 1938) *Die Weißköpfe* (N, 1939), *Unsere Arbeit ist Glaube* (W, 1940), *Die Schafschur* (Co, 1944).

Grimm, Hans

March 22, 1875, Wiesbaden–September 27, 1959, Lippoldsberg on the Weser. Father: professor of law. Studied literature in Lausanne. Business training in England from 1895 to 1897; merchant in South Africa from 1897 to 1910. From 1911 to 1915, freelance writer. Studied political science in Munich and at the Colonial Institute in Hamburg. Military service after 1916, and freelance writer after 1918 at his estate in Klosterhaus in Lippoldsberg, the location of the Lippoldsberg Writers' Meeting for the Promotion of *völkisch* Literature (with W. Beumelburg, R. G. Binding, E. G. Kolbenheyer, H. Carossa, and others). Acquaintance with Hitler, Goebbels, and Hugenburg. Received an honorary Ph.D. from Göttingen in 1927, and the Goethe Medal in 1932. Became a senator of the Prussian Academy of the Arts, Literature Section, in 1932 and a member of the governing body of the Chamber of Literature. German national author, taking his material from the German colonies. Nazi supporter (without a Party membership book) who, in his best-known work, provided the Nazis with the catchword "a people without space."

Works: *Südafrikanische Novellen* (S, 1913), *Der Gang durch den Sand* (Ss, 1916), *Die Olewagen-Saga* (S, 1918), *Der Ölsucher von Duala* (Di, 1918), *Volk ohne Raum* (N, 1926 and 1956), *Das deutsche Südwesterbuch* (W, 1929), *Der Richter in der Karu* (Ss, 1930), *Der Schriftsteller und die Zeit* (Es, 1931), *Lüderitzland* (Ss, 1943; retitled *Geschichten aus Südwest-Afrika,* 1951), *Englische Rede: Wie ich den Engländer sehe* (Sp, 1939).

Hagelstange, Rudolf

January 14, 1912, Nordhausen, Harz–August 5, 1984, Hanau. Father: merchant. Studied *Germanistik* from 1931 to 1933 in Berlin; from 1936 to 1938, training as the editor of the feuilleton at the Nordhausen newspaper. Served from 1940 to 1945 as a soldier in France and Italy. Editor of soldiers' newspapers. After 1945, freelance writer in Nordhausen, Hemer in Westphalia, and Unteruhldingen on the Bodensee. Poet, storywriter, and essayist.

Works: *Ich bin die Mutter Cornelias* (S, 1939), *Es spannt sich der Bogen* (P, 1943), *Venezianisches Credo* (P, 1945).

Haushofer, Albrecht (Jürgen Werdenfels)

January 7, 1903, Munich–April 23, 1945, Moabit Prison in Berlin. Father: geo-politician who supported National Socialism. Attended the Theresia Gymnasium, then studied history and geography in Munich, receiving a Ph.D. in 1924 and working as a university professor's assistant in Berlin. Was general secretary of the Society for Geography from 1925 to 1937; extensive travel. Qualification as a university professor (*Habilitation*) in 1933; head of the department of geo-politics at the Institute of Politics in Berlin. Became a professor of political geography and geo-politics in Berlin in 1940. Until 1941, the foreign policy advisor to Rudolf Heß, then worked with the Foreign Office. Together with his intellectual friends, distanced himself from the National Socialist regime; connections to the Kreisau circle of resistance and to the Christian resistance. In 1941, removed from office and briefly arrested; ban placed on speaking. After the conspiracy of July 20, 1944, arrested once again and then convicted for his participation. Shortly before the end of the war, shot to death by a specially assigned SS detail at Moabit prison. Editor of scientific journals. His works, poems and dramas in classic style, are evidence of the middle-class, humanistic resistance of an intellectual. Christian convictions. The *Moabiter Sonette* can be considered some of the most impressive documents of the literary battle against National Socialism.

Works: *Abend im Herbst* (P, 1927), *Richtfeuer* (P, 1932), *Scipio* (Dr, 1934), *Sulla* (Dr, 1938), *Gastgeschenk* (P, 1938), *Augustus* (Dr, 1939), *Chinesische Legende* (Dr, 1939–1940; published in 1949), *Moabiter Sonette* (P, 1946), "Die Makadonen" (Dr manuscript), *Allgemeine politische Geographie und Geopolitik* (W, 1951).

Jelusich, Mirko

December 12, 1886, Semil near Prague–June 22, 1969, Vienna. Father: Croatian railway official. Mother: Sudeten German. Studied philosophy, Slavic languages, and Sanskrit in Vienna. Received his Ph.D. in 1912. Decorated Austrian artillery officer from 1914 to 1916; then an invalid. Scriptwriter after 1916, then bank official and journalist. After the war, founded the "Fighting Association for German Culture." In 1923, editor of the cultural section of the *German-Austrian Daily News;* promoted *Anschluß.* In 1938, briefly commissary head of the Burgtheater, then a freelance writer. Received the Grillparzer Prize of the City of Vienna in 1943. Arrested after 1945, and released in 1949. Poetry, dramas, and especially novels about great leaders.

Works: *Caesar* (N, 1929), *Don Juan* (N, 1931), *Cromwell* (N, 1933; Dr, 1934), *Hannibal* (N, 1934), *Der Löwe* (N, 1936), *Der Ritter* (N, 1937), *Der Soldat* (N, 1939; retitled *Scharnhorst,* 1953), *Der Traum vom Reich* (N, 1940), *Eherne Harfe* (P, 1942), *Margareth und der Fremde* (S, 1942), *Samurai* (Dr, 1943), *Die unvollständige Kompanie* (S, 1944).

Johst, Hanns

July 8, 1890, Seershausen, Saxony–November 23, 1978, Ruhpolding, Upper Bavaria. Father: elementary school teacher. Attended Gymnasium in Leipzig. In 1907, medical orderly in the Bodelschwingh institutions in Bethel. Studied medicine, philology, and art history in Leipzig, Vienna, Munich, and Berlin. Actor for a brief period. War volunteer in 1914. After 1918, freelance writer in Oberallmannshausen, Lake Starnberg. In 1933, Prussian state counselor; from 1935 to 1945, president of the Reich Chamber of Literature and president of the German Academy of Literature, member of the Reich Culture Senate, SS *Brigadeführer;* Received the NSDAP Prize for Art and Science in 1935; holder of the Wartburg Poet's Rose. Classified in 1949 as a "main perpetrator." Storywriter, poet, and especially a dramatist; from expressionism to National Socialism.

Works: *Der junge Mensch* (Dr, 1916), *Wegwärts* (P, 1916), *Der Einsame* (Grabbe Dr, 1917), *Rolandsruf* (P, 1919), *Der König* (Dr, 1920), *Mutter* (P, 1921), *Kreuzweg* (N, 1922), *Propheten* (Dr, 1922), *Wechsler und Händler* (Co, 1923), *Lieder der Sehnsucht* (P, 1924), *Marmelade* (Co, 1926), *Thomas Paine* (Dr, 1927), *Ich glaube! Bekenntnisse* (W, 1928), *So gehen sie hin* (N, 1930), *Die Torheit der Liebe* (N, 1931), *Ave Eva* (S, 1932), *Schlageter* (Dr, 1933), *Maske und Gesicht* (Tb, 1935), *Ruf des Reiches, Echo des Volkes! Eine Ostfahrt* (W, 1940), *Die Straße* (P, 1941), *Fritz Todt* (Requiem, 1943).

Jünger, Ernst

March 29, 1895, Heidelberg–February 17, 1998, Riedlingen. Father: apothecary. Joined the foreign legion in 1913. War volunteer in 1914; later a lieutenant and received the "ordre pour le merite." *Reichswehr* from 1919 to 1923, then studied zoology and philosophy in Leipzig and Naples. After 1925, freelance writer. Co-editor of right-oriented newspapers. In the Second World War, *Hauptmann* (army officer); on the staff of the military high commander of Paris. In 1944, discharged for being "unworthy of army service," but commander of a unit of volunteer forces. In 1945, prohibited from publishing for a short period. No official function in the Third Reich. From 1959 to 1971, co-editor of the journal *Antaios.* Numerous honors and prizes: in 1955 the Culture Prize of the City of Goslar, in 1959 the Culture Prize of the City of Bremen, in 1959 the Great Cross of Merit of the Federal Republic, in 1960 the Literature Prize of German Industry, in 1965 the

Immermann Prize, in 1970 the Freiherr von Stein Medal, in 1974 the Schiller Memorial Prize, and in 1982 the Goethe Prize of the City of Frankfurt am Main. Storywriter and essayist. Representative of "heroic realism" and "steel romanticism," of "magic realism" and of "universal conservatism."

Works: *In Stahlgewittern* (Di, 1920; N, 1922 and 1934), *Der Kampf als inneres Erlebnis* (Es, 1922), *Das Wäldchen 125. Eine Chronik aus den Grabenkämpfen 1918* (Rep, 1925), *Das abenteuerliche Herz* (Es, 1929, 1932, and 1938), *Die totale Mobilmachung* (Es, 1931), *Der Arbeiter* (W, 1932), *Blätter und Steine* (Es, 1934), *Afrikanische Spiele* (N, 1936), *Auf den Marmorklippen* (N, 1939), *Gärten und Straßen* (Di, 1942), *Myrdun: Briefe aus Norwegen* (Le, 1943).

Jünger, Friedrich Georg

September 1, 1898, Hanover–July 20, 1977, Überlingen. Father: apothecary. Brother of Ernst Jünger. Spent his childhood in Hanover and the Steinhuder Sea. Served in the First World War. Then studied law in Halle and Leipzig, received his doctorate in law, and practiced with the courts and as a private attorney. From the beginning of the 1930s on, a freelance writer in Berlin. From 1937, in Überlingen on the Bodensee. In Berlin, belonged to the circle around Alfred Bäumler and Ernst Niekisch. In the 1920s, national revolutionary (see *Aufmarsch des Nationalismus*). In 1934, temporarily prohibited from publishing because of the poem "Der Mohn"; after that, watched by the Gestapo. Editor of the journal *Scheidewege*. Primarily a poet, novelist, storywriter, and essayist, with a broad spectrum of themes. Universal education, conservative, and guided by the models of classicism. Also active as an editor and translator.

Works: *Aufmarsch des Nationalismus* (Es, 1926), *Gedichte* (P, 1934), *Der verkleidete Theseus* (Dr, 1934), *Der Krieg* (Ep, 1936), *Über das Komische* (Es, 1936), *Der Taurus* (P, 1937), *Der Missouri* (P, 1940), *Griechische Götter: Appolon-Pan-Dionysos* (Es, 1943), *Die Titanen* (Es, 1944).

Kästner, Erich

February 3, 1899, Dresden–July 29, 1974, Munich. Lower middle-class origins. Started elementary school in 1906; attended the teachers' seminar in Dresden to be trained as an elementary school teacher in 1913. In 1917, inducted into the military. After being discharged in 1918, completed his teacher's training at the teachers' seminar; received a wartime *Abitur* (final examination at Gymnasium) in 1919. Studied *Germanistik*, history, philosophy, and theater history in Leipzig, Rostock, and Berlin. Received his Ph.D. in 1925 with the dissertation topic "Die Erwiderungen auf Friedrichs des Großen Schrift 'De la littérature allemande.'" After 1922, editor of the *Neue*

Leipziger Zeitung; various additional activities. In 1927, moved to Berlin and worked there as a freelance writer. Worked on various newspapers and was a theater critic. In 1933, his books were burned, and he was prohibited from publishing in Germany (extended to other countries in 1942). Kästner published abroad at the beginning of the National Socialist period and otherwise worked in the film industry. After the end of the war in 1945, he settled in Munich. From 1945 to 1948, feuilleton editor of the *Neue Zeitung* and worked with the cabaret "Die Schublade" (The Drawer). After 1946, became the editor of the journal for young people, *Der Pinguin.* Active in the West German PEN, and became president of that organization in 1951. Received the Literature Prize of the City of Munich in 1956, the Büchner Prize in Darmstadt in 1957, and the Hans Christian Andersen Medal of the International Curatorium for Children's Books in 1960. His works are for the most part geared toward children; satire and humor. Often pointedly polemical, but celebration of traditional values reduces criticism.

Works: *Herz auf Taille* (P, 1928), *Emil und die Detektive* (Cb, 1928), *Lärm im Spiegel* (P, 1929), *Leben in dieser Zeit* (Rp, 1929), *Ein Mann gibt Auskunft* (P, 1930), *Fabian* (N, 1931), *Pünktchen und Anton* (Cb, 1931), *Der 35. Mai* (Cb, 1931), *Gesang zwischen den Stühlen* (P, 1932), *Das fliegende Klassenzimmer* (Cb, 1933), *Drei Männer im Schnee* (N, 1934), *Emil und die drei Zwillinge* (Cb, 1934), *Die verschwundene Miniatur* (N, 1934), *Doktor Erich Kästners lyrische Hausapotheke* (P, 1936), *Georg und die Zwischenfälle* (N, 1938; 1949 as *Der kleine Grenzverkehr*), *Münchhausen* (Fi, 1942), *Zu treuen Händen* (Co, 1943), *Bei Durchsicht meiner Bücher* (P, 1946).

Klepper, Jochen

March 22, 1903, Beuthen–December 11, 1942, Berlin. Father: pastor. Studied theology without finishing. In 1927, editor for the Lutheran press association; in 1931, worked at Berlin radio, but let go because he was married to the Jewish woman Johanna Stein. Dismissed from Ullstein Publishers in 1935 for the same reason. Excluded from the Reich Chamber of Literature in 1937 and from the army in 1941 for being "related to Jews." Committed suicide in 1942 with his wife and stepdaughter, who were threatened with deportation.

Works: *Kahn der fröhlichen Leute* (N, 1933), *Der Vater* (N, 1937), *Kyrie* (Sg, 1939), *Der christliche Roman* (Es, 1940).

Kolbenheyer, Erwin Guido

December 30, 1878, Budapest–April 12, 1962, Munich. Father: Hungarian German ministerial architect. Studied natural history, philology, and psychology in Vienna from 1900 to 1905; Ph.D. in 1905. In the First World War, leader of a prisoner-of-war camp. From 1919 on, freelance writer.

Received the Stifter Prize in 1926; made a member of the Prussian Academy of Writers in 1938. Received the Goethe Medal in 1932, the Goethe Prize of the City of Frankfurt in 1937, the Eagle Shield of the German Reich in 1938, the Königsberg Kant Medal in 1941, an honorary degree in medicine from Tübingen, and the Grillparzer Prize of the City of Vienna in 1943. Member of the NSDAP; prohibition on writing from 1945 to 1950. Classified in 1948 as "implicated," then in 1950 as "less implicated." Received the Sudeten German Culture Prize in 1958. There is a Kolbenheyer Society for the promotion of his works. Philosopher ("Die Bauhütte"), poet, dramatist, and storywriter; primarily historical in the manner of antiquity.

Works: *Giordano Bruno* (T, 1903; retitled *Heroische Leidenschaften*, 1929), *Amor Dei* (Spinoza N, 1908), *Meister Joachim Pausewang* (N, 1910), *Montsalvasch* (N, 1912), *Paracelsus* (N trilogy: *Die Kindheit des Paracelsus,* 1917, *Das Gestirn des Paracelsus,* 1922, and *Das Dritte Reich des Paracelsus,* 1926; 3 volumes, 1927–1928), *Der Dornbusch brennt* (P, 1922), *Die Bauhütte: Elemente einer Metaphysik der Gegenwart* (W, 1925), *Das Lächeln der Penaten* (N, 1927), *Heroische Leidenschaften* (T, 1929), *Das Gesetz in dir* (Dr, 1931), *Jagt ihn — ein Mensch* (Dr, 1931), *Unser Befreiungskampf und die deutsche Dichtkunst* (Es, 1932), *Deutsches Bekenntnis* (poetry for speaking choruses, 1933), *Gregor und Heinrich* (Dr, 1934), *Das gottgelobte Herz* (N, 1938), *Die Bauhütte: Grundlage einer Metaphysik der Gegenwart* (W, 1939), *Vox humana* (P, 1940), *Das Geistesleben in seiner volksbiologischen Bedeutung* (Sp, 1942), *Menschen und Götter* (Dr, 1944).

Krauss, Werner

June 7, 1900, Stuttgart–August 28, 1976, Berlin (German Democratic Republic). Father: literary scholar. Studied literature and other subjects in Munich, Madrid, and Berlin. Received his Ph.D. in 1929 and his qualification as a university professor (*Habilitation*) in Marburg from Erich Auerbach (*Die ästhetischen Grundlagen des spanischen Schäferromans*) in 1931; became a professor of romance languages there in 1935. In 1940, sent to the training company for interpreters in Berlin. Contact with the resistance group "Red Orchestra." In detention from 1942 to 1945. After 1945, a professor for romance languages again, first in Marburg, then in Leipzig; retired in 1965. Krauss was one of the leading German experts in romance languages and literatures. Until 1948, he was the co-editor, with Karl Jaspers and Alfred Weber, of Dolf Sternberger's journal *Die Wandlung*. According to Franz Mehring, "the most important Marxist literary scholar" (*Literatur Lexikon*).

Works: *Corneille als politischer Dichter* (1936), *Die Lebenslehre Gracians* (1946). His only work of *belles lettres,* the novel *PLN: Die Passionen der halykonischen Seele,* was written from 1943 to 1944 in prison and was published in 1946 in Frankfurt am Main and in 1948 in the Soviet Zone of Occupation (new edition in 1981).

Kuckhoff, Adam

August 30, 1887, Aachen–August 5, 1943, Plötzensee. Father: needle manufacturer. Studied law, literature, and philosophy in Freiburg in Breisgau, Munich, Heidelberg, Berlin, and Halle. Was awarded his Ph.D. in 1912 with a dissertation on "Schiller's Theory of the Tragic to the Year 1784." Actor, director, dramatic advisor to the theaters at the front, in Krefeld, Frankfurt am Main, and Berlin; also a dramatist and filmmaker. Collaborator on the conservative journal *Die Tat* of Eugen Diederichs Publishers. In the Third Reich, freelance reader for German Publishers (previously Ullstein). After 1933, member in the anti-fascist resistance associated with the Harnack-Schultze-Boysen group ("Red Orchestra"); arrested in September of 1942 and executed on August 5, 1943.

Works: Countless articles, essays, and small prose texts for newspapers and journals (for example, "Das neue Theater. Gedanken zum Theater," in *Die Tat,* No. 3, 1928; "Das Streu-Engelchen zu Aachen," in the *Frankfurter Zeitung* of October 29, 1925). Editor of a popular edition of Büchner's works (1927), *Der Deutsche von Bayencourt* (Dr, written in 1915 with the title *Rufendes Land,* printed in 1915, and staged for the first time in 1918; published as a novel in 1937), *Disziplin* (Co, 1923), *Zwergnase* (children's play, written with his first wife Mie Paulun, 1919 and 1929), *Scherry* (S, 1931), *Wetter veränderlich* (Co, 1932, with Eugen Gürster), *Der Schieber* (translation from the French *K Turcaret,* 1933), *Rosen und Vergißmeinicht* (Co, 1933, with Otto Zoff), *Till Eulenspiegel* (Dr, 1941), *Strogany und die Vermißten* (N, 1941, with Peter Tarin).

Lange, Horst

October 6, 1904, Liegnitz, Lower Silesia–July 6, 1971, Munich. As a developing painter, member of the Bauhaus in Weimar, then studied art history in Breslau and Berlin. After interrupting his studies in 1931, worked as a radio and press journalist in Berlin. Member of the "Kolonne" circle around Martin Raschke. Married the poetess Oda Schaefer in 1933. Soldier from 1941 to 1945. Author of poems, radio plays, and prose works. Zuckmayer called his story "Die Leuchtkugel" (1944) the best German prose work of the Second World War. His epic main work, the novel *Schwarze Weide,* set in the vicinity of Liegnitz and provided with demonic overtones, appeared in 1937. His war diary appeared in 1979, edited by Hans Dieter Schäfer, who counts Lange among the "non-fascist authors of the 'young generation'" (in Denkler and Prümm, *Die deutsche Literatur im Dritten Reich.*)

Works: *Nachtgesang* (P, 1928), *Die Heimkkehr* (Rp, 1933), *Die Gepeinigten* (S, 1933), *Spuk in den zwölf Nächten* (Rp, 1934), *Der Zauberer Tepe* (Rp, 1934), *Der Nächtliche* (Rp, 1935), *Was kostet die Hölle?* (Rp, 1936), *Gesang hinter den Zäunen* (P, 1938), *Auf dem östlichen Ufer* (Ss, 1939) *Ulanenpatrouille* (S, 1940), *Das Irrlicht* (N, 1943).

Langenbeck, Curt

June 20, 1906, Elberfeld–August 5, 1953, Munich. Father: manufacturer. Training in his father's silk factory from 1925 to 1929, as well as in Switzerland, France, and the United States. Studied literature, theater, history, art history, and philosophy in Cologne, Freiburg in Breisgau, and Vienna from 1931 to 1933. Dramatic advisor at the Kassel State Theater from 1935 to 1938; after 1938, head dramatic advisor at the Munich State Theater. After 1945, freelance writer. Received the Immermann Prize in 1939 and the Reinish Prize for Literature in 1940. Dramatist, storywriter, and theoretician. Made efforts to restore the German historical tragedy "from the spirit of the times" in the tradition of the Greek tragedy.

Works: *Alexander* (T, 1934), *Heinrich IV* (T, 1936), *Der getreue Johannes: Eine Dichtung für die Bühne* (Dr, 1937), *Der Hochverräter* (T, 1938), *Das Schwert* (T, 1940), *Tragödie und Gegenwart* (Sp, 1940), *Wiedergeburt des Dramas aus dem Geist der Zeit* (Sp, 1940), *Frau Eleonore* (S, 1941), *Treue* (Dr, 1944).

Langgässer, Elisabeth (Elisabeth Hoffmann, nee Langgässer)

February 23, 1899, Alzey–July 25, 1950, Rheinzabern. Father: Jew and architect. Schooling in Darmstadt; *Abitur* (final examination at Gymnasium) in 1918, then pedagogical training at the teachers' seminar and various stints of practice teaching. Teacher at various Hessian schools from 1921 to 1928. After 1920, publication of poems and stories. Lecturer at the Anna von Gierke Women's School in Berlin from 1929 to 1930. From November of 1930 on, freelance writer. Received the Literature Prize of the Society of German Women Citizens in 1931 for the still unpublished story "Proserpina." In 1934, worked in children's radio for Berlin Radio. Married Wilhelm Hoffmann in 1935. In 1936, excluded from the Reich Chamber of Literature and was thus prohibited from practicing her profession, as Langgässer was half Jewish. In 1941, her daughter Cordelia from an earlier relationship with Hermann Heller had to wear the Jewish star because she was a "three-quarters Jew." In 1942, the first signs of multiple sclerosis. In 1943, narrowly escaped being arrested by the Gestapo. In 1944, her daughter Cordelia was taken away to Auschwitz, and Langässer was obligated to do forced labor service. In 1945, her residence was destroyed by bombing attacks. In 1946, Langgässer learned that her daughter Cordelia was alive.

In 1947, travel and first German Writers' Congress in Berlin. In 1948, moved to Rheinzabern. Awarded the Georg Büchner Prize posthumously in 1950. Her works are characterized by the Catholicism-inspired representation of a dualism between the Christian story of salvation and pagan, mystical events in nature. Also active as an editor.

Works: *Der Wendekreis des Lammes: Ein Hymnus der Erlösung* (P, 1924), *Triptychon des Teufels* (Ss, 1932), *Grenze: Besetztes Gebiet: Ballade eines Landes* (N, 1932), *Proserpina* (S, 1933), *Frauen als Wegbereiter: Amalie Dietrich* (Rp, 1933), *Der Sturz durch die Erdzeitalter* (Rp, 1933), *Flandrischer Herbst* (Rp, 1933), *Sterne über dem Palatin* (Rp, 1933), *Ahnung und Gegenwart* (Rp, 1934), *Der Gang durch das Ried* (N, 1936), *Die Tierkreisgedichte* (P, 1936), *Rettung am Rhein* (Ss, 1938), *Ich blase drei Federn in den Wind* (Le, 1945), *Das unauslöschliche Siegel* (N, 1946).

Lersch, Heinrich

September 12, 1889, Mönchgladbach–June 18, 1936, Remagen. Father: kettlemaker. Lersch was initially also a kettlemaker and spent his apprenticeship years traveling through Germany, Switzerland, Austria, Italy, Holland, and Belgium. Served in the First World War and was wounded. Then again worked in his father's kettlemaking business. A lung disease forced him to give up physical labor in 1925. He then made his living as a freelance writer. From 1932 on, lived in Bodendorf on the Ahr. Lersch was considered a "worker poet." On one hand, lamented the situation of the proletariat, and on the other, also saw labor as a challenge to the productive capabilities of the human being. Social, socialist, communist, anarchist, religious, national, and mythical elements come together in his works. The poem "Soldatenabschied" first made him known; national enthusiasm for war. Later adopted the National Socialist formulas of "people" and "community"; the Nazis had a positive attitude toward him. In 1933, invited to join the Prussian Academy of Writers. In 1935, received the Reinish Literature Prize. An edition of his works as late as 1944.

Works: *Abglanz des Lebens* (P, 1914), *Die heilige Not* (P, 1915), *Herz, aufglühe dein Blut* (P, 1916), *Vergiß du deines Bruders Not: Arbeitergedichte* (P, 1917), *Die arme Seele: Gedichte vom Leid des Krieges* (P, 1917), *Deutschland: Lieder und Gesänge von Volk und Vaterland* (P, 1918), *Das Land* (P, 1918), *Der preußische Musketier* (P, 1918), *Hauptmann und Soldaten* (P, 1919), *Mensch im Eisen: Gedichte von Volk und Werk* (P, 1924), *Stern und Amboß* (P, 1927), *Capri* (P, 1927), *Der grüßende Wald* (Ss, 1927), *Hammerschläge* (N, 1930), *Wir Werkleute* (Ss and P, 1934), *Die Pioniere von Eilenburg: Roman aus der Frühzeit der deutschen Arbeiterbewegung* (N, 1934), *Mit brüderlicher Stimme* (P, 1934), *Mut und Übermut* (S, 1934), *Deutschland muß leben!* (P, 1935), *Im Pulsschlag der Maschinen* (Ss, 1935).

Loerke, Oskar

March 13, 1884, Jungen, West Prussia–February 24, 1941, Berlin-Frohnau. Father: brick-works and farm owner. Spent his childhood and youth in the country. Attended the Gymnasium in Graudenz, then initially worked in agriculture and forestry. From 1903 to 1907, studied philosophy, *Germanistik*, music, and history in Berlin. After the appearance of the story *Vineta* (1907), made his living as a freelance writer. Received the Kleist Prize and a travel stipend in 1913. In 1914, dramatic advisor for a theater publisher. After 1917 until his death, reader for the publisher S. Fischer. Very active as a reviewer and editor. In 1926, a member of the senate, and in 1928 secretary of the Literature Section of the Prussian Academy of the Arts. Expelled from the academy by the Nazis in 1933. Lived withdrawn during the period of fascism. Loerke began with prose, but was especially significant as a poet and for the development of poetic style in the postwar period. Themes were especially nature but also poetry about the big city, musical themes, travel themes, introspective observations, and philosophical reflections; in the late phase somewhat resigned. In terms of form, predominantly rhymed poems with a fixed stanzaic form, in part with the character of songs.

Works: *Vineta* (S, 1907), *Franz Pfinz* (N, 1909), *Der Turmbau* (S, 1910), *Wanderschaft* (P, 1911), *Gedichte* (P, 1915), *Gedichte* (P, 1916; 1929, retitled *Pansmusik*), *Das Goldbergwerk* (N, 1919), *Die Chimärenreiter* (N, 1919), *Der Prinz und der Tiger* (S, 1920), *Der Oger* (N, 1921), *Pompeji* (P, 1921), *Die heimliche Stadt* (P, 1921), *Der längste Tag* (P, 1926), *Formprobleme der Lyrik* (Es, 1929), *Atem der Erde* (P, 1930), *Der Silberdistelwald* (G 1934), *Das unsichtbare Reich* (Es, 1935), *Das alte Wagnis des Gedichtes* (Ss, 1935), *Vom Reimen* (Ss, 1935), *Der Wald der Welt* (P, 1936), *Meine sieben Gedichtbücher* (Es, 1936), *Anton Bruckner: Ein Charakterbild* (Es, 1938), *Magische Verse* (P, 1938), *Der Steinpfad* (P, 1938–1941), *Kärntner Sommer* (P, 1939), *Hausfreunde: Charakterbilder* (Es, 1939), *Die Abschiedshand* (P, 1949).

Miegel, Agnes

March 9, 1879, Königsberg–October 26, 1964, Bad Salzuflen. Father: merchant in Königsberg. Attended boarding schools in Weimar (1894–1896) and Bristol (1902). Study trips to France and Italy; training as a teacher and journalist in Berlin. From 1920 to 1926, editor and directress of the feuilleton of the *Ostpreußische Zeitung* in Königsberg. Received an honorary doctorate from the University of Königsberg in 1924. After 1927, freelance writer there. In 1933, invited to join the "reorganized" Academy of Writers. In 1944, flight from Königsberg to a Danish camp. After 1948, in Bad Nenndorf and Bad Salzuflen; did not receive permission to publish again until 1949. After 1956, "honorarium" for life from the City of Hameln.

Received numerous literature prizes: the Kleist Prize in 1913, the Herder Prize in 1936, the Königsberg Literature Prize in 1939, the Goethe Prize of the City of Frankfurt in 1940, the Honorary Medal of the East German Cultural Council in 1957, and the Literature Prize of the Bavarian Academy of Fine Arts in 1959. Poetry and stories characterized by feelings for the homeland (at times nationalistically exaggerated) and Christian philosophy. Ties to the neo-romantic circle around Börries von Münchhausen.

Works: *Gedichte* (P, 1901), *Balladen und Lieder* (P, 1907), *Gedichte und Spiele* (P, 1920), *Herbstgesang* (P, 1923), *Heimat, Lieder und Balladen* (P, 1926), *Geschichten aus Alt-Preußen* (Ss, 1926), *Die schöne Malone* (S, 1926), *Gesammelte Gedichte* (P, 1927), *Die Auferstehung des Cyriakus* (S, 1928), *Dorothee Heimgekehrt* (Ss, 1931), *Die Fahrt der sieben Ordensbrüder* (S, 1933), *Der Geburtstag* (S, 1933), *Kirchen im Ordensland* (S, 1933), *Gang in die Dämmerung* (S, 1934), *Die Schlacht von Rudau* (Dr, 1934), *Weichnachtspiel* (Dr, 1934), *Deutsche Balladen* (P, 1935), *Kathrinchen kommt nach Hause* (S, 1936), *Noras Schicksal* (S, 1936), *Das Bernsteinherz* (S, 1937), *Meine alte Lina* (S, 1938), *Werden und Werk* (Aut, 1938), *Und die geduldige Demut der treuesten Freunde* (P, 1938), *Frühe Gedichte* (P, 1939), *Im Ostwind* (S, 1940), *Wunderliches Weben* (S, 1940), *Ostland* (P, 1940), *Die gute Ernte* (S, 1942), *Mein Bernsteinland und meine Stadt* (S, 1944).

Möller, Eberhard Wolfgang

January 6, 1906, Berlin–January 1, 1971, Bietigheim, Württemberg. Father: sculptor. Studied philosophy, literature and theater, music, and history in Berlin. In 1933, dramatic advisor in Königsberg. In 1934, theater expert at the Propaganda Ministry; member of the Reich Culture Senate and area leader on the staff of the Reich youth leadership. In the war, reporter for the Waffen SS; from 1945 to 1948, incarcerated. Friendship with Reich Dramatic Advisor Rainer Schlösser and Reich Youth Leader Baldur von Schirach. Author of the "Leader Book" of the Hitler Youth. Brought about the Paul Ernst renaissance and made efforts on behalf of the *Thingspiel* and National Socialist drama.

Works: *Bauern* (Dr, 1925), *Aufbruch in Kärnten* (Dr, 1928), *Douaumont* (Dr, 1929), *Kalifornische Tragödie* (Dr, 1929), *Panamaskandal* (Dr, 1930), *Rothschild siegt bei Waterloo* (Dr, 1934), *Die höllische Reise* (Dr, 1933), *Die Insterburger Ordensfeier: Heroldspiel von der Überwindung des Todes* (Dr, 1934), *Das Südender Weihnachtspiel* (Dr, 1934), *Die erste Ernte* (P, 1934), *Das Schloß in Ungarn* (N, 1935), *Berufung der Zeit: Kantaten und Chöre* (P, 1935), *Briefe der Gefallenen: Festliches Vortragspiel vom Krieg* (Le, Dr, 1935), *Volk und König* (Dr, 1935), *Das Frankenburger Würfelspiel* (Dr, 1936), *Der Sturz des Ministers* (Dr, 1937), *Der Untergang Karthagos* (Dr, 1941), *Das brüderliche Jahr* (P, 1941 and 1943), *Das Opfer* (Dr, 1941).

Molo, Walter von

June 14, 1880, Sternberg, Moravia–October 27, 1958, Murnau. Belonged to old German imperial nobility. Grew up in Vienna. After graduating from the Technical University of Vienna, became an engineer for Siemens and Halske, and was at the Patent Office until 1913, then became a freelance writer in Vienna and Berlin. Resigned as the president of the Literature Section of the Prussian Academy of the Arts in 1930. After the seizure of power in the spring of 1933, withdrew from Berlin and public life to Murnau in Upper Bavaria. After the war, defender of the Inner Emigration, especially in a letter to Thomas Mann. Storywriter, essayist, dramatist, and poet; religious and historical material. His historical, national themes put him close to *völkisch*-national views, but von Molo guarded himself against being taken in.

Works: four-volume Schiller novel: *Ums Menschentum* (1912), *Titanenkampf* (1913), *Die Freiheit* (1914), *Den Sternen zu* (1916); Romantrilogie: *Ein Volk wacht auf* (Vol. 1 *Fredericus,* 1918; Vol. 2, *Luise,* 1919; Vol. 3, *Das Volk,* 1921; appeared in 1924 as one volume called *Der Roman meines Volkes*); *Im ewigen Licht* (N, 1926); *Legende vom Herrn* (N, 1927); *Mensch Luther* (N, 1928); *Die Scheidung* (N, 1929); *Zwischen Tag und Traum* (Sp and Es, 1930); *Ein Deutscher ohne Deutschland* (N, 1931); *Holunder in Polen* (N, 1932); *Friedrich List* (Dr, 1934); *Der kleine Held: Geschichte meiner Jugend* (Aut, 1934); *Eugenio von Savoy* (N, 1936); *Geschichte einer Seele: Kleist Roman* (N, 1938); *Lyrisches Tagebuch* (Di, 1943).

Reck-Malleczewen, Friedrich

August 11, 1884, Malleczewen Estate, East Prussia–February 17, 1945, Dachau Concentration Camp. Father: estate owner. Pursued an officer's career, then studied medicine in Königsberg, earning his degree in medicine in 1911. Extended trip to South and North America. From 1913 on, freelance writer in Passing near Munich and the Poing Estate near Truchtlaching, Chiemgau. Rejected the Third Reich because of his monarchist, feudalistic point of view. Arrested in 1944, and died of typhoid in the concentration camp. Journalist and author of bestsellers.

Works: *Frau Übersee* (N, 1918), *Die Dame aus New York* (N, 1921), *Von Räubern, Henkern und Soldaten: Als Stabsoffizier in Rußland von 1917 bis 1919* (W, 1924), *Sif* (N, 1926), *Die Siedlung Unitrusttown* (N, 1925), *Bomben auf Monte Carlo* (N, 1930, filmed with Hans Albers and Heinz Rühmann), *Acht Kapitel für die Deutschen* (Es, 1934), *Ein Mannsbild namens Prack* (N, 1935), *Bockelson: Geschichte eines Massenwahns* (N, 1937), *Charlotte Corday: Geschichte eines Attentats* (N, 1938), *Der Richter* (N, 1940), *Diana Pontecorvo* (N, 1944), *Tagebuch eines Verzweifelten* (Di, posthumously, 1947).

Rehberg, Hans

December 25, 1901, Posen–June 20, 1963, Duisburg. Lived for a long time in Pieskow, Mark Brandenburg, then from 1941 on in Silesia. Friendship with Gerhard Hauptmann. Member of the NSDAP; for a time, official responsible for culture in the *Gau* Berlin. Enjoyed the protection of Gründgens, H. Johst, and Goebbels. In fleeing, lost all his manuscripts. In the Third Reich, a gifted but controversial dramatist, especially because of his Prussian dramas, which did not project the heroic image of the Prussian king demanded by the Nazis but were still very successful. After the war, he devoted himself primarily to the subjects of Maria Stuart and the Atrides.

Works: *Cecil Rhodes* (Dr, 1939), *Johannes Kepler* (Dr, 1933), *Der große Kurfürst* (Dr, 1934), *Der Tod und das Reich* (Dr, 1934), *Friedrich I* (Co, 1935), *Friedrich Wilhelm I* (Dr, 1935), *Kaiser und König* (Dr, 1937), *Der siebenjährige Krieg* (Dr, 1938), *Isabella, Königin von Spanien* (Dr, 1938), *Wallenstein* (Dr, 1941), *Gaius Julius Caesar* (Dr, 1942), *Heinrich und Anna* (Dr, 1942), *Karl V* (Dr, 1943), *Wölfe* (Dr, 1940).

Schauwecker, Franz

March 26, 1890, Hamburg–May 31, 1964, Günzburg. Father: senior customs inspector. Studied *Germanistik* and history in Munich, Berlin, and Göttingen. Soldier and company leader in the First World War; wounded. After the war, various professions, then freelance writer in Berlin and Günzburg. Especially stories and plots based on his war experiences.

Works: *Im Todesrachen* (N, 1919; retitled *Frontbuch,* 1927), *Weltgericht* (S, 1920), *Ghavati* (N, 1920), *Hilde Roxh* (N, 1922; retitled *Die Geliebte,* 1930), *Aufbruch der Nation* (N, 1930), *Der Spiegel* (P, 1930), *Die Entscheidung* (Dr, 1933), *Der Panzerkreuzer* (N, 1939), *Der weiße Reiter* (N, 1944).

Schenzinger, Karl Aloys

May 28, 1886, Neu-Ulm–July 4, 1962, Prien on the Chiemsee. Apprenticed as an apothecary, then studied medicine in Freiburg, Munich, and Kiel. Physician in Hanover; from 1923 to 1925 in New York. From 1928 on, freelance writer; his *Hitlerjunge Quex* (1932) was one of the most successful National Socialist youth novels.

Works: *Hinter Hamburg* (N, 1929), *Man will uns kündigen* (N, 1931), *Anilin* (N, 1936), *Metall* (N, 1939).

Schneider, Reinhold

May 13, 1903, Baden-Baden–April 6, 1958, Freiburg in Breisgau. Father: hotel owner. Spent his youth in Baden-Baden. Finished his *Abitur* (final examination at Gymnasium) in 1921. Business employee in Dresden. After a suicide attempt in 1922, extended travel abroad. From 1932 to 1937, freelance writer in Potsdam, then in Freiburg. Negative attitude toward National Socialism. Ties to the Kreisau circle of the German resistance. After 1940, no longer had approval to print his works. In 1945, the charge of high treason against him was not brought to trial because the war ended. After that, one of the most important representatives of the intellectual new beginning, but was soon disappointed in the political development of the new Germany. Schneider primarily wrote essays on culture, but also sonnets, stories, and dramas. Thematic focus is the Middle Ages. In the fifties, especially autobiographical writings.

Works: *Das Leiden des Camoës oder Untergang und Vollendung der portugiesischen Macht* (Es, 1930), *Portugal* (Tb, 1931), *Philipp II* (C, 1931), *Das Erdbeben* (S, 1932), *Geschichte eines Nashorns* (S, 1932), *Fichte, der Weg zur Nation* (Es, 1932), *Die Hohenzollern* (Es, 1933), *Auf Wegen deutscher Geschichte* (Es, 1934), *Der Tröster* (S, 1934 and 1943), *Kaiser Lothars Krone* (Es, 1937), *Las Casas von Karl V* (S, 1938), *Corneilles Ethos in der Ära Ludwigs XIV* (Es, 1939), *Sonette* (P, 1939), *Macht und Gnade* (Es, 1940), *Das Vaterunser* (S, 1941), *Der Abschied der Frau von Chantal* (S, 1942), *Der Kreuzweg* (S, 1942), *Der Dichter vor der Geschichte* (Hölderlin, Novalis) (S, 1942), *Stimme des Abendlandes* (Es, 1944), *Weltreich und Gottesreich* (Es, 1946), *Apokalypse* (P, 1946).

Schumann, Gerhard

February 14, 1911, Eßlingen on the Neckar–July 29, 1995, Bodmann. Father: high school teacher. Attended the Latin school in Ingelfingen and Lutheran theological seminars in Schöntal and Urach. After 1930, studied *Germanistik* in Tübingen. Was the National Socialist student leader and an SA *Oberführer* there. During the Third Reich, was the head dramatic advisor at the Württemberg State Theater. Member of the Reich Culture Senate, of the SA cultural circle, and of the Presidial Council of the Reich Chamber of Literature. Received the Swabian Poets' Prize in 1935 and the National Book Prize in 1936. After 1945, was the business manager of the European Book Club in Stuttgart. Founded Hohenstaufen Publishers in Eßlingen and moved with it to Bodmann on the Bodensee. Representative of Nazi literature of the blood-and-soil type. Predominantly poetry.

Works: *Ein Weg führt ins Ganze* (P, 1933), *Fahne und Stern* (P, 1934), *Die Lieder vom Reich* (P, 1935), *Siegendes Leben* (Dr and P, 1935), *Wir aber sind das Korn* (P, 1936), *Heldische Feier* (choral work, 1936), *Wir dürfen dienen* (P, 1937), *Schau und Tat* (P, 1938), *Volk ohne Grenzen* (cantata, 1938), *Entscheidung* (Dr, 1938), *Bewährung* (P, 1940), *Die Lieder vom Krieg* (P, 1941), *Gesetz wird zu Gesang* (P, 1943), *Gudruns Tod* (Dr, 1942).

Seidel, Ina

September 15, 1885, Halle–October 2, 1974, Ebenhausen near Munich. Father: physician; artistically gifted family. Grew up in Braunschweig, Marburg, and Munich. In 1907, married her cousin Heinrich Wolfgang Seidel, a writer and pastor. Lived in Berlin and Eberswalde, and after 1934 in Starnberg. In addition to writing, she was also an editor and translator. Poetry closely related to Romanticism, with feelings and reverence for nature. Narrative prose focuses in part on realms of experience of children and adolescents as well as of women and mothers. Christian elements, Protestant ethics, and religiously oriented, educated middle class.

Works: *Gedichte* (P, 1914), *Familie Mutz* (P, 1914), *Neben der Trommel her* (P, 1915), *Das Haus zum Monde* (N, 1917), *Weltinnigkeit* (P, 1919), *Hochwasser* (Ss, 1920), *Das Labyrinth: Ein Lebenslauf aus dem 18. Jahrhundert* (N, 1924), *Sterne der Heimkehr* (N, 1923), *Neue Gedichte* (P, 1927), *Brömseshof* (N, 1928), *Die Brücke* (Ss, 1929), *Der volle Kranz* (P, 1929), *Der vergrabene Schatz* (Ss, 1929), *Das Wunschkind* (N, 1930), *Das Geheimnis* (Ss, 1931), *Die tröstliche Begegnung* (P, 1932), *Die Entwicklung der Friedensbewegung in Europa* (Es, 1932), *Der Weg ohne Wahl* (N, 1933), *Dichter, Volkstum und Sprache* (Es, 1934), *Luise, Königin von Preußen* (Biog, 1934), *Das russische Abenteuer und ausgewählte Gedichte* (P, 1935), *Meine Kindheit und Jugend* (Aut, 1935), *Spuk in des Wassermanns Haus* (Ss, 1936), *Gesammelte Gedichte* (G, 1937), *Lennacker* (N, 1938), *Unser Freund Peregrin* (S, 1940), *Gedichte* (P, 1941), *Achim von Arnim* (Biog, 1944), *Bettina* (Biog, 1944), *Clemens Brentano* (Biog, 1944).

Stehr, Hermann

February 16, 1864, Habelschwerdt, Silesia–September 11, 1940, Oberschreiberhau, Silesia. Father: saddler. Attended the preparatory institute in Landeck. Elementary school teacher from 1887 on; because of his religious views, disciplined and transferred to far-removed villages. After 1915, freelance writer in Warmbrunn, Riesengebirge; after 1926 in Schreiberau. Received an honorary doctorate, the Goethe Prize in 1933, and the Eagle's Shield of the German Reich in 1934. Influence of naturalism and Silesian mysticism. Mystical seeker of God. Storywriter, and also a dramatist and poet. Declared his loyalty to National Socialism. H. Johst viewed him as the "greatest living German poet"; the Hermann Stehr Society promotes his memory.

Works: *Auf Leben und Tod* (Ss, 1898), *Der Schindelmacher* (S, 1899), *Leonore Griebel* (N, 1900), *Geschichten aus dem Mandelhause* (N, 1913; retitled *Das Mandelhaus,* 1953), *Der Heiligenhof* (N, 2 volumes, 1918), *Lebensbuch* (P, 1920), *Peter Brindeisener* (N, 1924), *Das Märchen vom deutschen Herzen* (Ss, 1926), *Das Geschlecht der Maechler* (N trilogy: *Nathanael Maechler,*

1929; *Die Nachkommen,* 1933; *Damian oder Das große Schermesser,* 1944),
Mythen und Märchen (F, 1929), *Meister Cajetan* (S, 1931), *Mein Leben*
(Aut, 1934), *Der Mittelgarten* (P, 1936), *Das Stundenglas* (Sp and Di,
1936), *Der Himmelsschlüssel* (S, 1939).

Strauß und Torney, Lulu von

September 20, 1873, Bückeburg–June 19, 1956, Jena. Father: Major general with the prince of Schaumberg-Lippe. Attended girls' high school in
Bückeburg, then became a freelance writer there. Traveled frequently
through Germany, England, France, Italy, Holland, and Scandinavia. Associated with the circle of writers around Börries von Münchhausen (publications in the *Göttinger Musenalmanach,* 1901–1905). Friendship with Agnes
Miegel. Married in 1916 to the publisher-bookseller Eugen Diederichs; she
was an influential reader with that publisher during the twenties. After
Diederichs death in 1930, primarily an editor and translator. Lulu von
Strauß und Torney, together with Agnes Miegel and Münchhausen, is
considered one of the most important composers of ballads. The pathos of
her "grain-and-field romanticism" foreshadows "blood-and-soil literature."
Primarily historical material in novels and novellas.

Works: *Gedichte* (P, 1898), *Bauernstolz* (Ss, 1901), *Als der Großvater die Groß-
mutter nahm* (S, 1901), *Aus Bauernstamm* (S, 1902), *Balladen und Lieder* (P,
1902), *Eines Lebens Sühne* (S, 1904), *Das Erbe* (N, 1905), *Ihres Vaters Tochter*
(N, 1905), *Die Dorfgeschichte in der modernen Literatur* (Es, 1906), *Neue
Balladen und Lieder* (P, 1907), *Lucifer* (N, 1907), *Der Hof am Brink — Das
Meerminneke* (Ss, 1907), *Sieger und Besiegte* (Ss, 1909), *Judas* (N, 1911; retitled
Der Judashof, 1937), *Aus der Chronik niederdeutscher Städte* (Es, 1912), *Reif
steht die Saat* (ballads and P, 1919), *Der Tempel: Ein Spiel aus der Renaissance*
(Dr, 1921), *Der jüngste Tag* (N, 1922), *Das Fenster* (S, 1923), *Auge um Auge*
(S, 1933), *Erde der Väter* (P, 1936), *Schuld* (N, 1940), *Das goldene Angesicht*
(P, 1943), *Das verborgene Angesicht* (Aut, 1943).

Thiess, Frank

March 13, 1890, Eluisenstein near Uexküll, Lithuania–December 22, 1977,
Darmstadt. Father: architect. Immigrated to Germany in 1893. Studied
Germanistik, history, and philosophy in Berlin and Tübingen; Ph.D. in
1913. Soldier from 1915 to 1919, editor for foreign policy with the *Berliner
Tageblatt.* In 1920/21, dramatic advisor and director at the Stuttgart Volks-
bühne; from 1921 to 1923, theater critic in Hanover. From 1923 on, freelance writer in Berlin (in winter) and Steinhude (in summer). In 1933
traveled to Rome via Vienna, then back to Vienna. In 1941, married for the
second time to a Frenchwoman. After the war, in Darmstadt; from 1952 to
1954, editor of the *Neue Literarische Welt.* In the Third Reich, several of his

works criticized but published anyway. Primarily a storywriter and writer of essays on cultural policy, but also a dramatist.

Works: *Der Tod von Falern* (N, 1921), *Die Verdammten* (N, 1923), *Das Gesicht des Jahrhunderts* (Es, 1923), *Der Leibhaftige* (N, 1924), *Abschied vom Paradies* (N, 1925), *Der Kampf mit den Engeln* (Ss, 1925), *Das Tor zur Welt* (N, 1926), *Frauenraub* (N, 1927), *Erziehung zur Freiheit* (Es, 1929), *Der Zentaur* (N, 1931), *Die Geschichte eines unruhigen Sommers* (Ss, 1932), *Die Zeit ist reif* (Sp, 1932), *Johanna und Esther* (N, 1933), *Der Weg zur Isabelle* (N, 1934), *Der ewige Taugenichts* (Co, 1935), *Tsushima* (N, 1936), *Stürmischer Frühling* (N, 1937), *Die Herzogin von Langeais* (T, 1938), *Das Reich der Dämonen* (N, 1941), *Caruso* (N, 2 volumes, 1942–1946: Vol. 1, *Neapolitanische Legende*, Vol. 2, *Caruso in Sorrent*).

Vesper, Will

October 11, 1882, Wuppertal-Barmen–March 14, 1962, Triangel Estate, Gifhorn District. Father: farmer; Protestant family. Attended the Gymnasium in Barmen. Studied *Germanistik* and history in Munich. In 1906, literary advisor with C. H. Beck Publishers in Munich. From 1911 on, also a freelance writer. From 1915 to 1918, served in the First World War; towards the end, technical assistant on the general staff. From 1918 to 1920, cultural editor with the *Deutsche Allgemeine Zeitung,* Berlin. Then a freelance writer. From 1923 to 1943, editor of the monthly *Die Schöne Literatur* (after 1931, renamed *Die Neue Literatur*). In 1933, became a member of the German Academy of Literature, *Gau* spokesman of the National Socialist Reich Association of German Writers; together with Hanns Johst, head of the Reich Chamber of Literature. From 1938, farm owner of Triangel Estate. Novels about the German past and Germanic prehistory; chauvinistic and nationalistic, anti-Semitic attitudes, later emphatically National Socialist. The literary journal that he edited became the leading literary journal of the Third Reich, repeatedly attacking exile writers. Many *Führer* poems. Mythicizing retellings of old sagas. Very active as an editor.

Works: *Der Segen* (S, 1905), *Tristan und Isolde* (N, 1911), *Parzival* (N, 1911), *Vom großen Krieg 1914–1915* (P, 1915), *Der blühende Baum* (P, 1916), *Martin Luthers Jugendjahre: Bilder und Legenden* (Ss, 1918), *Schön ist der Sommer* (P, 1918), *Der Balte* (N, 1919), *Annemarie* (N, 1920), *Mutter und Kind* (P, 1920), *Die Wanderung des Herrn Ulrich von Hutten* (Di-N, 1922), *Fröhliche Märchen* (F, 1922), *Die ewige Wiederkehr* (S, 1922), *Der arme Konrad* (S, 1924), *Das Recht der Lebenden* (Es, 1927), *Der Heilige und der Papst* (S, 1928), *Das harte Geschlecht* (N, 1931), *Sam in Schnabelweide* (S, 1931), *Kranz des Lebens* (P, complete edition, 1934), *Der entfesselte Säugling* (S, 1935), *Eine deutsche Feier* (Dr, 1936), *Rufe in die Zeit* (P, 1937), *Geschichten von Liebe, Traum und Tod* (Ss, complete edition,

1937), *Kämpfer Gottes* (Ss, complete edition, 1938), *Bild des Führers* (P, 1942), *Im Flug nach Spanien* (S, 1943), *Dennoch!* (P, 1944).

Wehner, Josef Magnus

November 14, 1891, Bermbach, Röhn–December 14, 1973, Munich. Father: elementary school teacher. Studied philology in Jena and Munich. War volunteer in 1914; severely wounded at Verdun. Editor and theater critic in Munich (*Münchner Zeitung* and *Münchner Neueste Nachrichten*). In 1943, freelance writer in Munich and Tutzing on Lake Starnberg. Member of the German Academy of Literature. Received the Poet's Prize of the City of Munich in 1928 and the Honorary Prize of the Foundation for the Promotion of Writing in 1937. Connected Catholicism to *völkisch* chauvinistic ideas. Storywriter and dramatist.

Works: *Der Weiler Gottes* (Ep, 1921), *Der blaue Berg* (N, 1922; retitled *Erste Liebe*, 1941; continuation, *Die Hochzeitskuh*, N, 1928), *Struensee* (Biog, 1924), *Das Gewitter* (Dr, 1926), *Land ohne Schatten* (Tb, 1930), *Sieben vor Verdun* (N, 1930), *Die Wallfahrt nach Paris: Eine patriotische Phantasie* (N, 1933), *Das unsterbliche Reich* (W, 1933), *Mein Leben* (Aut, 1934), *Schlageter* (Biog, 1934), *Geschichten aus der Rhön* (S, 1935), *Hindenburg* (Biog, 1935), *Stadt und Festung Belgerad* (N, 1936), *Hebbel* (Biog, 1938), *Als wir Rekruten waren* (S, 1938), *Elisabeth* (S, 1939), *Echnaton und Nofretete* (S, 1940).

Weinheber, Josef

March 9, 1892, Vienna–April 8, 1945, Kirchstetten, Lower Austria. Father: butcher and animal trader; tavernkeeper. After the early death of his parents, spent 1902 to 1908 in the Mödling orphanage. Attended the Gymnasium there. In 1911, postal official, other professions on the side, and extensive travel in the twenties. In 1927, conversion to Protestantism. After 1932, freelance writer. Despite literary recognition, always had financial problems. Awarded the title of professor in 1936; purchased a country house in Kirchstetten. Numerous prizes and awards during the period of National Socialism. After 1943, Weinheber distanced himself in his private correspondence from National Socialism. Suicide in 1945. Novels with in-depth analysis of society. Poetry modeled on classic forms; wide variety. On one hand *volkstümlich*, on the other, containing an elevated ideal of the poet and a heroic view of life.

Works: *Der einsame Mensch* (P, 1920), *Das Waisenhaus* (N, 1924), *Der Selbstmörder* (S, 1926), *Boot in der Bucht* (P, 1926), *Paradies der Philister* (N, 1928; retitled *Der Nachwuchs*, 1953), *Macht des Wortes* (S, 1930), *Der gejagte Teufel* (S, 1932), *Adel und Untergang* (P, 1934), *Die Ehescheidung* (S, 1935), *Vereinsamtes Herz* (P, 1935), *Wien wörtlich* (P, 1935), *Das Geschenk* (S, 1936), *Späte Krone* (P, 1936), *Deutscher Gruß aus Österreich* (P,

1936), *O Mensch, gib acht* (P, 1937), *Selbstbildnis* (P, 1937), *Zwischen Göttern und Dämonen* (P, 1938), *Kammermusik* (P, 1939), *Die hohen Zeichen* (Dr, 1939), *Den Gefallenen* (P, 1940), *Blut und Stahl* (P, 1941), *Himmelauen, Wolkenfluh* (P, 1941), *Ode an die Buchstaben* (P, 1942), *Gedichte* (P, 1944), *Hier ist das Wort* (P, 1944), *Dokumente des Herzens* (P, 1944).

Wiechert, Ernst

May 18, 1887, Forestry House Kleinort near Sensberg, East Prussia–August 24, 1950, Uerikon, Switzerland. Father: forester. Studied *Germanistik*, English, and geography in Königsberg; after 1911, high school teacher there. Served in the First World War on the eastern and western fronts. From 1930 to 1933, teacher at a Berlin Gymnasium. Lived after 1933 as a freelance writer in Ambach, Upper Bavaria. After 1948 lived in Switzerland because of disappointment with the course of development in the postwar years in Germany. Partly cautious and partly decisive rejection of National Socialism because of Christian and moral convictions. Incarcerated for two months in 1938 in Buchenwald Concentration Camp (see his autobiographical novel *Der Totenwald*, written in 1939 and published in 1946). Then publication prohibition and surveillance by the Gestapo. Ernst Wiechert is one of the authors of the Inner Emigration. Novels and stories represent topical moral conflicts and are usually set in the East Prussian countryside.

Works: *Die Flucht* (N, 1916), *Der Wald* (N, 1922), *Der Totenwolf* (N, 1924), *Die blauen Schwingen* (N, 1925), *Heinrich der Städtegründer* (S, 1925), *Die Legende vom letzten Wald* (S, 1925), *Der Knecht Gottes Andreas Nyland* (N, 1926), *Der silberne Wagen* (Ss, 1928), *Die kleine Passion* (N, 1929; first part of the novel trilogy *Passion eines Menschen*), *Die Flöte des Pan* (Ss, 1930), *Jedermann* (N, 1931; second part of the novel trilogy), *Die Magd des Jürgen Doskocil* (N, 1932; third part of the novel trilogy), *Der brennende Dornbusch* (S, 1932), *Das Spiel vom deutschen Bettelmann* (Dr, 1932), *Das Männlein* (S, 1933), *Der Jünger* (S, 1933), *Tobias* (S, 1933), *Die Majorin* (N, 1934), *Der Vater* (S, 1934), *Der Todeskandidat* (Ss, 1934), *Der verlorene Sohn* (Dr, 1934), *Hirtennovelle* (S, 1935), *Der Dichter und die Zeit* (Sp, 1935 and 1945), *Die goldene Stadt* (Rp, 1935), *Wälder und Menschen* (Aut, 1936), *Das heilige Jahr* (Ss, 1936), *Das einfache Leben* (N, 1938), *Der ewige Stern* (S, 1940), *Demetrius und andere Erzählungen* (Ss, 1945), *Rede an die deutsche Jugend* (Sp, 1945), *Die Totenmesse* (Dr and Rp, 1945), *Die Jerominkinder* (N, 1940–1941), *Der weiße Büffel oder von der großen Gerechtigkeit* (S, 1946).

Zerkaulen, Heinrich

March 2, 1892, Bonn–February 13, 1954, Hofgeismar. Father: shoemaker. Studied pharmacology in Munich and Marburg. War volunteer in 1914; seriously wounded. Journalist and feuilleton contributer in Düsseldorf and Essen. From 1931, freelance writer in Dresden; after 1945, in Greiz and Witzenhausen. Classified as a sympathizer. Poet of the Reinish homeland; wrote historical novels and dramas.

Works: *Weiße Ostern* (P, 1912), *Leyer und Schwert* (war songs, 1915), *Die Spitzweggasse* (Ss, 1918), *Ursula Bittgang* (N, 1921), *Die Insel Thule* (Ss, 1924), *Lieder vom Rhein* (P, 1927), *Rautenkranz und Schwerter* (N, 1927), *Die Welt im Winkel* (N, 1928; retitled *Der Strom der Väter,* 1937), *Das offene Fenster* (P, 1929), *Musik auf dem Rhein* (Beethoven N, 1930; 1949), *Osternothafen* (N, 1931; retitled *Anna und Sigrid,* 1934), *Die heimliche Fürstin* (N, 1933), *Jugend von Langemarck* (Dr, 1933), *Der arme Kumpel Doris* (N, 1935), *Der Sprung aus dem Alltag* (Co, 1935), *Gesegneter Tag* (P, 1935), *Hörnerklang der Frühe* (N, 1935), *Der Reiter* (Dr, 1936), *Herr Lukas aus Kronach* (N, 1938), *Brommy* (Dr, 1939), *Erlebnis und Ergebnis* (Aut, 1939), *Der feurige Gott* (Beethoven N, 1943; 1954).

Zöberlein, Hans

September 1, 1895, Nuremberg–February 13, 1964, Munich. Father: shoemaker. Mason, sculptor, and architect. Soldier in the First World War; wounded and decorated. Fought against the *Räterepublik* in Munich. Early member of the NSDAP and SA; SA *Brigadenführer.* Holder of the Blood Order and the Golden Badge of Honor of the NSDAP. Received the Poet's Prize of the City of Munich in 1933 and the Culture Prize of the SA in 1938. Sentenced to death in 1948 because of his participation in the Penzberg murders; sentence commuted to imprisonment for life in 1948, then early release. Herald of experiences at the front. *Völkisch* racist incendiary literature.

Works: *Der Glaube and Deutschland* (N, 1934), *Der Befehl des Gewissens* (N, 1937), *Der Druckposten* (S, 1939), *Der Schrapnellbaum* (N, 1939).

Selected Bibliography

General

Amann, Klaus, and Albert Berger, eds. *Österreichische Literatur der dreißiger Jahre* (Austrian Literature of the Thirties). Vienna and Cologne: Böhlau, 1985.

Benz, Wolfgang, ed. *Enzyklopedie des Nationalsozialismus* (Encyclopedia of National Socialism). Stuttgart: Klett-Cotta, 1997.

Bracher, Karl Dietrich. *Die deutsche Diktatur* (The German Dictatorship). Cologne and Berlin: Kiepenheuer & Witsch, 1969.

Brüdigam, Heinz. *Der Schoß ist fruchtbar noch . . . Neonazistische, militaristische, nationalistische Literatur und Publizistik in der Bundesrepublik* (The Womb is Still Fertile . . . Neonazi, Militaristic, Nationalistic Literature and Journalism in the Federal Republic). Frankfurt am Main: Röderberg, 1964.

Caemmerer, Christiane, and Walter Delabar, eds. *Dichtung im Dritten Reich? Zur Literatur in Deutschland 1933–1945* (Literature in the Third Reich? On Literature in Germany, 1933–1945). Opladen: Westdeutscher Verlag, 1996.

Daim, Wilfried. *Der Mann, der Hitler die Ideen gab: Jörg von Liebenfels* (The Man Who Gave Hitler the Ideas: Jörg von Liebenfels). 3rd expanded and improved edition. Vienna: Ueberreuter, 1994.

———. *Der Mann, der Hitler die Ideen gab: Von den religiösen Verirrungen eines Sektierers zum Rassenwahn des Dikators* (The Man Who Gave Hitler the Ideas: From the Religious Confusion of a Sectarian to the Racial Madness of a Dictator). Munich: Isar Verlag, 1958.

Delabar, Walter, Horst Denkler, and Erhard Schütz, eds. *Banalität mit Stil: Zur Widersprüchlichkeit der Literaturproduktion im Nationalsozialismus* (Banality With Style: Contradictions in the Literary Production in National Socialism). *Zeitschrift für Germanistik* (Journal for *Germanistik*), New Series, Supplementary Volume 1. Bern and New York: Lang, 1999.

Denkler, Hans, and Karl Prümm, eds. *Die deutsche Literatur im Dritten Reich: Themen-Traditionen-Wirkungen* (German Literature in the Third Reich: Themes-Traditions-Effects). Stuttgart: Reclam, 1976.

Deutschkron, Inge. *Ich trug den gelben Stern* (I Wore the Yellow Star). 15th edition. Stuttgart: dtv, 1998.

Erdmann, Karl Dietrich. *Deutschland unter der Herrschaft des Nationalsozialismus 1933–1939* (Germany under the Rule of National Socialism, 1933–1939). In Gebhardt, *Handbuch der deutschen Geschichte.* 9th newly revised edition. Volume 20. Edited by Herbert Grundmann. Munich: dtv, 1980.

Fechter, Paul. *Geschichte der deutschen Literatur: Von den Anfängen bis zur Gegenwart* (The History of German Literature: From the Beginnings to the Present). Berlin: Knaur, 1941.

Fest, Joachim C. *Hitler: Eine Biography* (Hitler: A Biography). Frankfurt am Main: Propyläen, 1973.

Hartung, Günter. *Deutschfaschistische Literatur und Ästhetik: Gesammelte Studien* (German Fascist Literature and Aesthetics: Collected Studies). Leipzig: Leipziger Universitätsverlag, 2001.

———. *Literatur und Ästhetik des deutschen Faschismus* (Literature and Aesthetics in German Fascism). Berlin: Akademie Verlag, 1983.

Heer, Friedrich. *Der Glaube des Adolf Hitler* (The Faith of Adolf Hitler). Munich and Eßlingen: Bechtle, 1968.

Hermand, Jost. *Geschichte der Germanistik* (History of *Germanistik*). Reinbek near Hamburg: Rowohlt, 1994.

Hermand, Jost, and Frank Trommler, eds. *Die Kultur der Weimarer Republik* (The Culture of the Weimar Republic). Münich: Nymphenburg Publishers, 1978.

Hillesheim, Jürgen, and Elisabeth Michael. *Lexikon nationalsozialistischer Dichter: Biographien-Analysen-Bibliographien* (Lexicon of National Socialist Writers: Biographies-Analyses-Bibliographies). Würzburg: Königshausen & Neumann, 1993.

Hofer, Walter. *Der Nationalsozialismus: Dokumente 1933–1945.* (National Socialism. Documents, 1933–1945). 351,000th to 375,000th copies printed. Frankfurt am Main: Fischer, 1962.

Hopster, Norbert, and Petra Josting, eds. *Literaturlenkung im "Dritten Reich": Eine Bibliographie* (Control of Literature in the "Third Reich": A Bibliography). Hildesheim, Zurich, and New York: Olms, 1993.

Huber, Karl Heinz. *Jugend unterm Hakenkreuz* (Youth Under the Swastika). Berlin: Ullstein, 1982.

Kaes, Anton, ed. *Manifeste und Dokumente zur deutschen Literatur 1919–1933* (Manifestos and Documents on German Literature, 1919–1933). Stuttgart: Metzler, 1983.

Kammer, Hilde, and Elisabet Bartsch, eds. *Lexikon Nationalsozialismus: Begriffe, Organisationen und Institutionen* (Lexicon, National Socialism: Terms, Organizations, Institutions). Reinbek bei Hamburg: Rowohlt, 1999.

Kershaw, Ian. *Hitler 1889–1936: Hubris.* New York and London: Norton, 1998, 1999.

———. *Hitler 1936–1945: Nemesis.* New York and London: Norton, 2000.

Ketelsen, Uwe-K. "Die Literatur des 3. Reichs als Gegenstand germanistischer Forschung" (The Literature of the Third Reich as a Topic for Research in *Germanistik*). In *Wege der Literaturwissenschaft* (Paths of Studies in Literature). Edited by Jutta Kolkenbrock-Netz, Gerhard Plumpe, and Hans Joachim Schrimpf. Bonn: Bouvier, 1985, 284–302.

———. *Literatur und Drittes Reich* (Literature and the Third Reich). Schernfeld: SH-Verlag, 1992. 2nd revised edition: Vierow near Greifswald, 1994.

———. "Probleme einer gegenwärtigen Forschung zur 'Literatur des Dritten Reichs'" (Problems of Current Research on the "Literature of the Third Reich"). *Deutsche Vierteljahresschrift für Literaturwissenschaft und Geistesgeschichte* (German Quarterly for Literature and Intellectual History), 64, 4 (1990), 707–25.

———. *Völkisch-nationale und nationalsozialistische Literatur in Deutschland 1890–1945* (*Völkisch* National and National Socialist Literature in Germany, 1890–1945). Stuttgart: Metzler, 1976.

Klemperer, Victor. *Ich will Zeugnis ablegen bis zum letzten* (I Shall Bear Witness Until the End). Volume 1: *Tagebücher 1931–1941* (Diaries, 1931–1941), Volume 2: *Tagebücher 1942–1945* (Diaries, 1942–1945). Edited by V. Walter Nowojski in association with Hadwig Klemperer. Berlin: Aufbau, 1995. English translation by Martin Chalmers as *I Will Bear Witness: A Diary of the Nazi Years 1933–1941* (New York: Random House, 1998) and *I Will Bear Witness: A Diary of the Nazi Years 1942–1945* (New York: Random House, 1999).

Lämmert, Eberhard. "Beherrschte Literatur: Vom Elend des Schreibens unter Diktaturen" (Controlled Literature: On the Misery of Writing in Dictatorships). In *Literatur in der Diktatur: Schreiben im Nationalsozialismus und DDR-Sozialismus* (Literature in Dictatorship: Writing Under National Socialism and the Socialism of the German Democratic Republic). Edited by Günther Rüther. Paderborn: Schöningh, 1997, 115–37.

Langewiesche, Dieter, and Heinz Elmar Tenorth, eds. *Handbuch der deutschen Bildungsgeschichte, Band V, 1918–1945: Die Weimarer Republik und die nationalsozialistische Literatur* (Handbook of the History of German Education, Volume V, 1918–1945: The Weimar Republic and National Socialist Literature). Munich: Beck, 1989.

Loewy, Ernst. *Literatur unterm Hakenkreuz: Das Dritte Reich und seine Dichtung: Eine Dokumentation* (Literature Under the Swastika: The Third Reich and Its Literature. Documentation). Frankfurt am Main: Fischer, 1969, 1983, and 1987 (1st edition, Frankfurt am Main: Europäische Verlagsanstalt, 1966).

Martin, Elaine. *Gender, Patriarchy, and Fascism in the Third Reich: The Responses of Women Writers*. Detroit: Wayne State UP, 1993.

Mosse, George L. *Nazi Culture: Intellectual, Cultural and Social Life in the Third Reich*. New York: Grosset & Dunlap, 1968.

Natter, Wolfgang. *Literature at War, 1914–1940: Representing the "Times of Greatness" in Germany*. New Haven and London: Yale UP, 1999.

Prümm, Karl. *Die Literatur des Soldatischen Nationalismus der 20er Jahre (1918–1933)* (The Literature of Soldierly Nationalism in the Twenties [1918–1933]). 2 volumes. Kronberg im Taunus: Scriptor, 1974.

Reichel, Peter. *Der schöne Schein des Dritten Reiches: Faszination und Gewalt des Faschismus* (The Beautiful Appearance of the Third Reich: Fascination and Violence of Fascism). Munich: Hanser, 1991.

Richards, Donald Ray. *The German Bestseller in the 20th Century: A Complete Bibliography and Analysis 1915–1940*. Bern: Lang, 1968.

Ritchie, Jame MacPhearson. *German Literature under National Socialism*. London and Canberra: Croom Helm, 1983; Totowa, NJ: Barnes & Noble, 1983.

Rothe, Wolfgang, ed. *Die deutsche Literatur in der Weimarer Republik* (German Literature in the Weimar Republic). Stuttgart: Reclam, 1974.

Rüther, Günther, ed. *Literatur in der Diktatur: Schreiben im Nationalsozialismus und DDR-Sozialismus* (Literature in Dictatorship: Writing Under National Socialism and the Socialism of the German Democratic Republic). Paderborn: Schöningh, 1997.

Sarkowicz, Hans. "Die literarischen Apologeten des Dritten Reichs. Zur Rezeption der vom Nationalsozialismus geförderten Autoren nach 1945" (The Literary Apologists of the Third Reich. On the Reception After 1945 of the Authors Supported by National Socialism). In *Leid der Worte: Panorama des literarischen Nationalsozialismus* (The Suffering of Words: Panorama of the Literary National Socialism). Edited by Jörg Thunecke. Bonn: Bouvier, 1987, 435–59.

Schäfer, Hans Dietrich. "Kultur als Simulation: Das Dritte Reich und die Postmoderne" (Culture as Simulation: The Third Reich and the Postmodern). In *Literatur in der Diktatur: Schreiben im Nationalsozialismus und DDR-Sozialismus* (Literature in Dictatorship: Writing Under National Socialism and the Socialism of the German Democratic Republic). Edited by Günther Rüther. Paderborn: Schöningh, 1997, 115–37, 215–45.

Schäfer, Hans Dietrich, ed. *Am Rande der Nacht: Moderne Klassik im Dritten Reich* (On the Edge of Night: Modern Classics in the Third Reich). Frankfurt am Main: Ullstein, 1984.

———, ed. *Das gespaltene Bewußtsein: Deutsche Kultur und Lebenswirklichkeit 1933–1945* (Divided Consciousness: German Culture and the Realities of Life, 1933–1945). Munich: Hanser, 1981.

Schnell, Ralf. "Was ist 'nationalsozialistische Dichtung'?" (What is "National Socialist Literature?"). In *Leid der Worte: Panorama des literarischen Nationalsozialismus* (The Suffering of Words: Panorama of the Literary National Socialism). Edited by Jörg Thunecke. Bonn: Bouvier, 1987, 28–45.

Schonauer, Franz. *Deutsche Literatur im Dritten Reich* (German Literature in the Third Reich). Olten and Freiburg: Walter-Verlag, 1961.

Schütz, Erhard, and Jochen Vogt, eds. *Einführung in die deutsche Literatur des 20. Jahrhunderts.* Band 2: *Weimarer Republik, Faschismus, und Exil* (Introduction to German Literature of the Twentieth Century. Volume 2: The Weimar Republic, Fascism, and Exile). Opladen: Westdeutscher Verlag, 1977.

Shirer, William L. *The Rise and Fall of the Third Reich.* New York: Fawcett, 1959 and 1960.

Theweleit, Klaus. *Männerphantasien* (Men's Fantasies). Frankfurt am Main: Verlag Roter Stern, 1978.

Thunecke, Jörg, ed. *Leid der Worte: Panorama des literarischen Nationalsozialismus* (The Suffering of Words: Panorama of the Literary National Socialism). Bonn: Bouvier, 1987.

Von der Decken, Godele. *Emanzipation auf Abwegen: Frauenkultur und Frauenliteratur im Umkreis des Nationalsozialismus* (Emancipation on the Wrong Track: Women's Culture and Women's Literature in the National Socialist Environment). Frankfurt am Main: Athenäum, 1988.

Wagener, Hans, ed. *Gegenwartsliteratur und Drittes Reich* (Literature of the Present and the Third Reich). Stuttgart: Reclam, 1977.

Weiss, Herman. *Biographisches Lexikon zum Dritten Reich* (Biographic Lexicon of the Third Reich). Frankfurt am Main: Fischer, 1998.

Wulf, Joseph. *Literatur und Dichtung im Dritten Reich: Eine Dokumentation* (Literature and Poetry in the Third Reich: Documentation). Frankfurt am Main: Ullstein, 1983.

Ideology

Bronder, Dietrich. *Bevor Hitler kam* (Before Hitler Came). Hanover: Pfeiffer, 1964.

Brose, Eric Dorn. "Genetic Fascism Revisited: Attitudes Toward Technology in Germany and Italy, 1919–1945." In *German Studies Review* 10, 2 (1987): 273–97.

Bullivant, Keith. "Aufbruch der Nation: Zur 'Konservativen Revolution'" (Emergence of the Nation: On the "Conservative Revolution"). In Keith Bullivant, *Das literarische Leben in der Weimarer Republik* (The Literary Life in the Weimar Republic). Königstein im Taunus: Scriptor, 1978, 28–49.

Chamberlain, Houston Stewart. *Die Grundlagen des neunzehnten Jahrhunderts* (The Foundations of the Nineteenth Century). 28th edition. 2 volumes. Munich: Bruckmann, 1942

Dinter, Artur. *Die Sünde wider das Blut* (The Sin Against Blood). 15th edition. Leipzig: Matthes und Trost, 1921

Flex, Walter. *Der Wanderer zwischen beiden Welten* (The Wanderer Between Two Worlds). 2nd edition. Munich: Beck, 1942

Gobineau, Arthur. *Versuch über die Ungleichheit der Menschenrassen* (Attempt on the Inequality of the Human Races). German translation of *Essai sur l'inegalité des races humaines*, 1853–55. Berlin: Kurt Wolff, 1935.

Greiffenhagen, Martin. *Das Dilemma des Konservatismus in Deutschland* (The Dilemma of Conservatism in Germany). Munich: Piper, 1977.

Grimm, Reinhold, and Jost Hermand, eds. *Faschismus und Avantgarde* (Fascism and the Avantgarde). Königstein im Taunus: Athenäum, 1980.

Hamann, Richard, and Jost Hermand. *Gründerzeit* (Founders' Period). Berlin: Akademie-Verlag, 1965.

———. *Stilkunst um 1900* (The Art of Style Around 1900). Berlin: Akademie-Verlag, 1967.

Härtl, Heinz. "Romantischer Antisemitismus. Arnim und die 'Tischgesellschaft'" (Romantic Anti-Semitism. Arnim and the "Table Society"). In *Weimarer Beiträge* (Weimar Essays), 33, 7 (1987), 1159–73.

Hartung, Günther. "Völkische Ideologie" (*Völkisch* Ideology). In *Weimarer Beiträge* (Weimar Essays), 33, 7 (1987), 1174–85.

Hermand, Jost. *Der alte Traum vom neuen Reich: Völkische Utopien und Nationalsozialismus* (The Old Dream of the New Reich: *Völkisch* Utopias and National Socialism). Frankfurt am Main: Athenäum, 1988. Translated by Paul Levesque in collaboration with Stefan Soldoveri as *Old Dreams of a New Reich: Volkish Utopias and National Socialism*. Bloomington and Indianapolis: Indiana UP, 1992.

———. "Ultima Thule. Völkische und faschistische Zukunftsvisionen" (Ultima Thule. Völkisch and Fascist Visions of the Future). In Jost Hermand, *Orte. Irgendwo. Formen utopischen Denkens* (Places. Somewhere. Forms of Utopian Thinking). Königstein im Taunus: Athenäum, 1981, 61–86.

———. *Von Mainz nach Weimar (1793–1919)* (From Mainz to Weimar (1793–1919)). Stuttgart: Metzler, 1969.

Hitler, Adolf. *Mein Kampf* (My Struggle). 27th printing of the popular edition. Munich: Eher, 1933.

Jung, Edgar J. *Die Herrschaft der Minderwertigen: Ihr Zerfall und ihre Ablösung* (The Rule of Inferior Beings: Its Decline and Its Dissolution). Berlin: Deutsche Rundschau, 1927.

Kaltenbrunner, Gerd Klaus, ed. *Konservatismus International* (International Conservatism). Stuttgart: Seewald, 1973.

Kühnl, Reinhard. *Deutschland zwischen Demokratie und Faschismus* (Germany Between Democracy and Fascism). Munich: Hanser, 1969.

Langbehn, Julius. *Rembrandt als Erzieher* (Rembrandt as an Educator). Weimar: Duncker, 1943 (first appeared in 1890 anonymously, "By a German").

Moeller van den Bruck, Arthur. *Das Dritte Reich* (The Third Reich). 3rd edition. Hamburg: Hanseatische Verlagsanstalt, 1931.

Mohler, Arnim. *Die konservative Revolution in Deutschland 1918–1932: Ein Handbuch* (The Conservative Revolution in Germany, 1918–1932: A Handbook). Darmstadt: Wissenschaftliche Buchgesellschaft, 1972.

Mosse, George L. *The Crisis of German Ideology: Intellectual Origins of the Third Reich*. New York: Grosset & Dunlap, 1964.

Nolte, Ernst. *Die Krise des liberalen Systems und die faschistischen Bewegungen* (The Crisis of the Liberal System and the Fascist Movements). Munich: Piper, 1968.

Nolte, Ernst, ed. *Theorien über den Faschismus* (Theories on Fascism). Cologne and Berlin: Kiepenheuer & Witsch, 1967.

Rosenberg, Alfred. *Gestaltung der Idee: Blut und Ehre II. Band.* (Giving Form to the Idea: Blood and Honor, volume II). 8th edition. Munich: Eher, 1938.

———. *Der Mythus des 20. Jahrhunderts* (The Myth of the Twentieth Century). Munich: Hoheneichen-Verlag, 1937.

Saage, Richard. *Faschismustheorien: Eine Einführung* (Fascism Theories: An Introduction). Munich: Beck, 1976.

Schulz, Gerhard. *Faschismus — Nationalismus: Versionen und theoretische Kontroversen 1922–1972* (Fascism — Nationalism: Versions and Theoretical Controversies, 1922–1972). Frankfurt am Main, Vienna, and Berlin: Propyläen, 1974.

Schwedhelm, Karl. *Propheten des Nationalsozialismus* (Prophets of National Socialism). Munich: List, 1969.

Sontheimer, Kurt. *Antidemokratisches Denken in der Weimarer Republik* (Anti-Democratic Thinking in the Weimar Republic). 2nd edition. Munich: Nymphenburger Verlagshandlung, 1968.

Travers, Martin. *Critics of Modernity: The Literature of the Conservative Revolution in Germany, 1890–1933*. New York, Bern, Berlin, Bruxelles, Frankfurt am Main, Oxford, and Vienna: Lang, 2001.

Vondung, Klaus. "Der literarische Nationalismus. Ideologische, politische und sozial-historische Wirkungszusammenhänge" (Literary National Socialism. Ideological, Political, and Social-Historical Interconnections). In *Deutsche Literatur im Dritten Reich: Themen — Traditionen — Wirkungen* (German Literature in the Third Reich: Themes — Traditions — Effects), edited by Horst Denkler and Karl Prümm (Stuttgart: Reclam, 1976), 44–65.

Wippermann, Wolfgang. *Europäischer Faschismus im Vergleich 1922–1982* (European Fascism Compared, 1922–1982). Frankfurt am Main: Suhrkamp, 1983.

———. *Faschismustheorien: Zum Stand der gegenwärtigen Diskussion* (Theories of Fascism: On the State of the Present Discussion). 5th completely revised edition. Darmstadt: Wissenschaftliche Buchgesellschaft, 1989.

Wippermann, Wolfgang, ed. *Kontroversen um Hitler* (Controversies About Hitler). Frankfurt: Suhrkamp, 1986.

Theodore Ziolkowski, "Der Hunger nach dem Mythos. Zur seelischen Gastronomie der Deutschen in den Zwanziger Jahren" (Hunger for Mythos. On the Spiritual Gastronomy of the Germans in the Twenties). In *Die sogenannten zwanziger Jahre* (The So-Called Twenties). Edited by Reinhold Grimm and Jost Hermand. Bad Homburg v.d.H.: Gehlen, 1970, 169–201.

National Socialist Literature and Culture Policies

Amann, Klaus. *Der Anschluß österreichischer Schriftsteller an das Dritte Reich: Institutionelle und bewußtseinsgeschichtliche Aspekte* (The Annexation of Austrian Writers and the Third Reich: Institutional Aspects and Aspects Relating to the History of Awareness). Frankfurt am Main: Athenäum, 1988.

Barbian, Jan Pieter. "Institutionen der Literaturpolitik im 'Dritten Reich'" (Institutions of Literature Policy in the "Third Reich"). In *Literatur in der Diktatur* (Literature in Dictatorship). Edited by Günther Rüther. Paderborn: Schöningh, 1997, 95–129.

———. *Literaturpolitik im "Dritten Reich": Institutionen, Kompetenzen, Betätigungsfelder* (Literary Policies in the "Third Reich": Institutions, Competencies, Fields of Activity). Frankfurt am Main: Buchhändler-Vereinigung GmbH, 1993; Munich: dtv, 1995.

Barner, Wilfried, and Christoph König, eds. *Zeitenwechsel: Germanistische Literaturwissenschaft vor und nach 1945* (Changing Times. The Study of German Literature Before and After 1945). Frankfurt am Main: Fischer, 1996.

Bartels, Adolf. *Geschichte der deutschen Literatur* (*History of German Literature*). 19th edition. Braunschweig: Westermann, 1943.

Brenner, Hildegard. *Die Kunstpolitik des Nationalsozialismus* (The Art Policy of National Socialism). Reinbeck: Rowohlt, 1963.

Conrady, Karl Otto. "Deutsche Literaturwissenschaft und Drittes Reich" (German Literature Studies and the Third Reich). In *Germanistik — eine deutsche Wissenschaft* (Germanistik — A German Scholarly Pursuit). Edited by Eberhard Lämmert. Frankfurt am Main: Suhrkamp, 1967, 71–109.

———. *Völkisch-nationale Germanistik in Köln: Eine unfestliche Erinnerung* (*Völkisch* National *Germanistik* in Cologne: An Un-Ceremonial Remembrance). Schernfeld: SH Verlag, 1990.

Cuomo, Glenn R. "Hanns Johst und die Reichsschriftumskammer: Ihr Einfluß auf die Situation des Schriftstellers im Dritten Reich" (Hanns Johst and the Reich Literature Chamber. Its Influence on the Situation of the Writer in the Third Reich). In *Leid der Worte: Panorama des literarischen Nationalsozialismus* (The Suffering of Words. Panorama of the Literary National Socialism). Edited by Jörg Thunecke. Bonn: Bouvier, 1987, 108–32.

Cuomo, Glenn R., ed. *National Socialist Cultural Policy*. New York: St. Martin's Press, 1995.

Ernst, Paul. "Das deutsche Volk und der Dichter von heute" (The German People and the Poet of Today). In *Des deutschen Dichters Sendung in der Gegenwart* (The Mission of the German Poet in the Present). Edited by Heinz Kindermann. Leipzig: Reclam, 1933, 19–28.

Fischer, Jens Malte. "'Zwischen uns und Weimar liegt Buchenwald.' Germanisten im Dritten Reich" (Between Weimar and Us Lies Buchenwald. Germanists in the Third Reich). In *Merkur* 41, 1 (January, 1987), 12–25.

Gilman, Sander L., ed. *NS-Literaturtheorie: Eine Dokumentation* (National Socialist Literature Theory. Documentation). Frankfurt am Main: Athenäum, 1971.

Herden, Werner. "Zwischen 'Gleichschaltung' und Kriegseinsatz. Positionen der Germanistik in der Zeit des Faschismus" (Between "Alignment" and Use in War: Positions of *Germanistik* in the Time of Fascism). In *Weimarer Beiträge* 33, 11 (1987), 1865–81.

Hermand, Jost. "Das junge Deutschland" (Young Germany). In Jost Hermand. *Von Mainz nach Weimar 1793–1919* (From Mainz to Weimar, 1793–1919). Stuttgart: Metzler, 1969, 152–73.

Hopster, Norbert. "Ausbildung und politische Funktion der Deutschlehrer im Nationalsozialismus" (The Training and Political Function of German Teachers in National Socialism). In *Wissenschaft im Dritten Reich* (Scholarship in the Third Reich). Edited by Peter Lundgren. Frankfurt am Main, Suhrkamp, 1985, 113–39.

Kater, Michael H. *Das "Ahnenerbe" der SS 1935–1945. Ein Beitrag zur Kulturpolitik des Dritten Reiches* ("Ancestor Research" of the SS, 1935–1945: A Contribution to the Cultural Policies of the Third Reich). Stuttgart: Deutsche Verlags-Anstalt, 1974.

Kindermann, Heinz. "Das Schriftum als Ausdruck des Volkstums" (Literature as the Expression of *Volkstum*). In *Kampf um die deutsche Lebensform* (Struggle for the German Way of Life). Edited by Heinz Kindermann. Vienna: Wiener Verlag, 1941 and 1944, 11–19.

Koch, Franz. *Geschichte der deutschen Dichtung* (The History of German Literature). 5th edition. Hamburg: Hanseatische Verlagsanstalt, 1942.

Lämmert, Eberhard, et al. *Germanistik — eine deutsche Wissenschaft* (*Germanistik* — A German Scholarly Pursuit). Frankfurt am Main: Suhrkamp, 1967.

Langenbucher, Hellmuth. *Volkhafte Dichtung der Zeit* (People's Literature of the Time), 6th edition. Berlin: Junker und Dünnhaupt, 1941 (1st edition, 1933).

Lerchenmüller, Joachim, and Gerd Simon. *Im Vorfeld des Massenmords: Germanistik und Nachbarfächer im 2. Weltkrieg: Eine Übersicht* (Leading up to Mass Murder: Germanistik and Related Fields in the Second World War. A Survey). Tübingen: Verlag der Gesellschaft für interdisziplinäre Forschung, 1997.

Oellers, Norbert. "Literatur und Volkstum. Der Fall der Literaturwissenschaft" (Literature and *Volkstum*. The Fall of Literary Scholarship). In *Literatur und Germanistik nach der Machtübernahme* (Literature and *Germanistik* After the Seizure of Power). Edited by Beda Allemann. Bonn: Bouvier, 1983, 232–54.

Osterkamp, Ernst. "Klassik-Konzepte: Kontinuität und Diskontinuität bei Walter Rehm und Hans Pyritz (Classicism Conceptions: Continuity and Discontinuity in Walter Rehm and Hans Pyritz." In *Zeitenwechsel: Germanistische Literaturwissenschaft vor und nach 1945* (Changing Times. The Study of German Literature Before and After 1945). Edited by Wilfried Barner and Christoph König. Frankfurt am Main: Fischer, 1996, 150–70.

Pinkerneil, Beate. "Vom kulturellen Nationalismus zur nationalsozialistischen Germanistik" (From Cultural Nationalism to National Socialist *Germanistik*). In *Am Beispiel "Wilhelm Meister." Einführung in die Wissenschaftsgeschichte der Germanistik* (Using the Example of "Wilhelm Meister." Introduction to the History of *Germanistik*), Volume 1, *Darstellung* (Description). Edited by Klaus L. Berghahn and Beate Pinkerneil. Königstein im Taunus: Athenäum, 1980, 75–97.

Schlösser, Rainer. "Das einfaltige Herz: Eichendorff als Geschichtsschreiber unseres Innern" (The Simple Heart: Eichendorff as the Historian of Our Interior Being). In *NS-Literaturtheorie* (National Socialist Literary Theory). Edited by Sander Gilman. Frankfurt am Main: Athenäum, 1071, 141–46.

Strothmann, Dietrich. *Nationalsozialistische Literaturpolitik: Ein Beitrag zur Publizistik im Dritten Reich* (National Socialist Literature Policies. A Contribution to Publishing in the Third Reich). 4th edition. Bonn: Bouvier, 1985.

Vondung, Klaus. *Völkisch-nationale und nationalsozialistische Literaturtheorie* (*Völkisch* National and National Socialist Literature Theory). Munich: List, 1973.

Voßkamp, Wilhelm. "Kontinuität und Diskontinuität. Zur deutschen Literatur-wissenschaft im Dritten Reich" (Continuity and Discontinuity. On the Study of German Literature in the Third Reich). In *Wissenschaft im Dritten Reich* (Science in the Third Reich). Edited by Peter Lundgren. Frankfurt am Main: Suhrkamp, 1985, 140–62.

Wulf, Joseph. *Literatur und Dichtung im Dritten Reich: Eine Dokumentation* (Literature and Poetry in the Third Reich. A Documentation) Frankfurt am Main: Ullstein, 1983.

Zeller, Bernhard, ed. *Klassiker in finsteren Zeiten: Eine Austellung des deutschen Literaturarchivs im Schiller-Nationalmuseum Marbach am Neckar* (Writers of German Classicism in Dark Times. An Exhibit of the German Literature Archive at the Schiller National Museum in Marbach on the Neckar). Volume 1. Marbach: Deutsche Schillergesellschaft, 1983.

The National Socialist Novel

Berens-Totenohl, Josefa. *Der Femhof* (The "Fehme" Farm). Jena: Diederichs, 1941.

Berman, Russel A. *The Rise of the Modern German Novel.* Cambridge, MA, and London: Harvard UP, 1986.

Beumelberg, Werner. *Geschichten vom Reich* (Stories of the Reich). Edited by Karl Plenzat. Leipzig: Hermann Eichblatt Verlag, 1941.

———. *Jörg.* Stuttgart: Verlag Deutsche Volksbücher GmbH, 1943 (published by the National Labor Front, National Socialist Association Kraft durch Freude [Strength through Joy]).

———. *Mont Royal* (Mount Royal). Published by the High Command of the Army, Internal Affairs Section, no date.

———. *Reich and Rom* (Reich and Rome). Oldenburg in East Frisia and Berlin: Stalling, 1937.

Blunck, Hans Friedrich. *Die Urvätersaga* (The Saga of the Forefathers). Jena: Eugen Diederichs, 1934.

Bohrer, Karl Heinz. *Die Ästhetik des Schreckens* (Aesthetics of Horror). Munich: Hanser, 1978.

Brecht, Bertolt. "Die Horst-Wessel-Legende" (The Horst Wessel Legend). In Bertolt Brecht. *Werke. Große kommentierte Berliner und Frankfurter Ausgabe* (Works. Large, Commented Berlin and Frankfurt Edition). Edited by Werner Hecht et al. Volume nineteen. Berlin, Weimar: Aufbau, 1997 and Frankfurt am Main: Suhrkamp, 1997, 381–89.

Brittmacher, Hans Richard. "Märtyer im Braunhemd. Hanns Heinz Ewers: *Horst Wessel: Ein deutsches Schicksal* (1932)" (Martyr in a Brown Shirt. Hanns Heinz Ewers: Horst Wessel. A German Fate, 1932). In *Dichtung im Dritten Reich? Zur Literatur in Deutschland 1933–1945* (Literature in the Third Reich? On Literature in Germany, 1933–1945). Edited by Christiane Caemmerer and Walter Delabar. Opladen: Westdeutscher Verlag, 1996, 215–30.

Dwinger, Edwin Eugen. *Die letzten Reiter* (The Last Cavalrymen). Jena: Diedrichs, 1935.

Eberhardt, Klaus. *Literatur-Sozialcharakter-Gesellschaft: Untersuchungen von präfaschistischen Erzählwelten zu Begin des 20. Jahrhunderts* (Literature-Social Character-Society: Studies on the Prefascist Story Worlds at the Beginning of the Twentieth Century). Frankfurt am Main, Bern, and New York: Lang, 1986.

Ewers, Hanns Heinz. *Horst Wessel: Ein deutsches Schicksal* (Horst Wessel: A German Fate). Stuttgart and Berlin: Cotta, 1933.

Grimm, Hans. *Volk ohne Raum* (People Without Space). Munich: Albert Langen and Georg Müller, 1926.

Gründer, Horst. *Geschichte der deutschen Kolonien* (History of the German Colonies). Paderborn: Schöningh Verlag, 1985.

Hofmann, Sebastian. "Konzept und Konstanz. Über das Konzept des geistigen und politischen Führertums bei Hans Grimm" (Concept and Consistency. On the Concept of Intellectual and Political Leadership as Used by Hans Grimm). In *Dichtung im Dritten Reich? Zur Literatur in Deutschland 1933–1945* (Literature in the Third Reich? On Literature in Germany, 1933–1945). Edited by Christiane Caemmerer and Walter Delabar. Opladen: Westdeutscher Verlag, 1996, 193–204.

Jaroslawski, Renate, and Rüdiger Steinlein. "Die 'politische Jugendschrift.' Zur Theorie und Praxis faschistischer deutscher Jugendliteratur" (The "Political Book for Young People." On the Theory and Practice of Fascist German Juvenile Literature). In *Die deutsche Literatur im Dritten Reich* (German Literature in the Third Reich). Edited by Horst Denkler and Karl Prümm. Stuttgart: Reclam, 1976, 305–29.

Jünger, Ernst. *In Stahlgewittern* (In Storms of Steel). 24th edition. Berlin: E. S. Mittler & Sohn, 1942.

———. *The Storm of Steel: From the Diary of a German Storm-Troop Officer on the Western Front*. Translated by Basil Creighton. London: Chatto & Windus, 1929.

Kaempfer, Wolfgang. *Ernst Jünger*. Stuttgart: Metzler, 1981.

Kiesel, Helmut. "Zwischen Kritik und Affirmation. Ernst Jüngers Auseinandersetzung mit dem Nationalsozialismus" (Between Criticism and Affirmation. Ernst Jünger's Dispute with National Socialism). In *Literatur in der Diktatur* (Literature in Dictatorship). Edited by Günther Rüther. Paderborn: Schöningh, 1997, 163–72.

Löns, Hermann. *Der Wehrwolf* (The Werewolf). Jena: Eugen Diederichs, 1926.

Prümm, Karl. "Das Erbe der Front. Der antidemokratische Kriegsroman der Weimarer Republik und seine nationalsozialistische Fortsetzung" (The Legacy of the Front. The Anti-Democratic War Novel and Its Continuation Under the National Socialists). In *Die deutsche Literatur im Dritten Reich* (German Literature in the Third Reich). Edited by Horst Denkler and Karl Prümm. Stuttgart: Reclam, 1976, 138–64.

Sachslehner, Johannes. *Führerwort und Führerblick: Mirko Jelusich: Zur Strategie eines Bestsellerautors in den Dreißiger Jahren* (Leader Words and Leader Looks: On the Strategy of a Bestseller-Author in the Thirties). Königstein im Taunus: Hain, 1985.

Schenzinger, Karl Aloys. *Hitlerjunge Quex* (Hitler Youth Quex). Berlin: Zeitgeschichte-Verlag Wilhelm Andermann, 1932.

Schweizer, Gerhard. *Bauernroman und Faschismus* (The Peasant Novel and Fascism). Tübingen: Tübinger Vereinigung für Volkskunde E. V. Schloss, 1976.

Vallery, Helmut. "Entheroisierte Geschichte. Der nationalsozialistische historische Roman" (History Without Heroes. The National Socialist Historical Novel). In *Leid der Worte* (The Suffering of Words). Edited by Jörg Thunecke (Bonn: Bouvier, 1987), 90–107.

Wagner, Jens Peter. "Die Kontinuität des Trivialen. Hans Friedrich Blunck (1888–1961)" (The Continuity of the Trivial. Hans Friedrich Blunck [1888–1961]). In *Dichtung im Dritten Reich? Zur Literatur in Deutschland 1933–1945* (Literature in the Third Reich? On Literature in Germany, 1933–1945). Edited by Christiane Caemmerer and Walter Delabar. Opladen: Westdeutscher Verlag, 1996, 245–64.

Wippermann, Wolfgang. "Geschichte und Ideologie im Roman des Dritten Reichs (History and Ideology in the Novel of the Third Reich). In *Die deutsche Literatur im Dritten Reich* (German Literature in the Third Reich). Edited by Horst Denkler and Karl Prümm. Stuttgart: Reclam, 1976, 183–206.

Zimmermann, Peter. *Der Bauernroman: Antifeudalismus-Konservatismus-Faschismus* (The Peasant Novel: Anti-Feudalism-Conservatism-Fascism). Stuttgart: Metzler, 1975.

————. "Kampf um den Lebensraum. Ein Mythos der Kolonial- und der Blut-und-Boden-Literatur (The Struggle for Living Space. A Myth of Colonial and Blood-and-Soil Literature). In *Die deutsche Literatur im Dritten Reich* (German Literature in the Third Reich). Edited by Horst Denkler and Karl Prümm. Stuttgart: Reclam, 1976, 168–82.

Zöberlein, Hans. *Der Befehl des Gewissens* (The Command of Conscience). 38th edition. Munich: Zentralverlag der NSDAP, Franz Eher Nachfolger, 1942.

The National Socialist Drama

Balfour, Michael, ed. *Theatre and War 1933–1945: Performance in Extremis.* New York: Berghahn, 2001.

Berghaus, Günter, ed. *Fascism and Theatre: Comparative Studies on the Aesthetics and Politics of Performance in Europe, 1925–1945.* Providence: Berghahn, 1996.

Bethge, Friedrich. *Marsch der Veteranen* (March of the Veterans). In *Zeit und Theater* (Times and Theater). Volume 3. Edited by Günther Rühle. Berlin: Propyläen, 1974, 196–258.

Breßlein, Erwin. *Völkisch-faschistoides und nationalsozialistisches Drama* (*Völkisch* Fascistoid and National Socialist Drama). Frankfurt am Main: Haag + Herchen, 1980.

Drewniak, Boguslaw. *Das Theater im NS Staat* (The Theater in the National Socialist State). Düsseldorf: Droste, 1983.

Dussel, Konrad. *Ein neues, ein heroisches Theater? Nationalsozialistische Theaterpolitik und ihre Auswirkungen* (A New, Heroic Theater? National Socialist Theater Policy and Its Effects). Bonn: Bouvier, 1988.

Eichberg, Henning, et al. *Massenspiele: NS-Thingspiel, Arbeiterweihespiel und olympisches Zeremoniell* (Mass Plays: National Socialist *Thingspiele,* Workers Initiation Plays, and Olympic Ceremonies). Stuttgart-Bad Cannstatt: frommann-holzboog, 1977.

Gadberry, Glen W. *Theater in the Third Reich, the Prewar: Essays on Theatre in Nazi Germany.* Westport, CT, and London: Greenwood Press, 1995.

Griese, Friedrich. *Der Mensch, aus Erde gemacht* (The Human Being, Made of Earth). Berlin: Bühnenvolksbund-Verlag, 1932.

Johst, Hanns. *Ich glaube: Bekenntnisse von Hanns Johst* (I Believe: Confessions of Hanns Johst). Munich: Langen, 1928.

————, *Schlageter*. In *Zeit und Theater* (Times and Theater). Volume 3. Edited by Günther Rühle. Berlin: Propyläen, 1974, 77–139.

Ketelsen, Uwe-K. *Heroisches Theater: Untersuchungen zur Dramentheorie des Dritten Reichs* (Heroic Theater: Studies on Drama Theory in the Third Reich). Bonn: Bouvier, 1968.

———. "'Die Jugend von Langemarck.' Ein poetisch-politisches Motiv der Zwischenkriegszeit ('The Youth of Langemarck.' A Poetic and Political Motif of the Period Between the Wars]." In *Mit uns zieht die neue Zeit — Der Mythos Jugend* (With Us Comes the New Era. The Myth of Youth). Edited by Thomas Koebner, et al. Frankfurt am Main: Suhrkamp, 1985, 68–96.

———. *Von heroischem Sein und völkischem Tod* (On Heroic Existence and *Völkisch* Death). Bonn: Bouvier, 1970.

Kirsch, Mechthild. "Heinz Kindermann — ein Wiener Germanist und Theaterwissenschaftler" (Heinz Kindermann — a Viennese Scholar of German Studies and Theater). In *Zeitenwechsel: Germanistische Literaturwissenschaft vor und nach 1945* (Changing Times: The Study of German Literature Before and After 1945). Edited by Wilfried Barner and Christoph König. Frankfurt am Main: Fischer, 1996, 47–59.

Kolbenheyer, Erwin Guido. *Gregor und Heinrich* (Gregory and Henry). In *Zeit und Theater* (Times and Theater). Volume 3. Edited by Günther Rühle. Berlin: Propyläen, 1974, 259–34.

Langenbeck, Curt. *Der Hochverräter* (The Man Who Committed High Treason). In *Zeit und Theater* (Times and Theater). Volume 3. Edited by Günther Rühle. Berlin: Propyläen, 1974, 379–438.

Lehnert, Herbert. "Langemarck — historisch und symbolisch" (Langemark — Historical and Symbolic). In *Orbis Litterarum* 42 (1987), 271–90.

Menz, Egon. "Sprechchor und Aufmarsch. Zur Entstehung des Thingspiels" (Speaking Chorus and Procession. The Evolution of the *Thingspiel*). In *Die deutsche Literatur im Dritten Reich* (German Literature in the Third Reich). Edited by Horst Denkler and Karl Prümm (Stuttgart: Reclam, 1976), 330–46.

Möller, Eberhard Wolfgang. *Frankenburger Würfelspiel* (Frankenburg Dice Game). In *Zeit und Theater,* Volume 3. Edited by Günther Rühle. Berlin: Propyläen, 1974, 335–78.

———. *Rothschild siegt bei Waterloo* (Rothschild Wins at Waterloo). Berlin: Langen-Müller, 1934.

Pfanner, Helmut. *Hanns Johst.* The Hague and Paris: Mouton, 1970.

Rehberg, Hans. *Der siebenjährige Krieg* (The Seven Years War). In *Zeit und Theater* (Times and Theater). Volume 3. Edited by Günther Rühle. Berlin: Propyläen, 1974, 439–500.

Rühle, Günther. *Theater für die Republik 1917–1933* (Theater for the Republic, 1917–1933). Frankfurt am Main: Fischer, 1967.

———. *Zeit und Theater: Diktatur und Exil 1933–1945* (Times and Theater: Dictatorship and Exile, 1933–1945). Volume 3. Berlin: Propyläen, 1974.

———. *Zeit und Theater: Von der Republik zur Diktatur 1925–1933* (Times and Theater: From the Republic to Dictatorship, 1925–1933). Volume 2. Berlin: Propyläen, 1972.

Stollmann, Rainer. "Theater im Dritten Reich" (Theater in the Third Reich). In *Leid der Worte* (The Suffering of Words). Edited by Jörg Thunecke. Bonn: Bouvier, 1987, 72–89.

Stommer, Rainer. *Die inszenierte Volksgemeinschaft: Die "Thing-Bewegung" im Dritten Reich* (The Staged Community of the People: The "Thing Movement" in the Third Reich). Marburg: Jonas, 1985.

Wanderscheck, Hermann. *Deutsche Dramatik der Gegenwart* (German Drama of the Present). Berlin: Bong, 1938.

Wardetsky, Jutta. *Theaterpolitik im faschistischen Deutschland: Studien* (Theater Policies in Fascist Germany. Studies). Berlin: Henschelverlag, 1983.

Wulf, Joseph. *Theater und Film im Dritten Reich: Eine Dokumentation* (Theater and Film in the Third Reich. Documentation). Frankfurt am Main, Berlin, and Vienna: Ullstein, 1983.

Zerkaulen, Heinrich. *Jugend von Langemarck* (Youth of Langemark). In *Zeit und Theater* (Times and Theater). Volume 3. Edited by Günther Rühle. Berlin: Propyläen, 1974, 141–94.

Zimmermann, Rainer. *Das dramatische Bewußtsein: Studien zum bewußtseinsgeschichtlichen Ort der Dreißiger Jahre* (The Dramatic Consciousness: Studies on the Situation in Terms of the History of Consciousness During the Thirties in Germany). Münster: Aschendorffsche Verlagsbuchhandlung, 1989.

National Socialist Poetry

Anacker, Heinrich. *Heimat und Front: Gedichte aus dem Herbst 1939* (Homeland and Front. Poems from the Fall of 1939). Munich: Eher, 1940.

———. *Über die Maas, über die Schelde und Rhein! Gedichte vom Feldzug im Westen* (Across the Maas, Across the Scheldt and Rhine! Poems of the Campaign in the West). Munich: Eher, 1942.

Atkinson, Jeanette Lee. "Joseph Weinheber: Sänger des Austrofaschismus?" (Joseph Weinheber: The Singer of Austrian Fascism?). In *Leid der Worte* (The Suffering of Words). Edited by Jörg Thunecke. Bonn: Bouvier, 1987, 403–19.

Benn, Gottfried. *Autobiographische Schriften* (Autobiographical Writings). In *Gesammelte Werke in acht Bänden* (Collected Works in Eight Volumes). Volume 8. Edited by Dieter Wellershoff. Wiesbaden: Limes, 1960.

————. *Gedichte* (Poems). In *Gesammelte Werke in acht Bänden* (Collected Works in Eight Volumes). Volume 3. Edited by Dieter Wellershoff. Wiesbaden: Limes, 1960.

Böhme, Herbert, ed. *Rufe in das Reich: Die heldische Dichtung von Langemarck bis zur Gegenwart* (Calls into the Reich: Heroic Poetry from Langemark up to the Present). Berlin: Verlag Junge Generation, 1934.

Bormann, Alexander von. "Das nationalsozialistische Gemeinschaftslied" (The National Socialist Community Song). In *Die deutsche Literatur im Dritten Reich* (German Literature in the Third Reich). Edited by Horst Denkler and Karl Prümm. Stuttgart: Reclam, 1976, 256–80.

George, Stefan. *Das neue Reich* (The New Empire). Reprint of volume 9 of the complete edition of 1928. Düsseldorf: Küpper, 1964.

Groppe, Carola. "Widerstand oder Anpassung? Der George-Kreis und das Entscheidungsjahr 1933" (Resistance or Adaptation? The George Circle and the Year of Decision, 1933). In *Literatur in der Diktatur* (Literature in Dictatorship). Edited by Günther Rüther. Paderborn: Schöningh, 1997, 59–92.

Hildebrand, Bruno, ed. *Über Gottfried Benn: Kritische Stimmen 1912–1956* (On Gottfried Benn: Critical Voices, 1912–1956). Frankfurt am Main: Fischer, 1987.

Ketelsen, Uwe-K. "Nationalsozialismus und Drittes Reich" (National Socialism and the Third Reich). In *Geschichte der politischen Lyrik in Deutschland* (History of Political Poetry in Germany). Edited by Walter Hinderer. Stuttgart: Reclam, 1978, 291–314.

Miegel, Agnes. *Ostland*. Jena: Diederichs, 1940 and 1943.

Münchhausen, Börries von. *Das Herz im Harnisch: Neue Balladen und Lieder* (The Heart in Armor: New Ballads and Songs). Stuttgart and Berlin: Deutsche Verlagsanstalt, 1935.

Piorreck, Anni. *Agnes Miegel: Ihr Leben und ihre Dichtung* (Agnes Miegel: Her Life and Her Poetry). Düsseldorf: Diederichs, 1967.

Reuschle, Max. "Der Sinn des Gedichtes in unserer Zeit" (The Meaning of the Poem in Our Time). In *Des deutschen Dichters Sendung in der Gegenwart* (The German Poet's Mission in the Present). Edited by Heinz Kindermann. Leipzig: Reclam, 1933, 213–17.

Schöne, Albrecht. *Über politische Lyrik im 20. Jahrhundert* (On Political Poetry in the Twentieth Century). Göttingen: Vandenhoeck & Ruprecht, 1965.

Schröder, Jürgen. "'Wer über Deutschland reden und richten will, muss hier geblieben sein.' Gottfried Benn als Emigrant nach innen" ("Anyone Who Wants to Talk About and Judge Germany, Must Have Stayed Here." Gottfried Benn as an Inner Emigrant). In *Literatur in der Diktatur* (Literature in Dictatorship). Edited by Günther Rüther. Paderborn: Schöningh, 1997, 131–44.

Schumann, Gerhard. *Die Lieder vom Reich* (Songs of the Reich). Munich: Langen Müller, 1935.

———. *Ruf und Berufung: Aufsätze und Reden* (Call and Calling: Essays and Speeches). Munich: Langen and Müller, 1943.

———. *Stachel-Beeren Auslese* (A Selection of Gooseberries). Stuttgart: Silberberg Verlag, 1960.

Strauß und Torney, Lulu von. *Reif steht die Saat* (The Seed is Ripe). Jena: Diederichs, 1926.

Weinheber, Josef. *Adel und Untergang* (Nobility and Decline). 6th edition. Vienna and Leipzig: Luser, 1934.

———. *Sämtliche Werke* (Complete Works), Volume 4: *Kleine Prosa* (Small Prose Works). Edited by Josef Nadler and Hedwig Weinheber. Salzburg: Otto Müller, 1954.

———. *Späte Krone: Gedichte* (Late Crown: Poems). Munich: Langen and Müller, 1936.

National Socialist Film

Albrecht, Gerd. *Nationalsozialistische Filmpolitik* (National Socialist Film Policies). Stuttgart: Ferdinand Enke Verlag, 1969.

Bathrick, David, and Eric Rentschler, eds. *Nazi Cinema: Special Issue of New German Critique* 74 (Spring-Summer, 1998).

Beyer, Friedemann. *Die UFA-Stars im Dritten Reich: Frauen für Deutschland* (The UFA-Stars in the Third Reich: Women for Germany). Munich: Heyne, 1991.

Courtade, Francis, and Pierre Cadars. *Geschichte des Films im Dritten Reich* (The History of Film in the Third Reich). Munich: Hanser, 1975.

Drewniak, Boguslaw. *Der deutsche Film 1938–1945: Ein Gesamtüberblick* (The German Film 1938–1945: An Overview). Düsseldorf: Droste, 1987.

Gregor, Ulrich. "Film in Berlin." In *Berlin 1910–1933*. Edited by Eberhard Roters. Translated into English by Marguerite Mounier. Secaucus, NJ: Wellfleet Press, 1982.

Hake, Sabine. *Popular Cinema of the Third Reich*. Austin: U of Texas P, 2001.

Harlan, Veit. *Im Schatten meiner Filme* (In the Shadow of my Films). Gütersloh: Mohn, 1966.

Hull, David Steward. *Film in the Third Reich*. Berkeley and Los Angeles: U of California P, 1969.

Klotz, Marcia. *An Interpretation of Three National Socialist Films: Jud Süss, Carl Peters, Ohm Krüger*. Basel, Switzerland: Basler Afrika Bibliographien, 1996.

Knilli, Friedrich. *Ich war Jud Süß. Die Geschichte des Filmstars Ferdinand Marian* (I Was Jew Suess: The Story of the Film Star Ferdinand Marian). Berlin: Henschel, 2000.

Kracauer, Siegfried. *From Caligari to Hitler: A Psychological History of the German Film.* Princeton: Princeton UP, 1947.

Kreimeier, Klaus. *The Ufa-Story: A History of Germany's Greatest Film Company 1918–1945.* Translated from the German (*Die Ufa-Story: Geschichte eines Filmkonzerns.* Munich and Vienna: Hanser, 1992) by Robert and Rita Kimber. New York: Hill and Wang, 1996.

Lange, Gabriele. *Das Kino als moralische Anstalt: Soziale Leitbilder und die Darstellung gesellschaftlicher Realität im Spielfilm des Dritten Reiches* (Cinema as Moral Institution: Social Models and the Depiction of Social Reality in Films of the Third Reich). Frankfurt am Main: Lang, 1994.

Leiser, Erwin. *"Deutschland erwache!" Propaganda im Film des Dritten Reiches* ("Germany, Awake!" Propaganda in the Film of the Third Reich). Reinbek near Hamburg: Rowohlt, 1968.

Lowry, Stephen. *Pathos und Politik: Ideologie in Spielfilmen des Nationalsozialismus* (Pathos and Politics: Ideology in Films of National Socialism). Tübingen: Niemeyer, 1991.

Moeller, Felix. *The Film Minister: Goebbels and the Cinema in the Third Reich.* Foreword by Volker Schlöndorff, translated from the German (*Der Filmminister: Goebbels und der Film im Dritten Reich.* Berlin: Henschel, 1998) by Michael Robinson. Stuttgart and London: Edition Axel Menges, 2000.

Noack, Frank. *Veit Harlan: "Des Teufels Regisseur"* (Veit Harlan: "The Devil's Director"). Munich: Belleville Verlag, 2000.

O'Brien, Mary-Elizabeth. *Nazi Cinema as Enchantment: The Politics of Entertainment in the Third Reich.* Rochester, NY: Camden House, 2003.

Reimer, Robert. *Nazi-Retro Film: How German Narrative Cinema Remembers the Past.* New York: Twayne, and Toronto and New York: Maxwell McMillan, 1992.

Reimer, Robert C., ed. *Cultural History through a National Socialist Lens: Essays on the Cinema of the Third Reich.* Rochester, NY: Camden House, 2000.

Rentschler, Eric. *The Ministry of Illusion: Nazi Cinema and its Afterlife.* Cambridge, MA, and London: Harvard UP, 1996.

Riefenstahl, Leni. *Hinter den Kulissen des Reichsparteitagfilms* (Behind the Curtains of the Reich Party Congress Film). Munich: Franz Eher Nachfolger, 1935.

———. *Memoiren* (Memoirs). Munich: Knaus, 1987.

Rother, Rainer. *Leni Riefenstahl: die Verführung des Talents* (Leni Riefenstahl: the Seduction of a Talent). Berlin: Henschel, 2000.

Schulte-Sasse, Linda. *Entertaining the Third Reich*. Durham & London: Duke UP, 1996.

———. "The Jew as Other Under National Socialism: Veit Harlan's Jud Süß." In *The German Quarterly,* 61, 1 (Winter, 1988), 22–49.

Welch, David. *Propaganda and the German Cinema, 1933–1945.* Oxford: Oxford UP, 1983 (paper 1985).

Witte, Karsten. "Die Filmkomödie im Dritten Reich" (The Film Comedy in the Third Reich). In *Die deutsche Literatur im Dritten Reich* (German Literature in the Third Reich). Edited by Horst Denkler and Karl Prümm. Stuttgart: Reclam, 1976, 347–63.

———. *Lachende Erben, toller Tag: Filmkomödie im Dritten Reich* (Laughing Heirs, Fantastic Day: Film Comedy in the Third Reich). Munich: Vorwerk, 1995.

———. "Major Tellheim nimmt Minna von Barnhelm in Dienst oder Wie der Nazifilm mit Klassikern mobil machte" (How Major Tellheim Takes Minna von Barnhelm into Service, or How Nazi Film Mobilized the Classic Writers). In *Neue Rundschau* 96, 1 (1985), 158–73.

Non-National Socialist Literature

Andres, Stefan. *Der Dichter in dieser Zeit: Reden und Aufsätze* (The Poet in These Times: Speeches and Essays). Munich: Piper, 1974.

———. "El Greco malt den Großinquisitor" (El Greco Paints the Grand Inquisitor). In *Novellen und Erzählungen* (Novellas and Stories). Munich: Piper, 1962.

Ausländer, Rose. *Die Erde war ein atlasweißes Feld: Gedichte 1927–1956* (The Earth Was a Satin-White Field: Poems, 1927–1956). Frankfurt am Main: Fischer, 1985.

Benz, Wolfgang, and Walter H. Pehile, eds. *Encyclopedia of German Resistance to the Nazi Movement.* New York: Continuum, 2001.

Bergengruen, Werner. *Dichtergehäuse: Aus den autobiographischen Aufzeichnungen* (Poet's Cabinet: From the Autobiographical Notebooks). Edited by Charlotte Bergengruen. Zurich: Arche, 1966.

———. *Der Großtyrann und das Gericht* (The Great Tyrant and the Court). Munich: Nymphenburger Verlagshandlung, 1951.

———. *Dies Irae* (Day of Anger). Munich: Zinnen-Verlag Kurt Desch, no date (1945).

———. *Schreibtischerinnerungen* (Writing Desk Memoirs). Zurich: Arche, 1961 (licensed edition in Germany by Nymphenburger Verlagshandlung).

Bock, Sigrid. "Arbeiterkorrespondenten und -schriftsteller bewähren sich. Jan Petersen: *Unsere Straße*" (Worker-Correspondents and Worker-Writers Prove Themselves. Jan Petersen: Our Street). In *Erfahrung Nazideutschland* (The Experience of Nazi Germany). Edited by Sigrid Bock und Manfred Hahn. Berlin, Weimar: Aufbau, 1987, 44–98.

———. "Kämpfer vor dem Sieg. Adam Kuckhoff: *Der Deutsche von Bayencourt*" (Fighter Before Victory. Adam Kuckhoff: The German from Bayencourt). In *Erfahrung Nazideutschland* (The Experience of Nazi Germany). Edited by Sigrid Bock and Manfred Hahn. Berlin, Weimar: Aufbau, 1987, 44–98.

Bock, Sigrid, and Manfred Hahn, eds. *Erfahrung Nazideutschland: Romane in Deutschland 1933–1945. Analysen* (The Experience of Nazi Germany: Novels in Germany, 1933–1945. Analyses). Berlin, Weimar: Aufbau, 1987.

Brekle, Wolfgang. "Die antifaschistische Literatur in Deutschland" (The Anti-Fascist Literature in Germany). In *Weimarer Beiträge* 11, 6 (1970), 67–128.

———. *Schriftsteller im antifaschistischen Widerstand 1933–1945 in Deutschland* (Authors in the Anti-Fascist Resistance from 1933 to 1945 in Germany). Berlin and Weimar: Aufbau, 1985.

Carossa, Hans. *Ungleiche Welten* (Unequal Worlds). Frankfurt am Main: Suhrkamp, 1978 (1st edition, Wiesbaden: Insel, 1951).

———. *Wirkungen Goethes in der Gegenwart* (The Influence of Goethe in the Present). Leipzig: Insel, 1938 and 1944.

Cuomo, Glenn. *Career at the Cost of Compromise: Günter Eich's Life and Work in the Years 1933–1945*. Amsterdam and Atlanta: Rodopi, 1989.

Delabar, Walter. "Unheilige Einfalt. Zu den Verhaltenskonzepten in den Romanen Ernst Wiecherts" (Unholy Simplicity. On the Concepts of Conduct in the Novels of Ernst Wiechert). In *Dichtung im Dritten Reich? Zur Literatur in Deutschland 1933–1945* (Literature in the Third Reich? On Literature in Germany, 1933–1945). Edited by Christiane Caemmerer and Walter Delabar. Opladen: Westdeutscher Verlag, 1996, 135–50.

Denkler, Horst. "Janusköpfig. Zur ideologischen Physiognomie der Zeitschrift *Das Innere Reich* (1934–1944)" (Janus-headed. On the Ideological Physiognomy of the Journal The Inner Realm [1934–1944]). In *Die deutsche Literatur im Dritten Reich* (German Literature in the Third Reich). Edited by Horst Denkler and Karl Prümm. Stuttgart: Reclam, 1976, 382–405.

Donahue, Neil H., and Doris Kirchner, eds. *Flight of Fantasy: New Perspectives on Inner Emigration in German Literature, 1933–1945*. New York: Berghahn: 2003.

Döring, Jörg. "Eulenspiegel schreibt Gespenstergeschichten, Wolfgang Koeppen im Dritten Reich" (Eulenspiegel Writes Ghost Stories, Wolfgang Koeppen in the Third Reich). In *Dichtung im Dritten Reich? Zur Literatur in Deutschland 1933–1945* (Literature in the Third Reich? Literature in Germany, 1933–1945). Edited by Christiane Caemmerer and Walter Delabar. Opladen: Westdeutscher Verlag, 1996, 97–119.

Edvardson, Cordelia. *Gebranntes Kind sucht Feuer* (Burned Child Seeks Fire). Translated from Swedish by Anna Liese Kornitzky. Munich and Vienna, 1986 (Swedish original: *Bränt barn söker sig till elden,* 1984; English translation: *Burned Child Seeks Fire: A Memoir.* Translated by Joel Agee. Boston: Beacon Press, 1997).

Elm, Theo. "Aufklärung als Widerstand. Oskar Loerke's Gedicht 'Das Auge des Todes'" (Education as Resistance. Oskar Loerke's poem "The Eye of Death," 1934). In *Oskar Loerke: Marbacher Kolloquium 1984* (Oskar Loerke: Marbach Colloquium, 1984). Edited by Reinhard Tgahrt. Mainz: Hase & Koehler, 1986, 89–105.

Emmerich, Wolfgang. "Die Literatur des antifaschistischen Widerstandes" (The Literature of the Anti-Fascist Resistance). In *Die deutsche Literatur im Dritten Reich* (German Literature in the Third Reich). Edited by Horst Denkler and Karl Prümm. Stuttgart: Reclam, 1976, 427–58.

Felsmann, Barbara, and Karl Prümm. *Kurt Gerron: Gefeiert und gejagt, 1897–1944: Das Schicksal eines deutschen Unterhaltungskünstlers: Berlin, Amsterdam, Theresienstadt, Auschwitz* (Kurt Gerron: Celebrated and Hunted, 1897–1944: The Fate of a German Entertainer: Berlin, Amsterdam, Theresienstadt, Auschwitz). Berlin: Edition Hentrich, 1992.

Goltschnigg, Dietmar, ed. *Büchner im "Dritten Reich": Mystifikation-Gleichschaltung-Exil: Eine Dokumentation* (Büchner in the "Third Reich": Mystification-*Gleichschaltung*-Exile: A Documentation). Bielefeld, Aisthesis: 1990.

Grimm, Reinhold. "Im Dickicht der inneren Emigration" (In the Thicket of Inner Emigration). In *Die deutsche Literatur im Dritten Reich* (German Literature in the Third Reich). Edited by Horst Denkler and Karl Prümm. Stuttgart: Reclam, 1976, 406–26.

Grimm, Reinhold, and Jost Hermand, eds. *Exil und Innere Emigration* (Exile and Inner Emigration). Frankfurt am Main: Athenäum, 1972.

Groll, Gunter, ed. *De Profundis: Deutsche Lyrik in dieser Zeit: Eine Anthologie aus zwölf Jahren* (De Profundis: German Poetry in These Times: An Anthology from Twelve Years). Munich: Desch, 1946.

Grosser, J. F. G., ed. *Die große Kontroverse: Ein Briefwechsel um Deutschland* (The Great Controversy: A Correspondence about German). Hamburg: Nagel, 1963.

Hagelstange, Rudolf. "Die Form als erste Entscheidung" (The Form as the First Decision). In *Mein Gedicht ist mein Messer: Lyriker zu ihren Gedichten* (My Poem is My Knife: Poets on Their Poems). Edited by Hans Bender. Munich: List, 1964, 37–47.

———. "Venezianisches Credo" (Venetian Credo). Munich: Insel, 1946.

Haushofer, Manfred. *Moabit Sonnets*. German-English edition, translated by M. D. Herter Norton. London and New York: Norton, 1978.

Hofen, Nikolaus. *Reinhold Schneiders Las Casas vor Karl V. im Deutschunterricht der gymnasialen Oberstufe* (Reinhold Schneider's Las Casas Before Charles V in the Higher Classes of the Gymnasium). Frankfurt am Main: Lang, 2001.

Hoffmann, Charles Wesley. "Opposition Poetry in Nazi Germany, 1933–1945." Diss. University of Illinois, 1956.

Jünger, Ernst. *Auf den Marmorklippen* (On the Marble Cliffs). Frankfurt am Main: Ullstein, 1980.

Kesaris, Paul L., ed. *The Rote Kapelle: The CIA's History of Soviet Intelligence and Espionage Networks in Western Europe, 1936–1945*. Washington, DC: University Publications of America, Inc., 1979.

Klausnitzer, Ralf. *Blaue Blume unterm Hakenkreuz: Die Rezeption der deutschen literarischen Romantik im Dritten Reich* (The Blue Flower Under the Swastika: The Reception of German Literary Romanticism in the Third Reich). Paderborn: Schöningh, 1999.

Klüger, Ruth. *Weiter leben: eine Jugend*. Göttingen: Hallstein, 1992. English translation: *Still Alive: A Holocaust Girlhood Remembered*. New York: Feminist Press at the University of New York, 2001.

Krauss, Werner. *PLN: Die Passionen der halykonischen Seele* (ZIP Code: The Passions of the Halyconian Soul). Frankfurt am Main: Klostermann, 1946.

Kuckhoff, Adam. *Der Deutsche von Bayencourt* (The German from Bayencourt). Berlin: Rowohlt, 1937.

———. *Fröhlich bestehen, Adam Kuckhoff: Prosa, Lyrik, Dramatik* (Happily Exist. Adam Kuckhoff: Prose, Poetry, Drama). Edited by Werner Jung. Aachen: Alano, 1985.

Kuckhoff, Greta, ed. *Adam Kuckhoff zum Gedenken: Novellen, Gedichte, Briefe* (In Memory of Adam Kuckhoff: Novellas, Poems, Letters). Berlin: Aufbau, 1946.

Langbein, Hermann. *Against all Hope: Resistance in the Nazi Concentration Camps, 1938–1945*. New York: Continuum, 2001.

Langmann, Peter. *Sozialismus und Literatur — Jura Soyfer: Studien zu einem österreichischen Schriftsteller der Zwischenkriegszeit* (Socialism and Literatur — Jura Soyfer: Studies on an Austrian Writer of the Period Between the Wars). Frankfurt am Main: Hain Meisenheim, 1986.

Loerke, Oskar. *Die Gedichte* (The Poems). Edited by Peter Suhrkamp. Frankfurt am Main: Suhrkamp, 1958.

———. *Tagebücher 1903–1939* (Diaries, 1903–1939). Edited by Hermann Kasack. Heidelberg and Darmstadt: Schneider, 1956.

Moll, Michael. *Lyrik in einer entmenschten Welt: Interpretationsversuche zu deutschsprachigen Gedichten aus nationalsozialistischen Gefängnissen, Ghettos und KZ's* (Poetry in a Dehumanized World: Attempts at Interpretation of Poems from National Socialist Prisons, Ghettos, and Concentration Camps). Frankfurt am Main: R. G. Fischer, 1988.

Müller, Karlheinz. *Elisabeth Langgässer: Eine biographische Skizze* (Elisabeth Langgässer: A Biographical Sketch) Darmstadt: Gesellschaft Hessischer Literaturfreunde, 1990.

Perrault, Gilles. *L'orchestre rouge* (The Red Orchestra). Paris: Fayars, 1967. German: *Auf den Spuren der Roten Kapelle*. Translated by E. and R. Thomsen. Vienna and Zurich: Europa Verlag, 1990. English translation by Peter Wiles as *The Red Orchestra*. New York: Simon and Schuster, 1969.

Reiner, Guido. *Ernst Wiechert im Dritten Reich: Eine Dokumentation* (Ernst Wiechert in the Third Reich: Documentation). Paris: Self-Published, 1974.

Schäfer, Hans Dieter. "Die nichtfaschistische Literatur der 'jungen Generation' im nationalsozialistischen Deutschland" (Non-fascist Literature of the 'Young Generation' in National Socialist Germany). In *Die deutsche Literatur im Dritten Reich* (German Literature in the Third Reich). Edited by Horst Denkler and Karl Prümm. Stuttgart: Reclam, 1976, 459–503.

Schäfer, Hans Dieter, ed. *Am Rande der Nacht: Moderne Klassik im Dritten Reich: Ein Lesebuch* (On the Edge of the Night: Modern Classics in the Third Reich: A Reader). Frankfurt am Main: Ullstein, 1984.

Schlösser, Manfred, ed. *An den Wind geschrieben: Lyrik der Freiheit 1933–1945* (Written to the Wind: Poetry of Freedom, 1933–1945). 2nd edition. Darmstadt: Agora, 1961.

Schneider, Reinhold. *Las Casas vor Karl V.* (Las Casas Before Charles V). In *Gesammelte Werke* (Collected Works). Volume 3: *Der Große Verzicht* (The Great Renunciation). Edited by Edwin Maria Landau. Frankfurt am Main: Insel, 1978.

———. *Lyrik* (Poetry). Selection and foreword by Christoph Perels. In *Gesammelte Werke* (Collected Works). Volume 5. Edited by Edwin Maria Landau. Frankfurt am Main: Insel, 1981.

———. *Zwei autobiographische Werke: Verhüllter Tag; Winter in Wien* (Two Autobiographical Works: Enshrouded Day; Winter in Vienna). In *Gesammelte Werke* (Collected Works). Volume 10: *Die Zeit in uns* (The Time in Us). Edited by Edwin Maria Landau. Frankfurt am Main: Insel, 1978.

Schnell, Ralf. *Literarische Innere Emigration 1933–1945* (Literary Inner Emigration, 1933–1945). Stuttgart: Metzler, 1976.

Soyfer, Jura. *Das Gesamtwerk* (The Complete Works). Edited by Horst Jarka. Vienna: Europa Verlag, 1980.

Thiess, Frank. *Jahre des Unheils: Fragmente erlebter Geschichte* (Year of Calamity: Fragments of Experienced History). Vienna: Zsolnay, 1972.

Van Roon, Ger. *Widerstand im Dritten Reich: Ein Überblick* (Resistance in the Third Reich: An Overview). 4th reworked edition. Munich: Beck, 1987.

Vaßen, Florian. "'Das illegale Wort.' Literatur und Literaturverhältnisse des Bundes proletarisch-revolutionärer Schriftsteller nach 1933" ("The Illegal Word." Literature and Literary Circumstances of the Union of Proletarian Revolutionary Writers After 1933). In *Kunst und Kultur im deutschen Faschismus* (Art and Culture in German Fascism). Edited by Ralf Schnell. Stuttgart: Metzler, 1978, 285–93.

Vieregg, Axel. "Der eigenen Fehlbarkeit begegnet? Günter Eich's Verstrickung im 'Dritten Reich'" (Faced with His Own Fallibility? Günter Eich's Entanglement in the "Third Reich"). In *Literatur in der Diktatur* (Literature in Dictatorship). Edited by Günther Rüther. Paderborn: Schöningh, 1997, 173–94.

Wehdeking, Volker. "Zwischen Exil und 'vorgeschobenem Posten' der Kulturnation. Thomas Mann als Projektionsfigur für die im Land gebliebenen Nichtfaschisten" (Between Exile and an "Outpost" of the Culture Nation. Thomas Mann as a Projection Figure for the Non-Fascists Who Remained in the Country). In *Literatur in der Diktatur* (Literature in Dictatorship). Edited by Günther Rüther. Paderborn: Schöningh, 1997, 145–62.

Weisenborn, Günther, ed. *Der lautlose Aufstand: Bericht über die Widerstandsbewegung des deutschen Volkes 1933–1945* (The Soundless Revolution. Report on the Resistance Movement of the German People, 1933–1945). Hamburg: Rowohlt, 1953.

Weiss, Peter. *Die Ästhetik des Widerstands* (The Aesthetics of Resistance). Volume 3. Frankfurt am Main: Suhrkamp, 1981.

Wiechert, Ernst. *Jahre und Zeiten: Erinnerungen* (Years and Times: Memoirs). In *Sämtliche Werke in zehn Bänden* (Complete Works in Ten Volumes). Volume 9. Vienna: Desch, 1957.

———. *Der Totenwald: Ein Bericht* (The Forest of the Dead: A Report). In *Sämtliche Werke in zehn Bänden* (Complete Works in Ten Volumes). Volume 9. Vienna: Desch, 1957, 197–329.

———. "Der weiße Büffel. Oder von der grossen Gerechtigkeit" (The White Buffalo. Or the Great Justice). In *Sämtliche Werke in zehn Bänden* (Complete Works in Ten Volumes). Volume 6. Vienna: Desch, 1957, 553–625.

Wirth, Günter. "Eine Stimme für die Gleichberechtigung der Völker. Reinhold Schneider: 'Las Casas vor Karl V. Szenen aus der Konquistadorenzeit" (A Voice for Equality of the Peoples. Reinhold Schneider: "Las Casas Before Charles V. Scenes from the Time of the Conquistadors"). In *Erfahrung Nazideutschland* (The Experience of Nazi Germany). Edited by Sigrid Bock and Manfred Hahn. Berlin, Weimar: Aufbau, 1987, 298–334.

Zimmermann, Ingo. *Reinhold Schneider: Weg eines Schriftstellers* (Reinhold Schneider: Path of a Writer). Berlin: Union Verlag, 1982.

Ziolkowski, Theodor. "Form als Protest. Das Sonett in der Literatur des Exils und der Inneren Emigration" (Form as Protest. The Sonnet in the Literature of Exile and the Inner Emigration). In *Exil und Innere Emigration* (Exile and Inner Emigration). Edited by Reinhold Grimm and Jost Hermand. Frankfurt am Main: Athenäum, 1972, 153–72.

Language in the Third Reich

Berning, Cornelia. *Vom 'Abstammungsnachweis' zum 'Zuchtwart.' Vokabular des Nationalsozialismus* (From "Proof of Ancestry" to the "Guardian of Breeding." Vocabulary of National Socialism). Berlin: de Gruyter, 1964.

Brackmann, Karl Heinz, and Renate Birkenhauer. *NS-Deutsch. "Selbstverständliche" Begriffe und Schlagwörter aus der Zeit des Nationalsozialismus* (National Socialist German. "Obvious" Concepts and Slogans from the Period of National Socialism). Straelen, Lower Rheine: Straelener Manuskripte Verlag, 1988.

Hutton, Christopher M. *Linguistics and the Third Reich: Mother-Tongue Fascism, Race, and the Science of Language.* London: Routledge, 1999.

Klemperer, Victor. *LTN: Notizbuch eines Philologen* (LTN: Notebook of a Philologist). 5th edition. Leipzig: Reclam, 1978.

Maas, Utz. *"Als der Geist der Gemeinschaft eine Sprache fand." Sprache im Nationalsozialismus* ("As the Spirit of the Community Found a Language." Language in National Socialism). Opladen: Westdeutscher Verlag, 1984.

Schmitz-Berning, Cornelia. *Vokabular des National-Sozialismus* (Vocabulary of National Socialism). Berlin and New York: de Gruyter, 1998.

Sternberger, Dolf, Gerhard Storz, and Wilhelm Süskind. *Aus dem Wörterbuch des Unmenschen* (From the Dictionary of the Beast). Frankfurt am Main: Ullstein, 1989.

Translator's Note

TRANSFERRING THOUGHTS AND concepts originally expressed in German into the words and cultural environment of American English always presents special challenges. The fact that the thoughts and concepts under discussion, as well as the associated vocabulary lie three-quarters of a century in the past in a very different world only makes those challenges greater. The core problem is that there are no true equivalents in English for much of the vocabulary that was created and then took on a life of its own in the German language before and during the Third Reich. Such concepts are in fact so significantly and specifically enmeshed in the ideology of the Third Reich that they defy translation, especially as the meaning of the German words themselves has changed since that era. Essentially, exact translation is clearly impossible, but with the objective of making the study *Literatur im Dritten Reich* accessible to English speakers, I have sought to find solutions to individual translation problems that reproduce accurately what Karl-Heinz Schoeps (and the wide variety of German writers he quotes) is seeking to convey.

In terms of vocabulary, a typical and critical area is the large family of words surrounding the concept of *Volk*. As George L. M. Mosse points out, "to German thinkers ever since the birth of German Romanticism in the late eighteenth century 'Volk' signifies the union of a group of people with a transcendental 'essence.'"[1] The concept took on even greater importance in the Third Reich. The term signifies the German people, but in a manner totally unlike its English-language cousin "folk," the word acquired highly charged political relevance with mythical overtones. In essence, *Volk* referred in that period to "the entirety of the German nation as a political, racial, cultural, and fated 'community by blood.'"[2] In the Nazi political theory of the time, this new conception of "*Volk*" was the "basic political value" in the life of the nation and state.[3] The term saturated the propaganda language and literature of the time, spinning off myriad related terms, for example, "Volkheit," "Volkstum," "volkhaft," "völkisch," "volkstümlich," "volklich," "volksam," and so on, most of which slipped into oblivion after 1945 or retained meaning only as associated with the Third Reich. The subtle differences in meaning, which probably were less than clear during the Nazi period, are often indistinguishable today. So, in the interest of simplicity, *Volk* has been translated as "people," and most of the frequently used derivatives of *Volk* have been rendered with an appropriate construction using "people." Several key derivatives, however, have been left in German: *Völkisch* originally entered the German language with the meaning "national," acquiring the sense of national on the basis of blood and race, and was used by Hitler as the opposite of "Jewish" and "international";[4] *Volkstum* refers to the distinct community of a people as determined by history, culture and language, and *volkstümlich* is the adjective form of that term.[5] The reader will become aware, if only on the basis of repetition alone, of just how overused this politicized family of words became among Nazi supporters within the Third Reich.

A variety of other terms have been left in German for the sake of linguistic economy. *Gleichschaltung,* meaning forced adaptation of countries and organizations to Nazi policies, and *Anschluß,* meaning annexation of occupied territories, particularly Austria, by the Nazis, have become accepted technical terms for those particular historical phenomena. *Reich* is generally accepted to apply to the governmental entity of the Third Reich, although the translation "empire" is used for earlier such entities. *Germanistik* connotes much more specifically the scholarly study of German language and literature in the German context than does "German studies," a term that developed later in English and covers a much broader spectrum of endeavor. Finally, *Thingspiel,* as a very specific dramatic form limited to the Nazi era, is most appropriately left in German.

A few words must be said about the handling of the many textual examples that provide the concrete basis for this study. All texts, verse and prose, have been translated to facilitate the comprehension of readers, especially those who know little or no German. Prose texts, however, have been dealt with somewhat differently from poetry. As prose allows a good deal more latitude in formulation during the translation process, prose texts have been quoted directly in English translation, without inclusion of the original German. In contrast, the examples of poetry and verse are quoted first in German, followed by a translation in brackets. The chief objective of the poetry translations is to give a clear rendering of the poem's content. No attempt is made to reproduce exactly the rhyme schemes or meter of the poetry — that would involve creating a new poem on the same theme in English, which does not suit the purposes of this study. At the same time, the translations have meter and are verse-like to convey the important sense that they are, after all, poetry and not prose. The translations, except for those of the *Moabiter Sonette* presented in the chapter on non-National Socialist literature, are mine, for better or for worse.

In the same spirit of accommodating the reader, English translations are included after German book titles the first time that they appear in each chapter and in the bibliography as well. Specialized concepts, such as *Wandervogel,* or *Blaue Blume,* which require no explanation for German readers, are clarified in the text or by endnotes. Names of organizations, at least the lesser-known ones, are supplied in German and English. In these and other ways, every attempt has been made to ensure accessibility.

In preparing this translation, I have had the good fortune to collaborate directly with the author of the work, who has advised and corrected as needed. Ultimately, however, I take full responsibility for any and all errors and misinterpretations and hope only that none are so egregious as to detract from the worth of the study itself.

Notes

[1] George L. Mosse, *The Crisis of German Ideology: Intellectual Origins of the Third Reich* (New York: Grosset & Dunlap, 1964 and 1971), 4.

[2] Karl Heinz Brackmann and Renate Birkenhauer, *NS-Deutsch. "Selbstverständliche" Begriffe und Schlagwörter aus der Zeit des Nationalsozialismus* (National Socialist German. "Obvious" Concepts and Slogans from the Period of National Socialism) (Straelen, Lower-Rhine: Straelener Manuskripte Verlag, 1988), 193.

[3] Cornelia Schmitz-Berning, *Vokabular des National-Sozialismus* (Vocabulary of National Socialism) (Berlin and New York: de Gruyter, 1998), 643.

[4] See Brackmann and Birkenhauer, 194; see also Schmitz-Berning, 645–47.

[5] See Brackmann and Birkenhauer, 198; see also Schmitz-Berning, 675–79.

Index